Psychosocial Factors at Work in the Asia Pacific

Akihito Shimazu · Rusli Bin Nordin
Maureen Dollard · Jodi Oakman
Editors

Psychosocial Factors at Work in the Asia Pacific

From Theory to Practice

Springer

Editors
Akihito Shimazu
Department of Mental Health
Graduate School of Medicine
The University of Tokyo
Bunkyō, Tokyo
Japan

Rusli Bin Nordin
Jeffrey Cheah School of Medicine and Health Sciences
Clinical School Johor Bahru
Monash University
Johor Bahru
Malaysia

Maureen Dollard
School of Psychology, Social Work and Social Policy
Asia Pacific Centre for Work Health and Safety
A World Health Organization Collaborating Centre in Occupational Health
University of South Australia
Magill, SA
Australia

Jodi Oakman
Department of Public Health
Centre for Ergonomics and Human Factors
La Trobe University
Bundoora, VIC
Australia

ISBN 978-3-319-44399-7 ISBN 978-3-319-44400-0 (eBook)
DOI 10.1007/978-3-319-44400-0

Library of Congress Control Number: 2016947757

Printed on acid-free paper

This Springer imprint is published by Springer Nature
The registered company is Springer International Publishing AG Switzerland

Contents

Part I
Policy and Practice Framework in the Asia Pacific and Beyond

Chapter 1
State of the Art: The Context of Psychosocial Factors at Work in the Asia Pacific?

Jodi Oakman, Maureen Dollard, Akihito Shimazu and Rusli Bin Nordin

Abstract The Asia Pacific is a rapidly growing region with a diverse range of countries, both developing and developed. Across the region there are significant cultural variations and different work practices, creating a range of challenges for those charged with the management of workplace health. This book addresses an important gap, by focusing on research in the Asia-Pacific region that explores psychosocial work environment issues that have a significant influence on worker health and productivity. Most research concerning psychosocial factors at work is from Europe or North America and the generalizability of the research and practical implications is not clear. Consequently, managers, occupational health and safety personnel, human resource professionals, occupational health psychology practitioners, and public health professionals in the Asia Pacific have relied on an evidence basis with largely untested validity. This book extends the work of the first edition, "Psychosocial Factors at Work in the Asia Pacific," applies and tests new and emerging theories, provides insights into different workplace issues pertinent to the Asia Pacific, and practical insights into the management of psychosocial factors in the workplace.

Keywords Psychosocial · Working conditions · Asia Pacific · Worker health · Hazards · Policy

J. Oakman (✉)
Center for Ergonomics and Human Factors, School of Psychology and Public Health, La Trobe University, Melbourne, Australia
e-mail: J.Oakman@latrobe.edu.au

M. Dollard
Asia-Pacific Center for Work Health and Safety, School of Psychology, Social Work, and Social Policy, University of South Australia, Adelaide, Australia

A. Shimazu
Graduate School of Medicine, Department of Mental Health, The University of Tokyo, Tokyo, Japan

R.B. Nordin
Jeffrey Cheah School of Medicine and Health Sciences, Monash University Malaysia, Bandar Sunway, Malaysia

A. Shimazu et al. (eds.), *Psychosocial Factors at Work in the Asia Pacific*,
DOI 10.1007/978-3-319-44400-0_1

Introduction

Work is good for health, but poor working conditions can result in health erosion. As expounded in the (2008) Seoul Declaration on Safety and Health at Work, access to safe and healthy workplaces is a fundamental human right. However, large discrepancies are found in relation to worker health status and exposures to workplace risk factors between and within countries across the Asia Pacific.

This is the second book on psychosocial factors at work in the Asia Pacific. It builds on the content from the first book, Psychosocial Factors at Work in the Asia Pacific (Dollard et al. 2014). The aim of both books is to address a gap in the knowledge about psychosocial factors at work particularly in the Asia Pacific. This large and economically diverse region has a wide range of working conditions, from very good to very poor along with high levels of job insecurity. Despite the region being the most populous, most research in the field has been undertaken in areas outside the region. Prior research suggests that, for example, in the area of occupational health psychology, only 10 % of the global knowledge published in English emerges from the Asia Pacific (Kang et al. 2008). A major challenge across a range of occupational and health-related disciplinary research approaches (e.g., occupational health psychology, occupational behavioral medicine, public health and occupational health and safety) is to produce knowledge that is relevant and practical, within and across national contexts. Both books are intended to help build a knowledge platform for the region, and this second edition particularly focuses on practical applications.

Psychosocial hazard and risk factors at work refer to those aspects of work organizations that are of human design and construction, with the potential to cause psychological or physical harm. Often, these factors also involve human relations. Psychosocial hazard and risk factors include the organization and management of work, the social and relational aspects of work, and job design (Cox and Griffiths 2005). Psychosocial risk factors at work, such as poor organizational climate, work pressure, job insecurity, bullying, violence, and work stress in general, are increasingly recognized as threats to workers' psychological and physical health and safety, as well as to organizational performance and productivity (Commission on Social Determinants of Health 2008).

A lack of awareness and understanding of the relationship between the work environment and worker psychosocial wellbeing has hampered the development of policy and occupational health services for work-related psychosocial health in nonindustrialized countries (Houtman et al. 2007). In 2010, experts from the Asia-Pacific region met in Darwin, Australia, and agreed that a much greater cooperative effort was needed to build a stronger evidence base to address the issues and contribute to global and local knowledge development, and policies and practice in the region. The first book was a first step to take stock of knowledge, produce new knowledge, and publish material in a common language to increase awareness of psychosocial factors at work in the Asia Pacific. This second book builds on this project, extending the range of psychosocial risks under investigation, and has a particular focus on practical examples of interventions and actions being undertaken in the region to address issues relating to psychosocial factors at work in the Asia Pacific.

The Asia-Pacific Region

For the purpose of this book and the researchers involved in the various projects, the Asia-Pacific region has been defined as follows. We have integrated regions specified by the International Labor Organization (ILO) (2014) and the World Health Organization (WHO) (2014). We combined the ILO Asia and Pacific Region classification with the WHO Western Pacific Region, and the WHO South-East Asia Region. These groupings are defined as the Asia-Pacific region. In addition, Taiwan has been added as an area of significance (see Table 1.1). Figure 1.1 features the significant areas (Christensen 2014).

The Asia-Pacific region is very diverse, culturally, ethnically, religiously, and economically, and combines some of the richest countries as well as two-thirds of

Table 1.1 Areas of the Asia Pacific

1. Afghanistan (The Islamic State of)	22. Philippines
2. Australia	23. Republic of Korea
3. Brunei Darussalam	24. Samoa
4. Cambodia (The Kingdom of)	25. Singapore (The Republic of)
5. China (The People's Republic of)	26. Solomon Islands
6. Cook Islands	27. Tonga
7. Fiji	28. Tuvalu
8. Iran (Islamic Republic of)	29. Vanuatu
9. Japan	30. Viet Nam (The Socialist Republic of)
10. Kiribati	31. Bangladesh (The People's Republic of)
11. Lao People's Democratic Republic	32. Bhutan
12. Malaysia	33. Korea (The Republic of)
13. Marshall Islands	34. India
14. Micronesia (Federated States of)	35. Indonesia
15. Mongolia	36. Maldives (The Republic of)
16. Nauru	37. Myanmar
17. New Zealand	38. Nepal
18. Niue	39. Sri Lanka
19. Pakistan	40. Taiwan
20. Palau (The Republic of)	41. Thailand (The Kingdom of)
21. Papua New Guinea	42. Timor-Leste

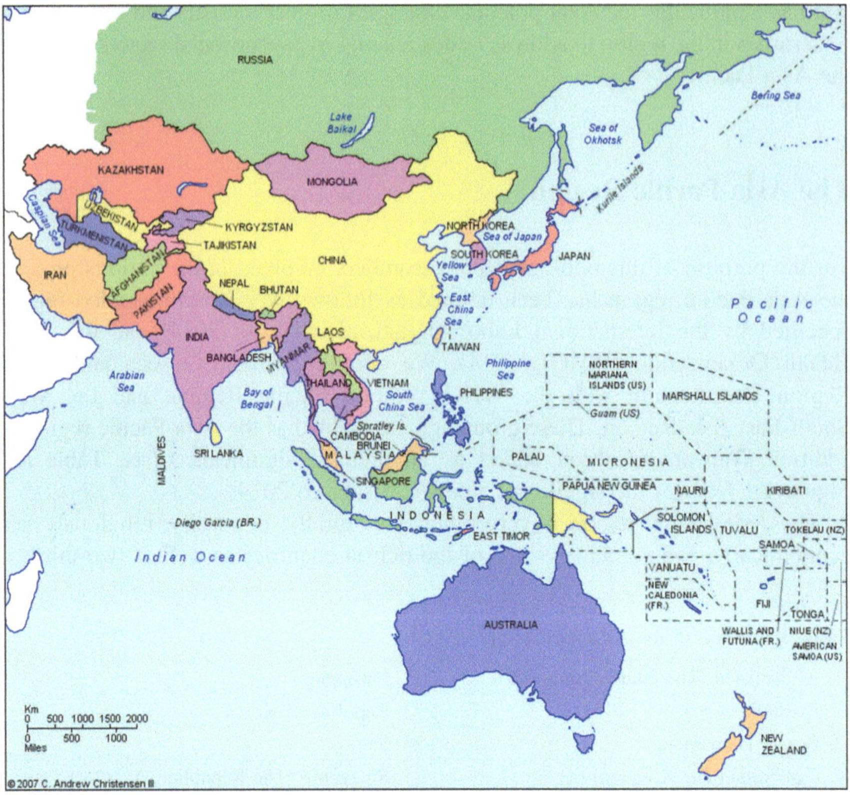

Fig. 1.1 Map of the Asia-Pacific region

the world's poor (ILO 2014). The Asia Pacific combines advanced industrialized economies (e.g., Japan, Australia), with emerging or newly industrialized (e.g., India, China) and developing economies (e.g., Vietnam). The regulatory frameworks are very different across the regions (see Chaps. 2, 3, 4, 5, and 10) and the subsequent management of psychosocial factors in the workplace varies too (Chaps. 11, 12, 14, 15, 16, and 17).

Job design is important in the development of effective preventative strategies to reduce psychosocial hazards and risk in the workplace (see Chap. 7). However, in countries with high levels of job insecurity, having a poorly designed job is better than no job. For economically advanced countries such as Australia, New Zealand, and Japan, discussion about the role of job design and the importance of reducing psychosocial hazards is made possible through the much higher levels of job security, although this is not uniform across all sectors.

Psychosocial Factors at Work

In the previous book, new learning emerged about the issues of psychosocial factors at work. The importance of culturally specific tools was explored which found the need to consider the adaptation of tools and methods to ensure accurate data is collected in this area.

The kinds of issues facing the Asia-Pacific workplaces in developed economies (e.g., Japan, Australia) are common in some respects to other areas of the world. A powerful force shaping the nature of work in the Asia Pacific is globalization (Dollard 2007). Taking into account macro or external factors (e.g., national politics, national policies, income inequality, employment conditions), organizational and individual factors is of key importance to the management of psychosocial factors at work (see Fig. 1.2). As an example, Chap. 2 in this book provides a comprehensive coverage of an important external factor, regulatory frameworks, and explores these in a range of countries and provides a background to where the next steps might be in risk management of the psychosocial work environment in the Asia Pacific.

As was presented in the previous book (Dollard et al. 2014), challenges which the Asia Pacific face are numerous and linked to neoliberal policies which have stimulated global trade, freed up markets, and increased competition. For developed economies in the Asia Pacific, this has led to changing labor markets (e.g., unstable labor markets, job insecurity, and precarious contracts), new forms of production

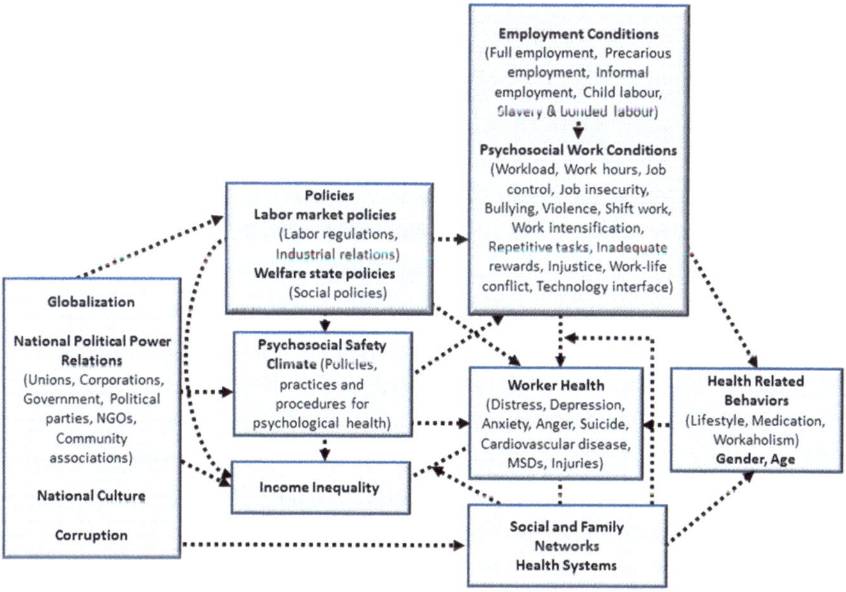

Fig. 1.2 Multilevel model of psychosocial factors at work

(e.g. lean production), and in turn work intensification, long working hours, increased workload, work pressure, and poor work-life balance (Van den Bossche et al. 2006). Organizations have adapted by downsizing and restructuring to flatter structures to improve flexibility and competitiveness (Kawakami 2000). We extend exploration of these issues and interventions in this book.

Asia-Pacific Academy for Psychosocial Factors at Work

Asia-Pacific Academy for Psychosocial Factors at Work was established in 2012 following a series of expert meetings across the Asia-Pacific region. The overarching aim of the Academy is to bring together academics, practitioners, and policy makers from the Asia-Pacific region and beyond, and contribute to better working arrangements in the region. The academy provides a forum to discuss psychosocial factors at work, to share and generate knowledge, to deliver education and training, to build greater networks, and to foster opportunities to prevent work injury. The academy is multidisciplinary in outlook.

The executive comprises:

- Foundation President-elect Professor Maureen Dollard and Area Representative of Australia
- Vice President, Professor Rusli Bin Nordin, and Area Representative of Malaysia
- Vice President, Associate Professor Akihito Shimazu, and Area Representative of Japan
- Executive Officer, Tessa Bailey, Australia
- Chair Research and Development, Dr. Michelle Tuckey, Australia
- Chair Education and Training, Professor Rusli Bin Nordin, Malaysia
- Conference Chair, Assistant Professor Sara Arphorn, Area Representative, Thailand
- Membership Officer Professor Paula Brough, Australia
- External Relations Officer, Mikaela Owen, Australia
- Publications officer, Wes McTernan, Australia
- Finance Director, Annabelle Neal, Australia
- Area Representative, Professor Jeong-Ho Chae, South Korea
- Area Representative, Associate Professor Junming Dai, China
- Area Representative, Dr. Pham Minh Khuê, Vietnam
- Area Representative, Dr. Yawen Cheng, Taiwan

There is also an International Advisory Committee comprising Professor Norito Kawakami, Japan; Professor Christian Dormann, Germany; and Dr. Loic Lerouge, France.

In April 2014, the Academy was invited to sign a Memorandum of Understanding with The European Academy of Occupational Health Psychology

Fig. 1.3 Signing the MOU, April 16th 2014; Professor Sergio Iavicoli, President, European Academy of Occupational Health Psychology; Professor Maureen Dollard, President, Asia-Pacific Academy for Psychosocial Factors at Work; Professor Stavroula Leka, Chair European Academy of Occupational Health Psychology Conference London

(EAOHP), on scientific and professional collaboration in the field of occupational health psychology (signed in London on the 16th April 2014 at the European Academy of Occupational Health Psychology conference). The MOU includes collaboration for the promotion and development of occupational health psychology at national, international and global levels within the limits of their missions, strategies, competencies, and resources. We very much look forward to this working with the EAOHP to achieve better work conditions for people in the Asia Pacific (Fig. 1.3).

The Academy also has a relationship with ICBM (International Society of Behavioral Medicine), whereby Professor Norito Kawakami is a past president. In 2014, their official journal, the International Journal of Behavioral Medicine, convened a special issue on behavioral medicine in the Asia Pacific. Guest editors were Akihito Shimazu, Akizumi Tsutsumi, and Kazuhiro Yoshiuch.

The Academy has organized six international expert workshops held consecutively in Australia, Malaysia, Japan, Thailand, Australia, and Korea. These have been highly successful in coordinating and organizing efforts to understand and address psychosocial factors at work in the Asia Pacific. Many of the plans formulated in the meetings have been implemented with great success. They include:

1. A Special Issue of the International Journal of Stress Management titled *Theory and Methods to Prevent and Manage Occupational Stress: Innovations From and Around the Globe* published in the first journal's issue of 2014, and edited by Professor Paula Brough, Professor Maureen Dollard, and Dr. Michelle Tuckey;
2. A successful Australian Research Council grant between the University of South Australia (Professor Dollard and Dr. Tuckey) and the University of Malaya (Dr. Awang Idris). Titled *The dynamic interplay of physical and psychosocial safety in frontline healthcare workplaces in Australia and Malaysia,* the grant has initiated international collaborative research arrangements on psychosocial factors at work.
3. The book, *Psychosocial Factors at Work in the Asia Pacific*, Dordrecht, The Netherlands; Springer International Publishing, edited by Maureen Dollard, Akihito Shimazu, Rusli Bin Nordin, Paula Brough, and Michelle Tuckey.
4. A second book (this volume), Psychosocial Factors at Work in the Asia Pacific: From theory to practice edited by Akihito Shimazu, Rusli Bin Nordin, Maureen Dollard, and Jodi Oakman.

History of the Academy and Coordination in the Asia Pacific

In this section, we briefly recap activities until 2013 (these are elaborated in the first book), and then outline the activities of the Academy since then. Coordinated efforts for dialogue on psychosocial factors at work in the Asia Pacific began in 2010 (8–9 July) when an expert meeting was convened in Darwin by Professor Maureen Dollard and Dr. Michelle Tuckey and Professor Paula Brough, from Australia. Twenty-one experts from Australia, New Zealand, Malaysia, Japan, and Germany, including industry regulators, policy makers, and academics from a range of disciplines met for two days to discuss psychosocial factors at work in the Asia Pacific.

The Second Asia-Pacific Expert Workshop on Psychosocial Factors at Work was held in Johor Bahru, Malaysia on 7–8 July 2011, hosted by Professor Rusli Bin Nordin and Ms Cindy Biding Ahin, from the Jeffrey Cheah School of Medicine & Health Sciences, Clinical School Johor Bahru at Monash University Malaysia. Twenty-eight delegates from Australia, Japan, and different parts of Malaysia including Sabah and Sarawak attended the workshop.

The Third Expert Workshop on Psychosocial Factors at Work in the Asia Pacific was held at the University of Tokyo. It was chaired by Associate Professor Akihito Shimazu, and was attended by 46 participants. A major outcome of the meeting was the official launch of the *Asia-Pacific Academy for Psychosocial Factors at Work* on 3 August, 2012.

The Fourth Expert Workshop on Psychosocial Factors at Work in the Asia Pacific was held in Phra Nakhon Sri Ayutthaya Province, Thailand, on 28–29 November 2013, convened by Assistant Professor Sara Arphorn. It was hosted by the cooperation of Thai academic institutions: the Research Center for Informal Workers, Department of Occupational Health and Safety, Faculty of Public Health, Mahidol University and the Rajamagala University of Technology, Suan Dusit Rajabhat University, Suansaranrom Psychiatric Hospital, and Naresuan University. The goals of the workshop were successfully achieved by bringing together academics from the Asia-Pacific region and beyond to discuss psychosocial factors at work and establish expert networking. The workshop welcomed 35 participants from 6 countries: Japan, Australia, China, France, Malaysia, and Thailand. The program included a special lecture on participatory action-oriented training for the prevention of psychosocial risks at work in different sectors. The lecture consisted of a talk by Dr. Kazutaka Kogi, the President of ICOH, the achievement report from Prof. Dr. Maureen Dollard, 2 focus group forums on Education and Training and Research and Practice and 22 oral presentations. All participants experienced Thai Massage on the last day of workshop. The workshop ended with good atmosphere of friends for better working arrangements in the region.

The Fifth meeting took place in Adelaide, South Australia as part of the International Congress of the International Commission on Occupational Health: Work, Organizational, and Psychosocial Factors (ICOH-WOPS), 17–19 September 2014, Adelaide Convention Center. The conference committee was as follows: Conference Chair, Prof. Maureen Dollard; Scientific Committee Chair, Dr Michelle Tuckey; Organizing Committee Chair, Ms Tessa Bailey; Social Committee Chair, Prof Tony Winefield; Social Committee Member, Annabelle Neal; Social Committee Member and Media Support, Wesley McTernan; Finance, Mirela Garaplija; Chloe Lidiard, Marketing; Committee Member, Sharron Skelly; and Committee Member, Karen O'Brien.

The conference explored a number of themes including: Psychosocial factors at work and their relationship with productivity and health; Psychosocial research in developing countries; Integrative and interdisciplinary approaches; Prevention and interventions for workers at risk; 'Hot topics' such as workplace bullying, sickness absence, aging workforce; Organizational factors that promote wellbeing; Managing workers with chronic health disorders and mental health issues; Focus on industries/occupations at risk, e.g., health workers; Worker health: From research to practice.

The ICOH-WOPS conference featured three preconference workshops for attendees as described below:

- *Longitudinal designs* by Prof. Christian Dormann (Johannes Gutenberg-Universität Mainz, Mainz, Germany) and Professor Dieter Zapf (Johann Wolfgang Goethe-University, Frankfurt, Germany). *This workshop aimed to contribute to the use of statistical methodology in the field of occupational health psychology by providing a brief overview of reasons for and types of longitudinal designs.*

- *Theory development in work stress research: A meta-theoretical approach* by Prof. Jan de Jonge (Eindhoven University of Technology, The Netherlands). This workshop aimed to analyze and evaluate theoretical models in the area of work stress from a meta-theoretical perspective.
- *Precarious employment: Understanding an emerging social determinant of health* by Prof. Joan Benach (Pompeu Fabra University, Barcelona, Spain).

The conference also featured keynote presentations by:

- Professor Robert Karasek (University of Massachusetts Lowell, USA), *From the Demand/Control Model to a Feasible Economy of Innovative and Healthy Work.*
- Professor Norito Kawakami (University of Tokyo, Japan), *Mainstreaming positive mental health among workers: A new evidence-based approach*?
- Professor Stavroula Leka, (University of Nottingham, United Kingdom), *Are current policy and practice frameworks appropriate to tackle psychosocial risks and promote mental health in the workplace*?
- Professor Sharon Parker (University of Western Australia, Australia), *Designing Work That Works: Future Directions for Job Design Research and Practice.*

And a State of the Art Address by:

- Associate Professor Joan Benach (Pompeu Fabra University, Spain), *Health Inequities: solutions for our Worst Public Health Epidemic.*

More information on each of the keynote presenters as well as the abstracts for each talk can be viewed at http://www.unisa.edu.au/Research/Asia-Pacific-Center-for-Work-Health-Safety/International-Congress-for-Occupational-Health-and-Work- Organization-and-Psychosocial-Factors11/Keynote-Presentations/.

A standout feature of the conference was *Burning Questions*. Members of the audience asked preprepared questions of an expert audience comprising:

- Prof. Michael Quinlan, School of Organization and Management, University of New South Wales, Australia (Labour relations Australia)
- Sandra Dann, Director, Working Women's Centre, South Australia, Australia (Women at work, bullying)
- Mr. Michael Borowick, Assistant Secretary, Australian Council of Trade Unions (Industrial relations)
- Prof. Maureen Dollard, University of South Australia, Chair
- Prof. Akinori Nakata, University of Occupational and Environmental Health, Japan (Public Health, Asia Pacific)
- Prof. Stavroula Leka, Professor of Work, Health and Policy, Director, Center for Organizational Health and Development, University of Nottingham, UK (International policy, Europe)
- Prof. Peter Schnall, Professor of Medicine, Director, Center for Social Epidemiology, University of California, Irvine, US (Cardiovascular disease and work stress) (Fig. 1.4)

Fig. 1.4 The International Congress of the International Commission on Occupational Health: Work, Organizational, and Psychosocial Factors (ICOH-WOPS), 17–19 September 2014, Adelaide Convention Centre

The conference program also featured oral presentations, symposia, and poster presentations from 187 contributing authors. Awards were given for the best student oral paper, and the best student poster. This year's winners were:

Best student oral paper award: Irene Niks (Eindhoven University of Technology, Eindhoven, The Netherlands), with her coauthors Jan De Jonge, Josette Gevers, and Irene Houtman for the paper entitled *DISCovery: evaluating tailored work-oriented interventions in hospital care*.

Best student poster award: Yuya Shimojo (Tohoku University Graduate School of Medicine, Japan), with his coauthors Kyouko Asakura, Miho Sato, Ikue Watanabe for the poster entitled, *Relationships between work-family organizational culture, organizational commitment, and intention to stay in Japanese registered nurses*.

The proposal for this current book was developed at the Adelaide meeting.

The 6th meeting took place in South Korea in 2015. On May 30 2015, members of the Korean Society of Occupational Stress (KSOS) and APA-PFW met for a joint conference in city of Seoul (Campus of Seoul National University, College of Nursing) with the theme of *Suicide at work and psychosocial health management*. Twenty-six experts from 4 countries, Australia, Japan, Malaysia, and Korea participated. Prof. Mina Ha (President of KSOS, Dankook University, Korea) and Prof. Jungsun Park (Advisor of KSOS, Daegu Catholic University) gave the welcoming address speeches. Prof. Maureen Dollard gave opening remarks and an achievement report on the APA-PFW. The morning joint conference session was moderated by Dr. Sarven McLinton (University of South Australia) and the 6 orals and 3 posters were presented, which covered a broad scope of psychosocial factors at work and its management including topics such as "*The roles of personal resource of job satisfaction*," "*The effect of psychosocial safety climate on workers' emotion*," "Impact of job demand," "The effects of proximity on work and home relationships," and "Workholism versus work engagement."

A special lecture, "*Recommendations for individual participant data (IPD) meta-analyses on work stressors and health outcomes: comments on IPD-Work Consortium papers*" by Prof. Bongkyoo Choi (University of California, Irvine) was presented with a hot discussion ensuing. At the afternoon conference, two keynote presentations were given: "Towards healthy employees in a healthy organization: From a perspective of work engagement"" by Prof. Akihoto Shimazu (University of Tokyo), and "*The integration of the assessment of mental health among workers into the management*" by Prof. Jong-Min Woo (Inje University).

It was a day filled with excellent presentations in both English and Korean. There was also time for discussions about actions for the Academy with many excellent outcomes. As an exercise to help foster collaboration between present parties, groups were assembled and discussed the possibility of a training program (accredited by the APA-PFW) for psychosocial safety across the Asia Pacific. Current region-specific programs exist, and therefore a more universal program was proposed.

During discussion, members pooled their knowledge and proposed a strategy for program development and deployment. The following is a brief synthesis of these ideas. Identifying key steps for any training development programs that are undertaken by a collaboration of academy members and colleagues were recommended as follows: (1) Create a program steering committee; (2) Identify target audience; (3) Identify the essence of pre-existing programs; (4) Critique current programs; (5) Tool selection and development; and 6) Trainers to deliver program.

Best poster presentation award was given to "*The implementation of mental health care program for the unemployed: from its development to evaluation*" by Miho Takahashi from University of Tokyo.

Also at the workshop it was suggested that a database of skills to be created for those members and colleagues willing to collaborate on projects. The database has since been created by Dr Sarven McLinton and can be accessed via: https://docs.google.com/spreadsheets/d/1A4Goi2MnFZo9S_zLZ1Lhi5YQTtTn0COCpm01wl-rudnY/edit?usp=sharing.

We welcome members and colleagues to use this information as a reference point for seeking partners in the Asia Pacific to collaborate with ongoing projects, papers, and presentations.

The 7th meeting will take place in October 2016 in Shanghai China, hosted by Professor Junming Dai.

The Current Book

This second book builds on the issues raised in the first book and provides further discussion of psychosocial factors at work in the Asia Pacific. It has a particular focus on practical approaches to developing and then managing health workplaces, to improve the psychosocial working conditions.

The book is presented in 6 parts:

I. Introduction
II. Policy and practice frameworks in the Asia Pacific and beyond
III. Psychosocial factors at work in the Asia Pacific
IV. Practical approaches toward developing healthy workplaces and workers
V. Practical approaches to the management of psychosocial risk
VI. Conclusions

We are delighted that experts have contributed their knowledge and expertise for this book project. We have continued our ethos of encouraging authors for their region to work together to produce the chapter, some for the first time, others building on collaborations developed in the first book. This book aims to increase research capacity in the region, so authors were invited to contribute based on knowledge of their joint interests. The book features inputs from 46 academics, 44 from 7 countries across the Asia Pacific.

Content

Part I: Introduction

Each chapter introduces the issue, outlines its importance, and provides an overview of relevant theoretical perspectives to psychosocial factors at work in a range of countries across the region. The specific intent is to place the issue in the context of the Asia Pacific. Case studies, proposed guidelines, and examples of interventions are used to highlight the specific issues in the Asia Pacific. Each chapter then provides a discussion on the overall findings and concludes with highlights and future directions in research, policy, and practice for the region.

Part II: Policy and Practice Frameworks in the Asia Pacific and Beyond

In the second part of this book, three chapters are presented which examine policy and recommendations for the management of psychosocial factors at work. Chapter 2 by Leka and Jain reviews international policy and practice initiatives for the management of psychosocial risks and the promotion of mental health in the workplace. It provides a relevant institutional framework including international organizations, regional institutions, stakeholder associations, networks, and professional bodies. Regulatory and nonbinding policy approaches are outlined which are applicable at the international level. Examples of good practice in terms of practical tools are presented from several countries before an overall evaluation is offered on the current state of the art and whether the right balance has been achieved in policy and practice in this area.

Chapter 3 by Tsutsumi and Shimazu focused on preventive measures for workplace mental health and the development of guidelines for the primary prevention for mental health at work. These guidelines were developed following a systematic review of primary prevention measures for occupational mental health and a consensus meeting by experts and practitioners in the occupational health field. These guidelines for primary prevention for mental health at work consider three preventive strategies—workplace improvement, self-care training, and supervisor training. The guidelines proposed take into account different levels of research evidence, and are considered as recommendations for those charged with managing psychosocial factors in the workplace.

Insights from the Asia Pacific are provided in Chap. 4 from Bailey, Cheng, Idris, and Arphorn, where policy and practice were discussed in a focus group with representatives from Australia, Taiwan, Malaysia, and Thailand. Differences in regulatory approaches were discussed, and in some countries, policy in the area of psychosocial factors at work was very limited, suggesting the need for translation of evidence into policy.

Focusing specifically on South Korea, Chap. 5 by Park, introduces how work-related cardiovascular and cerebrovascular diseases and job stress are handled in South Korea and presents the statistics, guidelines, and policies related to these issues and describes strategies to prevent and manage them. South Korea lags behind other developed countries in the development of guidelines for occupational safety and health, but nevertheless has made some progress in terms of reducing work-related cardiovascular and cerebrovascular diseases, but not job stress.

Part III: Psychosocial Factors at Work in the Asia Pacific

In Chap. 6, Yulita, Idris, and Dollard present a systematic narrative review of a facet-specific climate for psychosocial safety (psychosocial safety climate [PSC]) that has been featured in the literature. PSC refers to policies, practices, and procedures for the protection of workers' psychological health and safety (Dollard and Bakker 2010, p. 580). The review considered PSC in terms of its history, role, impact, and research trend. Thirteen peer-reviewed journal articles qualified for the review. For comparative purposes, the review also considered 75 other peer-reviewed journal articles on safety-related work climates [safety climate (n = 59), psychological safety climate (n = 16)], published from 1980 to 2016. The researchers identify the specificity of outcome related to PSC (e.g., physical health, psychological health, work motivation, work conditions). They also consider the main theorization of the PSC, whether as an antecedent, mediator, or moderator of work stress processes. To obtain a greater understanding of PSC and its future role in workers' psychological health and work outcomes, the chapter considers some future challenges such as the simultaneous use of multiple climates, multilevel modeling, research time lags, advanced research designs, and data analysis tools.

In Chap. 7, Parker and Zhang highlight the importance of designing work in the contemporary work context of uncertainty and complexity. Much research shows that good work design has positive outcomes for individuals and organizations. Their chapter provides a state of the art review on the development of work design theory and research, especially providing a brief overview of two popular work design perspectives: designing motivating work; and, designing safe and healthy work. However, the primary goal of the chapter is to identify some important future research directions due to the remarkable changes in the nature of workplace and workforce.

The issue of workplace violence is increasingly recognized as an important occupational health issue. Despite this, empirical studies on workplace violence are limited in Taiwan. Chapter 8 is an investigation by Cheng and Pien into the workplace violence problem and policy debates concerning workplace violence in Taiwan. The chapter presents empirical findings on the workplace violence distributions, trends, antecedents, and associated health risks, based on large-scale survey data of the general working population, in 2010 (N = 17,286) and 2013 (N = 18,030). They investigate four types of violence: physical violence, verbal violence, psychological violence, and sexual harassment. In particular, they pay attention to workplace violence exposures by gender and occupation. In an innovative approach, they go further and contextualize workplace violence in terms of prevailing climate (neighborhood-level workplace violence), and estimate its effects on mental health using multilevel analyses. They finalize the chapter by considering improvements in workplace violence measures, study designs to investigate the casual mechanisms of workplace violence, and health consequences of the strategies for effective prevention of workplace violence.

In Chap. 9, Oakman, Maakip, and Keegel address the issue of psychosocial hazards in the development of musculoskeletal disorders (MSDs). They consider the question about whether workplace factors vary by sociocultural factors and consider the context of office workers in Malaysia and Australia. MSDs are considered to be a major occupational health problem contributing significantly to absenteeism, disability, and loss of productivity. The majority of studies related to MSDs have been conducted in developed countries such as Australia, and it is proposed that contributing factors linked with MSDs development might function differently in developing countries like Malaysia, as a result of sociocultural differences.

A key issue in the development of MSDs is the contribution of psychosocial factors; however, this is not reflected in current management practices, which tend to focus predominately on physical factors. Malaysia and Australia have very different societal structures, which influence the way work is organized and the expectations employees have at their workplaces. Therefore, it is plausible that the contribution of workplace factors to MSDs development might differ. The researchers use a survey tool to assess a range of workplace and personal factors, including work-life balance, job satisfaction, physical hazards, coping strategies, and psychosocial hazards. Analysis was undertaken to assess relevant predictors for each population and then a comparison undertaken to identify key differences between the populations. Despite similarities in the prevalence of musculoskeletal discomfort in both the Australian and Malaysian populations, differences were identified in the relative contribution of factors. The chapter also discusses the results from a qualitative study of female Malaysian office workers who were asked about their coping strategies for persistent musculoskeletal pain.

Chapter 10 covers the area of PSC; Afsharian, Zadow, and Dollard investigate the concept from two different cultural perspectives in the Asia Pacific: Iranian and Australian healthcare contexts. PSC may be conceptualized as the organizational practices, policies, and procedures for the protection of workers' psychological health and safety. To date, PSC theory has not been investigated at the boundaries of the Asia Pacific. For the first time, these investigators examined PSC as a theoretical construct in Iran, a developing country in the heart of the Middle East. The PSC-12 scale was translated into Farsi and administered among 33 work groups in an Iranian hospital (n = 257) then compared with a sample of Australian hospital employees (n = 239, across 21 work groups). The researchers explore how PSC behaves as a group level phenomenon cross culturally, how PSC levels and job design factors vary by country, how PSC as a group level phenomenon relates to job design, psychological health and work outcomes.

Part IV: Practical Approaches Toward Developing Healthy Workplaces and Workers

In Chap. 11, Potter, Fattori, and Dollard critically review eleven psychosocial risk management tools (e.g., the Canadian Implementation Guide (Standard), the UK HSE Management Standards) that are publicly available from the European Union, Canada and Australia for organizations, offering practical guidelines for organizations to readily adopt in order to decrease the impact of psychosocial risks (WHO 2010) and addresses the WHO's Global Plan of Action (GPA) on Worker Health (2008–2017) (WHO 2013). The main objective is, therefore, twofold: (1) to provide a resource that identifies and critically evaluates existing psychosocial risk management toolkits, and therefore enables organizations to determine the most suitable tool for their needs; and (2) to facilitate the distribution and transference of knowledge on these accessible organizational resources to all world regions, particularly in the Asia-Pacific region. Thus, this critical review aims to address an objective of the GPA, and responds to an appeal to identify, collect, and disseminate tools (and resources) for the evaluation and improvement of personal health resources and global psychosocial work environments (WHO 2007).

In Chap. 12, Inoue and colleagues examine the reliability and construct validity of a new version of the Brief Job Stress Questionnaire (New BJSQ), which measures an extended set of psychosocial factors at work by adding new scales/items to the current version of the BJSQ. Additional scales/items were extensively collected from theoretical models of job stress and similar questionnaires in several countries. Scales/items were field-tested and refined through a pilot internet survey. Finally, an 84-item standard version questionnaire, a 63-item recommended set, and a 23-item short version (141, 120, and 80 items in total when combined with the current 57-item BJSQ) were developed. In Japan, the number of workers with mental health problems is increasing and thus primary prevention of mental health problems is a high priority for both employers and employees. Previous studies have shown that "assessing and improving work environment" effectively reduces mental health problems (Semmer 2006); thus, the BJSQ and Job Stress Assessment Diagram (JSAD) have been developed with an aim to assess and improve the Japanese working environment. The BJSQ and JSAD have been widely used in research and practice in the field of mental health in the Japanese workplace (e.g., Kobayashi et al. 2008; Umanodan et al. 2009).

In Chap. 13, Nordin and Biding review research of Malaysian organizations to examine the role of coping strategies (employee-based) and organizational intervention (organizational-based) in preventing and alleviating psychological distress at work. Since appropriate coping strategies are known to be effective in controlling psychosocial stressors and may be the only measures available in most organizations, organizations are particularly encouraged to promote more coping skills training among their employees as part of their legal and corporate responsibility (OSHA 1994).

In Chap. 14, Imamura and colleagues investigate an innovative way to deliver Cognitive Behavioral Therapy based (CBT-based) treatment that is currently, widely practiced using computerized CBT [CCBT via Internet (iCBT)] technology. The authors review and introduce three recent iCBT intervention studies, and discuss the possibility of utilization of iCBT program in the workplace. Reasons for the increasing popularity of iCBT have been the focus of constant attention on improving symptoms or preventing onset of mental disorders. It is proposed that iCBT may be useful for people not able to access face-to-face therapies due to geographical or other challenges.

In Chap. 15, Martin presents findings from a quasi-experimental simulation study which examines how attitudes move toward employees with depression (affective, cognitive and behavioral forms of stigma) are influenced by contextual cues by reflecting an organization's support for mental health and how these attitudes and context are associated with performance ratings of a depressed employee. There is a high prevalence of depression in working adults (lifetime prevalence estimates are one in five people or greater) (WHO 2009) which presents significant social and economic issues for organizations. Development of strategies for workplaces to utilize in assisting those in management positions to employees with mental health issues is needed.

Part V: Practical Approaches to the Management of Psychosocial Risk

In this section, a range of practical approaches to managing psychosocial factors in the workplace are presented. These interventions are undertaken in Japan, China, and Australia.

In Chap. 16, Moriguchi, Sakuragi, and Ikeda discuss psychosocial factors in small-scale enterprises in Japan and the Asia-Pacific region. In many countries, occupational health service activities for small-scale and micro-scale enterprises are often insufficient as they have limited access to human, economic, and technical resources. The demands of employers in those enterprises in relation to mental health activities and established measures for improving the existing situation in Japan are discussed.

Chapter 17 presents a review of health issues of workers engaged in operations related to the accident at the Fukushima Daiichi Nuclear Power Plant (NPP)—a mega-earthquake and subsequent tsunami occurred in 11 March 2011, followed by a nuclear accident in northern Japan at the NPP of the Tokyo Electric Power Company (TEPCO). A large number of workers were impacted and a range of health issues are described along with the actions taken to solve them. A summary of lessons learned from the experience for the disasters in the future is included.

In Chap. 18 Hu, Schaufeli, and Taris address the effect of a nation-specific stressor on wellbeing by focusing on Guanxi (i.e., human network, connection) in the Chinese workplace. Guanxi has been considered as a product of Confucian values and is inherent in the work ethics of the Chinese people. This chapter describes the conceptual and cross-cultural development of the Job Demands Resource model (Schaufeli and Bakker 2004) proposed in western cultures and how the Chinese interpersonal phenomenon of Guanxi is incorporated.

Finally, in Chap. 19, McTernan, Dollard, Tuckey, and Vandenberg discuss the impacts of remote work on workers and their families in Australian mines. Australia's vast landscape is abundant in valuable mineral deposits. However, these resources are largely dispersed inland at a great distance from Australia's coastal urban populations. Although a review of the literature investigating health hazards in the mining industry found quite an extensive range of research published, little research was found specifically investigating psychosocial risks to health. In the chapter, key demands pertinent to remote and nonremote mining workers, the key resources that help workers manage job demands, and the form the job strain manifests are discussed.

Part VI: Conclusion

In the conclusion, a synthesis of the evidence is presented and some insights into challenges and future directions for research, interventions, and policy development are provided.

This book is an exciting contribution to the field and it is **For You**! If you are working in the field of occupational health and safety, human resource management, occupational health psychology, organizational psychology, or ergonomics, this book will provide valuable insights for your practice.

The specific focus on the Asia Pacific makes it particularly relevant for those working in the region. The chapter provides specific detail on a topic, explains current research and thinking, outlines practical implications, but importantly also provides direction to further research in the related area. It will be a valuable resource for academics, students, and practitioners across the Asia Pacific.

This second book on psychosocial factors in the Asia Pacific is a must to have on your desk for relevant and up to date information of a range of psychosocial issues across the region.

References

Christensen III, C. A. (2014). Map of the Asia Pacific © 2007. Retrieved from http://www.worldmonitor.info/aboutwm.html (22 Jan 2014).

Commission on Social Determinants of Health. (2008). *Closing the gap in a generation: Health equity through action on the social determinants of health (Final Report of the Commission on Social Determinants of Health)*. Geneva: World Health Organization.

Cox, T., & Griffiths, A. (2005). The nature and measurement of work-related stress: theory and practice. In J. R. Wilson & N. Corlett (Eds.), *Evaluation of human work* (3rd ed.). London: CRS Press.

Dollard, M. (2007). Necrocapitalism: Throwing away workers in the race for global capital. In J. Houdmont & S. McIntyre (Eds.), *Occupational health psychology: European perspectives on research, education and practice* (Vol. 2, pp. 169–193). Maia: ISMAI Publishers.

Dollard, M. F., & Bakker, A. B. (2010). Psychosocial safety climate as a precursor to conducive work environment, psychological health problems, and employee engagement. *Journal of Occupational and Organizational Psychology, 83*, 579–599.

Dollard, M. F., Shimazu, S., Nordin, R. B., & Brough, P. (2014). Chapter 1 The context of psychosocial factors at work in the Asia Pacific. In M. F. Dollard, A. Shimazu, R. B. Nordin, P. Brough, & M. R. Tuckey (Eds.), *Psychosocial factors at work in the Asia Pacific* (pp. 3–27). Dordrecht: Springer International Publishing.

Houtman, I., Jettinghoff, K., & Cedillo, L. (2007). *Raising awareness of stress at work in developing countries: A modern hazard in a traditional working environment.* Geneva: WHO (Protecting Workers' Health series No. 6). Geneva: World Health Organization (WHO).

International Labour Organization. (2014). Regions. Retrieved from http://www.ilo.org/global/regions/lang–en/index.htm (4 Mar 2015).

Kawakami, N. (2000). Preface. Job stress in East Asia: Exchanging experiences among China, Japan, Korea, Taiwan and Thailand. In *Proceedings of the First East-Asia Job Stress Meeting, Waseda University International Conference Centre Japan* (pp. 1–2).

Kang, S. Y., Staniford, A., Dollard, M. F., & Kompier, M. (2008). Knowledge development and content in occupational health psychology: A systematic analysis of the Journal of Occupational Health Psychology, and Work & Stress, 1996–2006. In J. Houdmont & S. Leka & (Eds.), *Occupational health psychology: European Perspectives on Research, Education and Practice* (Vol. 3, pp. 27–63). Maia: ISMAI Publishers.

Kobayashi, Y., Kaneyoshi, A., Yokota, A., & Kawakami, N. (2008). Effects of a worker participatory program for improving work environments on job stressors and mental health among workers: A controlled trial. *Journal*

OSHA. (1994). *Laws of Malaysia. Act 514: Occupational Safety and Health Act 1994*. Kuala Lumpur: Government of Malaysia.

Schaufeli, W. B., & Bakker, A. B. (2004). Job demands, job resources, and their relationship with burnout and engagement: A multisample study. *Journal of Organizational Behavior, 25*, 293–315.

Semmer, N. K. (2006). Job stress interventions and the organization of work. *Scandinavian Journal of Work, Environment & Health, 32*, 515–527.

Seoul Declaration on Safety and Health at Work. International Labour Organization, International Safety and Security Organization, Korean Occupational Safety and Health Agency, 2008. http://www.seouldeclaration.org/index.php.

Umanodan, R., Kobayashi, Y., Nakamura, M., Kitaoka-Higashiguchi, K., Kawakami, N., & Shimazu, A. (2009). Effects of a worksite stress management training program with six short-hour sessions: A controlled trial among Japanese employees. *Journal of Occupational Health, 51*, 294–302.

Van den Bossche, S., Smulders, P., & Houtman, I. (2006). *Trends and risk groups in working conditions*. Hoofddrop: TNO Work & Employment.

World Health Organization. (2007). *Workers' health: Global plan of action. Sitieth World Health Assembly*. Geneva: WHO Press.

World Health Organization. (2009). *Depression: What is depression*? Retrieved from http://www.who.int/topics/depression/en/ (4 Mar 2015).

World Health Organization. (2010). *WHO healthy workplace framework and model: Background and supporting literature and practices*. Geneva: WHO Press.

World Health Organization. (2013). *WHO Global Plan of Action on Workers' Health (2008–2017): Baseline for implementation. Global Country Survey 2008/2009. Executive Summary and Survey Findings*. Geneva: WHO Press.

Chapter 2
International Initiatives to Tackle Psychosocial Risks and Promote Mental Health in the Workplace: Is There a Good Balance in Policy and Practice?

Stavroula Leka and Aditya Jain

Abstract This chapter reviews international initiatives for the management of psychosocial risks and the promotion of mental health in the workplace. The chapter first presents the relevant institutional framework including international organizations, regional institutions, stakeholder associations, networks, and professional bodies. It then proceeds to outline regulatory and nonbinding policy approaches applicable at the international level. Finally, an overall evaluation is offered on the current state of the art and whether the right balance has been achieved in policy and practice in this area.

Keywords Psychosocial risks · Mental health in the workplace · Policy · Practice

Introduction

Work-related psychosocial factors refer to aspects of work organization, design and management such as work demands, organizational support, rewards, and interpersonal relationships. When these factors are not managed well in the workplace they can represent hazards that have the potential to cause harm on individual health, safety, and wellbeing, on organizations (e.g., through sickness absence, reduced productivity, human error) and on society (e.g., increased disability pensions, healthcare costs, etc.) (e.g., WHO 2008). Psychosocial risk refers to the potential of psychosocial hazards to cause harm (BSI 2011).

Work-related stress is closely associated with exposure to psychosocial hazards and is defined, for example, on the UK Health & Safety Executive website as

S. Leka (✉)
Centre for Organizational Health and Development, School of Medicine, University of Nottingham, Nottingham, UK
e-mail: stavroula.leka@nottingham.ac.uk

A. Jain
Nottingham University Business School, Nottingham, UK

A. Shimazu et al. (eds.), *Psychosocial Factors at Work in the Asia Pacific*,
DOI 10.1007/978-3-319-44400-0_2

"the adverse reaction people have to excessive pressures or other types of demand placed on them at work." The European Agency for Safety & Health at Work (EU-OSHA) website states that "people experience stress when they perceive that there is an imbalance between the demands made of them and the resources they have available to cope with those demands." When pressure at work is chronic and unmanageable, it results in work-related stress which is recognized as a negative experience resulting from exposure to poor working conditions (psychosocial and/or physical) (Cox 1993; Cox and Griffiths 2010; WHO 2008).

International Initiatives to Prevent and Manage Psychosocial Risks

A number of significant developments toward the prevention and management of psychosocial risks have been achieved at the international, regional (e.g., European), and national level. These include both regulatory approaches such as ILO conventions, European Union directives, and national legislation, as well as 'non-binding/voluntary' approaches which may take the form of specifications, guidance, social partner agreements, and standards. This chapter clarifies the institutional framework of relevance to the prevention of psychosocial risks, identifying the key institutions which play a role in managing psychosocial risks, and highlights the key regulatory and nonregulatory approaches taken by these institutions.

Institutional Framework

International Organizations

A number of international organizations such as the International Labor Organization (ILO), World Health Organization (WHO), International Social Security Association (ISSA), Organization for Economic Cooperation and Development (OECD), and World Bank have been active in the prevention and management of psychosocial risks and promotion of mental health through research and advocacy, as well as through the development and implementation of specific initiatives. The contributions of the ILO, and the WHO, in this area, have been the most significant at the global level and are discussed in the next sections on regulatory and nonregulatory/voluntary approaches.

The ILO has been committed to the prevention and management of work-related stress and psychosocial risks since the 1970s, and has developed a number of policy instruments as well as guidance, tools, and training material. The current work of the WHO on occupational health is governed by the Global Plan of Action on

Workers' Health 2008–2017, endorsed by the World Health Assembly in 2007. Objective two of the global plan, specifies actions "to protect and promote health at the workplace," and states that "the assessment and management of health risks at the workplace should be improved by: defining essential interventions for prevention and control of mechanical, physical, chemical, biological and psychosocial risks in the working environment" (WHO 2007a, p. 6). The WHO has contributed to this area through publication of research and guidance documents, and development of tools and resources.

Proactive and preventive social security is a pillar of ISSA's vision, and involves the promotion of health and support of employment and activity. ISSA recognizes that while prevention efforts over the past decades have resulted in many positive outcomes, numerous challenges to workers' health remain such as the increasing prevalence of psychosocial issues which require more complex approaches to prevention; therefore the ISSA has been calling and advocating for a more holistic approach toward promoting health and safety (ISSA 2012).

The OECD recognizes that tackling mental ill-health of the working-age population is a key issue for labor market and social policies in OECD countries, whose governments are increasingly recognizing that policy has a major role to play in keeping people with mental ill-health in employment or bringing those outside of the labor market back to it, and in preventing mental illness. The OECD Mental Health and Work Project is examining how the broader education, health, social, and labor market policy challenges for mental health and work are being tackled in a number of OECD countries (OECD 2012).

The World Bank works to enhance the awareness and understanding of mental and psychosocial health as a development concern by ensuring that mental and psychosocial health are incorporated into operations within the development of more long-term policies, strategies, plans, and resources to ensure sustainability (Rockhold and McDonald 2008). However, its activities in this area are not solely focused on work and employment, but on broader issues, particularly those in the context of conflict affected countries.

Regional Institutions

A number of regional organizations have adopted or intend to adopt policies that may lead to integration of national activities at the regional level. Regional institutions include the European Union (EU), African Union (AU), Association of Southeast Asian Nations (ASEAN), Commonwealth of Independent States (CIS), Caribbean Community (CARICOM), Cooperation Council for the Arab States of the Gulf (CCASG), South Asian Association for Regional Cooperation (SAARC), Union of South American Nations (UNASUR), and the Economic Cooperation Organization (ECO) among others. While a number of regional institutions have developed broad framework strategies which are relevant to workers' safety, health, and wellbeing (for example the UNASUR Health Institute—ISAGS, the AU's

Social Policy Framework for Africa), only the European Union has developed laws and policies that apply throughout the member states of the EU.

At the European level, the decision-making process in general and the co-decision procedure in particular involve three main institutions: the European Parliament, the Council of the EU, and the European Commission (EC). In addition to the main EU institutions, the EU has a number of other institutions and bodies that play specialized roles. Two tripartite specialized institutions, the European Agency for Safety and Health at Work (EU-OSHA), and the European Foundation for the Improvement of Living and Working Conditions (Eurofound), play an important role in managing psychosocial risks and promoting mental health in the workplace. Key policy initiatives from the EU are also reviewed in the following sections on regulatory and nonregulatory/voluntary approaches.

Stakeholder Associations, Networks, and Professional Bodies

Social dialogue is a mode of governance in the area of social policies, including policies on occupational safety and health. It comprises discussions, consultations, negotiations, and joint actions undertaken by social partner or stakeholder organizations such as federations of employers and workers, as well as experts in the field to participate in social policy decision making at international, regional, and sectoral level (Lawrence and Ishikawa 2005). There are a number of stakeholder organizations active in the field of managing psychosocial risks and promoting mental health at work.

The International Trade Union Confederation (ITUC) is the global voice of the world's working people. Its main areas of activity include trade union and human rights; economy, society, and the workplace; equality and nondiscrimination; and international solidarity. In 2010, the ITUC Congress Resolutions on Decent Work, called on the ITUC and regional organizations, working together with Global Unions partners and affiliates to "work with the ILO to campaign for the extension of social protection to all; work for the improvement of occupational health and safety in all countries, including as relates to exposure to hazardous chemicals, psychosocial hazards and other occupational injuries and accidents" (ITUC 2010, p. 17).

The International Organization of Employers (IOE) is the largest network of the private sector in the world. In social and labor policy debate taking place in the ILO, across the UN and multilateral system, and in the G20 and other emerging processes, the IOE is the recognized voice of business. The IOE supports national business organizations in guiding corporate members in matters of international labor standards, business and human rights, corporate social responsibility (CSR), occupational safety and health (OSH), and international industrial relations. The IOE has a number of guides and factsheets for employers to raise awareness of issues and to promote good practice in workers' safety, health, and wellbeing (e.g. IOE 2010, 2012).

The World Economic Forum (WEF) is an independent international organization for promoting public–private cooperation. The World Economic Forum is committed to improving the state of the world by engaging business, political, academic, and other leaders of society to shape global, regional, and industry agendas. The WEF established the Global Agenda Council on Wellbeing and Mental Health, which gives wellbeing and mental health recognition within a broader health context, and included them as a specific agenda on the UN's post-2015 development charter. The Council's current activities are focused on wellbeing and mental health in the workforce (WEF 2013).

The International Organization for Standardization (ISO) is the world's largest developer of voluntary international standards, which are developed through global consensus. International standards give state of the art specifications for products, services, and good practice, helping to make industry more efficient and effective. The ISO 10075 series standards which establish principles and requirements for the measurement and assessment of mental workload and specify the requirements for measurement instruments are relevant to this field of work (ISO 2004).

In addition to these organizations, a number of international professional bodies/associations are active in the field of managing work-related stress and promoting wellbeing at work. These include the International Commission on Occupational Health (ICOH), the International Ergonomics Association (IEA), and a number of regional associations. ICOH is an international nongovernmental professional society whose aims are to foster the scientific progress, knowledge and development of occupational health and safety in all its aspects ICOH is recognized by the United Nations as a nongovernmental organization (NGO), and has close working relationships with ILO, WHO, and ISSA. In 1996, the International Commission on Occupational Health created its scientific committee on Work Organization and Psychosocial Factors (ICOH-WOPS). In 1999, the European Academy of Occupational Health Psychology (EAOHP) was established and in 2005, the Society for Occupational Health Psychology (SOHP) was founded in the United States. Other regional associations have been formed since which include the Asia-Pacific Academy for Psychosocial Factors at Work, the Latin American Research Network of Researchers on Psychosocial Factors at Work (RIFAPT), and the Ibero-American Network for Work-related Psychosocial Risks (RIPSOL).

The following sections outline regulatory and nonregulatory/voluntary approaches and instruments developed by some key institutions of the ones outlined above of relevance to the prevention of psychosocial risks.

Regulatory Approaches

The regulatory approach, typically characterized by 'legal instruments', is defined as a policy relying primarily on the authority and power of the state—ultimately its legitimate monopoly on the means of coercion—in the construction, operation, and implementation, including enforcement of arrangements at international, national, or subnational level (Kirton and Trebilcock 2004). Statutes or regulations in national legal systems are generally taken as prototypical of legal instruments (Abbott et al. 2000). At the intergovernmental level they can take the form of legally binding treaties, conventions, and directives.

ILO Conventions

International labor standards are legal instruments drawn up by the ILO's constituents (governments, employers, and workers) and set out basic principles and rights at work. These standards can be either conventions or recommendations. ILO Conventions are legally binding international treaties that may be ratified by member states, which lay down the basic principles of a labor standard to be implemented by ratifying countries. They differ from recommendations, which serve as nonbinding guidelines. Recommendations can be used to supplement a Convention by providing more detailed guidelines on how it could be applied or they can be autonomous, i.e., not linked to any Convention. ILO Conventions relevant to the prevention and management of psychosocial risks are presented in Table 2.1.

Table 2.1 ILO Conventions relevant to the prevention and management of psychosocial risks

Document	Description of relevance
C155 Occupational Safety and Health Convention, ILO, 1981 and its Protocol of 2002	The Convention provides for the adoption of a coherent national occupational safety and health policy, as well as action to be taken by governments and within enterprises to promote occupational safety and health, and to improve working conditions The Convention states that "each Member shall, in the light of national conditions and practice, and in consultation with the most representative organizations of employers and workers, formulate, implement and periodically review a coherent national policy on occupational safety, occupational health, and the working environment" The policy should take into account, "relationships between the material elements of work and the persons who carry out or supervise the work, and adaptation of machinery, equipment, working time, organization of work and work processes to the physical and mental capacities of the workers"
C159 Vocational Rehabilitation and Employment (Disabled Persons) Convention, ILO, 1983	This Convention provides for the adoption of a policy at the national level which shall aim to ensure that appropriate vocational rehabilitation measures are made available to all categories of disabled persons, and at promoting employment opportunities for disabled persons in the open labor market. This policy shall be developed by taking into consideration national conditions and practice and the representative organizations of employers and workers

(continued)

Table 2.1 (continued)

Document	Description of relevance
	(including representative organizations of and for disabled persons) shall be consulted on the implementation According to the Convention, "the term disabled person means an individual whose prospects of securing, retaining and advancing in suitable employment are substantially reduced as a result of a duly recognized physical or mental impairment"
C111 Discrimination (Employment and Occupation) Convention, ILO, 1958	The Convention concerning discrimination in respect of employment and occupation (which include access to vocational training, access to employment and to particular occupations, and terms and conditions of employment) provides for the adoption of a policy at the national level which shall promote, by methods appropriate to national conditions and practice, equality of opportunity and treatment in respect of employment and occupation, with a view to eliminating any discrimination. For the purpose of this Convention the term discrimination includes (a) any distinction, exclusion, or preference made on the basis of race, color, sex, religion, political opinion, national extraction, or social origin, which has the effect of nullifying or impairing equality of opportunity or treatment in employment or occupation (b) such other distinction, exclusion, or preference which has the effect of nullifying or impairing equality of opportunity or treatment in employment or occupation as may be determined by the Member concerned after consultation with representative employers' and workers' organizations, where such exist, and with other appropriate bodies
C187 Promotional Framework for Occupational Safety and Health Convention, ILO, 2006	This Convention aims at promoting a preventative safety and health culture and progressively achieving a safe and healthy working environment. It requires ratifying States to develop, in consultation with the most representative organizations of employers and workers, a national policy, national system, and national program on occupational safety and health. The national policy shall be developed in accordance with the principles of Article 4 of the Occupational Safety and Health Convention, 1981 (No. 155), and the national systems and programs shall be developed taking into account the principles set out in relevant ILO instruments

European Union Legislation

The main piece of legislation on health and safety in the EU is the Framework Directive 89/391/EEC on Safety and Health of Workers at Work. Even though the Directive does not include the terms 'work-related stress' or 'psychosocial risk', it asks employers to ensure workers' health and safety in every aspect related to work. It requires employers to "adapt the work to the individual, especially as regards the design of work places, the choice of work equipment and the choice of working and production methods, with a view, in particular, to alleviating monotonous work and working at a predetermined work-rate, developing a coherent overall prevention policy which covers technology, organization of work, working conditions, social relationships and the influence of factors related to the working environment." In this sense, there is an indirect reference to, and provision for, risks related to the psychosocial work environment (Ertel et al. 2010; Leka et al. 2011). However, there are several other pieces of legislation in the EU that are relevant to the prevention of psychosocial risks (for a full list see Leka et al. 2015).

Nonbinding/Voluntary Approaches

In addition to regulatory approaches, 'non-binding/voluntary' approaches which directly refer to psychosocial risks, and work-related stress have been initiated including social partner agreements in the EU, standards as well as guidance and tools. These initiatives have taken place partly due to the growing recognition that good psychosocial risk management also goes beyond legal requirements (Jain et al. 2011). Examples of nonbinding approaches take the form of recommendations, resolutions, agreements, and guidance developed by international organizations such as the ILO, WHO, and the European Commission, among others.

ILO Initiatives

Key nonbinding initiatives and approaches developed by the ILO to address work-related stress and psychosocial risks, include the ILO OSH-MS, ILO recommendation—R194, the SOLVE programme, and the Stress Checkpoints.

Psychosocial Factors at Work: Recognition and Control

This report of the Joint ILO/WHO Committee on Occupational Health (ILO 1986) examined the subject of psychosocial factors at work and their consequences, emphasizing health issues. It describes the nature of such factors as related to health and the methods of identifying psychosocial factors. It also examines the means of preventing, reducing, or eliminating the psychosocial problems that arise in workplaces. It proposes a series of measures which could be taken at the enterprise level, national and international levels, with a view to giving greater importance to the psychosocial aspects of programs for the improvement of working conditions and environment and the promotion of the health and wellbeing of workers.

Preventing Stress at Work: Conditions of Work Digest

The conditions of work digest on preventing stress at work is a guidance document which provides an introduction to the issue of work-related stress, identifies trends and issues in an international perspective, and includes an analysis of 19 case studies on stress prevention programs from across the ILO regions. It is considered as essential reading for policy-makers in government agencies, employers' and workers' organizations, health professionals, trainers, consultants, managers, and workers' representatives concerned with the complex and challenging problem of work-related stress (ILO 1993).

ILO-OSH 2001 Guidelines on Occupational Safety and Health Management Systems

The ILO-OSH 2001 guidelines present practical approaches and tools for assisting organizations, national institutions, employers, and workers in establishing, implementing, and improving occupational safety and health (OSH) management systems, with the aim of reducing work-related injuries, ill health, diseases, incidents, and deaths, specifically defined 'as negative impacts on employee health arising from exposure to chemical, biological, physical, work-organizational, and psychosocial factors at work' (ILO 2001). Implementation of the guidelines would, therefore, also enable national institutions and organizations to put in place systems to prevent and manage psychosocial risks.

Violence at Work

This guidance document examines aggressive acts that occur in workplaces bullying, mobbing, and verbal abuse. It provides information and evidence about the incidence and severity of workplace violence in countries around the world, evaluates various causal explanations and details social and economic costs. "It evaluates the effectiveness of workplace anti-violence measures and responses such as regulatory innovations, policy interventions, workplace design that may reduce risks, collective agreements and various best practice options worldwide" (ILO 2006, p. 362).

ILO Recommendation: R194 Revised Annex

On 25 March 2010, the governing board of the ILO approved a new list of occupational diseases which has been designed to assist countries in the prevention, recording, notification and, if applicable, compensation of diseases caused by work. With the publication of R194—Recommendation concerning the List of Occupational Diseases and the Recording and Notification of Occupational Accidents and Diseases, for the first time mental and behavioral disorders in the workplace have been recognized as occupational diseases, which result from psychosocial hazards. Section 2.2.4 of ILO recommendation—R194 revised annex is titled "Mental and behavioural disorders," and includes:

- "2.4.1. Post-traumatic stress disorder"
- "2.4.2. Other mental or behavioural disorders not mentioned in the preceding item where a direct link is established scientifically, or determined by methods appropriate to national conditions and practice, between the exposure to risk factors arising from work activities and the mental and behavioural disorder(s) contracted by the worker" (ILO 2010).

SOLVE

The ILO's SOLVE program, is an interactive educational program, based on the recognition of the interdependent relationships between psychosocial factors and other health-related behaviors and their underlying causes in the workplace (work organization, working conditions, labour relations). The program promotes the design of enterprise level policies and intervention programs to improve working conditions and reduce work-related stress from an occupational safety and health perspective by incorporating psychosocial hazards into the risk assessment and risk management strategy, involving both employers and workers through bipartite OSH committees at the workplace level.

Stress Checkpoints

The ILO Stress Checkpoints manual (ILO 2012) has been prepared to reflect the increased necessity for measures to deal with problems causing stress in the workplace. The 50 checkpoints included in the manual are based on the experiences of the experts who contributed to its review and preparation for implementation of stress prevention in the workplace. The checkpoints represent simple, low-cost workplace improvements readily applicable in different working situations. As the checkpoints cover broad areas, users of the manual are encouraged to take multi-faceted actions that take into account local situations.

Initiatives in the European Union

Participants in European social dialogue—ETUC (trade unions), BUSINESSEUROPE (private sector employers), UEAPME (small businesses), and CEEP (public employers)—have concluded a number of agreements that have been ratified by the Council of Ministers and are now part of European legislation such as parental leave (1996), part-time work (1997) and fixed-term contracts (1999). The social partners have also concluded 'voluntary' agreements on telework (2002), work-related stress (2004), and harassment and violence at work (2007). Other relevant recent initiatives include the European Pact for Mental Health (2008) and the related European Parliament resolution on Mental Health (2009).

Framework Agreement on Work-Related Stress

The framework agreement on work-related stress clarifies the relevance of the Framework Directive 89/391/EEC for the management of work-related stress and psychosocial risks. The agreement states that "Stress is a state, which is accompanied by physical, psychological or social complaints or dysfunctions and which results from individuals feeling unable to bridge a gap with the requirements or expectations placed on them." Under the agreement, the responsibility for determining the appropriate measures rests with the employer. These measures are carried out with the participation and collaboration of workers and/or their representatives. These measures can be collective, individual, or both. They can be introduced in the form of specific measures targeted at identified stress factors or as part of an integrated stress policy encompassing both preventive and responsive measures (European Social Partners 2004).

Framework Agreement on Harassment and Violence at Work

The Framework Agreement on Harassment and Violence at Work states that "Harassment and violence are due to unacceptable behaviour by one or more individuals and can take many different forms, some of which may be more easily identified than others. The work environment can influence people's exposure to harassment and violence." The agreement aims to increase awareness and understanding of employees, workers, and their representatives of workplace harassment and violence, and to provide employers, workers, and their representatives at all levels with an action-oriented framework to identify, manage, and prevent problems of harassment and violence at work. According to the agreement, enterprises need to have a clear statement outlining that harassment and violence will not be tolerated. The procedures to be followed where cases arise should be included (European Social Partners 2007).

European Pact for Mental Health and WellBeing

In 2008, a high level conference finalized the development of the European Pact for Mental Health and Wellbeing which recognized that mental health and wellbeing are a key resource for the success of the EU as a knowledge-based society and economy and for the realization of the objectives of the Lisbon strategy, on growth and jobs, social cohesion and sustainable development. The purpose of the Pact was to establish an EU-level framework for exchange and cooperation on mental health challenges and opportunities. The Pact has five priorities, with 'Mental Health in Workplace Settings' being one of them. It stated that "employment is beneficial to physical and mental health…action is needed to tackle the steady increase in work absenteeism and incapacity, and to utilise the unused potential for improving productivity that is linked to stress and mental disorders" (European Pact for Mental Health and Wellbeing 2008). The Pact also called on the EC to issue a proposal for a Council Recommendation on Mental Health and Wellbeing.

European Parliament Resolution T6-0063/2009 on Mental Health

In 2009, the European Parliament passed a nonlegislative resolution on mental health. The resolution, called on "the Member States to encourage research into the working conditions which may increase the incidence of mental illness, particularly among women;" it called on "employers to promote a healthy working climate, paying attention to work-related stress, the underlying causes of mental disorder at the workplace, and tackling those causes," and it called on "the Commission to require businesses and public bodies to publish annually a report on their policy and work for the mental health of their employees on the same basis as they report on physical health and safety at work" (European Parliament 2009).

WHO Initiatives

The WHO has also developed guidance on how to address psychosocial risks at work, work-related stress, violence and psychological harassment as discussed next.

Work Organization and Stress

This guidance document provides practical advice on how to deal with work stress. It is aimed at informing and raising awareness of management of work-related stress for employers, managers, and trade union representatives. It discusses the nature of stress at work, the causes and effects of stress, as well as prevention strategies, risk assessment, and management methods. The guide also discusses the role of organizational culture in this process and the resources to be drawn upon for managing work stress. The guidance includes lists of common causes and effects of stress for illustrative purposes (WHO 2003a).

Raising Awareness of Psychological Harassment at Work

This guidance document aims at raising awareness of harassment at work by, "providing information on its characteristics, such as its definition, differences between normal conflicts and psychological harassment at work, the ways it is practiced, and the consequences it can produce on health and society. Special attention is devoted to the causes that lead to its development and the measures to be adopted in order to combat it and react to it" (WHO 2003b, p. 4). Since psychological harassment is widespread in all occupational sectors, this guidance document is aimed at promoting health and safety at work among health professionals, decision makers, managers, human resources directors, the legal community, unions, and workers worldwide (WHO 2003b).

Raising Awareness of Stress at Work in Developing Countries: A Modern Hazard in a Traditional Working Environment: Advice to Employers and Worker Representatives

The purpose of this guidance document is to, "raise awareness for employers and worker representatives on work-related stress in developing countries. Work-related stress is discussed as an issue of growing concern in developing countries due to important developments in the modern world of work; two of the most significant being globalization and the changing nature of work. Raising awareness at an early stage seems critical because work-related stress is also a problem which is far from being resolved in developed and industrialized countries" (WHO 2007b, p. 1). It addresses the need to resolve the division between working conditions and the (physical) work environment which makes psychosocial risks at work harder to identify by most occupational health and safety professionals (WHO 2007b).

PRIMA-EF: Guidance on the European Framework for Psychosocial Risk Management: A Resource for Employers and Worker Representatives

This document provides guidance on the European framework for psychosocial risk management (PRIMA-EF) and concerns the management of psychosocial risks in the workplace, aiming at the prevention of work-related stress, workplace violence and bullying (WHO 2008). PRIMA-EF was built on the basis of a review, critical assessment, reconciliation, and harmonization of methods that have proved valid in the EU for the management of psychosocial risks and the promotion of mental health and wellbeing in the workplace. The PRIMA-EF model is relevant to both the enterprise and the wider macro policy level and can be used as a guidance tool for the development of further methods both in Europe and internationally and provide a benchmark for validation of existing and new methods. Two priorities identified on the basis of PRIMA-EF for the future of psychosocial risk management and the promotion of mental health in the workplace in Europe were the development of training for different stakeholders, and the development of a guidance standard on psychosocial risk management in the workplace. As a result, the PRIMA-EF consortium worked with the British Standards Institution to develop Publicly Available Specification 1010 (PAS1010): Guidance on the management of psychosocial risks in the workplace (BSI 2011). This was the first guidance standard in this area to be introduced worldwide. The Canadian national standard in psychological health and safety developed in 2013 (see Potter et al. chapter in this volume) is aligned with PAS1010. In addition, a training course has been developed, PRIMA-eTraining (PRIMAeT) that includes specific modules for employers, employees, employee representatives, and OSH practitioners. The training is offered free of charge through a flexible online platform that can be adapted for use by different stakeholders.

WHO Healthy Workplaces Framework—Healthy Workplaces: A Model for Action: For Employers, Workers, Policymakers and Practitioners

Drawing on existing good practice tools and methodologies, the WHO, on the basis of the Global Plan of Action on Workers' Health, in April 2010, launched the Global Framework for Healthy Workplaces. In identifying common denominators across all regions, it aims to provide global guidance on how to create a healthy workplace, which takes into account the different aspects of the work environment and the potential hazards. The framework also highlights the benefits of creating healthy workplaces comprehensively and strategically aligned with the core objectives of an enterprise. The WHO defines a healthy workplace as "one in which workers and managers collaborate to use a continual improvement process to protect and promote the health, safety and well-being of all workers and the sustainability of the workplace by considering the following, based on identified needs:

- health and safety concerns in the physical work environment;
- health, safety and well-being concerns in the psychosocial work environment, including organization of work and workplace culture;
- personal health resources in the workplace; and
- ways of participating with all stakeholders to improve the health of workers, their families and other members of the community" (WHO 2010, p. 6).

Other International Initiatives

Other international initiatives include the relevant standards developed by ISO and various standards and instruments developed to promote CSR or responsible business practices.

ISO 10075 Series Standards

The ISO 10075 series standards establish principles and requirements for the measurement and assessment of mental workload and specify the requirements for measurement instruments. The standards are intended for use mainly by ergonomic experts, psychologists, occupational health specialists, and/or physiologists, with appropriate training in the theoretical background and usage of such methods, and in the interpretation of the results (ISO 2004).

ISO 10075-1 outlines the general terms and definitions of ergonomic principles related to workload. The standard defines mental stress as "the total of all assessable influences impinging upon a human being from external sources and affecting it mentally." The standard states that mental strain results from immediate effect of mental stress within the individual (not the long-term effect) depending on his/her individual habitual and actual preconditions, including individual coping styles (ISO 1991). ISO 10075-2 provides the design principles of the ergonomic principles related to workload, specifically "sources of fatigue: intensity of mental workload and temporal distribution of mental workload." Factors of temporal distribution of mental workload include "duration of working hours, time off between successive work days or shift, time of day, shift work, breaks and rest pauses, changes in task activities with different task demands or kinds of mental workload" (ISO 1996). ISO 10075-3 provides information for choosing appropriate methods and on aspects of assessing and measuring mental workload to improve communication among the parties involved (ISO 2004).

It should also be noted that an ISO occupational health and safety standard, 45001, is currently being finalized and will be launched in 2017.

Sustainability and Corporate Social Responsibility Instruments and Standards

More than 200 standards and instruments to promote sustainability, responsible business practices, or corporate social responsibility (CSR) have been developed (McKague and Cragg 2007). These include a number of instruments that have specific labor dimensions and are applicable globally. Some key instruments include: the United Nations Global Compact, United Nations Guiding Principles on Business and Human Rights, OECD Guidelines for Multinational Enterprises, ILO Tripartite declaration of principles concerning multinational enterprises and social policy, the Global Reporting Initiative (GRI), and ISO 26000.

The ILO's Tripartite Declaration of Principles concerning Multinational Enterprises and Social Policy (MNE Declaration), includes recommendations concerning occupational health and safety which encourage multinational enterprises to maintain the highest standards of worker health, taking into account relevant experience from operations in other countries. It calls on multinational and national enterprises to incorporate, where appropriate, matters relating to health and safety in agreements with workers' representatives and organizations. As far as governments are concerned, the MNE Declaration recommends applying international labor standards in order to ensure that both multinational and national enterprises provide adequate health and safety standards for their employees (ILO 2006).

Jain et al. (2014) carried out a study to examine which psychosocial factors, and related issues such as work-related stress, violence, bullying, and harassment are covered in Sustainability and CSR instruments and standards. The findings clearly indicate that these instruments and standards provide a broad coverage of several psychosocial factors. Since most standards and instruments cover labor dimensions and working conditions, which include basic labor themes originating from international labor standards and regulations, a number of psychosocial factors are directly or indirectly addressed by these instruments.

Is There the Right Balance in Policy and Practice?

An interesting policy mix can be observed at an international level in relation to psychosocial risks and work-related stress. This includes not only legislation in several countries but also additional nonbinding/voluntary policy initiatives including guidance, social partner agreements, and, since 2011, even standards. It can also be observed that the introduction of different types of policies such as legislation, agreements, guidance, and a national standard in the case of Canada, has spurred organizational action. The chapter by Potter et al. in this volume presents further national initiatives that can be considered alongside the international initiatives presented here to draw conclusions on the current state of the art in psychosocial risk management policy and practice.

For example, in the UK where extensive work has been carried out to implement the good practice approach of the Management Standards for work-related stress (that is also now used in Ireland and Italy), prioritization of psychosocial risks and work-related stress has suffered in recent years due to a lack of political will to address these issues and limited use of the evidence base (Leka et al. 2015). In many countries it seems that lack of action might be the result of lack of political will, deregulation, poor social dialogue practices, and lack of resources—key barriers that affect policy development, research, and organizational practices. However, overall, across countries, legislation has indeed acted as a catalyst for the prioritization of psychosocial risks and work-related stress. In fact, especially where awareness and expertise on these issues are limited, legislation has been highlighted as a necessary precondition to spur action (Kortum et al. 2011).

Another issue highlighted by experts and stakeholders is the lack of specificity in terminology used in existing legislation in relation to psychosocial risks and work-related stress (e.g., Ertel et al. 2010; Leka et al. 2015). This has been reported to negatively impact on practice even though complementary guidance might be available that clarifies the relevance of such legislation to these issues (for example, this is the case in the EU in relation to its key health and safety directive which also applies to psychosocial risks according to guidance from the European Commission and to the European social partner framework agreement on work-related stress; Leka et al. 2011).

Of course, what has been highlighted repeatedly is that legislation is no good without appropriate enforcement (Quinlan and Sheldon 2011). Appropriate enforcement is only possible where there are adequately resourced and competent inspectorates. However, in many countries it is observed that budget cuts have negatively affected inspectorates both in terms of manpower and resources to develop and promote new initiatives. In addition, competence of inspectorates in relation to psychosocial risks and work-related stress prevention has been widely criticized (e.g., Johnstone et al. 2011; Lippel et al. 2011; Rasmussen et al. 2011). Efforts have been made in some countries to address this gap and tools developed could be used in other countries too (such as the tools developed through the Senior Labor Inspectors Committee (SLIC) campaign on psychosocial risks that can serve as a good practice example for countries outside Europe). The second issue in relation to enforcement of legislation concerns the low frequency of inspection visits in SMEs. This raises concerns about an over reliance on a legislative approach, even in countries where it exists.

A further issue is the information generated through the lists of occupational diseases and compensation systems used across countries. Although the ILO (2010) has led the way including mental and behavioral disorders in R194—Recommendation concerning the List of Occupational Diseases and the Recording and Notification of Occupational Accidents and Diseases, it is still early to appreciate the level of consequent action that will result at national level. However, the EU, for example, has also put effort in exploring this possibility in terms of their respective list (EC 2013).

Even though legislation has been reported as being the main driver to engage businesses in good practice in health and safety in general, and in particular, psychosocial risk management (e.g., EU-OSHA 2010), others advocate that business and ethical case are stronger drivers (e.g., Bevan 2010; Jain et al. 2011). Approaches like PAS1010 by BSI and the Canadian national standard on psychological health and safety aim at showcasing that psychosocial risk management should be integrated in business operations and is good management practice. They offer a process, guidance, and tools to complement management systems used in companies in order to address psychosocial risks. Additional good practice examples include tools specifically developed for smaller businesses at national and sectoral level, promoted by the social partners, sectoral, and professional associations, both through the internet and more traditional means of communication. The promotion of an integrated approach through occupational health and safety management systems should be pursued at organizational level. At the same time, an integrated approach at policy level (e.g., bringing together the OSH and health promotion perspectives) should be promoted.

There is, however, also the case of developing countries where many believe that other much more urgent and serious issues need to be addressed (for example accidents and communicable diseases). Since evidence has been building in developing countries to indicate that psychosocial risks and work-related stress are real problems accentuated by processes of globalization and requiring urgent attention (e.g., Kortum and Leka 2013), the question arises of whether the models used in industrialized countries are appropriate for application in the developing country context. It is widely acknowledged that any good practice approach would require adaptation in any other country than the one where it was developed. The parameters of the psychosocial work environment are universal in any workplace. What will differ are their relative importance in the specific organizational context, and their interaction with other factors in the work environment, including physical aspects as well as the socioeconomic, and even the political, context in each country (e.g. Maakip et al. in this volume). As such it has been suggested that the models used to address psychosocial risk and work-related stress in developing countries must be more comprehensive and consider macro factors (e.g., Benach et al. 2007; Kortum and Leka 2013).

Although the picture across the world varies considerably, it is fair to say that several actions have been taken at different levels to address psychosocial risks and work-related stress across countries. Sharing of good practices and critical evaluation of different approaches is missing so that these can be used for future planning. Some examples exist where good practices have been adapted and used in other countries (for example, the Management Standards for work-related stress in the UK, Ireland, and Italy, and ISTAS21 in Spain and Chile).

Since there are several approaches and tools available, it is important that key stakeholders further develop, and actively work in, strategic partnerships to advance sharing of good practices and evaluation in different contexts. International organizations and key regional bodies should work in closer collaboration with national stakeholders and professional associations to coordinate and promote good practice. A lot of knowledge is available in this area already and it is evident that limited success can be achieved by isolated efforts. Coordinated actions in strategic partnerships in policy and practice are needed.

An innovative policy mix, including regulatory and nonbinding/voluntary approaches, promoted through partnerships and networks, and supported by the availability of tools and access to competent support are crucial for the future, in order to tackle psychosocial risks and work-related stress in a preventive manner and to achieve the right balance in policy and practice.

References

Abbott, K. W., Keohane, R. O., Moravcsik, A., Slaughter, A.-M., & Snidal, D. (2000). The Concept of Legalization. *International Organization, 54*(3), 401–419.

Benach, J., Muntaner, C., & Santana, V. (2007). Employment conditions and health inequalities. *Final report to the WHO Commission on Social Determinants of Health (CSDH) Employment Conditions Knowledge Network (EMCONET).* Geneva: World Health Organization.

Bevan, S. (2010). *The business case for employee health and well-being.* A report prepared for Investors in People. London: The Work Foundation.

British Standards Institution (BSI). (2011). *Guidance on the management of psychosocial risks in the workplace: PAS1010.* London: BSI.

Cox, T. (1993). *Stress research and stress management: Putting theory to work.* Sudbury: HSE Books.

Cox, T., & Griffiths, A. (2010). Work-related stress: A theoretical perspective. In S. Leka & J. Houdmont (Eds.), *Occupational health psychology* (pp. 31–55). Chichester: Wiley-Blackwell.

Ertel, M., Stilijanow, U., Iavicoli, S., Natali, E., Jain, A., & Leka, S. (2010). European social dialogue on psychosocial risks at work: Benefits and challenges. *European Journal of Industrial Relations, 16*(2), 169–183.

European Agency for Safety and Health at Work (EU-OSHA). (2010). *Mainstreaming OSH into business management*. Luxembourg: Office for Official Publications of the European Communities.
European Commission (EC). (2013). Report on the current situation in relation to occupational diseases' systems in EU Member States and EFTA/EEA countries, in particular relative to Commission Recommendation 2003/670/EC concerning the European Schedule of Occupational Diseases and gathering of data on relevant related aspects. Available at: http://ec.europa.eu/social/BlobServlet?docId=9982&langId=en.
European Pact for Mental Health and Wellbeing. (2008). EU high level conference 'Together for mental health and wellbeing'. Brussels, 12–13 June 2008.
European Parliament. (2009). European Parliament resolution of 19 February 2009 on Mental Health T6-0063/2009, Reference 2008/2209(INI). Available at: http://www.europarl.europa.eu/oeil/FindByProcnum.do?lang=en&procnum=INI/2008/2209.
European Social Partners. (2004). *Framework agreement on work-related stress*. Brussels: European Social Partners—ETUC, UNICE (BUSINESSEUROPE), UEAPME and CEEP.
European Social Partners. (2007). *Framework agreement on harassment and violence at work*. Brussels: Social Partners—ETUC, BUSINESSEUROPE, UEAPME and CEEP.
International Labour Organization (ILO). (1986). Psychosocial factors at work: Recognition and control. Report of the Joint International Labour Office and World Health Organization on Occupational Health, Ninth Session, Geneva, 18–24 September 1984. Occupational Safety and Health Series No. 56. Geneva: ILO.
International Labour Organization (ILO). (1993). *Preventing stress at work (Conditions of work digest 2/92)*. Geneva: ILO.
International Labour Organization (ILO). (2001). *Guidelines on occupational safety and health management systems (ILO-OSH 2001)*. Geneva: ILO.
International Labour Organization (ILO). (2006). *Violence at work* (3rd ed.). Geneva: ILO.
International Labour Organization (ILO). (2010). *Recommendation concerning the list of occupational diseases and the recording and notification of occupational accidents and diseases ILO recommendation R194 revised annex*. Geneva: ILO.
International Labour Organization (ILO). (2012). *Stress prevention at work checkpoints: Practical improvements for stress prevention in the workplace*. Geneva: ILO.
International Organisation of Employers (IOE). (2010). *IOE helping employers: Make the business case for investing in occupational safety and health (OSH)*. Geneva: IOE.
International Organisation of Employers (IOE). (2012). *IOE helping employers: Manage employees' work-related health risks*. Geneva: IOE.
International Organization for Standardization (ISO). (1991). ISO 10075:1991. Ergonomic principles related to mental work-load—General terms and definitions. Geneva: ISO.
International Organization for Standardization (ISO). (1996). ISO 10075-2:1996. Ergonomic principles related to mental workload—Part 2: Design principles. Geneva: ISO.
International Organization for Standardization (ISO). (2004). ISO 10075-3:2004. Ergonomic principles related to mental workload—Part 3: Principles and requirements concerning methods for measuring and assessing mental workload. Geneva: ISO.
International Social Security Association (ISSA). (2012). ISSA section for a culture of prevention. *ISSA Newsletter, 01*.
International Trade Union Confederation (ITUC). (2010). *ITUC Congress Resolutions on Decent Work*. Brussels: ITUC.
Jain, A., Leka, S., & Zwetsloot, G. (2011). Corporate social responsibility and psychosocial risk management in Europe. *Journal of Business Ethics, 101*(4), 619–633.
Jain, A., Ripa, D., & Herrero, (2014). An analysis of the coverage of psychosocial hazards at work in corporate social responsibility instruments and standards. In S. Leka & R. Sinclair (Eds.), *Contemporary occupational health psychology: Global perspectives on research and practice* (Vol. 3). Chichester: Wiley-Blackwell.
Johnstone, R., Quinlan, M., & McNamara, M. (2011). OHS inspectors and psychosocial risk factors: Evidence from Australia. *Safety Science, 49*(4), 547–557.

Kirton, J. J., & Trebilcock, M. J. (Eds.). (2004). *Hard choices, soft law: Voluntary standards in global trade, environment and social governance*. Aldershot: Ashgate Publishing Ltd.

Kortum, E., & Leka, S. (2013). Tackling psychosocial risks and work-related stress in developing countries: The need for a multi-level intervention framework. *International Journal of Stress Management, 21*(1), 7–26.

Kortum, E., Leka, S., & Cox, T. (2011). Perceptions of psychosocial hazards, work-related stress and workplace priority risks in developing countries. *Journal of Occupational Health, 53*, 144–155.

Lawrence, S., & Ishikawa, J. (2005). *Social Dialogue Indicators Trade union membership and collective bargaining coverage: Statistical concepts, methods and findings*. Working Paper No. 59. Geneva: International Labour Office.

Leka, S., Jain, A., Iavicoli, S., & Di Tecco, C. (2015). An evaluation of the policy context on psychosocial risk and mental health in the workplace in the European Union: Achievements, challenges and the future. *BioMed Research International, id.213089*, 1-18. Available at: http://dx.doi.org/10.1155/2015/213089.

Leka, S., Jain, A., Iavicoli, S., Vartia, M., & Ertel, M. (2011). The role of policy for the management of psychosocial risks at the workplace in the European Union. *Safety Science, 49* (4), 558–564.

Lippel, K., Vézina, M., & Cox, R. (2011). Protection of workers' mental health in Québec: Do general duty clauses allow labor inspectors to do their job? *Safety Science, 49*, 543–546.

McKague, K., & Cragg, W. (2007). Compendium of Ethics Codes and Instruments of Corporate Responsibility. Available at: http://www.yorku.ca/csr/_files/file.php?fileid=fileCDOICwJiei&filename=file_Codes_Compendium_Jan_2007.pdf.

Organization for Economic Co-operation and Development (OECD). (2012). *Sick on the Job? Myths and realities about mental health and work*. Paris: OECD.

Quinlan, M., & Sheldon, P. (2011). The enforcement of minimum labour standards in an era of neo-liberal globalisation: An overview. *Economic and Labour Relations Review, 22*(2), 5–32.

Rasmussen, M. B., Hansen, T., & Nielsen, K. T. (2011). New tools and strategies for the inspection of the psychosocial working environment: The experience of the Danish Working Environment Authority. *Safety Science, 49*, 565–574.

Rockhold, P., & McDonald, L. (2008). The World Bank's work on mental and psychosocial health in the context of conflict affected countries. *Intervention, 6*(3/4), 314–322.

World Economic Forum WEF. (2013). *Global Agenda Councils - Health & Well-being. Network of Global Agenda Councils Reports 2011 – 2012*. Geneva: World Economic Forum.

World Health Organization. (WHO) (2003a). *Work organization and stress*. Protecting Workers' Health Series, No. 3. Geneva: WHO.

World Health Organization (WHO) (2003b). *Raising awareness to psychological harassment at work*. Protecting workers' health series; no. 4. Geneva: WHO.

World Health Organization (WHO). (2007). *Workers' health: global plan of action*. Geneva: WHO

World Health Organizatio.n (WHO) (2007b). *Raising awareness of stress at work in developing countries: A modern hazard in a traditional working environment: advice to employers and worker representatives*. Protecting Workers' Health Series, No. 6. Geneva: WHO.

World Health Organization. (WHO) (2008). *PRIMA-EF Guidance on the European Framework for Psychosocial Risk Management: A Resource for Employers and Worker Representatives*. Protecting Workers' Health series, number 9. Geneva: WHO.

World Health Organization (WHO). (2010). *Healthy workplaces: a WHO global model for action*. Geneva: WHO.

Chapter 3
Macro-Level Policy and Practice Relating to Psychosocial Factors at Work in the Asia Pacific

Tessa S. Bailey, Yawen Cheng, Awang Idris and Sara Arphorn

Abstract The Asia-Pacific region contains more than a third of the world's total labour force (CIA, 2014), and yet there are limited collaborative approaches towards managing psychosocial factors at work. While countries such as Japan, Korea and Australia have laws and regulations specific in addressing work-related psychosocial risk aspects many other countries do not (Kawakamiet al. 2014). This chapter examines answers from a focus group of industry experts representing Australia, Taiwan, Malaysia and Thailand regarding industry, state and national policy and initiatives relating to management of work-related psychosocial risk factors. While specific laws relating to worker wellbeing, including compensation systems attributable to psychosocial risk factors such as workload and stressful work conditions, have been established in Australia and Taiwan, other countries are yet to develop clear legal processes. In Malaysia there is a general requirement for employers to provide a safe working environment; however, this is usually interpreted only in relation to physical health. For Thailand laws protecting worker wellbeing are limited to very specific issues such as chemical exposure and muscular–skeletal disorders (MSDs) but no clear expectations exist regarding psychosocial aspects. Socialised expectation to obey authority is identified as a barrier to better psychosocial risk management at work for both Malaysia and Thailand. Awareness of psychosocial factors and their impact on worker health appears to be growing in the region. For example a recently introduced model Workforce Health and Safety Act in Australia specifically refers to

T.S. Bailey (✉)
Asia Pacific Centre for Work Health and Safety,
University of South Australia, Adelaide, Australia
e-mail: Tessa.bailey@unisa.edu.au

Y. Cheng
Institute of Health Policy and Management, National Taiwan University, Taipei, Taiwan

A. Idris
Department of Anthropology and Sociology, Faculty of Arts and Social Sciences,
University of Malaya, Kuala Lumpur, Malaysia

S. Arphorn
Department of Occupational Health and Safety, Faculty of Public Health,
Mahidol University, Phutthamonthon, Thailand

A. Shimazu et al. (eds.), *Psychosocial Factors at Work in the Asia Pacific*,
DOI 10.1007/978-3-319-44400-0_3

psychological health and in Taiwan since 2008 mental disorders have been classified as compensable, if due to stressful work conditions. However even in countries with formal legal and compensation systems in place, barriers such as limited enforcement and lack of focus on prevention of psychosocial risk factors continue to suppress the protection of worker health and wellbeing.

Keywords Psychosocial · Risk · Macro-level · Policy · Law · Initiatives

Introduction

Following the success of the '3rd Expert Workshop on Psychosocial Factors at Work in the Asia Pacific', held in Japan, and the creation of the 'Asia Pacific Academy for Psychosocial Factors at Work', development commenced on a book featuring work from members of the academy and participants at the workshops. The book titled 'Psychosocial Factors at Work in the Asia Pacific' (Dollard et al. 2014) was intended to bring to light current developments relating to this important work safety issue in a region that receives limited exposure in the western world. While the Asia Pacific possesses a vast proportion of workers in the world CIA (2014), there is minimal systematic collaboration between countries to measure and assess the impact of psychosocial risk factors at work in the region. The efforts of Dollard et al. (2014) have provided a step towards better understanding the latest innovations and barriers in a diverse and at times challenging landscape.

In relation to macro-level (industry, state, national) policy in Book 1 of the series, Chap. 2 titled 'National Status of Psychosocial Factors at Work in Japan, Korea, Australia and China' (Kawakami et al. 2014) provided an in depth summary of current developments for some of the countries in the region. It showed that while most of the countries (Japan, Korea, and Australia) that were examined in the chapter have laws and regulations specific in addressing work-related psychosocial risk management, China is still lacking in this area with the focus on more traditional (physical) occupational hazards. Also while Japan, Korea and Australia have systems in place for workers to claim financial compensation for physical or psychological injuries that are due to psychosocial risk factors, this is also absent in China. However it was noted that only Japan and Korea have clearly established compensation practices for Cardio Vascular Disease (CVD) due to overwork. Further China is also the only country, out of those included in the chapter that does not have a national surveillance system for work-related psychosocial risk and/or psychological health outcomes. It was also discussed that while employee assistance programmes exist in each country the actual figures regarding how many and who has access to them is limited and these programmes often exist only in medium to large organisations.

The chapter provided a much needed insight into the status of psychosocial factors at work and their management at a national level in countries across the Asia Pacific. While Japan and Australia share similarities on a range of psychosocial factors including long working hours, awareness of risks and hazards, national surveillance and compensation for work-related stress, there is recognition of some laws and regulation in Korea and growing awareness in China. More analysis of comparisons between developing, emerging and developed economies is needed to further understand the macro-level influences on psychosocial factors at work in this diverse region.

Method

In November 2013 during the 4th Expert Workshop on Psychosocial Factors at Work in Asia Pacific, Thailand, a focus group was held on macro-level factors that affect psychosocial risk management and psychological health at work. Questions were developed to reflect research previously conducted by Leka et al. (2010) to evaluate macro-level psychosocial risk management initiatives in Europe. Their investigations covered a range of aspects including legislation, sectorial initiatives, awareness raising, social dialogue and difficulties with implementation.

The focus group session for the current study included 10 people (5 from Malaysia, 4 from Australia, 1 from Thailand) separated into groups of 3 or 4 individuals, where each group included people from different countries to promote discussions and comparisons. Following the session the results were sent to expert representatives from Australia, Malaysia and Thailand to review the details and add further relevant information. A representative, Yawen Cheng, with over 10 years experience in the field was also invited to add details on macro-level factors at work in Taiwan to provide a broader perspective from the region.

Results

"Are There Laws in Your Region that Relate to Worker Psychological Health and Safety"?

Australia

In Australia, employers are responsible for worker health and safety in general and are required to adhere to legislation within their state. While the laws are intended to cover psychological health, the focus is primarily on physical health and well-being. The recent introduction of a model Workforce Health and Safety Act, adopted by most states and territories, clearly states that the definition of 'Health' includes both 'Psychological' as well as 'Physical' (Safe Work Australia 2012).

Also in Australian regulatory bodies endorse a number of guidelines relating to psychosocial factors but some difficulties exist in enforcing the laws that cover worker psychological health, especially in terms of prevention. Australia also has an extensive workers' compensation claim system for both public and private employees with a number of compensation claims attributed to psychological injury (see Table 3.1).

Taiwan

In Taiwan, cardiovascular and cerebrovascular diseases (CVDs) attributed to excessive workloads have been recognised as compensable occupational diseases since 2006. From 2008, mental disorders caused by stressful work conditions are also considered compensable (Cheng et al. 2012). In 2013, 68 cases of occupational CVDs and 3 cases of occupational mental disorders attributed to work stress were recognised and compensated.

In July 2013, the Occupational Safety and Health Act (OSHAct) was amended which for the first time imposes a duty on employers to prevent health risks caused by psychosocial hazards: Article 6 of the OSHAct states that "employers shall adequately plan and adopt the necessary safety and health measures for the following items", which include "to prevent ailments induced by exceptional workloads such as working shifts, working at night and long working hours" and "to prevent physical or mental harms caused by wrongful actions of others during the execution of job duties". Employers who fail to adopt necessary actions shall be subject to a fine in the range of NTD 30,000–150,000 (USD 1000–5000).

In September 2014, two implementation guidelines were promulgated by the Occupational Safety and Health Administration. One for the prevention of ailments induced by exceptional workloads, and the other for the prevention of physical and mental harms caused by wrongful actions of others during the "execution of job duties". In the former, "exceptional workloads" are defined as having rotating shifts, night shifts, irregular shifts, overtime work in excess of 37 h per month on average within the past 6 months (over the regular working hours of 168 h per month), frequent business travel, uncomfortable work environment or other stressful working conditions. According to this guideline, employers are encouraged to conduct risk assessment and adopt health management programmes for stress-related health risks, mostly for cardiovascular diseases. In the second guideline, wrongful actions are referred to workplace violence, which could be in forms of physical assault, threatening behaviours, verbal abuse, intimidation and sexual harassment. Employers are encouraged to publically endorse the principle of "zero tolerance for workplace violence" in occupational safety and health policy and to incorporate necessary actions to prevent workplace violence.

Malaysia

For Malaysia some laws exist that can be related to worker psychological health, although they are under the general laws regarding employer duty of care to provide a safe work environment. The focus of the general law is mostly on physical health,

Table 3.1 Comparison of Australia, Taiwan, Malaysia, Thailand: National and organisational approaches to work stress prevention and management

	WHS/OHS[a] legislation covers psychosocial risk	WHS/OHS legislation covers psychological health	Workers compensation for work related mental health problems	Worker compensation for work related physical health problems due to psychosocial risk	National surveillance for psychosocial risk	National surveillance for mental health of workers	Employee Assistance Programmes for mental health
Australia	Yes, indirectly the requirement of employers to provide an environment without 'risk' to physical and psychological health includes psychosocial factors. However, the term'psychosocial' is not stated specifically	Yes, WHS Act states employers are responsible for providing a 'working environment that is safe and without risk to health' and that the definition of 'health' encompasses both the 'physical' and 'psychological'	Yes, in 2012–2013 financial year 6980 claims for mental disorders were awarded representing 5.9 % of claims (Safe Work Australia 2014)	Yes, 35 claims for physical injuries/diseases as a result of mental stress on for 201213 (0.5 % of all accepted claims) (Safe Work Australia 2014)	Australian Workplace Barometer 2009, 2010, 2011 (limited states), and in 2014/2014 (all states and territories)	Australian Workplace Barometer 2009, 2010, 2011 (limited states), in 2014/2014 (all states and territories)	Often present in medium to large organisations. No formal requirement. No recording systems of use of EAPs
Taiwan	Yes	Yes	Yes	Yes (CVDs)	Yes. National surveillance of psychosocial work content every 3 years since 2001, covering job demands, job control, workplace justice, job insecurity, workplace violence, work–family conflict, etc.	Yes. National surveillance of psychosocial work content every 3 years since 2001, covering self-rated health, burnout, psychosomatic problems, physician-diagnosed diseases, work ability, etc.	Yes; promoted by the government but adopted mainly in large enterprises

(continued)

Table 3.1 (continued)

	WHS/OHS[a] legislation covers psychosocial risk	WHS/OHS legislation covers psychological health	Workers compensation for work related mental health problems	Worker compensation for work related physical health problems due to psychosocial risk	National surveillance for psychosocial risk	National surveillance for mental health of workers	Employee Assistance Programmes for mental health
Malaysia	Yes the OSHA Act that informs general rules for employers to protect employees from workplace hazards (including psychosocial)	No, except for PTSD	No, except for PTSD	No	No	No	Yes. There are some initiatives by Ministry of Health to promote healthy lifestyle including mental health
Thailand	No	Yes, but it only mentioned the meaning of health which cover physical and mental health	No	No	No	No	No

Table adapted with permission from 'Psychosocial Factors at Work in the Asia Pacific' (Kawakamiet al. 2014)
[a]*WHS* work, health and safety, *OHS* occupational health and safety

and a major issue is the lack of these laws being enforced. The practical translation of how these laws protect worker psychological health has not yet been visibly undertaken. Supportive efforts by workplace managers and supervisors relating to the management of psychosocial issues are limited with minimal practical examples made towards psychosocial risk management on a day-to-day basis. Leadership support is also severely lacking in that they would rather not be made aware of psychosocial issues whereby they generally demonstrate an attitude of "no news is good news" as stated by one of the focus group participants.

Malaysia is also different to Australia and Taiwan as no specific mechanism exists to claim compensation for psychological injury at work. Focus group participants outlined many examples where workers had suffered psychological health issues due to their work, but no instance where a successful compensation claim was lodged or awarded. In Malaysia, a general concern exists for workers who suffer from physical injury but not for psychological health issues. It was suggested that this may be because psychological illness related to factors at work are not necessarily immediately identifiable and therefore more difficult to prove. If a diagnosis does not link work-related factors to the outcome, then it will appear as though there is no evidence to substantiate that the injury was caused by workplace factors, even for cases of depression.

Historically, psychiatrists were the only professionals who could provide a diagnosis and treatment in relation to psychological illness, and psychologists were rarely employed outside of universities. In the recent years psychologists have increasingly been employed in several government agencies. Their brief is to work with the public, and employees' who suffer psychological injuries due to work, family and other related problems. And recently the Malaysian Government, in particular the Ministry of Health has introduced an initiative promoting intervention strategies to create awareness about mental health issues in society, including in workplaces and schools. It was also noted that in Malaysia guidelines and laws now exist which recognise cases of workplace sexual harassment.

Thailand

Currently, in Thailand no laws exist which directly relate to psychological issues at work. Laws are in place for physical health issues such as chemical exposure, MSD and ergonomics but not for any other psychosocial factors. There are many psychosocial pressures on workers in Thailand such as high demands, low pay, lack of opportunity, lack of job security and precarious employment. However a key issue in Thailand is job security. Their collectivist culture does mean that social connections are strong and their collectivist network such as family and friends provide some emotional and financial support. However this generally only occurs outside of work contexts. It was noted that informal dialogue has recently commenced in relation to areas such as work-related stress but this has not yet seen a change in law, which therefore limits any progression on formal prevention practices.

"Are There Any Industry Based Initiatives that Address Psychosocial Factors at Work Within Your Region"?

Australia

In Australia wide ranging regulation results in a number of industry based initiatives towards prevention and intervention of psychosocial hazards such as fatigue, work-life balance, violence at work, bullying and harassment. However there continues to be issues in Australia, in particular relating to evidence-based assessment and prevention as well as enforcement of regulations at the industry level due to lack of clarity in the laws. The new federal WHS laws and subsequent regulation may assist industry regulators to provide better enforcement of psychosocial risk prevention and intervention practices.

Taiwan

Health promotion programmes have been encouraged and supported financially by the government of Taiwan since the 1990s. However self-initiated health promotion programmes are still quite limited and largely restricted to large enterprises. In response to the new regulations concerning psychological work hazards, Employee Assistance Programmes (EAP) with emphasis on stress management and psychological counselling are also gaining popularity among large enterprises.

Malaysia

In Malaysia some larger employers have developed initiatives related to psychosocial factors at work. However this is not replicated in small businesses. Large organisations have a stronger regulation culture with greater enforcement of policies relating to psychosocial factors. This includes more training in the form of workshops and access to counseling. Focus group participants suggested this is because the implementation of such initiatives are financially driven so only occur in companies with financial resources available to implement and enforce policies.

Thailand

In Thailand since 2012 industry based initiatives have been undertaken by the Ministry of Industry to develop standards and guidelines on health examinations relating to chemical and physical risk factors in workplaces. However this is still in its early stages of development and no other examples could be recalled by focus group participants.

"What Forms of Social Dialogue (Communication) Exist to Inform Employers and Employees About Psychosocial Risk Factors in Your Region"?

Australia

Many examples of social dialogue could be recalled by Australian focus group participants such as advertising campaigns, media reports, promotions by regulatory bodies, conferences, online materials, education and training. Safe Work Australia provides online material relevant to laws, compensation claims, and prevention of psychological injuries. State-based regulators such as SafeWork SA provide printed and online material as well as information sessions regarding psychosocial factors at work including fatigue management and bullying prevention.

Taiwan

Since the early 1990s in Taiwan, physical and psychological impacts of adverse psychosocial work conditions have been widely reported and heatedly discussed in the media. The labour authority has taken various actions at the policy levels to address public's concerns over work-related stress, especially on sudden death caused by heavy workloads. In the recent years, work-related burnout and mental health problems caused by work stress have been studied and research findings have been published in journals and in the media. Education and training courses are routinely offered by professional groups and sponsored by the Occupational Safety and Health Administration to disseminate information, knowledge, on regulations and guidance concerning psychosocial work hazards.

Malaysia

Focus group participants from Malaysia stated that while some examples such as seminars and training regarding the importance of psychosocial factors do exist that it is infrequent and very reactive rather than proactive, mostly in response to complaints. It was suggested that differences between Australia and Malaysia in relation to enforcement and regulation could be related to unions and workers being unwilling to raise their concerns. In Malaysia most of the complaints remain anonymous and behind closed doors. It was suggested that cultural differences in relation to power imbalance could be part of the issue where workers in Malaysia tend to just accept what is happening in their workplace without complaint.

Thailand

The focus group participant from Thailand could not recall any examples of wide ranging social dialogue in relation to psychosocial factors. From personal experience, they reported that workers in some communities appear to be more openly discussing factors related to workplace stress, such as workload.

"Do Any Awareness Raising Campaigns Regarding Work-Related Psychosocial Risk Factors Occur in Your Region"?

Australia

Examples of awareness raising campaigns in Australia include media campaigns regarding being safe at work. While some of the media advertising is quite general about being safe at work, guidance material exists regarding more specific aspects such as bullying and fatigue at work. Also a range of presentations on psychosocial factors such as risk surveillance and psychosocial safety climate have been included during promotions in annual events such as safe work week.

Some state-based agencies also make efforts to raise awareness by providing seminars and presentations on psychosocial factors at work and are active in linking researchers with industry via grant opportunities to address these issues. For instance SafeWork SA has supported a range of projects on bullying and psychosocial safety climate with one of the aims being to increase industry awareness. In addition some industry groups, for instance Shop Distributive and Allied Employees' Association (SDA), and union groups host seminars to educate members on psychosocial risk surveillance, prevention and hazard management.

Taiwan

In recent years, slogans such as "anti-sweatshop economy" and "anti overwork" have been widely used in Labour Day March and in other occasions by labour rights groups. While non-governmental organisations exert strong influence in promoting issues concerning health risks associated with heavy workloads and other psychosocial hazards, governmental officials of the Occupational Safety and Health Administration gain momentum and play an important role in drafting new regulations and initiating policies.

Malaysia

Focus group participants from Malaysia agreed that awareness about the issue of psychosocial risk factors is wide ranging amongst workers. However there is a lack of willingness by employers and governing bodies to actively address, regulate or undertaken appropriate prevention activities.

Thailand

The representative from Thailand could not think of any formal examples of awareness raising campaigns related to psychosocial factors at work. Although there are some informal talks starting to happen for instance some organisations will invite a member from the Ministry of Public Health to talk to safety officers in an organisation and occasionally this will include some aspects relating to psychosocial factors and how they can impact on worker health and wellbeing.

"Are You Aware of Any Other Strategies for Psychosocial Based Prevention and Intervention at the Industry, Sector or Regional Level"?

Australia

Focus group participants from Australia agreed that initiatives focusing on prevention are limited. Most of the focus from national groups and regulatory bodies is on reduction of compensation claims. Recent initiatives such as surveillance conducted by the Australian Workplace Barometre have highlighted industries and groups at risk; however, records of actual practices or regulation of employers to conduct prevention activities is limited.

Taiwan

Several occupational groups have been identified as high risk for stress-related illnesses and workplace violence, including health care workers, social workers, truck drivers, engineers, security guards, convenient store workers etc. The labour inspectors of the central government and local governments have expanded the scope and intensity of labour inspection, targeting workers from these sectors as a prevention strategy.

Malaysia

In Malaysia minimal examples of policy exist in relation to psychosocial factors and/or government prevention and intervention, although, some organisations are taking their own initiative to implement psychosocial risk management programmes. There are some recent developments in relation to a harassment Act that was implemented due to pressure from non-government organisations such as the Women's Association in order to protect female employees. However, it was implemented quite recently and while awareness is increasing there is still the ongoing issue of enforcement. Often it is only the researchers in this field that are aware of government policy.

Thailand

Thailand was described as having little to no policy driving prevention or intervention. However, they have also had some industry based committee working towards standards for protection of female workers, which suggests awareness is improving in the area of psychosocial factors.

"What Are the Main Barriers to Worker Psychological Injury Prevention and Intervention in Your Region"?

Australia

Participants suggested that some barriers stem from industry. For instance male dominated industries with a culture where aggressive behaviour is accepted and other industries, such as health care settings, suffer from wide spread bullying and harassment cultures. Strategies are needed to change these cultures towards improving wellbeing and focus more on prevention of psychosocial hazards.

Other barriers include the lack of clear and specific laws relating to psychosocial factors which then limits the capacity of regulatory bodies to enforce better workplace practices. In addition, practical tools for surveillance, risk prevention and hazard management or standards with clear steps given on when and how to utilise the tools that are available are limited.

Taiwan

For the prevention of psychosocial hazards at work, effective governmental interventions combining labour participation should be essential. In Taiwan, the main barriers include insufficient labour inspection, low unionisation rates, lack of collective bargaining power of workers and insufficient labour participation.

Malaysia

For Malaysia it was suggested that issues related to limited awareness and a culture of no reporting where subordinates are reluctant to address issues relating to their psychological health. It was stated that this could be reflective of wider cultural norms from childhood regarding obeying authority i.e., you obey your parents, your teachers, your boss. There needs to be more education about worker rights and what workers need to be psychologically healthy rather than just suppressing emotions and accepting current conditions.

Leadership is also an issue as they often react negatively to workers who do speak up and express their opinions. In addition, there are some barriers related to traditional beliefs where some psychological problems are perceived as something derived from 'supernatural power'. Thus, to remove the psychological illness such as depression and anxiety, the only way is to remove a bad spirit. Another issue is due to Malaysian culture where the emphasis is on 'collective feeling', rather than individual interest. Thus, individual employees are not keen to voice their problems as this could be considered uncomfortable to others.

Thailand

It was stated that there are cultural issues similar to those in Malaysia that act as a barrier in Thailand whereby workers are expected to obey authority without question. This attitude of general acceptance limits progress towards development of laws as well as enforcement and regulation relating to psychosocial factors.

Challenges and Future Directions

Some countries, particularly developing economies such as Thailand, are relatively new to the process of establishing laws specific to protecting worker health from the detrimental impacts of psychosocial risk factors, however, awareness appears to be growing. While in countries such as Malaysia, laws are intended to protect workers from psychological illness and injuries resulting from workplace factors, those laws tend to be only interpreted in relation to physical health and wellbeing. Resourcing for prevention is often only available in larger organisations. In addition, the collectivist culture, which has a tendency to teach youth to obey authority figures, can act as a barrier preventing individuals from being willing to question their superiors or report inappropriate behaviours.

Even in more developed economies challenges exist in the form of enforcing the laws that do exist. In particular, the area of prevention where employers are required to promote safe workplace practices that have a positive impact on worker psychological health rather than only reacting once a situation has resulted in illness, injury and/or compensation claim. Addressing some of the main barriers such as lack of consistent regulation, low unionisation rates, limited collective bargaining power of workers and insufficient labour participation, at a macro-level through government practices, industry regulatory bodies and organisational policy regarding health and safety practices would contribute to improving workplace conditions.

It needs to be made clear by academics and practitioners to governing bodies, employers and workers alike that participation in addressing psychosocial risk factors at work will not only improve employee health and wellbeing but will also have a significant impact on productivity outcomes through increased engagement, reduced presenteeism and sickness absence. A more collaborative approach across the Asia-Pacific region to achieve these goals would benefit a major percentage of the world's workforce in countries where some of the world's most disadvantaged people reside.

Conclusion

Clear differences exist in the standards for psychosocial risk prevention and worker psychological health across countries in the Asia-Pacific region. While it appears more developed economies such as Australia and Taiwan have clearer laws and penalties, issues with enforcement and prevention are common across the region. Focus group participants across all countries agreed that stronger government regulation is needed for intervention and surveillance to promote psychosocial risk prevention. In addition, limited formal translation into practice and lack of focus on psychosocial risk prevention practices are ongoing issues across most countries. It is possible that establishing global guidelines for psychosocial health at work demonstrating a unified agreement for best practice across the world would be a positive step towards addressing these issues.

References

Central Intelligence Agency (CIA). (2014). *The world fact book.* https://www.cia.gov/library/publications/the-world-factbook/rankorder/2095rank.html. Accessed 4 Feb 2016.

Cheng, Y., Park, J., Kim, Y., & Kawakami, N. (2012). The recognition of occupational diseases attributed to heavy workloads: Experiences in Japan, Korea and Taiwan. *International Archives of Occupational and Environmental Health, 85*(7), 791–799.

Dollard, M. F., Shimazu, A., Bin Nordin, R., Brough, P., & Tuckey, M. R. (2014). The context of psychosocial factors at work in the Asia Pacific. In M. F. Dollard, A. Shimazu, R. B. Nordin, P. Brough, & M. Tuckey (Eds.), *Psychosocial factors at work in the Asia Pacific*. New York: Springer.

Kawakami, N., Park, J., Dollard, M.F., & Dai, J. (2014). National status of psychosocial factors at work in Japan, Korea, Australia, and China. In M.F. Dollard, A. Shimazu, R.B. Nordin, P. Brough, M. Tuckey (Eds.), *Psychosocial factors at work in the Asia Pacific*. Springer.

Leka, S., Jain, A., Zwetsloot, G., & Cox, T. (2010). Policy-level interventions and work-related psychosocial risk management in the European Union (Special Issue on Organisational Interventions for the Management of Work-related Stress). *Work and Stress, 24*(3), 298–307.
Safe Work Australia. (2012). *Guide to the WHS Act*. http://www.safeworkaustralia.gov.au/sites/SWA/about/Publications/Documents/717/Guide-to-the-WHS-Act.pdf. Accessed 5 May 2013.
Safe Work Australia. (2014). *Compendium of workers' compensation statistic*s Australia 2012–13. Retrieved from http://www.safeworkaustralia.gov.au/sites/swa/about/publications/pages/australian-workers-compensation-statistics-2012-13, May 2015.

Chapter 4
Guidelines for Primary Prevention for Mental Health at Work

Akizumi Tsutsumi and Akihito Shimazu

Abstract Occupational health experts' and practitioners' evaluated systematic reviews of primary prevention measures for occupational mental health. A consensus meeting was held with the intent of developing primary prevention guidelines for mental health at work. Three preventive strategies were developed—improving the psychosocial work environment, self-care training, and supervisor training. For improving the psychosocial work environment, eight recommendations and four proposed items were developed across four domains. These four domains are planning and organization development, basic rules of implementation, proposals for effective improvement measures, and continued implementation. The guidelines for self-care training consist of four steps that coincide with the process of formulating and implementing measures to help individuals cope with stress (self-care) in the workplace. These four steps are planning and preparing, deciding what self-care entails, and making subsequent efforts. Six recommendations and four proposed items are provided for these four steps. The evidence-based guidelines for supervisor mental health training include ten recommendations and four proposed items. These guidelines recommend providing training to all supervisors, with a particular focus on high-priority populations, and on the needs and situation in the workplace. The training content should be tailored to the different management levels of supervisor groups but also provide basic information, such as explaining the national guidelines and the major occupational stress models. The training should aim to change supervisors' behaviors and not just issue warnings. The guidelines also recommend providing supervisor training periodically (annually), because there is no evidence that the training effect lasts more than 6 months. We expect these guidelines to help to promote the adoption of evidence-based preventive strategies for the management of occupational mental health.

A. Tsutsumi (✉)
Department of Public Health, Kitasato University School of Medicine, Sagamihara, Japan
e-mail: akizumi@kitasato-u.ac.jp

A. Shimazu
Department of Mental Health, The University of Tokyo, Tokyo, Japan

A. Shimazu et al. (eds.), *Psychosocial Factors at Work in the Asia Pacific*,
DOI 10.1007/978-3-319-44400-0_4

Keyword Best available evidence · Evidence-based guidelines · Self-care training · Supervisor training · Workplace improvement

Introduction

For a range of reasons, public health programs, including occupational health programs, may not reach their stated goals for success. Reasons for this failure include: (1) choosing an intervention approach which is not supported by evidence as being effective; (2) selecting a potentially effective program but with weak evidence; (3) conducting an inadequate evaluation that does accurately assess the effectiveness of a program; and (4) paying inadequate attention to the adaptation of an intervention to the population and context of interest (Brownson et al. 2010).

As is well known, scientific evidence is graded, with randomized controlled studies are considered the gold standard. However, randomized control studies are challenging to successfully implement in workplaces. Therefore, the rigorous investigation of strategies for the primary prevention of mental health problems among workers has been challenging.

Although evidence is limited, organizing recommendations about what should be done first at the workplace is useful to promote effective occupational health practices. We developed guidelines for the primary prevention of mental health problems at work for three relevant prevention strategies—improving the psychosocial work environment, self-care training, and supervisor training (see Fig. 4.1). The guidelines are based on a review of research, which has utilized

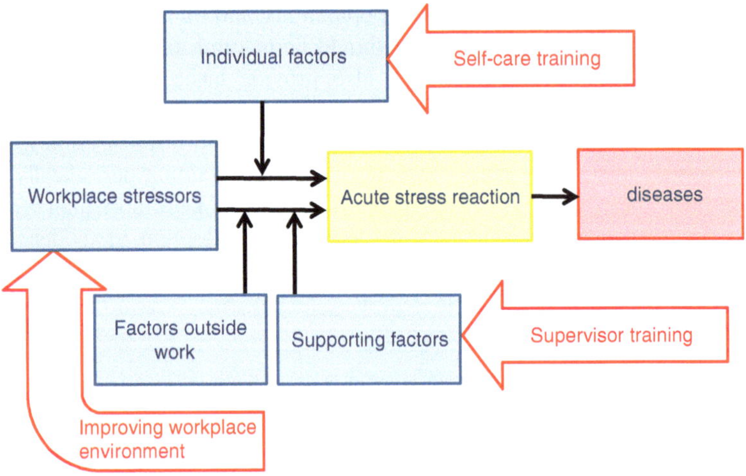

Fig. 4.1 Evidence-based guideline for primary prevention practices. Based on NIOSH occupational stress model (Hurrell and McLaney 1988)

studies that have investigated the psychological stress responses of workers as the study outcomes. In addition, expert opinions have been attained and incorporated into the suggested guidelines.

Implementing Preventive Measures for Workplace Mental Health in the Asia-Pacific Region

To improve workplace mental health, international organizations such as the WHO, the ILO, and the EU have adopted a common strategy to disseminate useful tools, such as guidelines and manuals based on evidence and best practices (ILO 2012; Leka et al. 2011; World Health Organization 2014). Although the major program adopted by the above organizations is risk management, similar strategies are appropriate for the development of practical measures for workplaces to improve the psychosocial work environment and employee training. The guidelines presented in this chapter were developed based on the best evidence currently available and are proposed for application in workplaces across the Asia-Pacific region. However, because evidence and guidelines of this kind are limited in the field of occupational health, the addition of relevant local information, specific to the cultural context of the work environment is suggested. Thus, the guidelines should be regularly reviewed and refined through the incorporation of new evidence and good practices, as they emerge particularly from the Asia-Pacific region.

Guidelines for Improving the Psychosocial Work Environment

Guidelines to facilitate improvement in the psychosocial work environment in terms of the primary prevention of mental health problems among workers were developed by Yoshikawa et al. (2013), who drew examples of good practices from 17 case reports and documents specific to Japan (Yoshikawa and Kogi 2010) and 33 documents identified through two systematic reviews (Egan et al. 2007; Lamontagne et al. 2007). These systematic reviews assessed the impact of improving psychosocial work environments associated with workplace organization, such as working methods or working conditions, and the physical and chemical environment, including human relations in the workplace, on psychological and physical health factors. In the present study, guidelines about four domains of improving the psychosocial work environment were developed. These guidelines consisted of 12 items, including eight recommended items whose validity was confirmed and four proposed items for which scientific grounds were limited but whose validity was supported by expert consensus (Table 4.1).

Table 4.1 Guideline for improving workplace environment for occupational mental health (Outline version)

Domain	Recommendations (R) and proposed items (P)
Planning and organization	Build consensus on aims and establish steering group (R) Engage in way of problem-solving manner (not problem-indicative manner) (R) Elicit proactive involvement of organizational and division heads (P)
Basic rules of implementation	Refer to good practices inside and outside the workplace (R) Facilitate workers participation in all the process (R) List and prioritize a broad range of issues related to workers' mental health (R)
Proposals for effective improvement measures	Take into account the workplace resources and do not disturb the ordinal activities of the organization (R) Employ appropriate tools to support workers (R) Use workplace mechanisms that already exist (P) Adopt an approach in accordance with the readiness of the organization (P)
Continued implementation	Sustain the autonomous activities by producing short-term wins (R) Incorporate the activity into PDCA cycle (P)

Planning and Organizational Development

Consensus building is required in the workplace with respect to the aims of improving the psychosocial work environment. The participation of workers in the process of change and planning assists with improving the mental health of the workers (Kobayashi et al. 2008). It has been confirmed that common processes such as policy setting, planning, implementation, and evaluation promote improvements in the psychosocial work environment. It has also been observed that clarification of internal company policies, development of a system, and division of roles are important to ensure ongoing improvements. Additionally, decision making that incorporates workers' participation and interventions that improve the psychosocial work environment have been shown to improve psychosocial and physical health indicators (Egan et al. 2007; Kawakami et al. 1997; Kobayashi et al. 2008; Lamontagne et al. 2007; Tsutsumi et al. 2009).

Efforts should be made to adopt a problem-solving approach. A review of improvements made to psychosocial work environments in 17 cases revealed that organizations engaged in improving psychosocial work environments emphasized the problem-solving approach (Yoshikawa and Kogi 2010). Further, the subjective work performance improved for workers in the manufacturing industry who participated in activities intended to improve the psychosocial work environments based on the problem-solving approach (Tsutsumi et al. 2009).

It is important to gain the proactive involvement of organizations and divisions that implement measures to improve psychosocial work environments. The support and commitment of the top management, such as the president or the plant manager, is an important step in developing effective stress management programs through improvements in psychosocial work environments. With respect to initiating improvements in psychosocial work environments, it is also important to encourage dialogue with management and human resources about what is required to improve the psychosocial work environment. Highlighting the significance and benefits of activities related to improving psychosocial work environments is required to educate and gain commitment from senior management.

Basic Rules of the Implementation Procedure

A common step in stress management through improving psychosocial work environments includes identification of good practices in the workplace or elsewhere in similar industries and professions. These examples can be provided to workers, to demonstrate what is possible to achieve in improving the psychosocial work environments.

It is important to enable workers to participate in the whole process of the activity. A body of scientific evidence supports that the participation of the workers has a positive influence on the health of the individual and the organization, such as psychosocial indicators (e.g., sense of control, subjective performance) and health indicators (e.g., decrease in rate of absenteeism) (Bond and Bunce 2001; Bourbonnais et al. 2006; Hertting et al. 2003; Maes et al. 1998; Mikkelsen and Saksvik 1999; Smith et al. 1998).

It is recommended that working environments and working conditions related to physical and mental burden should be adapted extensively and improvement measures prioritized and examined. Through a multifactorial approach to the improvement of working environments and conditions related to physical and mental burden, health indicators have been demonstrated to improve (Mikkelsen and Saksvik 1999; Mikkelsen et al. 2000; Tsutsumi 2011; Smith et al. 1998).

Proposal of Effective Improvement Measures

It is recommended that planning states take into consideration workplace conditions, timing, and resources. Those charged with improving the psychosocial work environment activities should consider the workplace conditions when developing training or meeting schedules. When business conditions are unfavorable, it is difficult to obtain beneficial effects from improvements in the participation in activities conducted. Encouraging proposals tailored to the workplace conditions, with consideration to financial management is suggested.

It is recommended to take advantage of tools that encourage proposals that can easily be implemented by drawing out awareness and ideas about the workplace. Many constructive proposals can be obtained from the workplace using a tool that organizes workplace-level discussions to identify immediate, low-cost improvements in the workplace (Tsutsumi et al. 2009). It has been shown that showing examples of good practices promotes improvements in psychosocial work environments (Yoshikawa and Kogi 2010).

To establish systems for continuous improvement, the use of existing workplace mechanisms is suggested. Such mechanisms include safety and health committees or stress reduction committees consisting of staff members, supervisors, human resources workers, and medical personnel, as well as combined programs by relevant labor and management organizations including the supervisor training division. The implementation of these programs is facilitated by the gradual progress of improving psychosocial work environments and readiness of the organization.

Continued Implementation

It is recommended that timelines be set to review implementation status and results with interim reports submitted to ensure the continued implementation of workplace environment improvements. Through participatory activities for improving the psychosocial work environment based on a step-by-step problem-solving approach, the work performance of the employees engaged in the manufacturing line has been shown to improve (Tsutsumi et al. 2009). Additionally, efforts have been made for continued implementation of improvements to psychosocial work environment activities such as workshops for the follow-up of management and supervisor training, as well as regular meetings for determining psychosocial stressors and presenting proposals for solutions to management and workers.

Improving the psychosocial work environment initiatives should preferably include a cycle of planning, implementation, assessment, and review. It is also preferable that these initiatives are implemented continuously. The worker participation type program can be incorporated in the planning, risk assessment, workplace improvement, recording, and review in the occupational safety and health management system. There are also workplace improvement efforts for stress management that can be positioned, planned, implemented, and evaluated as part of the labor safety and health management system.

Guidelines for Self-Care Training

The guidelines for self-care training consist of four steps: planning and preparing to implement self-care, determining what self-care entails, selecting the forms of self-care, and carrying out subsequent efforts (Shimazu 2013; Table 4.2).

Six recommendations and four proposed items are provided for the aforementioned four steps, and have been developed by taking into account evidence levels. Evidence substantiating each recommendation is provided, and the consensus view

Table 4.2 Guideline for self-care training for occupational mental health (Outline version)

Domain	Recommendations (R) and proposed items (P)
Planning and preparation	Include at least two training sessions and one follow-up session (R) Trainers may be specialists in occupational mental health or occupational health professionals (R) Feedback a worker profile of stress assessment in combination with stress management training (R) Start with groups that are most in need of that training, on the limited condition (P) Wrap up a session within 2 h (P)
What self-care entails Forms of self-care	Apply cognitive-behavioral techniques, combined with relaxation techniques if appropriate (R) Select the training format (group training or individual training) in accordance with characteristics of and conditions in the workplace and characteristics of and circumstances faced by participants (R) Create conditions in the workplace to encourage participants to apply what they have learned (P)
Subsequent efforts	Conduct a follow-up session where workers can reflect on the program (R) Encourage workers to apply learned knowledge and acquired skills into daily life (P)

that led to each proposed item is described. Approaches to implement recommendations and proposed items smoothly in the workplace are presented as key aspects of implementation. The guidelines have the following characteristics:

1. A total of ten suggestions (six recommendations and four proposed items) are presented in the guidelines. These suggestions are arranged, following the steps involved in formulating and implementing measures to help individuals cope with stress. Those in control of developing measures to help workers cope with stress can immediately see which actions they should take.
2. Suggestions in the guidelines are classified into recommendations and proposed items based on the scientific evidence available. This distinction in the level of a suggestion (recommendation vs. proposed item) allows individuals overseeing the formulation of measures to help workers cope with stress to more easily prioritize measures in accordance with feasibility in the workplace.
3. For each suggestion, proposed measures are presented, along with their rationale and key aspects of their implementation. The effectiveness of measures to help workers cope with stress in the workplace, based on existing scientific evidence, has been taken into account.

Planning and Preparation

Self-care training could potentially lead to reduced psychological distress through the use of newly acquired knowledge and skills. Self-care training may be provided by specialists in worker self-care or by occupational health staff members in the workplace. When an outside specialist provides care, the specialist should be provided with information regarding workplace characteristics and needs of potential program participants. If training is conducted by an occupational health staff member with little experience in implementing self-care, this staff member should be trained in the necessary knowledge and skills.

Many workplaces use questionnaires to assess stress levels of their workers. Simply informing workers of their results on these assessments is not an appropriate method of reducing stress levels. Workers need to be informed of their results along with specific strategies (training) to reduce stress.

When self-care training is implemented in the workplace, various constraints on time, expense, and personnel can arise. In such instances, identification of groups most in need of the training can be identified, and the training can begin with those groups. In selecting a certain group, a high level of interest in self-care, conditions in the workplace (whether conditions facilitate the use of what has been learned), and the level of stress should be considered.

In light of conditions in the workplace, the burden placed on participants, and fatigue, the duration of a training session should be a maximum of 2 h. If a single session does not allow adequate time for the training, self-care training can be implemented over multiple sessions.

Deciding What Self-Care Entails

Review articles on individual stress management in the workplace (Ganster and Murphy 2000; Richardson and Rothstein 2008; van der Klink et al. 2001) have indicated that the most effective programs are those involving cognitive-behavioral training or cognitive-behavioral training in combination with relaxation techniques. A range of cognitive-behavioral training and relaxation techniques exist and as such the techniques to be taught should be chosen in accordance with the needs and circumstances of potential program participants during program planning and formulation.

An appropriate format should be chosen, taking into account the circumstances of participants, the trainer and relative advantages and disadvantages of each program format. Programs can be conducted as group training, as individual training, or through e-learning. There are advantages and disadvantages of each format. As an example, group training allows a large number of participants to be trained at one time, but participation tends to be more passive and may be challenging to meet the diverse needs of participants. Individual training involves one-on-one interaction between trainer and the participant. This method allows a flexible approach to meeting the participant's needs, but is more costly (labor costs, as well as the allocation of a location and time). Web-based independent learning (e-learning) is unaffected by time and place constraints that hamper individual training and group training, and allows participants to learn at their own pace. However, web-based learning participants have few chances to interact with other participants, and participants can only learn in places equipped with a computer.

The effectiveness of self-care training stems from the repeated use of learned knowledge and acquired skills in everyday life. Thus, creating conditions in the workplace that encourage workers to apply the learned skills is crucial. In a workplace where workers are given appropriate discretion, opportunities to apply their newly acquired knowledge and skills will occur, enhancing the likelihood that training will be effective. Thus, self-care training should be accompanied by measures to increase worker discretion in the workplace.

Subsequent Efforts

Self-care training should lead to reduced psychological distress by teaching both knowledge and skills and by encouraging the use of this newly acquired knowledge and skills in everyday life. Following the training, a session should be conducted to have participants reflect on what they have learned, encourage them to remember the knowledge they have gained and the skills they have acquired, and to encourage participants to apply their newly acquired knowledge and skills in everyday life. This approach will help to increase the effectiveness of the training. During the follow-up session, trainers will encourage participants to reflect on what they learned during the training sessions, and whether participants are able to use the skills acquired in training. Trainers will then identify factors that encourage participants to use these techniques to cope with stress and those that prevent participants from doing this.

Even if the training is understood intellectually, failure to apply what has been learned to everyday life will not prevent mental health problems from occurring or help to sustain or improve health. Thus, the approach should encourage participants to apply the knowledge they have learned to their own problems and circumstances (e.g., by assigning homework to the participants).

Guidelines for Supervisor Training

Supervisor training is regarded as an important strategy for the primary prevention of mental health problems among workers. However, because the effectiveness of primary prevention strategies has not been sufficiently validated, supervisor training has been carried out based on the empirical values of occupational health staff members. Determining the contents and methods of training given to supervisors to improve mental health conditions of workers in the workplace remains important for developing the primary prevention system in the workplace.

Table 4.3 Guideline for supervisor training for occupational mental health (Outline version)

Domain	Recommendations (R) and proposed items (T)
Selection of training participants	Identify population with an increased need for education and prioritize their training (R) Plan training focused of the needs and circumstances of the target workplace (R) Provide mental health training to all personnel in managerial positions (R) Stratify the target management position according to needs in training content (P)
Contents and format	Include items recommended in the National Guideline and items relevant to major occupational stress models (R) Aim for behavioral modification of supervisors (R) Seek the effective way to promote better understandings of managers (R) Incorporate participatory training to develop listening and advising techniques (R) Provide training on administrative procedure of returning to work, arrangement of work condition, and procedure to cooperate with other insiders (R) Present issues and data of the workplace (P) Present case examples to increase motivation in training participation (P)
Frequency	Provide training once a year (R) Provide training periodically (not only once) (R) Plan stepwise training (P)

A review of literature identified that, at least in the short term, providing supervisors with information and techniques related to mental health contributed to beneficial effects in occupational stress factors, workers' mental health state, insomnia, and work performance (Tsutsumi 2011). Although most findings supported the hypothesis that supervisor training improves the mental health of workers, the significant results from randomized controlled studies were based on the subanalyzes or different stress responses from the primary outcomes. In developing the guidelines presented in this chapter, the characteristics of the subjects, contents, and format of the training, training period, and evaluation period were considered. Subsequently, recommended content for inclusion in training took into account experts' consensus on effectiveness (Tsutsumi 2011) (Table 4.3).

Selection of Training Participants

A body of evidence suggests that higher rates of supervisors participating in training sessions lead to more effective outcomes (Tsutsumi et al. 2005). In other words, effectiveness throughout the organization may not be entirely achieved without the participation of a certain number of supervisors. Furthermore, the cases that have shown positive effects of supervisor training had a certain background that required mental health management, such as the presence of a population with concerns about the future prospects of their company.

According to the experts, providing training for those who supervise people on how to deal with these people and to cooperate with occupational health staff members can be meaningful. The experts also noted that, for business managers, education to ensure the significance of establishing a system for mental health support is important.

Contents and Format of the Training

Learning content indicated in the "Guideline for maintenance and improvement of workers' mental health" published by the Ministry of Health, Labor, and Welfare (2006) has been shown to be effective (Tsutsumi 2011). The effectiveness of providing knowledge of major occupational stress models along with work environment improvement methods has also been demonstrated. Furthermore, past studies have suggested that the outcome of training was achieved through enhancing knowledge and favorable behavioral changes of supervisors (Tsutsumi et al. 2005).

Online training is considered an efficient method of imparting information, because it allows course participants to learn at their own pace, without time and place restrictions that may be problematic in individual or group education.

Some attitudes and behaviors of supervisors that may impact workers with mental health problems returning to work were identified. These include knowledge about symptoms of mental health problems and administrative procedures to return to work, appropriate responses and an empathic attitude, adjustment and reallocation of job responsibilities, consideration of other workers, and cooperation with occupational health staff and external organizations (Johnston et al. 2015).

No studies were identified which evaluated the effects of active listening in improving the mental health of workers. However, previous studies have indicated that workers supervised by supervisors with good listening skills and attitudes showed responses to psychological stress that were favorable overall, compared with workers under the supervision of supervisors with poorer listening skills and attitudes (Mineyama et al. 2007). A study employing a before–after comparison design without any control groups showed favorable changes in attitudes of supervisors brought about by proactive listening training (Kubota et al. 2004). The potential of participatory training to improve active listening skills among supervisors has been suggested.

Experts' opinions suggested that incorporating data or cases specific to a particular workplace into the education program may capture the interests of participants.

Evaluation Period for the Training and its Effectiveness

Long-term effects of training greater than one year have not been fully investigated. One randomized controlled study suggested that training effects on supervisors' knowledge or behavior are of benefit for only six months following training take (Nishiuchi et al. 2007). The experts also pointed out that attempting to convey an excessive amount of information may reduce the educational effects. This evidence suggests that training needs to be repeated to maintain the effects, and it is recommended to provide training at least once each year.

During the repeated training sessions, each workplace should consider the topics to be covered. The knowledge and attitudes acquired by supervisors takes time to develop. Attempting to convey excessive amounts of information may reduce the effect of training.

Challenges and Future Directions

We acknowledge that the proposed guidelines are not ideal. The small number of previous studies, minimal effects shown, and methodological limitations, limit the conclusions that can be drawn and as such further studies with rigorous design are needed to evaluate the effects of the primary prevention measures for mental health support. The guidelines need to be enriched by incorporating positive outcomes of the cases that have not yet been published but are often seen in occupational health sites. More evidence from the Asia-Pacific region is required, as most of the intervention research to date has been conducted in Western Europe and North America, with the exception of research on supervisor training (Dollard et al. 2014). However, challenges arise in conducting randomized controlled trials in occupational settings. Intervention effects may vary by workplace or social conditions, due to a range of obstacles to implementing the intervention (e.g., type of organization, prospects, lack of resources, or insufficient skill of practitioner).

Despite the methodological challenges, we need to accumulate the evidence in occupational health interventions in particular around the area of psychosocial management. Interventions should be theory-based with provision for appropriate evaluations. Process evaluations using quantitative and qualitative methods will provide useful information on the interventions (Tashakkori and Teddlie 2010).

Guidelines are systematically developed statements to assist practitioners and patients in making decisions about appropriate health care for specific clinical circumstances. In the field of occupational health, it is the practitioner who chooses and adapts recommendations so that they are appropriate for the workplace. However, this requires an adequately skilled practitioner to use the guidelines efficiently. Evidence suggests that training of practitioners in occupational health is limited (World Health Organization 2013).

It is possible that not all of the measures of a multimodal intervention will be accepted in the workplace. Guideline developers should provide an assessment of the strength of each individual recommendation so that the practitioners can choose the recommendations more easily (Andrews et al. 2013).

Conclusion

Understanding what needs to be done first in developing organizational health interventions is challenging. The guidelines presented in this chapter are proposed to provide a range of standardized evidence informed recommendations for use in workplaces across the Asia Pacific and beyond.

References

Andrews, J., Guyatt, G., Oxman, A. D., Alderson, P., Dahm, P., Falck-Ytter, Y., et al. (2013). GRADE guidelines: 14. Going from evidence to recommendations: The significance and presentation of recommendations. *Journal of Clinical Epidemiology, 66*(7), 719–725.

Bond, F. W., & Bunce, D. (2001). Job control mediates change in a work reorganization intervention for stress reduction. *Journal of Occupational Health Psychology, 6*(4), 290–302.

Bourbonnais, R., Brisson, C., Vinet, A., Vézina, M., & Lower, A. (2006). Effectiveness of a participative intervention on psychosocial work factors to prevent mental health problems in a hospital setting. *Occupational and Environmental Medicine, 63*(5), 335–342.

Brownson, R. C., Baker, E. A., Leet, T. L., Gillespie, K. N., & True, W. R. (2010). *Evidence-based public health* (2nd ed.). New York: Oxford University Press.

Dollard, M. F., Shimazu, S., Nordin, R. B., & Brough, P. (2014). The context of psychosocial factors at work in the Asia Pacific. In M. F. Dollard, A. Shimazu, R. B. Nordin, P. Brough, & M. R. Tuckey (Eds.), *Psychosocial factors at work in the Asia Pacific* (pp. 3–27). Dordrecht: Springer International Publishing.

Egan, M., Bambra, C., Thomas, S., Petticrew, M., Whitehead, M., & Thomson, H. (2007). The psychosocial and health effects of workplace reorganisation. 1. A systematic review of organisational-level interventions that aim to increase employee control. *Journal of Epidemiology and Community Health, 61*(11), 945–954. doi:10.1136/jech.2006.054965.

Ganster, D. C., & Murphy, L. R. (2000). Workplace interventions to prevent stress-related illness: Lessons from research and practice. In C. L. Cooper & E. A. Locke (Eds.), *Industrial and Organizational Psychology* (pp. 34–51). Oxford: Blackwell.

Hertting, A., Nilsson, K., Theorell, T., & Larsson, U. S. (2003). Personnel reductions and structural changes in health care, work-life experiences of medical secretaries. *Journal of Psychosomatic Research, 54*, 161–170.

Hurrell, J. J, Jr., & McLaney, M. A. (1988). Exposure to job stress—A new psychometric instrument. *Scandinavian Journal of Work and Environmental Health, 14*(suppl I), 27–28.

ILO. (2012). *Stress prevention at work checkpoints—Practical improvements for stress prevention in the workplace*. Geneva: ILO.

Johnston, V., Way, K., Long, M. H., Wyatt, M., Gibson, L., & Shaw, W. S. (2015). Supervisor competencies for supporting return to work: A mixed-methods study. *Journal of Occupational Rehabilitation, 25*(1), 3–17. doi:10.1007/s10926-014-9511-z.

Kawakami, N., Araki, S., Kawashima, M., Masumoto, T., & Hayashi, T. (1997). Effects of work-related stress reduction on depressive symptoms among Japanese blue-collar workers. *Scandinavian Journal of Work & Environmental Health, 23*(1), 54–59.

Kobayashi, Y., Kaneyoshi, A., Yokota, A., & Kawakami, N. (2008). Effects of a worker participatory program for improving work environments on job stressors and mental health among workers: A controlled trial. *Journal of Occupational Health, 50*(6), 455–470.

Kubota, S., Mishima, N., & Nagata, S. (2004). A study of the effects of active listening on listening attitudes of middle managers. *Journal of Occupational Health, 46*(1), 60–67.

Lamontagne, A. D., Keegel, T., Louie, A. M., Ostry, A., & Landsbergis, P. A. (2007). A systematic review of the job-stress intervention evaluation literature, 1990-2005. *International Journal of Occupational and Environmental Health, 13*(3), 268–280. doi:10.1179/oeh.2007.13.3.268.

Leka, S., Jain, A., Cox, T., & Kortum, E. (2011). The development of the European framework for psychosocial risk management: PRIMA-EF. *Journal of Occupational Health, 53*(2), 137–143.

Maes, S., Verhoeven, C., Kittel, F., & Scholten, H. (1998). Effects of a Dutch work-site wellness-health program: The Brabantia Project. *American Journal of Public Health, 88*(7), 1037–1041.

Mikkelsen, A., & Saksvik, P. Ø. (1999). Impact of a participatory organizational intervention on job characteristics and job stress. *International Journal of Health Services, 29*(4), 871–893.

Mikkelsen, A., Saksvik, P. Ø., & Landsbergis, P. (2000). The impact of a participatory organizational intervention on job stress in community health care institutions. *Work and Stress, 14*(2), 156–170.

Mineyama, S., Tsutsumi, A., Takao, S., Nishiuchi, K., & Kawakami, N. (2007). Supervisors' attitudes and skills for active listening with regard to job stress and psychological stress reactions among subordinate workers. *Journal of Occupational Health, 49*(2), 81–87.

Ministry of Health, Labor and Welfare. (2006). *Japanese guideline for workers' mental health in the workplace*. http://www.mhlw.go.jp/new-info/kobetu/roudou/gyousei/anzen/101004-3.html.

Nishiuchi, K., Tsutsumi, A., Takao, S., Mineyama, S., & Kawakami, N. (2007). Effects of an education program for stress reduction on supervisor knowledge, attitudes, and behavior in the workplace: A randomized controlled trial. *Journal of Occupational Health, 49*(3), 190–198.

Richardson, K. M., & Rothstein, H. R. (2008). Effects of occupational stress management intervention programs: A meta-analysis. *Journal of Occupational Health Psychology, 13*, 69–93.

Shimazu, A. (2013). Guidelines for self-care training in occupational mental health. *Job Stress Research, 20*, 124–133.

Smith, L., Hammond, T., Macdonald, I., & Folkard, S. (1998). 12-h shifts are popular but are they a solution? *International Journal of Industrial Ergonomics, 21*, 323–331.

Tashakkori, A., & Teddlie, C. (2010). *Handbook of mixed methods in social and behavioral research* (2nd ed.). Thousand Oaks, CA: Sage.

Tsutsumi, A. (2011). Development of an evidence-based guideline for supervisor training in promoting mental health: Literature review. *Journal of Occupational Health, 53*, 1–9.

Tsutsumi, A., Nagami, M., Yoshikawa, T., Kogi, K., & Kawakami, N. (2009). Participatory intervention for workplace improvements on mental health and job performance among blue-collar workers: A cluster randomized controlled trial. *Journal of Occupational and Environmental Medicine, 51*, 554–563.

Tsutsumi, A., Takao, S., Mineyama, S., Nishiuchi, K., Komatsu, H., & Kawakami, N. (2005). Effects of a supervisory education for positive mental health in the workplace: A quasi-experimental study. *Journal of Occupational Health, 47*(3), 226–235.

van der Klink, J. J. L., Blonk, R. W. B., Schene, A. H., & van Dijk, F. J. H. (2001). The benefits of interventions for work-related stress. *American Journal of Public Health, 91*, 270–276.

World Health Organization. (2013). *WHO Global Plan of Action on Workers' Health (2008–2017): Baseline for implementation. Global Country Survey 2008/2009*, Executive summary and survey findings. Geneva, WHO.

World Health Organization. (2014). *Workers' Health Tool Kits*. http://www.who-toolkit.org/.

Yoshikawa, T., & Kogi, K. (2010). Roles in stress prevention of good practices for workplace improvements and the use of action support tool. *Job Stress Research, 17*, 267–274.

Yoshikawa, T., Yoshikawa, E., Tsuchiya, M., Kobayashi, Y., Shimazu, A., Tsutsumi, A., et al. (2013). Development of evidence-based medicine guideline for improving the workplace environment by means of primary job stress prevention. *Job Stress Research, 20*, 135–145.

Chapter 5
Strategies to Prevent Work-Related Stress and Cardiovascular Diseases in South Korea

Jungsun Park

Abstract The first KOSHA guideline that dealt with preventing work-related stress was the "Guidelines on the Occupational Stressor Scale for Korean Workers (KOSS 2006)." KOSS was developed by the Korean Society of Occupational Stress and supported by KOSHA. In 2008, KOSHA developed health management guidelines for shift workers. Thereafter, during 2011–2012, KOSHA developed stress management guidelines for various high stress working groups. In 2014, in response to increasing social concerns about the mental health of workers who engage in emotional labor in Korea, the Korean government and KOSHA developed the "Guidelines on Assessment for Emotional Labor for Korean Workers." In the future, the Korean government should take into account the underlying reasons why work-related stress is not properly managed in workplaces. The suggested points here should be considered when developing and disseminating standard risk assessment tools for work-related stress.

Keywords Work-related stress · Work-related cardiovascular diseases · South Korea · Strategy

Introduction

South Korean society first began to deal with work-related cardiovascular and cerebrovascular diseases in 1999, and to be concerned about work-related stress in 2003, when the phrase "work-related stress" first appeared in Korean Regulations on Occupational Safety and Health. This review presents the statistics, guidelines, and policies associated with work-related stress and work-related cardiovascular and cerebrovascular diseases in South Korea and describe strategies to prevent and manage these problems.

J. Park (✉)
Department of Occupational Health, Catholic University of Daegu, Gyonsan-si, Gyeongsangbuk-do, Republic of Korea
e-mail: jsunpark@chol.com

A. Shimazu et al. (eds.), *Psychosocial Factors at Work in the Asia Pacific*,
DOI 10.1007/978-3-319-44400-0_5

Prevention of Work-Related Cerebrovascular and Cardiovascular Diseases

Statistics on Disease Due to Overwork: Cerebrovascular and Cardiovascular Diseases (CVDs)

South Korea is one of few countries in the world to classify cerebrovascular and cardiovascular diseases (CVDs) as work-related diseases (Park et al. 2012). When CVDs were first classified by the Ministry of Labor as work-related in 1982, only accidental CVDs, such as intracranial hemorrhage and sudden cardiac death that were clearly work associated, were recognized as occupational diseases, and only a few such patients were compensated yearly. In December 1994, the criteria for work-related CVDs fell under the enforcement ordinances of the Industrial Accident Compensation Insurance Act, a higher level of regulation. These criteria have since been modified several times. Hemorrhagic cerebrovascular diseases tended to be regarded easily as work-related CVDs if they occurred while working in the workplace; i.e., "in-the-course-of-work-stipulation."

Since then, the number of work-related CVDs has increased dramatically, from 252 in 1996 to 1214 in 1999, peaking at 2358 in 2003 (Park et al. 2011). However, the number of Work-related CVDs decreased steadily to 639 in 2009, following amendment of Rules regarding Health Standards of MOEL in 2003. It decreased further since 2008, following revision of the "in-the-course-of-work-stipulation." The number of compensated work-related CVDs was 579 in 2012, increasing to 676 in 2014 (Fig. 5.1).

Criteria for Recognition of Work-Related CVDs in Korea

The criteria for recognition of work-related CVDs in South Korea are shown in Table 5.1, and detailed ministerial rules on recognition are shown in Table 5.2. The number of hours worked per week is essential for the recognition of CVDs. Chronic overwork was defined by ministerial rules in July 2013 as ≥60 h work per week for at least 12 weeks before the onset of disease. In the context of a normal workweek of 40 h, an average work week of ≥60 h in Korea is similar to the Japanese criteria for monthly overwork, defined as ≥80 h per month for 2–6 months before the onset of disease.

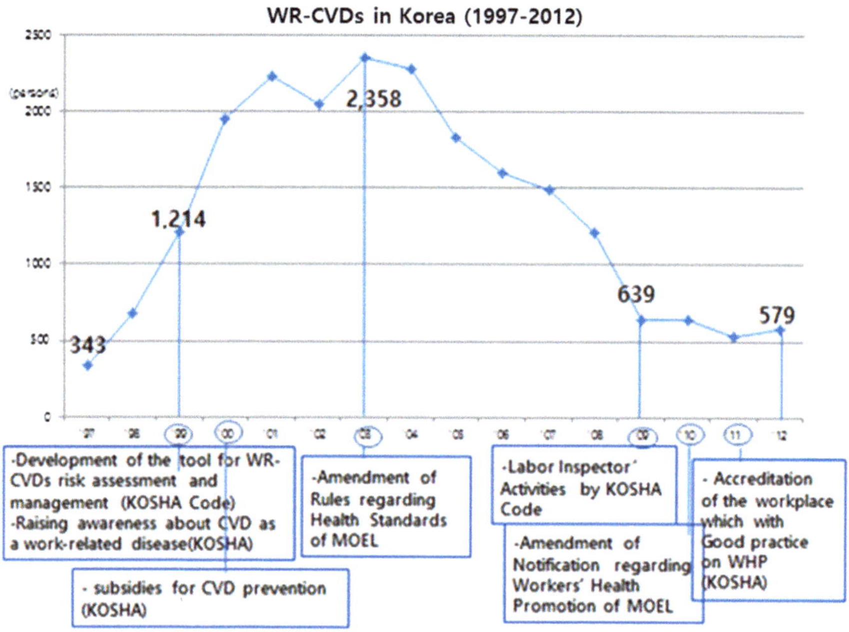

Fig. 5.1 The number of work-related CVDs (1997–2012) and prevention activities by year (Source: Park 2014, Presentation at WPRO, WHO)

Table 5.1 Criteria for Recognition of Work-related CVDs in South Korea

A. If a worker experiences any type of intracerebral hemorrhage, subarachnoid hemorrhage, cerebral infarction, myocardial infarction, or dissecting aneurysm of the aorta, and this disease meets any of the criteria below, it will be considered a work-related disease. Conditions that result from natural pathological processes will not be considered work-related 1. Situations that cause significant physiological changes in workers who have experienced unexpected accidental strain, agitation, fear, shock, or dramatic changes in work environment just prior to the onset of disease 2. Situations that cause mental and physical exhaustion as a result of increased workload, working hours, work intensity, job responsibility or changes in work environment for brief periods before the onset of disease 3. Situations that cause mental and physical overload due to chronic overwork, followed by a change in workload, working hours, work intensity, job responsibility, or work environment
B. A condition can also be considered work-related if any cerebrovascular or cardiovascular diseases not mentioned above are triggered or aggravated in a chronological or medical manner
C. Instructions necessary for the evaluation of work-relatedness according to A and B shall be prescribed by Notification of the Minister of MOEL

Table 5.2 Detailed notice on the recognition of CVDs in South Korea

1. "Situations that cause significant physiological changes in workers who have experienced unexpected accidental strain, agitation, fear, shock, or dramatic changes in work environment" in A-1 (see above) of the enforcement ordinances of the Industrial Accident Compensation Insurance Act indicate that sudden and unexpected situations related to work occurring within 24 h prior to the onset of disease, with those situations contributing to the accelerated progression of CVDs beyond natural processes
2. "Situations that cause mental and physical exhaustion as a result of increased workload, working hours, work intensity, job responsibility or changes in work environment" in A-2 of the enforcement ordinances of the Industrial Accident Compensation Insurance Act indicate that >30 % increases in workloads or working hours, or increases in work intensity, job responsibility or changes in the work environment that changed for similar workers in similar jobs difficult to adapt to within 1 week before the onset of disease. In addition, determination of 'excessive overwork during a brief period' requires comprehensive consideration of workloads, working hours, work intensity, job responsibility, days off and holidays, work patterns, changes in work environment, adaptation period, age, gender, and health status
3. "Situations that cause mental and physical overload due to chronic overwork followed by a change in work load, working hours, work intensity, job responsibility, or work environment" in A-2 of the enforcement ordinances of the Industrial Accident Compensation Insurance Act indicate the need to continuously and objectively identify situations for 3 months before the onset of disease. Determination of 'chronic overwork' requires comprehensive consideration of workloads, working hours, work intensity, job responsibility, days and holidays, patterns of work such as shiftwork or night work, psychological strain, sleeping time, work environment, age, gender, and health status. In evaluating working hours, the following should be considered (1) An average of ≥60 h per week for 12 weeks, or ≥64 h per week for 4 weeks, should indicate a strong association between working hours and disease development (2) Even if average weekly working hours are lower than these cutoffs, the association between working hours and disease development should be regarded as increasing with increasing working hours. Furthermore, night work, including shift work at night, should be considered more burdensome than day work

Activities to Prevent Work-Related CVDs

Various measures have been shown to contribute to a rapid decline in the number of work-related CVDs (see Fig. 5.1). Preventive measures include:

1. Periodic medical checkups of workers for early detection of risk factors for CVDs.
   The Occupational Safety and Health Act mandated that employers should provide periodic general medical examination to workers for free since 1982. Targets of periodic general medical examination changed from early detection of pulmonary tuberculosis to early detection of risk factors for CVDs, such as obesity, hypertension, diabetes, and dyslipidemia. Periodic general medical examinations have been provided to workers for free by the National Health Insurance Corporation since 1995.

2. Development and dissemination of risk assessment and management guidelines on Work-related CVDs.
   Risk assessment and management guidelines on work-related CVDs were first developed by the Korea Occupational Safety and Health Agency (KOSHA) in 1999, and have since been revised slightly several times. These guidelines included the World Health Organization (WHO) guidelines on hypertension, but focused on workplace-rather than individual-based management. Workers were categorized into four groups based on their risks of work-related CVDs: normal, low-risk, moderate-risk, and high-risk groups. With the goal of lowering risk grade, workers in the moderate- and high-risk groups are advised to modify their lifestyles and to continue hypertension control. They are also evaluated on fitness for work and may be changed to other jobs if necessary.
3. Government-subsidized activities to prevent CVDs in workers in small-sized businesses.
   Since 2000, KOSHA has provided subsidies, sourced from workers' compensation funds, to private occupational health service institutes to perform activities to prevent CVDs in workers in small-sized companies, defined as having fewer than 50 employees.
4. Revised rules on Health Standards include assessing the risks of work-related CVDs.
   In July 2003, the Ministry of Employment and Labor drastically revised its rules on Health Standards. These rules included assessment of the risks of work-related CVDs although risk assessment is not a legal requirement, but a recommendation.
5. Development of a manual for labor inspectors to prevent work-related CVDs in workers.
   The Ministry of Employment and Labor developed a manual on the prevention of work related CVDs and provided it to labor inspectors in 2009. This manual was based on risk assessments and management guidelines regarding work-related CVDs.
6. Drastic revision of ministerial rules regarding workers' health promotion.
   In 2010, the Ministry of Employment and Labor drastically revised its rules regarding workers' health promotion. The rules aimed to prevent work-related CVDs, work-related musculoskeletal disorders, and work-related stress, and mandated that health promotion activities include activities in the workplace to prevent these health problems.
7. Introduction of a certification program for good practices of workplace health promotion.
   KOSHA began to certify workplaces performing workplace health promotion activities in 2011. Workplaces that apply to KOSHA for good practices of workplace health promotion, are evaluated and may be acknowledged, based on predetermined criteria, as good practices of workplace health promotion. If so, they are given a plaque certifying good practice.

In sum, South Korea established a unique strategy for prevention of work-related CVDs in workers. The South Korean government aimed to detect workers at high-risk for CVDs in their early stages, encouraging these workers to modify their lifestyles and control their underlying diseases. Workers may also be evaluated on fitness for work and may be changed to other jobs if necessary. These strategies differed from those in Japan, which focused on decreasing overtime work.

Future Direction of Policies

South Korea's population is aging more rapidly than that of any other country, due to a low birth rate and an increase in mean life expectancy. This aging trend will have a significant impact on the quantity and quality of labor force with work ability. Aging is the most important risk factor for noncommunicable diseases (NCDs) that cannot be cured but must be managed throughout life. Customized preventive strategies are therefore needed, depending on labor life cycle. These goals require the collaboration of governmental agencies at the central and local levels. At the central level, the common goal should be the reinforcement of follow-up measures in general medical examinations and the promotion of healthy lifestyles for workers, by the signing of a Memorandum of Understanding by the Ministry of Employment and Labor and the Department of Health and Welfare. At the local level, activities should be promoted by collaborations among Worker's Health Centers, Health Promotion Centers, and community health centers.

Prevention of Work-Related Stress

Exposure to Work-Related Stressors

KOSHA, a government affiliated organization, conducted Korean Working Conditions Surveys (KWCS) in 2006, 2010, 2011, and 2014. In 2006 and 2010, 10,000 workers each were targeted for at-home interviews; whereas in 2011 and 2014, 50,000 targeted workers were interviewed. The contents and methods of the KWCS were similar to those of the Working Conditions Survey of the European Union. The results of the KOSHA surveys are considered to represent working conditions throughout South Korea (Park and Lee 2009; Kim et al. 2013).

The 2006, 2010, 2011 and 2014 KWCS found that 44.4, 25.4, 27.1, and 10.4 % of respondents, respectively, reported hiding any emotionally hurt feelings while at work. The 2010 survey found that 31.3 % of respondents, including 32.6 % of males and 29.4 % of females, answered "Yes" to the question, "Do you have stress at work?" In 2011, 26.1 % of respondents answered "Yes" to this question, including 26.5 % of males and 24.5 % of females.

The 2010, 2011, and 2014 KWCS found that 3.7, 4.4, and 6.6 % of respondents, respectively, reported being verbally abused during the month prior to the survey, while 0.3, 0.6 and 0.5 % of respondents, respectively, answered "Yes" to the question, "Were you physically abused during the past month?"

The 2006, 2010, 2011, and 2014 KWCS found that 19.4, 47.0, 45.8, and 50.1 % of the respondents, respectively, said that they were supported by their coworkers, while 20.7, 48.8, 49.8, and 47.4 %, respectively, reported being supported by their bosses.

According to the 2010, 2011, and 2014 KWCS, 21.3, 23.5, and 26.1 % of respondents, respectively, reported presenteeism.

According to the 2014 KWCS, 23.4 % of workers (22.5 % of males and 24.4 % of females) reported a WHO-5 index score below 13, which indicated poor mental well-being and suggests the need to test for depression.

The above results strongly indicate that work-related stress management in the workplace and promotion of mental health in workers are becoming increasingly more important in Korea.

Regulations and Guidelines on Work-Related Stress

In December 2002 amendment to the Occupational Safety and Health Act, the Ministry of Labor stipulated that employers should prevent employee health problems due to physical fatigue and mental stress (Article 5). Immediately afterward, the ministry completely revised its regulations on occupational health standards (Ordinance of the Ministry of Labor No. 195) and, in July 2003, the Ministry established a new rule [Countermeasures on health problems due to work-related stress] in Article 259.

This rule, however, focused more on preventing work-related CVDs rather than preventing work-related stress by managing work-related factors. In July 2011, when the rules on occupational safety and occupational health standards were combined and revised, this rule became Article 669 of the new Regulations.

Article 669 [Countermeasures to deal with health problems caused by work-related stress]
An employer shall take any of the following countermeasures to prevent health problems due to work-related stress pursuant to Item 1, Article 5 of the Act when any of his/her employees is involved with work that causes physical fatigue and mental stress, such as shift work including night work and working long hours, driving a taxi or bus, or monitoring work in the control room: (a) assessing possible stress factors, such as work environment, work content, and working hours, and planning and implementing countermeasures, such as reducing working hours and rotating tasks; (b) considering employees' opinions when formulating working plans based on work load and work schedule; (c) improving working conditions by allocating work hours and break times properly; (d) doing his/her best to secure the welfare of employees related to work

(continued)

(continued)

activities; (e) placing employees in positions based on the results of medical checkups and counseling, and providing enough explanation to the employee concerned about factors associated with work-related stress, the possibility of health problems and countermeasures; f) implementing health promotion programs to encourage employees to quit smoking and manage hypertension after assessing their CVD risks

Recently, concerns have been raised on mental health issues in workers involved in emotionally stressful labor (emotional labor), such as call center workers and salespersons in department stores, who should always respond kindly to customers with a smiling face, while hiding their own emotions. The Korean Ministry of Employment and Labor is preparing regulations to prevent work-related stress in these workers that will meet the expectations of labor groups and members of congress.

The first KOSHA guidelines that dealt with preventing work-related stress were developed by the Korean Society of Occupational Stress and supported by KOSHA. These Guidelines on the Occupational Stressor Scale for Korean Workers (KOSS), first made available in 2006, described the nature and use of KOSS, which was developed to address increased demands for tools that could assess stressors unique to Korean workers and be applied alongside widely used tools developed in Western countries (e.g., the JCQ and ERI).

In 2008, KOSHA developed health management guidelines for shift workers, followed by the development, during 2011–2012, of stress management guidelines for various high stress working groups, including taxi and bus drivers, building cleaners, food service workers, saleswomen, call center operators, nurses, nursing home workers, emotional laborers, posttraumatic stress disorder (PTSD) patients, workers with depression, workers working long hours, construction workers, bank tellers, hotel employees, airline cabin crews, train engineers, and caddies.

In 2014, in response to increasing social concerns about the mental health of workers who engage in emotional labor in Korea, the Korean government and KOSHA developed the "Guidelines on Assessment for Emotional Labor for Korean Workers."

Although the Korean government and KOSHA have developed various guidelines on work-related stress, most workplaces do not have measures in place to manage work-related stress and/or have difficulties managing work-related stress. This is largely due to the following.

First, employers know less about work-related stress than chemical or physical hazards, and they are often not concerned with the (non-mandatory) regulations on work-related stress.

Second, there are no assessment tools or management guidelines for sector-specific stressors, as even KOSS can only assess general work-related stressors.

Third, while the KOSHA guidelines provide guidance regarding the management of work-related stress in high-risk industrial sectors or occupations, they are not sufficiently detailed or concrete to be useful in individual work environments.

Fourth, few occupational health professionals are available to help manage work-related stress.

Therefore, employers tend to deal with job-related stress by using a personal approach for secondary or tertiary prevention rather than focusing on primary prevention.

Future Directions

To protect workers, the South Korean government recently introduced a risk assessment scheme to complement the Korean Occupational Safety and Health Act. This risk assessment scheme was introduced in December 2013 and has been in effect since January 2014. The government and KOSHA provide industry- and occupation-specific standard models and an electronic system for risk assessment in the workplace. However, the guidelines on risk assessment for work-related stress are not yet available.

In the future, the Korean government should take into account the reasons underlying why work-related stresses are not properly managed in workplaces. The following points should be considered when developing and disseminating standard risk assessment tools for work-related stress.

First, risk assessment tools for work-related stress should involve workers' group activities, because, in contrast to objective and quantifiable hazards (e.g., physical or chemical), work-related stress is subjective and qualitative (Encourage participation)

Second, the tools should be simple and easy to use without the support of professionals, because such professionals are not always available (Use an action checklist).

Third, the tools should suggest solutions intuitively rather than generate criticism, because most employers are reluctant to openly deal with work-related stress issues (Use a positive approach).

Fourth, the tools should be tailored to individual workplaces (Use a practical approach).

In addition, the successful implementation of these tools should be actively supported through long-term campaigns stressing the importance of primary prevention of work-related stress, training of facilitators who can support workplace risk assessment, continuous development and dissemination of industry- and occupation-specific tools, and identification and reporting of good practices.

References

http://www.kosha.or.kr/main.do?chk=1.

http://www.kosha.or.kr/jsp/kwcs/index.do?menuId=7598&fw=list.

http://www.kosha.or.kr/board.do?menuId=4828.

Kim, Y. S., Rhee, K. Y., Oh, M. J., & Park, J. (2013). The validity and reliability of the second Korean working conditions survey. *Safety and Health at Work, 4*(2), 111–116.

Park, J. (2014). *Workers and improving access to health services: An example from Korea.* Presentation material at Manila, WHO WPRO meeting.

Park, J., Kim, Y., & Hisanaga, N. (2011). Work-related cerebrovascular and cardiovascular diseases (work-related CVDs) in Korea. *Industrial Health, 49*, 3–7.

Park, J., Kim, Y., Cheng, Y., & Horie, S. (2012). A comparison of the recognition of overwork-related cardiovascular disease in Japan, Korea, and Taiwan. *Industrial Health, 50*, 17–23.

Park, J., & Lee, N. (2009). First Korean working conditions survey: A comparison between South Korea and EU Countries. *Industrial Health, 47*, 50–54.

Part II
Psychosocial Factors at Work in the Asia Pacific

Chapter 6
Psychosocial Safety Climate: Past, Present, and Future Research

Yulita, Mohd. Awang Idris and Maureen Dollard

Abstract A systematic review was conducted on the facet-specific climate for psychosocial safety [psychosocial safety climate (PSC)] that has been featured in the literature. Specifically, we sought answers regarding the roles, impacts, research trend, and challenges for PSC research. From our search of three databases, 113 articles peer-reviewed journal articles were identified of which 13 PSC articles qualified for the review. For comparative purposes we also considered research on other climate facets, safety climate (n = 59), and psychological safety climate (n = 16), published from 1980 to 2016. Although safety climate remains the dominant research interest, PSC surpassed psychological safety climate in terms of publications from 2010. We found that PSC has its own specific outcomes, whereby PSC was predominantly associated with psychological health. Evidence strongly supported the dual function of PSC, as an antecedent and moderator (rather than mediator) of the work stress process. Around half the studies were longitudinal, and all were published in either Australia or Malaysia. The review provides a better understanding of PSC research and shows that the climate for psychosocial safety is crucial for improving health and work quality. Given its important implications for working conditions, health, and engagement, we encourage further research on PSC. We provide insights into future research requirements to advance the field of PSC research such as the simultaneous use of multiple climates, multilevel modeling, research time lags, advanced research designs, and data analysis tools.

Keywords Psychosocial safety climate · Systematic literature review

---

Yulita (✉) · Mohd.A. Idris
Department of Anthropology and Sociology, Faculty of Arts and Social Sciences, University of Malaya, Kuala Lumpur, Malaysia
e-mail: yulitayuyu@gmail.com

Yulita · Mohd.A. Idris · M. Dollard
Asia Pacific Centre for Work Health and Safety, A WHO Collaborating Centre in Occupational Health, School of Psychology,, Social Work and Social Policy, University of South Australia,, Magill, Australia

A. Shimazu et al. (eds.), *Psychosocial Factors at Work in the Asia Pacific*,
DOI 10.1007/978-3-319-44400-0_6

Introduction

Safety risks at work are a global concern due to their hefty human and economic costs (EU-OSHA 2014). For example, in 2008, approximately 2.5 million workers died due to work-related injuries and diseases, and about 317 million workers suffered from non-fatal accidents at work (International Labour Organization 2011). From 1999 to 2007, over 20 million European workers experienced health problems due to work, with workplace accidents leading to death reaching over 5500 cases in 2007 (Eurostat 2010). European countries have estimated economic losses due to work-related physical problems. For example, the cost of work-related back pain among workers in France was estimated as EUR 1300 million (Aptel et al. 2002). For musculoskeletal disorders in the Netherlands costs were nearly EUR 3000 million (European Foundation for the Improvement of Living and Working Conditions 2005). Given the considerable costs of work injuries and fatalities, greater attention must be given to workers' safety within organizations.

Although there are several ways to measure workplace safety, the most common method is the safety climate approach; the assumption is that poor safety climate is a precursor to physical injuries and health (Zohar 1980, 2000). Workplace injuries are, however, not limited to physical injuries and physical health, but also to psychologically related injuries and health. Psychological distress also affects accidents and injuries (Clarke 2010). In the European Union, nearly 20 % of workers believe that work-related stress is a risk to their health (EASHW 2007). In Australia, stress-related absenteeism and presentism is estimated to cost AUD 14.8 billion per year, or 1.78 % of GDP (Medibank Private Ltd 2008). A specific organizational climate to explain psychosocial risks and psychological health and injuries emerged a decade ago. It began with the initiative of researchers from the University of South Australia who developed a new (and the only) tool to measure psychosocial safety climate (PSC) at work. Within a short period of time, since the first publication about PSC in 2010 (Dollard and Bakker 2010), the theoretical framework of PSC as a precursor to psychosocial working conditions has attracted researchers to explore how PSC can explain psychological health and injuries at work. In the current paper, we review the new emerging climate construct, psychosocial safety climate (PSC) (Dollard and Bakker 2010). This review enables us to identify research conducted to date on PSC and to examine the issues that need to be answered regarding the roles, impacts, level of measurement, research designs, sample selection, and future challenges of PSC research.

Psychosocial Safety Climate

Historically, the term "safety climate" was introduced in 1980, with its emphasis on physical injury and risks to safety (Zohar 1980, 2000). However, more recently, scholars argue that the concept of safety needs further clarification, as workplace injuries do not solely refer to physical injuries, but also to a wide range of psychosocial aspects, including psychological injuries. Unlike physical safety, PSC is a specific organizational climate that is a precursor to a conducive working environment (i.e., manageable job demands and higher job resources) which, in turn, influences positive individual and work outcomes (Dollard and Bakker 2010; Idris et al. 2012).

In their seminal work on PSC, Dollard and Bakker (2010) explain the definition of PSC as "policies, practices, and procedures for the protection of worker psychological health and safety" (p. 580). The only aspect that distinguishes safety climate from PSC is the focus on specific outcomes. While safety climate focuses on physical safety or preventative procedures that keep employees safe from any physical harm, PSC is focused on a preventative strategy to avoid psychological harm or damage to the employee well-being. In other words, while safety climate attempts to reduce or prevent any physical threat at work (Zohar and Luria 2005), PSC is concerned with reducing psychosocial hazards (Dollard and Bakker 2010).

Psychosocial safety climate is characterized by four major domains (Hall et al. 2010). First, management priority concerns the role of managers/employers in prioritizing psychological health among employees where there are competing imperatives between employees' safety and organizational productivity. Second, management commitment emphasizes the protection of employees' psychological health and well-being by taking assertive and immediate actions to resolve problems. Third, organizational communication reflects the importance of good and effective communication between the organization and employees in regard to psychological health and safety. Finally, organizational participation refers to all members in the organization participating and being involved in ensuring psychological health in the organization is protected.

Psychosocial safety climate (PSC) may be explained using the fundamental approach of climate perceptions. In general, there are two main approaches to investigate work climate (Ostroff et al. 2003). As argued by Reichers and Schneider (1990), work climate should be defined as employees' shared perception of the work environment. Using this approach, scholars conceive that organizational climate should be measured by aggregating the collective perceptions from employees within the same work unit or organization (Kozlowski and Klein 2000). By contrast another school of thought considers work climate to be the individuals' cognitive representations of their work environments (James and Sells 1981). The difference between these two perspectives not only reflects the way in which work climates are defined, but has influenced the methodological approach for how the data are collected and the measurement tools that are used. For example, most shared perception work climate research has recommended a referent-shift approach, such as "in my team" (e.g., Idris et al. 2012), whereas the use of "I" is more obvious in the cognitive approach (e.g., Idris and Dollard 2011). Consequently, although most studies of organizational climate have used the group approach, other scholars have investigated this area of research using the individual level; this latter approach gives rise to the "psychological work climate."

The different approaches to "individual" and "shared" perceptions not only influence the definition of "climate", but also affect the way in which work climate is modeled in the research framework. For example, although some studies on PSC have utilized the cognitive approach of individual perceptions (e.g., Hall et al. 2013; Idris and Dollard 2011), the majority of these climate studies have used a shared perception approach (e.g., Idris et al. 2015). In addition, having been defined as employees' perceptions (regardless of whether these are individual or shared perceptions), these climates have been employed as the antecedents in predicting outcomes for the individual and work outcomes. For example, PSC has been used to predict psychological health and performance (Dollard and Bakker 2010; Idris et al. 2015). However, this climate may also mediate and/or moderate in predicting outcomes, thus leading to the complexity of PSC research.

Psychosocial safety climate has two functions in the work stress process. First, it plays a primary role as an antecedent of the work stress process; its secondary role is to alleviate the impact of job demands on psychological health outcomes (Dollard and McTernan 2011). As a primary function, PSC is a predictor that directly influences the unfavorable job conditions that lead to psychological health problems and low well-being. In this regard, PSC is also a social determinant of employees' health and productivity (Dollard and Neser 2013) as well as being a leading indicator and workplace bullying and harassment (Bond et al. 2010; Kwan et al. 2014; Law et al. 2011). In its secondary function, PSC moderates the relationships between job conditions and outcomes, particularly the effect of job demands and workplace bullying on psychological health (Dollard and Karasek 2010; Law et al. 2011). This secondary function also reflects that PSC acts as a safety signal, indicating to employees consequences and benefits, and whether it is safe or not safe to use resources (e.g., personal resources or job resources) to cope with job demands (Law et al. 2011).

Finally, we provide several challenges for future research improvement, in terms of climate usage, multilevel modeling, research time intervals, research designs, and data analysis tools.

Review Procedure

We included all climates for psychosocial safety, regardless of their level of analysis. We searched for published empirical studies that used the terms "psychosocial," "climate," and "safety." We conducted the search using several databases, specifically PsycARTICLES@EBSCOhost, Academic Search Complete, and ISI Web of Knowledge. The search was not limited by the year of publication. We used search strings which combined the terms "psychosocial safety climate" with all the terms entered simultaneously. Our search was restricted to only peer-reviewed journals. In addition, the selected journals were not limited to the management and psychology fields, but were also from other fields, such as business and occupational health, and were indexed in the Social Sciences Citation

Index. We omitted any articles on meta-analyses or systematic literature reviews. With these yielding 113 articles, we continued the search by reviewing the abstract and full-text review of each article: this yielded 13 articles from eight different journals, with 100 articles discarded due to their topic being irrelevant to the current review.

Several questions guided the review: "What are the impacts of PSC?"; "what are the roles (antecedent, mediator, and moderator) of PSC?"; "What is the research trend in PSC?"; and "What is its level of measurement?" We examined the research method applied, the sample selection, and the level of analysis used over time.

To provide comparative information about trends, we compared PSC studies against those concerning other workplace climates (safety climate and psychological safety climate) gathered from 1980 to 2016. Psychological safety climate represents the interpersonal risk-taking of the individual when considering whether it is safe or not safe to engage with work based on their own perception of the work environment (Edmondson 1999). In total, we retrieved 59 articles on safety climate research and 16 articles on psychological safety climate research, together with 13 articles on PSC research. The method used and all of the studies reviewed in comprehensive tables located in the appendix.

Table 6.1 presents descriptive information on the PSC research, including information about the sample; design of the study; level of analysis; the role as antecedent and its consequences; the mediation and moderation of analysis involved in the study; and a summary of key results.

Results

Descriptive Explanations of PSC Research

As mentioned previously, this review focuses on the PSC research by considering a total of 13 articles. In addition, three main roles were investigated for PSC, namely, antecedent, mediator, and moderator. From this selection, two out of the three were identified as the main roles of PSC, as the antecedent and as a moderator. The summary of climate roles is presented in Table 6.2.

The consequences of PSC were classified as (1) work-related outcomes and (2) individual-related outcomes (see Table 6.3 for the summary). In addition, one study focused on workers' compensation claims related to workplace injuries or occupational accidents. Some of the PSC studies also included both individual-related outcomes and work-related outcomes in their research framework.

We measured the trends of publications, ranging from 1980 until 2016, in the climate genres in terms of frequency. From 1980, safety climate was the most often published climate concept, followed by psychological climate. However, the trend of research changed dramatically with the introduction of PSC in 2010. Although

Table 6.1 Summary of psychosocial safety climate studies

	Author/s (Year)	Sample	Study design/analysis strategy/level of analysis	Antecedents	Consequences	Moderators/mediators	Key climate results
1.	Dollard and Bakker (2010)	209–288 Australian Education Department education workers	Three-wave longitudinal/HLM/individual level and school level	PSC	Psychological health problems (psychological well-being, emotional exhaustion); work engagement	Job demands (work pressure, emotional demands) and job resources (job demands-resources [JD-R]) as mediator between PSC predicting psychological health problems and work engagement; PSC as a moderator of job demands and job resources in predicting psychological health problems and work engagement	PSC was negatively related to psychological health problems via job demands. PSC acts as a moderator between emotional demands and emotional exhaustion. PSC was significantly related to engagement through job resources PSC was not a moderator of the relationship between job resources and work engagement
2.	Idris and Dollard (2011)	269 employees of public and private sectors in Selangor, Malaysia	Cross-sectional/SEM AMOS/individual level	PSC	Job demands, job resources; depression; anger; engagement	Job demands and job resources as mediators between PSC and anger, depression, and engagement	PSC was negatively related job demands and positively to job resources
3.	Law et al. (2011)	220 Australian employees from 30 organizations in South Australia	Cross-sectional/HLM/individual level and organization level (multilevel)	PSC	Workplace bullying, demands (harassment); resources (work rewards); work engagement; psychological health problems (psychological distress, emotional exhaustion); engagement	PSC as a moderator of the relationship between workplace bullying/harassment and psychological health problems, as well as of the negative relationship between workplace bullying/harassment and work engagement	PSC as a determinant of harassment/bullying and resources (rewards, justice, supervisor support). In predicting psychological health problems (health erosion pathway) and work engagement (motivational pathway). Organizational level of PSC was negatively related to workplace

(continued)

Table 6.1 (continued)

	Author/s (Year)	Sample	Study design/analysis strategy/level of analysis	Antecedents	Consequences	Moderators/mediators	Key climate results
							bullying/harassment and then influenced psychological health problems. PSC was positively associated with resources and, in turn, work engagement
4.	Dollard et al. (2012a)	Time 1: 202 and Time 2: 163 from 48 units of Australian nurses working in remote areas	Two-wave longitudinal/HLM/individual level and group level (multilevel)	PSC	Working conditions (workload, job control, and supervisor support), psychological strain (emotional exhaustion, psychological distress)	Working conditions (emotional demands, workload, job control, supervisor support) as a mediator of PSC and psychological strain	PSC was negatively related to workload, and positively related to job control and supervisor support. PSC was related to emotional exhaustion via emotional demands and workload. PSC was related to psychological distress via job control, but not via supervisor support
5.	Dollard et al. (2012b)	Time 1: 318 and Time 2: 139 police constables from 23 Australian police units (stations)	Two-wave longitudinal/HLM/individual level and group level (multilevel)	PSC	Workgroup distress	PSC as a moderator between the interaction of emotional demands and emotional resources in predicting workgroup distress	PSC as the main factor that moderates the effects between emotional demands and emotional resources in predicting workgroup distress
6.	Idris et al. (2012)	126 Australian health care workers (16 teams) and 130 Malaysian	Cross-sectional/HLM/individual level and group level (multilevel)	PSC, physical safety climate, team psychological climate,	Job demands (workload, emotional demands, and psychological demands), psychological health problems	Job demands (workload, emotional demands, and psychological demands) as a mediator of PSC and	PSC was the strongest predictor to psychological health problems among other climates. PSC was related to psychological

(continued)

Table 6.1 (continued)

	Author/s (Year)	Sample	Study design/analysis strategy/level of analysis	Antecedents	Consequences	Moderators/mediators	Key climate results
		industrial workers (31 teams)		perceived organizational support	(psychological distress and emotional exhaustion)	psychological health problems	distress (depression) and emotional exhaustion in the Malaysian context, but not in the Australian context. PSC was negatively related to workload, emotional demands, and psychological demands in the Malaysian sample only
7.	Hall et al. (2013)	2343 Australian workers in New South Wales and Western Australia	Cross-sectional/moderated structural equation modeling AMOS/individual level	PSC	Depression; positive organizational behavior (POB) (engagement and job satisfaction)	PSC as a moderator of the relationship between job demands and depression; PSC as a moderator of the relationship between depression and POB	PSC as an overarching climate that was related to job demands, depression, and POB. The study demonstrated the moderating effect of PSC on psychological and emotional job demands
8.	Garrick et al. (2014)	61 school teachers in Australia (*N* = 915 data points)	Diary study (3-wave longitudinal; 8 months; 15 entries)/HLM analysis using MLwiN 2.10/daily level, diary level, and individual level (three-level)	Job demands; recovery	Work engagement; acute fatigue	PSC as a moderator of the relationship between job demands and acute fatigue; between daily recovery and acute fatigue; between daily job demands and work engagement; and also between daily recovery and work engagement	PSC could buffer the negative impact of job demands on a daily basis. PSC could also strengthen daily recovery for teachers
9.	Idris et al. (2014)	117 employees (27 organizations) Malaysian private sector	Longitudinal/HLM/individual level and group level (multilevel)	PSC	Emotional demands, emotional exhaustion; depression	Emotional demands as mediators of the relationship between PSC and emotional exhaustion	PSC is a predictor to emotional demands and also directly related to emotional exhaustion

(continued)

Table 6.1 (continued)

	Author/s (Year)	Sample	Study design/analysis strategy/level of analysis	Antecedents	Consequences	Moderators/mediators	Key climate results
10.	Kwan et al. (2014)	20 Malaysian workers	Interviews (PSC was measured by using a questionnaire after the interview session)/grounded theory approach/a modified Exit, Voice, Acquiescence, and Neglect model (from the Exit, Voice, Loyalty, and Neglect [EVLN] model)	PSC	Coping strategies and workplace bullying		High PSC in the workplace activated employees' coping strategies in dealing with workplace bullying; low PSC escalated bullying experiences and led to passive coping strategies
11.	Bailey et al. (2015b)	Used three different samples: Sample 1 (Time 1): 2907 New South Wales and Western Australian participants Sample 2 (Time 2): 1156 New South Wales and Western Australian participants Sample 3: 1043 South Australian participants	Longitudinal and cross-sectional using telephone interview/regression analysis/individual level	PSC	Job strain; depression	Job strain as a mediator of the relationship between PSC and symptoms of depression	PSC was negatively related to job strain and symptoms of depression; the benchmark for optimal organization PSC was at the mean score of 41 with the study finding that participants experienced mild symptoms of depression (37.6)

(continued)

Table 6.1 (continued)

	Author/s (Year)	Sample	Study design/analysis strategy/level of analysis	Antecedents	Consequences	Moderators/mediators	Key climate results
12.	Bailey et al. (2015a)	1095 Australian workers	Longitudinal/SEM AMOS/individual level	PSC	Psychosocial risk factors (i.e., work pressure and harassment/bullying/violence), emotional exhaustion; musculoskeletal disorder symptoms (MSDs); workers' compensation claims	Emotional exhaustion as a mediator of the relationship between psychosocial risk factors and MSDs; emotional exhaustion and MSDs as mediators of the relationship between psychosocial risk factors and workers' compensation; Psychosocial risk factors as mediators of the relationship between PSC and MSDs; harassment/violence/bullying as mediators of the relationship between PSC and workers' compensation claims	PSC was related to psychosocial risk factors; PSC was indirectly associated with workers' compensation claims in the psychosocial–physical processes
13.	Idris et al. (2015)	427 employees (56 teams) Malaysian private sector	Cross-sectional/HLM/individual level and group level (multilevel)	PSC	Learning opportunities; work engagement; performance	Learning opportunities mediate the relationship between PSC and work engagement. Work engagement mediates the relationship between PSC and performance, and also between learning opportunities and performance	PSC as a pivotal climate which fosters work engagement and performance through learning opportunities. PSC was positively related to learning opportunities

Table 6.2 Summary of PSC roles

	Roles			Total (N = 13)[a]
	Antecedent	Mediator	Moderator	
Psychosocial safety climate	10	–	6	16

[a]Some studies fit into multiple role categories; therefore, the number of studies in Table 6.2 outweighs the total number of studies

Table 6.3 Summary of findings

	Types of outcomes	Description
1.	Work-related outcomes	*Positive*: coping strategies, job performance, work engagement, job satisfaction, learning opportunities, positive organizational behavior (POB), job control, supervisor support, work rewards *Negative*: workplace bullying, workload, job strain, workgroup distress, work pressure, emotional demands, psychological demands
2.	Individual-related outcomes	*Positive*: psychological well-being *Negative*: burnout (emotional exhaustion and depersonalization), depression, anger, psychological distress, acute fatigue, musculoskeletal disorder symptoms (MSDs)
3.	Other outcomes	Workers' compensation claims

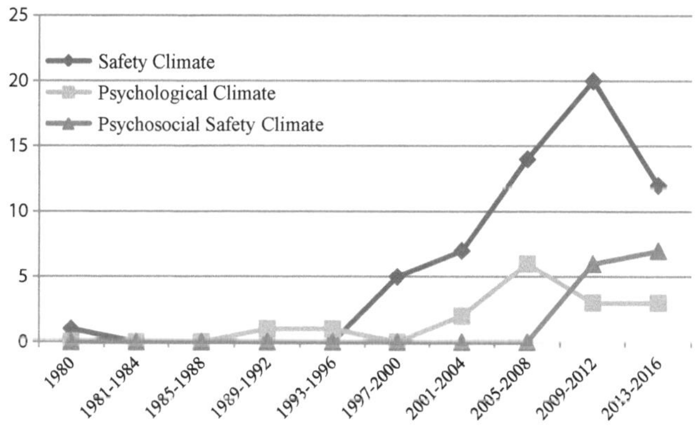

Fig. 6.1 Number and year of publication

safety climate remains the dominant research interest, since 2010, PSC has surpassed psychological climate. The summary of the growth in the number of articles, and their years of publication, for safety-related climate research is illustrated in Fig. 6.1.

Impacts of PSC

We found that the majority of PSC research investigated consequences to psychological health and well-being. All 13 published articles examined the impact of PSC on job conditions, particularly on job demands (e.g., workload, and emotional and psychological demands) and job resources (e.g., emotional resources, job control, supervisor support, and learning opportunities). Specifically, research of PSC on job resources (5 articles) was studied less compared to job demands (8 articles). Psychosocial safety climate (PSC) was negatively related to job demands and positively associated with job resources (e.g., Dollard and Bakker 2010; Dollard et al. 2012a; Idris and Dollard 2011; Idris et al. 2014). Interestingly, PSC was also identified as an indicator of negative workplace hazards, such as workplace bullying and harassment (2 articles; i.e., Kwan et al. 2014; Law et al. 2011). In relation to psychological health and work outcomes, studies have found that PSC is positively related to work engagement (article 1, 2, and 13) and performance (article 13), and negatively linked to burnout (article 4, 6, 9, and 12), psychological distress (article 1, 3, 4, and 6), depression (article 2 and 11), and anger (article 2), via job conditions (e.g., Dollard and Bakker 2010; Dollard et al. 2012a; Idris and Dollard 2011; Idris et al. 2014, 2015). The summary of the impacts of PSC is illustrated in Fig. 6.2.

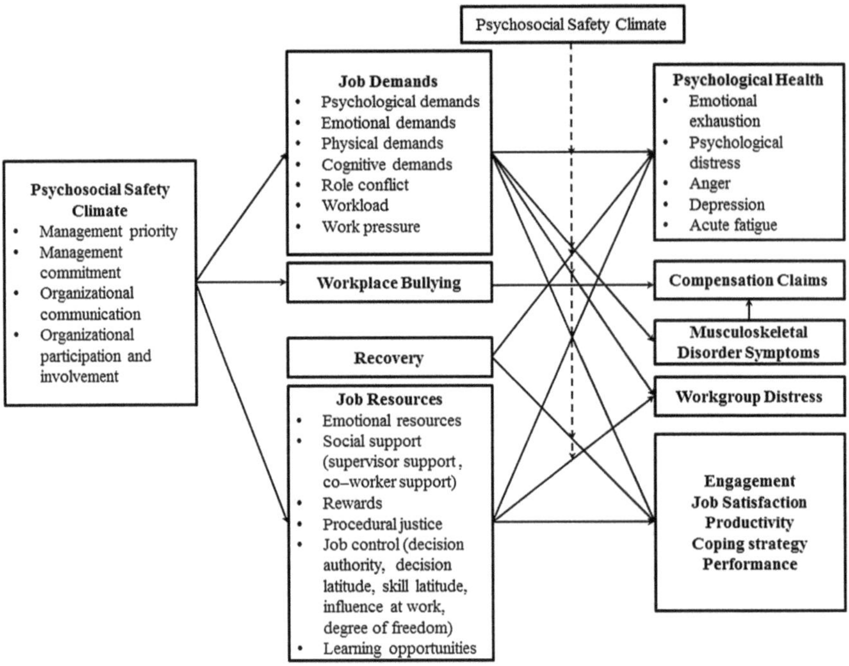

Fig. 6.2 PSC research framework

Roles of PSC

In relation to the antecedent role of PSC, we identified two types of antecedents: individual-level antecedents and multilevel antecedents (above individual-level antecedents).

Consistent with Reichers and Schneider (1990) argument that organizational climate is a "shared perception" of employees of their work environment, we discovered that the majority of PSC research used PSC as a group-level, team-level, or organizational-level antecedent (8 articles; e.g., Garrick et al. 2014; Law et al. 2011). Only a few studies from the PSC research employed PSC as an individual-level antecedent (4 articles; articles 2, 7, 11, and 12; e.g., Bailey et al. 2015a; Idris and Dollard 2011).

Psychosocial safety climate (PSC) was also treated as a moderator (5 articles; 1, 3, 5, 7, and 8), but none of the PSC researches used the PSC construct as a mediator. For instance, PSC moderated the relationship between workplace bullying and psychological health problems (Law et al. 2011). In addition, some studies used more than one role of PSC at a time. For example, Dollard and Bakker (2010) employed PSC as a group-level antecedent and also as a moderator in the same study.

Research Design

Overall, the survey design was the dominant research method (11 articles), with two studies using either a diary (1 article; i.e., Garrick et al. 2014) or interviews (1 article). Most survey research was either cross-sectional (6 articles; 2, 3, 6, 7, 11, and 13) or longitudinal (7 articles; 1, 4, 5, 8, 9, 11, and 12). One study combined individual surveys with interviews (i.e., Kwan et al. 2014).

Sample Selection

Most of the samples for PSC research were from public and private sectors (8 articles) with a few studies in the sectors of education (2 articles; 1 and 8), health care (2 articles; 4 and 6), and policing (1 article; 5). In terms of the geographic region, PSC research was dominated by Australia (9 articles) with a few studies in Asia, specifically, Malaysia (5 articles; 2, 6, 9, 10, and 13).

Challenges for Future Research

With the exception of the study by Idris et al. (2012), our review revealed that the majority of PSC research emphasized one specific role of PSC at a time. Idris et al. (2012) compared several types of climate, specifically using PSC, safety climate, team psychological climate, and perceived organizational support in predicting psychological health problems. Although the use of one single type of climate has been widely accepted as the best way to explain the climate–outcomes relationship, the question that springs to mind is what would be the findings if several types of climate were examined simultaneously. This is important as some of the climate consequences, such as job performance, job satisfaction, organizational trust, and commitment, are shared among several types of climate. The reason why it is important to consider the simultaneous use of multiple types of climate in this area of research was stated by Carr et al. (2003) in their meta-analytic study. They suggested that greater understanding of the effectiveness of the climate–outcomes relationship would possibly be achieved by investigating multiple types of climate simultaneously. Therefore, we urge that future research should consider multiple climate research.

Multilevel research is potentially important, and is widely used, in PSC research. Many research studies on PSC have focused on the relationship between upper level (i.e., unit, group, and organization levels) and lower level (i.e., individual level) entities, and on examining the cross-level climate–outcomes relationship. Most PSC research has relied on two levels of analysis, that is, individual level and organizational level (7 articles), while a few studies have focused on the individual level (4 articles) on its own. Indeed, Bryk and Raudenbush (1988) suggest that three levels of analysis offer a comprehensive understanding of a multilevel framework (e.g., individuals nested in teams that are nested in organizations). Although one study employed three levels of analysis (i.e., Garrick et al. 2014), the study did not represent the hierarchical influences on climate within organizations (e.g., three-level analysis that consists of organization → team → individual; Mathieu et al. 2007). Recently, Yulita et al. (under review) have used a diary study and a three-level model to test the effect of school level PSC on daily level PSC via individual level PSC. While this design is of interest, future research may test how the district level may affect school level and individual level.

How "espoused" PSC (what managers say) interrelates with "enacted" PSC (what managers do) should also be taken into consideration in future research (Zohar 2010). Our current unpublished (Yulita et al. under review) suggests that espoused and enacted PSC interaction to predict emotional exhaustion—it is only when there is alignment between what managers say and do that emotional exhaustion is reduced. However, as our research has relied heavily on individual perceptions, that is, a single source of data, future research could measure espoused PSC and enacted PSC using multiple sources of data. For example, espoused PSC could be measured using top management ratings, whereas enacted PSC could be assessed by employees, and objective outcome variables could be used (e.g., performance ratings, health status, psychological injuries).

Most PSC research has been analyzed using hierarchical linear modeling (HLM) software. Although this is one of the best tools for examining multilevel data, the tool is unable to test several variables simultaneously (Zhang et al. 2009). In addition, inaccuracy in variance estimates during the mediation process has limited the use of HLM (Zhang et al. 2009) software. Thus, future research needs to consider using more advanced tools such as multilevel structural equation modeling (MSEM). However, this requires using a sample size at the upper level of at least 100 groups, to ensure that they are able to estimate accurately (Hox and Maas 2001).

Bailey et al. (2015b) established PSC benchmarks (range 12–60) for low-risk (PSC at 41 or above) and high-risk (PSC at 37 or below) of employee job strain and depressive symptoms. They found using the population attributable risk (PAR) that improves PSC in organizations to above 37 could reduce 14 % of job strain and 16 % of depressive symptoms. This practical tool can be used by organizations to indicate risk levels for PSC, and take action accordingly. Further research is required to assess the validity of these benchmarks internationally.

Appendix

Review Procedure

We included all possible types of facet-specific climates for safety, regardless of their level of analysis. We searched for published empirical studies that used the terms "work," "climate," and "safety." We conducted a series of searches using several databases, specifically PsycARTICLES@EBSCOhost, Academic Search Complete, and ISI Web of Knowledge. The search was not limited by the year of publication. We formulated a set of search strings which combined the terms "organizational climate," "work climate," and "safety climate" with all the terms entered simultaneously. Our search was restricted to only peer-reviewed journals. In addition, the selected journals were not limited to the management and psychology fields, but also came from other fields, such as business and occupational health, and were indexed in the Social Sciences Citation Index. We omitted any articles on meta-analyses or systematic literature reviews; this yielded 218 articles; we continued the search by reviewing the abstract and full-text review of each article: this yielded 75 articles from 26 different journals, with 143 articles discarded due to being on irrelevant topics (Tables 6.4, 6.5).

Table 6.4 Summary of safety climate studies

Author/s (Year)	Sample	Study design/analysis strategy/level of analysis	Antecedents	Consequences	Moderators/Mediators	Key climate results
Zohar (1980)	20 industrial organizations in Israel	Cross-sectional and interview/multiple-range test/organizational level		Safety program effectiveness		'Perceptions of management about safety' and 'perceptions of the relevance of safety' were two of the eight safety climate dimensions that were highly correlated with safety program effectiveness
Cheyne et al. (1998)	915 employees from a manufacturing organization in the UK and France	Cross-sectional/structural equation modeling (SEM) and analysis of variance (ANOVA) and multivariate analysis of variance (MANOVA)/individual level	Organizational variables (safety management and safety standards); environmental evaluation (physical work environment and workplace hazards); attitudes to group process variables (personal involvement, individual responsibility, and communication)	Safety activity	Safety management as a mediator of the relationship between safety standards and workplace hazards	Safety standards and goals were positively related to safety management and personal involvement. Safety management was positively related to personal involvement, communication and physical work environment, and negatively related to workplace hazards. Personal involvement, communication and workplace hazards were positively associated with individual responsibility.

(continued)

Table 6.4 (continued)

Author/s (Year)	Sample	Study design/analysis strategy/level of analysis	Antecedents	Consequences	Moderators/Mediators	Key climate results
						Individual responsibility and physical work environment were positively related to safety activities
Griffin and Neal (2000)	Study 1: 1403 employees from 7 Australian manufacturing and mining organizations Study 2: 326 employees from 3 Australian manufacturing organizations	Cross-sectional/SEM/individual level	Safety climate	Study 1: safety knowledge; safety performance (safety compliance and safety participation) Study 2: safety knowledge; motivation (compliance motivation and participation motivation); safety performance (safety compliance and safety participation)	Study 1: safety knowledge as a mediator of the relationship between safety climate and safety performance Study 2: safety knowledge and motivation as mediators of the relationship between safety climate and safety performance	Safety climate was positively associated with safety knowledge, motivation, and safety performance
Rundmo (2000)	730 respondents of 13 plants in the USA and Canada	Cross-sectional/SEM	Safety climate	Risk behavior		Safety climate was positively related to safety behavior and negatively related to risk behavior
Varonen and Mattila (2000)	508 employees in 1990 and 548 employees in 1993 from 8 wood-processing	Cross-sectional/correlation matrix and factor analysis (Kaiser–Meyer–Olkin test index)/individual level	Safety climate	Safety practices; safety of work environment; occupational accidents		Safety climate was more strongly correlated with the safety of the work environment than with the safety practices of

(continued)

Table 6.4 (continued)

Author/s (Year)	Sample	Study design/analysis strategy/level of analysis	Antecedents	Consequences	Moderators/Mediators	Key climate results
	companies in Southern Finland					the company. High safety climate reduced the accident rate at the company
Zohar (2000)	534 production workers in 53 work groups in a manufacturing company	Cross-sectional/hierarchical linear modeling (HLM)/multilevel	Safety climate perception	Subunit injury and personal injury		The perception of safety climate influenced injury at the subunit level and the individual level. Safety climate predicted micro-accident records over 5 months
Gillen et al. (2002)	255 injured construction workers in California (union membership = 27 %)	Telephone interview/hierarchical multiple regression/individual level	Perceptions of workplace safety climate measure score	Decision latitude; social support; injury severity; union status		Union workers reported a higher level of safety climate perception than non-union workers. There was a negative relationship between safety climate measure score and social support
Zohar (2002)	411 production workers (42 work groups) in a metal processing plant company in Israel	Cross-sectional/SAS mixed procedure/group level and department level	Leadership style (transformational, laissez-faire, corrective transactional, and constructive)	Injuries	Safety climate as a mediator of the relationship between leadership style and injury; assigned safety priority as a moderator of the relationship between leadership style and safety climate	The corrective and laissez-faire leadership were negatively related to safety climate, whereas the transformational and constructive transactional leadership were positively associated with safety climate

(continued)

Table 6.4 (continued)

Author/s (Year)	Sample	Study design/analysis strategy/level of analysis	Antecedents	Consequences	Moderators/Mediators	Key climate results
Hofmann et al. (2003)	94 individuals in 25 teams in the US Army transportation unit	Cross-sectional/HLM/multilevel	Leader–member exchange	Safety citizenship behavior; safety citizenship role definitions	Safety citizenship role definitions as a mediator of the relationship between leader–member exchange and safety citizenship behavior; safety climate as a moderator of the relationship between leader–member exchange and safety citizenship role definitions	In a condition of positive safety climate, safety behaviors are seen as responsibilities that need to be done, whereas the relationship was not found if safety climate was not positive
Mearns et al. (2003)	682 employees (Year 1) and 806 employees (Year 2) in 13 UK Continental Shelf oil and gas installations	Longitudinal/multilevel	Safety climate	Safety performance; self-reported accident; official accident reports		Safety climate as a leading indicator of safety performance and also related to lower proportions of self-reported accident involvement and also official accident reports in Year 1 only, not in Year 2
DeJoy et al. (2004)	2208 employees of a large national retail chain in 21 locations in the USA	Cross-sectional/hierarchical, multiple regression analysis	Work situation (environmental conditions, safety-related policies and program, organizational climate)	Perceived work safety	Safety climate as a mediator of the relationship between work situation and perceived safety at work	Exposure to hazardous environment was negatively related to safety climate

(continued)

Table 6.4 (continued)

Author/s (Year)	Sample	Study design/analysis strategy/level of analysis	Antecedents	Consequences	Moderators/Mediators	Key climate results
Probst (2004)	136 manufacturing employees in the Pacific Northwest USA	Cross-sectional/multivariate multiple regression analysis	Job security	Safety outcomes (safety knowledge, safety compliance, accidents, and injuries)	Safety climate as a moderator of the relationship between job insecurity and safety outcomes	Safety climate was positively related to safety knowledge and safety compliance, and negatively associated with accidents and workplace injury
Siu et al. (2004)	Sample 1: 18 qualitative in-depth interviews Sample 2: 374 construction workers on 27 construction sites in Hong Kong	Cross-sectional/EQS program	Safety climate (safety attitudes and communication)	Safety performance (accident rates and occupational injuries)	Psychological distress as a mediator of the relationship between safety attitude and accident rates	Safety attitudes were negatively related to occupational injuries and not to accident rates
Katz-Navon et al. (2005)	632 employees in 47 hospital units from 3 hospitals in Israel	Cross-sectional/EQS program 6.0 and SEM/unit level	Safety climate (safety performance, safety information flow, managerial safety practices, and priority of safety)	Treatment errors on patient safety; unit safety performance	Safety priority as a moderator of the relationship between safety procedure and safety performance, and between safety information flow and safety performance	Perceived safety procedures, safety information flow, and perceived managerial safety practices were significantly related to unit safety performance in a curvilinear relationship
Naveh et al. (2005)	Phase 1: 241 staff members in 21 medical units of acute care in general hospital, with this cross-validated in Phase 2	Cross-validated/hierarchical moderated regression analysis/unit level	Safety climate dimensions: safety procedures suitability and safety information flow (independent variables), managerial safety practices	Treatment errors at unit level	Managerial safety practices as a moderator of the relationship between safety information flow and treatment errors; as well as between safety	Safety climate dimensions (i.e., safety procedures) were negatively related to unit's rate of treatment errors

(continued)

Table 6.4 (continued)

Author/s (Year)	Sample	Study design/analysis strategy/level of analysis	Antecedents	Consequences	Moderators/Mediators	Key climate results
	Phase 2: 218 staff members in 15 units in another hospital		(moderating variable), and priority to safety (mediating variable)		procedures suitability and treatment errors Priority to safety as a mediator of the relationship for both safety procedures and safety information flow on treatment errors	
Zohar and Luria (2005)	3952 production workers in 401 work groups from 36 small to medium-sized manufacturing plants	Cross-sectional/organizational level and group level (multilevel)	Organization-level safety climate; group-level safety climate	Safety behavior; climate variability	Group-level safety climate as a mediator of the relationship between organization-level safety climate and safety behavior. Routinization as a moderator of the relationship between organization-level safety climate and group-level safety climate	Organization-level safety climate strength was negatively related to between-group climate variability
Hofmann and Mark (2006)	1127 nurses in 81 general medical-surgical nursing units in 41 hospitals in the USA	Longitudinal/unit level	Safety climate	Medication errors; nurse and patient outcomes (nurse back injuries, patient urinary tract infections, patient satisfaction, patient perceptions of nurse responsiveness, and nurse satisfaction)	Patient complexity as a moderator of the negative relationship between safety climate and both nurse back injuries and medication errors	The positive safety climate was related to fewer incidents and errors, and higher satisfaction and perception levels

(continued)

Table 6.4 (continued)

Author/s (Year)	Sample	Study design/analysis strategy/level of analysis	Antecedents	Consequences	Moderators/Mediators	Key climate results
Huang et al. (2006)	2680 employees in 18 manufacturing, construction, service, and transportation companies in the USA	Cross-sectional/SEM AMOS 4.0	Safety climate (management commitment to safety, return-to-work policies, post-injury administration, and safety training)	Self-reported occupational injury	Safety control as a mediator of the relationship between safety climate and self-reported injury	Safety climate was positively related to safety control
Neal and Griffin (2006)	135 employees from 33 work groups in Australian hospitals	Longitudinal/MLwiN/individual level and group level (multilevel)	Safety climate	Lagged effect on individual safety motivation		Group-level safety climate was positively related to individual-level safety motivation
Smith et al. (2006)	33 industrial companies in the USA	Cross-sectional survey and objective data/linear regression analysis	Safety climate	Objective data of injury rates		Higher and positive safety climate was associated with lower injury rates
Wallace et al. (2006)	9429 delivery drivers in 253 centers (work groups)	One-month survey, and accident data collected for the next 12 months/LISREL 8.54/group level	Organizational support climate; management–employee relations climate	Occupational accidents	Safety climate as a mediator of the relationship between organizational support climate and occupational accidents; safety climate as a mediator of the relationship between management–employee relations and occupational accidents	Safety climate was negatively related to accident rate

(continued)

Table 6.4 (continued)

Author/s (Year)	Sample	Study design/analysis strategy/level of analysis	Antecedents	Consequences	Moderators/Mediators	Key climate results
Wills et al. (2006)	323 employees of 3 organizations: local government councils, state government agency; and private industrial in Queensland, Australia	Cross-sectional/hierarchical regression analysis/individual level	Safety climate factors (communication, work pressures, relationships, driver training, management commitment, and safety rules)	Work-related driving behavior		Several aspects of safety climate (safety rules, communication, and management commitment) were strongly related to work-related driving behavior
Huang et al. (2007)	1351 employees of 16 companies in 6 industries	Prospective design: cross-sectional survey and objective data injury frequencies)/STATA 8.0/individual level and company level (multilevel)	Safety climate	Perceived injury risk	Safety climate as a moderator of the relationship between work shift and perceived injury risk	Safety climate was related to perceived injury risk among night shift workers
Lee et al. (2007)	121 employees in 113 facilities in Taiwan	Cross-sectional/regression analysis	Safety climate	Organizational citizenship behavior	Job satisfaction and organizational commitment as mediators of the relationship between safety climate and organizational citizenship behavior	Safety climate was positively related to work attitude (job satisfaction and organizational commitment)
Mark et al. (2007)	1st round: 4911 nurses (collected workplace information) 2nd round: 3689 nurses (collected organizational structure and safety climate information)	Three-wave longitudinal/Mplus/multilevel	Safety climate; organizational structure (work engagement and work conditions)	Organizational effectiveness (needle sticks and back injuries)	Safety climate as a moderator of the relationship between work engagement and needle sticks; safety climate as a moderator of the relationship between work conditions and needle	Safety climate was positively related to work engagement and work conditions, and negatively related to back injuries

(continued)

Table 6.4 (continued)

Author/s (Year)	Sample	Study design/analysis strategy/level of analysis	Antecedents	Consequences	Moderators/Mediators	Key climate results
	3rd round: 3272 nurses (collected organizational effectiveness information) Data collected from 281 nursing units in 143 hospitals in the USA				sticks; safety climate as a moderator of the relationship between work conditions and back injuries	
Lu and Tsai (2008)	291 seafarers in 31 vessel companies in Taiwan	Cross-sectional/logistic regression analysis/individual level	Safety climate (management safety practices dimension, supervisor safety practices, safety attitude, safety training, job safety and co-worker safety practices)	Vessel accidents		Job safety was the strongest predictor on vessel accidents, followed by safety practices and safety training dimension
Probst et al. (2008)	1390 employees of 38 construction companies in the Northwestern USA	Cross-sectional/simple regression analysis	Safety climate	Workplace injury and illness rates; underreported injury rates		Safety climate was negatively related to workplace injury rates and unreported injury rates
Baba et al. (2009)	485 major international airline employees in China	Cross-sectional/moderated linear hierarchical regression/individual level	Proactive personality	Individual performance; organizational citizenship behavior (conscientiousness and altruism)	Safety climate as a moderator of the relationship between proactive personality and individual performance; emotional exhaustion together with safety climate as	The perceived safety climate was positively related to organizational citizenship behavior

(continued)

Table 6.4 (continued)

Author/s (Year)	Sample	Study design/analysis strategy/level of analysis	Antecedents	Consequences	Moderators/Mediators	Key climate results
					moderators of the relationship between proactive personality and role overload (three-way interactions)	
Cavazza and Serpe (2009)	345 blue-collar workers of 3 industrial companies in North Italy	Cross-sectional/SEM AMOS 4.0/individual level	Safety climate (company safety concern, senior managers' safety concern, supervisors' attitudes toward safety, and work pressure)	Safety norm violations (unsafe behavior) toward personal protective equipment	Individual ambivalence as a mediator of the relationship between safety climate and safety norm violations regarding the use of personal protective equipment	Company safety concern, senior managers' safety concern, and supervisors' attitudes toward safety were positively related to individual ambivalence, whereas work pressure was negatively related to individual ambivalence
Cigularov et al. (2009)	244 adolescent farm workers from 202 farm families in Colorado, USA	Telephone survey (cross-sectional)/moderated regression analysis/individual level	Safety climate; safety locus of control	Open communication about errors at work	Safety climate as a moderator of the relationship between safety locus of control and open error communication	Safety locus of control and safety climate were positively related to open error communication
Keren et al. (2009)	117 employees of a manufacturing facility in Iowa, USA	Survey Monkey/linear regression/individual level	Safety climate	Safety orientation in decision making; selection of safer choices		Safety climate was not significantly related to decision making, but positively related to selection of safer choices

(continued)

Table 6.4 (continued)

Author/s (Year)	Sample	Study design/analysis strategy/level of analysis	Antecedents	Consequences	Moderators/Mediators	Key climate results
Vinodkumar and Bhasi (2009)	1806 employees in 8 chemical industrial units in Kerala, India	Cross-sectional/SEM AMOS 4.0/individual level	Safety climate	Accident rates		Safety climate was negatively related to self-reported accident rates
Hope et al. (2010)	9601 offshore workers of 52 offshore installations on the Norwegian Continental Shelf	Cross-sectional/hierarchical multiple regression/individual level	Risk perception; safety climate	Sleep quality		Higher risk perception and negative safety climate were significantly associated with poor subjective sleep quality
Jiang et al. (2010)	23 work units of 631 participants in 2 petroleum and chemical companies in China	Cross-level/HLM/individual level and unit level (multilevel)	Safety climate	Safety behaviors (safety compliance and safety participation); safety performance (self-report injuries and self-report near-misses)	The unit level of safety climate as a moderator of the relationship between perceived safety knowledge/behavior and safety behavior; safety behaviors as moderators of the relationship between perceived safety knowledge/behavior and injuries, but not with near-misses	Higher levels of safety climate increased the effect of perceived safety knowledge/behavior on safety behavior
Kath et al. (2010a)	599 grocery store employees of 97 work groups in New England, USA	Cross-sectional/HLM/individual level and department level (multilevel)	Safety climate (group upward safety communication and group management attitudes toward safety)	Organizational trust; organizational outcomes (safety motivation, job satisfaction, and turnover intentions)	Individual organizational trust as a mediator of the relationship between safety climate on safety motivation and job satisfaction (partial	Group-level safety climate was related to individual-level organizational trust, job satisfaction, and safety motivation

(continued)

Table 6.4 (continued)

Author/s (Year)	Sample	Study design/analysis strategy/level of analysis	Antecedents	Consequences	Moderators/Mediators	Key climate results
					mediation); individual organizational trust as a mediator of the relationship between safety climate and turnover intentions (full mediation); job safety relevance as a moderator of the relationship between safety climate and organizational trust	
Kath et al. (2010b)	636 railway workers of the Canadian Pacific Railway	Cross-sectional/hierarchical multiple regression analysis	Safety climate (management safety attitudes, safety peer pressure, and safety job demands); leader–member exchange; organizational support	Upward safety communication		Management safety attitudes and safety job demands were positively related to upward safety communication
Mearns et al. (2010)	1932 employees from 31 offshore installations of 7 oil and gas companies in the UK	Cross-sectional/*R 1.6.2* software/worksite level and individual level (multilevel)	Health investment practices; safety climate; health climate	Safety compliance; commitment		Worksite level of safety climate was positively associated with individual safety compliance and commitment
Morrow et al. (2010)	421 mechanical workers of a large North American railroad	Cross-sectional/SEM and Probability SAS Macro/individual level	Safety climate (management safety, co-worker safety, and work–safety tension)	Unsafe behavior		Safety climate was related to unsafe behavior

(continued)

Table 6.4 (continued)

Author/s (Year)	Sample	Study design/analysis strategy/level of analysis	Antecedents	Consequences	Moderators/Mediators	Key climate results
Payne et al. (2010)	7728 manufacturing employees from 62 sites	Online survey and organizational data of site incidents one year before (lagging) and after (leading) online survey/site level (group level) and individual level (multilevel)	Safety climate as leading and lagging indicator (employees' beliefs about systems and processes to prevent large backlogs, good routine housekeeping, and employees' perceptions about prompt correction health safety issues)	Incidents (environmental impact, fire/explosion and property damage)		The lagging and leading indicators of good routine housekeeping and employees' perceptions about prompt correction health safety issues were negatively related to environmental impact incidents and fire/explosion
Probst and Estrada (2010)	425 employees from various industries and organizations in the USA	Cross-sectional/individual level	Safety climate	Unreported accidents	Safety climate as a moderator of the relationship between reported and unreported accidents	Safety climate was negatively related to reported and unreported accidents
Nielsen et al. (2011)	986 Norwegian offshore workers of 2 major unions	Cross-sectional/hierarchical regression analysis/individual level	Safety climate; risk perception	Job satisfaction	Safety climate as a moderator of the relationship between risk perception and job satisfaction	Safety climate was positively related to job satisfaction
Tomás et al. (2011)	1234 employees in industries in Valencia, Spain (individual level) 544 employees from 91 organizations (same participants as above-mentioned) (group level)	Cross-sectional/SEM with latent variables/individual level and company (group) level (multilevel)	Safety climate (safety management, personal involvement, communication, and individual responsibility)	Accident occurrence (near-misses, minor accidents, accidents with three days off and severe accidents with three or more days off); safety climate and attitude	Individual attributes as a mediator of the relationship between safety climate and accident occurrence	Safety climate was positively related to safety behavior and attitude

(continued)

Table 6.4 (continued)

Author/s (Year)	Sample	Study design/analysis strategy/level of analysis	Antecedents	Consequences	Moderators/Mediators	Key climate results
Wu et al. (2011)	521 employees from 23 plants in 7 departments of petrochemical companies in Taiwan	Cross-sectional SEM AMOS 5.0/individual level	Safety leadership	Safety performance	Safety climate as a mediator of the relationship between safety leadership and safety performance	Safety climate was positively associated with safety performance
Arcury et al. (2012)	300 Latino migrant farmworkers from North Carolina, USA	Cross-sectional/SAS 9.2/individual level	Safety climate	Health problems (musculoskeletal discomfort and depression); safety (working while injured)		Farmworkers perceived work safety climate to be poor and it related to musculoskeletal discomfort and safety
Brondino et al. (2012)	Cross-sectional/991 blue-collar workers from 91 work groups in 5 Italian manufacturing companies	Cross-sectional/Mplus 5.2/individual level and work group level (multilevel)	Safety climate (organizational, supervisor, and co-workers' safety climate)	Safety behaviors	Supervisor safety climate as a mediator of the relationship between organizational safety climate and co-workers' safety climate at the individual level; co-workers' safety climate as a mediator of the relationship between organizational safety climate and safety behaviors, and between supervisor safety climate and safety behaviors at the individual level	Organizational safety climate was significantly related to supervisor and co-workers' safety climate at both individual and group levels

(continued)

Table 6.4 (continued)

Author/s (Year)	Sample	Study design/analysis strategy/level of analysis	Antecedents	Consequences	Moderators/Mediators	Key climate results
Fernández-Muñiz et al. (2012)	131 firms in Spain	Cross-sectional/SEM/group level	Safety climate (management commitment, incentives and rewards, and organizational communication)	Safety behaviors; incentives for safety behaviors; work pressure; effect on communication and information transmission		Management commitment was positively related to incentives for safety behaviors and communication, and negatively related to work pressure. Communication was positively related to safety behaviors
Fugas et al. (2012)	356 transportation workers in Spain	Cross-sectional/SEM AMOS 17.0/individual level	Safety climate	Safety attitude; perceived behavioral control over safety; safety behaviors (compliance and proactive safety behaviors)	Co-workers' descriptive safety norms and safety attitudes as mediators of the relationship between safety climate and proactive safety behaviors; supervisors' injunctive safety norms and perceived behavioral control over safety as mediators of the relationship between safety climate and compliance safety behaviors	Safety climate was directly and positively related to co-workers' descriptive safety norms, supervisors' injunctive safety norms, safety attitudes, and perceived behavioral control over safety

(continued)

Table 6.4 (continued)

Author/s (Year)	Sample	Study design/analysis strategy/level of analysis	Antecedents	Consequences	Moderators/Mediators	Key climate results
Bosak et al. (2013)	856 non-management employees of a chemical manufacturing company in South Africa	Cross-sectional/hierarchical regression analysis/individual level	Safety climate (management commitment to safety, priority to safety, and pressure for production)	Self-reported risk behaviors	Priority to safety and pressure for production as moderators of the relationship between management commitment and risk behaviors (three-way interaction)	All safety climate dimensions were significantly related to risk behaviors
Khandan et al. (2013)	134 employees from Iranian petrochemical company	Cross-sectional/SEM/individual level	Safety climate	Ergonomic behaviors		Safety climate was positively related to ergonomic behaviors
Kwon and Kim (2013)	131 manufacturing industry employees in South Korea	Cross-sectional/Smart PLS 2.0/individual level	Safety climate dimensions (safety knowledge, safety compliance, safety motivation, and safety participation)	Safe working environment		Safety compliance and safety participation were positively related to safe working environment
McCaughey et al. (2013)	218 health care providers in hospitals in Western Canada	Cross-sectional/multiple regression/individual level	Workplace injury or illness	Job stress; turnover intentions; job satisfaction	Safety climate as a mediator of the relationship between workplace injury or illness and job stress; safety climate as a mediator of the relationship between workplace injury or illness and turnover intentions; safety climate as a mediator of the relationship	Safety climate was negatively related to job stress

(continued)

Table 6.4 (continued)

Author/s (Year)	Sample	Study design/analysis strategy/level of analysis	Antecedents	Consequences	Moderators/Mediators	Key climate results
					between workplace injury or illness and job satisfaction	
Tholén et al. (2013)	289 construction workers in 43 units in Sweden	Four-wave longitudinal (7-month time interval)/MLwiN 2.22/individual level and group level (multilevel)	Psychosocial conditions; safety climate	Individual safety behavior		Safety climate was positively related to safety behavior
Clark et al. (2014)	168 nurses and 103 peer surveys from 2 hospitals in the Midwestern USA with a total dataset of 94 matched dyads used in the study	Dyad study/hierarchical multiple moderated regression analysis	Safety climate	Organizational citizenship behavior	Role definition as a moderator of the relationship between safety climate and organizational citizenship behavior	Safety climate was positively associated with peer-rated organizational citizenship behavior
Golubovich et al. (2014)	464 full-time employees in a university in southern USA	Cross-sectional/Mplus 6.0/multilevel	Safety climate	Work-related musculoskeletal complaints; frustration	Psychological hardiness as a moderator of the relationship between safety climate and frustration; frustration as a mediator of the relationship between safety climate and work-related musculoskeletal complaints	Safety climate was negatively related to frustration

(continued)

Table 6.4 (continued)

Author/s (Year)	Sample	Study design/analysis strategy/level of analysis	Antecedents	Consequences	Moderators/Mediators	Key climate results
Huang et al. (2014)	1831 truck drivers and matched with 219 of their supervisors from 4 trucking companies in the USA	Cross-sectional/paired sample *t* tests and mixed effect ANOVA/organizational level and group level	Employees' safety climate; supervisors' safety climate	Lost work days/injury severity (objective measurement); safety behavior (subjective measurement)	Safety behavior as a mediator of the relationship between organization-level employee safety climate and lost work days; and also between-group-level employee safety climate and lost work days	Both organization and group levels of employee perception on trucking safety climate were significantly related to safety behavior
Zohar et al. (2014)	3207 long-haul truck drivers from a national trucking company in the USA	Prospective design (cross-sectional survey with hard braking data 6 months before and after survey)/Mplus 6.0	Dispatcher leadership (leader–member exchange); work ownership; safety climate	Safety driving behavior; hard braking	Safety driving behavior as a mediator of the relationship between safety climate and hard braking	Safety climate was positively related to safety driving behavior
Zohar and Polachek (2014)	364 mid-sized manufacturing company workers of 26 work teams	Randomized field study (experimental group and control group, pre- and post-interventions)/SAS 9.3/multilevel	Perceived supervisory messages	Safety climate; safety behavior; workload; teamwork; safety audit		After receiving feedback or supervisory messages, there were significant changes for higher safety climate, higher safety behavior, lower perceived workload, higher teamwork, and higher safety audit scores among the experimental group. No changes were found among the control group

(continued)

Table 6.4 (continued)

Author/s (Year)	Sample	Study design/analysis strategy/level of analysis	Antecedents	Consequences	Moderators/Mediators	Key climate results
Barbaranelli et al. (2015)	Sample 1: 616 employees from 21 industrial organizations in the USA Sample 2: 738 employees from 20 industrial organizations in Italy	Cross-sectional/Mplus 7.1	Safety climate	Safety behavior (safety compliance and safety participation)	Safety knowledge and safety motivation as mediators of the relationship between safety climate and safety compliance with higher impact among US participants than Italian participants; safety knowledge and safety motivation as mediators of the relationship between safety climate and safety participation with the same effect between the two countries	Safety climate was positively related to safety knowledge and safety motivation
Lee and Dalal (2016)	964 employees from 17 manufacturing organizations in South Korea	Cross-sectional/SAS 9.2/individual level and organization level (multilevel)	Conscientiousness	Safety behavior (safety compliance and safety helping)	Safety climate as a moderator of the relationship between conscientiousness and safety compliance; safety climate as a moderator of the relationship between conscientiousness and safety helping	The positive relationship between conscientiousness and both dimensions of safety behavior were stronger in conditions of weak safety climate

Table 6.5 Summary of psychological climate studies

Author/s (Year)	Sample	Study design/analysis strategy/level of analysis	Antecedents	Consequences	Moderators/mediators	Key climate results
Day and Bedeian (1991)	483 public, industrial, and government accountants in the USA	Cross-sectional/hierarchical regression analysis	Work orientation; psychological climate	Job performance	Psychological climate as a moderator of the relationship between work orientation and job performance	High work orientation was more strongly positively associated with job performance than low work orientation when the psychological climate was positive
Brown and Leigh (1996)	Sample 1: 178 salespeople from 3 companies Sample 2: 161 sales representatives from a medical products company	Cross-sectional/LISREL/individual level	Psychological climate	Job involvement; effort; performance	Job involvement as a mediator of the relationship between psychological climate and effort	The perceived psychological climate was positively related to job involvement
Baer and Frese (2003)	47 mid-sized industrial and service sectors companies in Germany	Longitudinal/LISREL 8 and moderated hierarchical regression analysis/organizational level	Initiative climate; psychological safety climate	Company performance (goal achievement and return on assets)	Initiative climate and psychological safety climate as moderators of the positive relationship between process innovations and company performance	Initiative climate and psychological safety climate were positively related to company performance
Carless (2004)	174 customer service employees in Australia	Cross-sectional/SEM AMOS 4.0/individual level	Psychological climate	Psychological empowerment; job satisfaction	Psychological empowerment as a mediator of the relationship between psychological climate and job satisfaction	Negative affectivity was moderately negatively related to psychological climate

(continued)

Table 6.5 (continued)

Author/s (Year)	Sample	Study design/analysis strategy/level of analysis	Antecedents	Consequences	Moderators/mediators	Key climate results
Byrne et al. (2005)	139 part-time restaurant employees	Cross-sectional/moderated multiple regression (MMR)	Work effort; psychological climate; conscientiousness	Job performance	Work effort and psychological climate subgroup as moderators of the relationship between conscientiousness and job performance in the three-way interaction effect	Psychological climate was positively related to job performance
Martin et al. (2005)	Sample 1: 779 public hospital employees (for Study 1) Sample 2: 877 public sector employees (for Study 2)	Cross-sectional/SEM EQS program v5.7b/individual level	Study 1: psychological climate (patient care, employee relationships, and supervisor support) Study 2: psychological climate (customer service, leader vision, and supervisor support)	Adjustment indicators (Study 1: psychological well-being and job satisfaction; Study 2: organizational commitment, turnover intentions, and absenteeism)	Study 1: change appraisal in terms of self-efficacy as a mediator of the relationship between psychological climate and adjustment indicators; change appraisal in terms of change stress as a mediator of the relationship between employee relationships and psychological well-being Study 2: change appraisal (change control and change self-efficacy) as a mediator of the relationship between psychological climate and adjustment indicators	Psychological climate was positively related to favorable change appraisals and better adjustment
Martin and Bush (2006)	106 sales managers and 313 sales representatives (matched data) in the USA	Dyad study/LISREL 8.3/individual level	Sales manager psychological climate; sales representatives' psychological climate	Sales manager empowerment; sales representatives' empowerment; sales representatives' customer-oriented selling; sales representative performance		Some psychological climate dimensions (3 dimensions) of sales managers and sales representatives were related to their own empowerment perceptions (sales manager

(continued)

Table 6.5 (continued)

Author/s (Year)	Sample	Study design/analysis strategy/level of analysis	Antecedents	Consequences	Moderators/mediators	Key climate results
						empowerment and sales representative empowerment). Some psychological climate dimensions (3 dimensions) of sales managers influenced transformational leadership
D'Amato and Zijlstra (2008)	406 hospital employees in North Italy	Cross-sectional/SEM/individual level	Psychological climate and self-efficacy	Work outcomes (quality of performance and emotional exhaustion)	Organizational citizenship behavior as a mediator of the relationship between psychological climate and work outcomes; and as a mediator of the relationship between self-efficacy and work outcomes	Psychological climate was positively related to organizational citizenship behavior
Larsson et al. (2008)	189 blue-collar construction workers in Sweden	Cross-sectional/SEM AMOS 4.0/individual level	Psychological climate	Self-reported safety behavior (structural safety behavior, interactive safety behavior, and personal safety behavior); workplace commitment; job satisfaction; safety motivation; safety knowledge	Safety motivation and safety knowledge as mediators of the relationship between psychological climate and personal safety behavior; safety motivation as a mediator of the relationship between psychological climate and interactive safety behavior	Psychological climate was positively related to three aspects of safety behavior
Tordera et al. (2008)	383 non-supervisor employees in 33 health care centers of Regional Public Health Service in Spain	Cross-sectional/hierarchical multiple regression analysis and SEM/individual level	Leader–member exchange	Role overload	Psychological climate dimensions (innovation, goals orientation, and rules orientation) as moderators of the relationship between leader–member exchange and role overload	

(continued)

Table 6.5 (continued)

Author/s (Year)	Sample	Study design/analysis strategy/level of analysis	Antecedents	Consequences	Moderators/mediators	Key climate results
Baltes et al. (2009)	639 non-government, non-profit fitness and community service organization employees in 28 Midwest locations, USA	Cross-sectional/hierarchical regression/individual level	Psychological climate with an organizational referent (PCo) and an individual referent (PCi)	Job satisfaction		Both PCo and PCi were positively related to job satisfaction
Bradley et al. (2012)	561 undergraduate students from a Midwestern university (117 project teams)	Participants were assigned to complete different tasks for one semester (in weeks 2, 4, 8, 10, and 13)/moderated hierarchical regression analysis/group level	Psychological safety climate; task conflict	Team performance	Psychological safety climate as a moderator of the relationship between task conflict and team performance	Task conflict and team performance were positively related under conditions of high psychological safety climate
Leroy et al. (2012)	Stage 1: 580 nurses in 54 nursing departments in Belgian hospitals Stage 2: 54 head nurses from same nursing departments as above (collected 6 months after Stage 1 survey)	Dyad study/Mplus/team (group) level	Leader behavioral integrity for safety; priority of safety; psychological safety	Reported treatment errors	Psychological safety as a moderator of the relationship between priority of safety and reported treatment errors; both priority of safety and psychological safety as mediators of the relationship between leader behavioral integrity for safety and reported treatment errors	The negative relationship of priority of safety to safety on reported treatment errors became stronger under conditions of higher psychological safety
Bedi et al. (2013)	1893 hospital employees in Canada	Cross-sectional/SEM AMOS/individual level	Interpersonal aggression	Burnout (emotional exhaustion, diminished personal accomplishment and depersonalization)	Psychological climate partially mediated the relationship between interpersonal aggression	Psychological climate was negatively associated with three dimensions of burnout (emotional

(continued)

Table 6.5 (continued)

Author/s (Year)	Sample	Study design/analysis strategy/level of analysis	Antecedents	Consequences	Moderators/mediators	Key climate results
					and two dimensions of burnout (emotional exhaustion and depersonalization)	exhaustion, diminished personal accomplishment, and depersonalization)
Wang et al. (2014)	Sample 1: 135 part-time MBA students with full-time employment in China Sample 2: 86 supervisors of industrial firms near the university studied in Sample 1 (answered by supervisors) A total of 193 valid sets used for the analysis (28 were excluded)	Cross-sectional/hierarchical multiple regression	Harmony enhancement; disintegration avoidance	Psychological climate for communication safety; innovative performance	Psychological climate as a mediator of the relationship between harmony enhancement and innovative performance; job autonomy as a moderator of the relationship between harmony enhancement and psychological climate	Psychological climate was positively associated with innovative performance
Lee and Ok (2015)	394 entry-level employees and managers from 4 areas of hotel operations in the USA	Cross-sectional/SEM AMOS 20 and SPSS 20/individual level	Core self-evaluation; psychological climate (customer orientation of management, managerial support, internal service, and information and communication)	Employee engagement		Psychological climate was positively related to employee engagement. Psychological climate did not moderate the relationship between core self-evaluations and employee engagement

References

Aptel, M., Aublet-Cuvelier, A., & Cnockaert, J. C. (2002). Work-related musculoskeletal disorders of the upper limb. *Joint Bone Spine, 69*(6), 546–555.

Arcury, T. A., O'Hara, H., Grzywacz, J. G., Isom, S., Chen, H., & Quandt, S. A. (2012). Work safety climate, musculoskeletal discomfort, working while injured, and depression among migrant farm workers in North Carolina. *American Journal of Public Health, 102*(S2), S272–S278. doi:10.2105/AJPH.2011.300597.

Baer, M., & Frese, M. (2003). Innovation is not enough: Climates for initiative and psychological safety, process innovations, and firm performance. *Journal of Organizational Behavior, 24*(1), 45–68. doi:10.1002/job.179.

Bryk, A. S., & Raudenbush, S. W. (1988). Toward a more appropriate conceptualization of research on school effects: A three-level hierarchical linear model. *American Journal of Education, 97*(1), 65–108.

Brown, S. P., & Leigh, T. W. (1996). A new look at psychological climate and its relationship to job involvement, effort, and performance. *Journal of Applied Psychology, 81*(4), 358–368. doi:10.1037/0021-9010.81.4.358.

Baba, V. V., Tourigny, L., Wang, X., & Liu, W. (2009). Proactive personality and work performance in China: The moderating effects of emotional exhaustion and perceived safety climate. *Canadian Journal of Administrative Sciences, 26*(1), 23–37. doi:10.1002/CJAS.90.

Bailey, T. S., Dollard, M. F., McLinton, S. S., & Richards, P. A. M. (2015a). Psychosocial safety climate, psychosocial and physical factors in the aetiology of musculoskeletal disorder symptoms and workplace injury compensation claims. *Work and Stress, 29*(2), 190–211. doi:10.1080/02678373.2015.1031855.

Bailey, T. S., Dollard, M. F., & Richards, P. A. M. (2015b). A national standard for psychosocial safety climate (PSC): PSC 41 as the benchmark for low risk of job strain and depressive symptoms. *Journal of Occupational Health Psychology, 20*(1), 15–26. doi:10.1037/a0038166.

Bond, S. A., Tuckey, M. R., & Dollard, M. F. (2010). Psychosocial safety climate, workplace bullying, and symptoms of posttraumatic stress. *Organization Development Journal, 28*, 37–56.

Baltes, B. B., Zhdanova, L. S., & Parker, C. P. (2009). Psychological climate: A comparison of organizational and individual level referents. *Human Relations, 62*(5), 669–700. doi:10.1177/0018726709103454.

Barbaranelli, C., Petitta, L., & Probst, T. M. (2015). Does safety climate predict safety performance in Italy and the USA? Cross-cultural validation of a theoretical model of safety climate. *Accident Analysis and Prevention, 77*, 35–44. doi:10.1016/j.aap.2015.01.012.

Bedi, A., Courcy, F., Paquet, M., & Harvey, S. (2013). Interpersonal aggression and burnout: The mediating role of psychological climate. *Stress and Health, 29*(5), 350–359. doi:10.1002/smi.2476.

Bosak, J., Coetsee, W. J., & Cullinane, S.-J. (2013). Safety climate dimensions as predictors for risk behavior. *Accident Analysis and Prevention, 55*, 256–264. doi:10.1016/j.aap.2013.02.022.

Bradley, B. H., Postlethwaite, B. E., Klotz, A. C., Hamdani, M. R., & Brown, K. G. (2012). Reaping the benefits of task conflict in teams: The critical role of team psychological safety climate. *Journal of Applied Psychology, 97*(1), 151–158. doi:10.1037/a0024200.

Brondino, M., Silva, S. A., & Pasini, M. (2012). Multilevel approach to organizational and group safety climate and safety performance: Co-workers as the missing link. *Safety Science, 50*(9), 1847–1856. doi:10.1016/j.ssci.2012.04.010.

Byrne, Z. S., Stoner, J., Thompson, K. R., & Hochwarter, W. (2005). The interactive effects of conscientiousness, work effort, and psychological climate on job performance. *Journal of Vocational Behavior, 66*(2), 326–338. doi:10.1016/j.jvb.2004.08.005.

Carr, J. Z., Schmidt, A. M., Ford, J. K., & DeShon, R. P. (2003). Climate perceptions matter: A meta-analytic path analysis relating molar climate, cognitive and affective states, and individual level work outcomes. *Journal of Applied Psychology, 88*(4), 605–619. doi:10.1037/0021-9010.88.4.605.

Clarke, S. (2010). An integrative model of safety climate: Linking psychological climate and work attitudes to individual safety outcomes using meta-analysis. *Journal of Occupational and Organizational Psychology, 83*(3), 553–578. doi:10.1348/096317909X452122.

Carless, S. A. (2004). Does psychological empowerment mediate the relationship between psychological climate and job satisfaction? *Journal of Business and Psychology, 18*(4), 405–425. doi:10.1023/B:JOBU.0000028444.77080.c5.

Cavazza, N., & Serpe, A. (2009). Effects of safety climate on safety norm violations: Exploring the mediating role of attitudinal ambivalence toward personal protective equipment. *Journal of Safety Research, 40*(4), 277–283. doi:10.1016/j.jsr.2009.06.002.

Cheyne, A., Cox, S., Oliver, A., & Tomás, J. M. (1998). Modelling safety climate in the prediction of levels of safety activity. *Work and Stress, 12*(3), 255–271. doi:10.1080/02678379808256865.

Cigularov, K. P., Chen, P. Y., & Stallones, L. (2009). Error communication in young farm workers: Its relationship to safety climate and safety locus of control. *Work and Stress, 23*(4), 297–312. doi:10.1080/02678370903416679.

Clark, O. L., Zickar, M. J., & Jex, S. M. (2014). Role definition as a moderator of the relationship between safety climate and organizational citizenship behavior among hospital nurses. *Journal of Business and Psychology, 29*(1), 101–110. doi:10.1007/s10869-013-9302-0.

Dollard, M. F., & Bakker, A. B. (2010). Psychosocial safety climate as a precursor to conducive work environments, psychological health problems, and employee engagement. *Journal of Occupational and Organizational Psychology, 83*, 579–599. doi:10.1348/096317909X470690.

Dollard, M. F., & Karasek, R. A. (2010). Building psychosocial safety climate: Evaluation of a socially coordinated PAR risk management stress prevention study. In J. Houdmont & S. Leka (Eds.), *Contemporary occupational health psychology: Global perspectives on research and practice* (pp. 208–234). Chichester: Wiley.

Dollard, M. F., & McTernan, W. (2011). Psychosocial safety climate: A multilevel theory of work stress in the health and community service sector. *Epidemiology and Psychiatric Science, 20*(4), 287–293. doi:10.1017/S2045796011000588.

Dollard, M. F., & Neser, D. Y. (2013). Worker health is good for the economy: Union density and psychosocial safety climate as determinants of country differences in worker health and productivity in 31 European countries. *Social Science and Medicine, 92*, 114–123. doi:10.1016/j.socscimed.2013.04.028.

Dollard, M. F., Opie, T., Lenthall, S., Wakerman, J., Knight, S., Dunn, S., et al. (2012a). Psychosocial safety climate as an antecedent of work characteristics and psychological strain: A multilevel model. *Work and Stress, 26*(4), 385–404. doi:10.1080/02678373.2012.734154.

Dollard, M. F., Tuckey, M. R., & Dormann, C. (2012b). Psychosocial safety climate moderates the job demand-resource interaction in predicting workgroup distress. *Accident Analysis and Prevention, 45*, 694–704. doi:10.1016/j.aap.2011.09.042.

D'Amato, A., & Zijlstra, F. R. H. (2008). Psychological climate and individual factors as antecedents of work outcomes. *European Journal of Work and Organizational Psychology, 17*(1), 33–54. doi:10.1080/13594320701307420.

Day, D. V., & Bedeian, A. G. (1991). Predicting job performance across organizations: The interaction of work orientation and psychological climate. *Journal of Management, 17*(3), 589–600. doi:10.1177/014920639101700304.

DeJoy, D. M., Schaffer, B. S., Wilson, M. G., Vandenberg, R. J., & Butts, M. M. (2004). Creating safer workplaces: Assessing the determinants and role of safety climate. *Journal of Safety Research, 35*(1), 81–90. doi:10.1016/j.jsr.2003.09.018.

EASHW. (2007). *Expert forecast on emerging psychosocial risks related to occupational safety and health*. Luxembourg: Office for Official Publications of the European Communities.

Edmondson, A. C. (1999). Psychological safety and learning behavior in work teams. *Administrative Science Quarterly, 44*(2), 350–383. doi:10.2307/2666999.

EU-OSHA. (2014). *Estimating the cost of accidents and ill-health at work: A review of methodologies*. Luxembourg: Publications Office of the European Union.

European Foundation for the Improvement of Living and Working Conditions. (2005). *Work-related stress*. Luxembourg: Office for Official Publications of the European Communities.

Eurostat. (2010). *Health and safety at work in Europe (1999–2007): A statistical potrait*. Luxembourg: Publications Office of the European Union.

Fernández-Muñiz, B., Montes-Peón, J. M., & Vázquez-Ordás, C. J. (2012). Safety climate in OHSAS 18001-certified organisations: Antecedents and consequences of safety behaviour. *Accident Analysis and Prevention, 45*, 745–758. doi:10.1016/j.aap.2011.10.002.

Fugas, C. S., Silva, S. A., & Meliá, J. L. (2012). Another look at safety climate and safety behavior: Deepening the cognitive and social mediator mechanisms. *Accident Analysis and Prevention, 45*, 468–477. doi:10.1016/j.aap.2011.08.013.

Garrick, A., Mak, A. S., Cathcart, S., Winwood, P. C., Bakker, A. B., & Lushington, K. (2014). Psychosocial safety climate moderating the effects of daily job demands and recovery on fatigue and work engagement. *Journal of Occupational and Organizational Psychology, 87*(4), 694–714. doi:10.1111/joop.12069.

Gillen, M., Baltz, D., Gassel, M., Kirsch, L., & Vaccaro, D. (2002). Perceived safety climate, job demands, and coworker support among union and nonunion injured construction workers. *Journal of Safety Research, 33*(1), 33–51. doi:10.1016/S0022-4375(02)00002-6.

Golubovich, J., Chang, C.-H., & Eatough, E. M. (2014). Safety climate, hardiness, and musculoskeletal complaints: A mediated moderation model. *Applied Ergonomics, 45*(3), 757–766. doi:10.1016/j.apergo.2013.10.008.

Griffin, M. A., & Neal, A. (2000). Perceptions of safety at work: A framework for linking safety climate to safety performance, knowledge, and motivation. *Journal of Occupational Health Psychology, 5*(3), 347–358. doi:10.1037/1076-8998.5.3.347.

Hall, G. B., Dollard, M. F., & Coward, J. (2010). Psychosocial safety climate: Development of the PSC-12. *International Journal of Stress Management, 17*(4), 353–383. doi:10.1037/a0021320.

Hall, G. B., Dollard, M. F., Winefield, A. H., Dormann, C., & Bakker, A. B. (2013). Psychosocial safety climate buffers effects of job demands on depression and positive organizational behaviors. *Anxiety, Stress and Coping, 26*(4), 355–377. doi:10.1080/10615806.2012.700477.

Hox, J. J., & Maas, C. J. M. (2001). The accuracy of multilevel structural equation modeling with pseudobalanced groups and small samples. *Structural Equation Modeling, 8*(2), 157–174. doi:10.1207/S15328007SEM0802_1.

Hofmann, D. A., & Mark, B. (2006). An investigation of the relationship between safety climate and medication errors as well as other nurse and patient outcomes. *Personnel Psychology, 59*(4), 847–869. doi:10.1111/j.1744-6570.2006.00056.x.

Hofmann, D. A., Morgeson, F. P., & Gerras, S. J. (2003). Climate as a moderator of the relationship between leader–member exchange and content specific citizenship: Safety climate as an exemplar. *Journal of Applied Psychology, 88*(1), 170–178. doi:10.1037/0021-9010.88.1.170.

Hope, S., Øverland, S., Brun, W., & Matthiesen, S. B. (2010). Associations between sleep, risk and safety climate: A study of offshore personnel on the Norwegian continental shelf. *Safety Science, 48*(4), 469–477. doi:10.1016/j.ssci.2009.12.006.

Huang, Y. H., Chen, J. C., DeArmond, S., Cigularov, K., & Chen, P. Y. (2007). Roles of safety climate and shift work on perceived injury risk: A multi-level analysis. *Accident Analysis and Prevention, 39*(6), 1088–1096. doi:10.1016/j.aap.2007.02.006.

Huang, Y. H., Ho, M., Smith, G. S., & Chen, P. Y. (2006). Safety climate and self-reported injury: Assessing the mediating role of employee safety control. *Accident Analysis and Prevention, 38*(3), 425–433. doi:10.1016/j.aap.2005.07.002.

Huang, Y. H., Robertson, M. M., Lee, J., Rineer, J., Murphy, L. A., Garabet, A., et al. (2014). Supervisory interpretation of safety climate versus employee safety climate perception: Association with safety behavior and outcomes for lone workers. *Transportation Research Part F: Traffic Psychology and Behaviour, 26*, 348–360. doi:10.1016/j.trf.2014.04.006.

Idris, M. A., & Dollard, M. F. (2011). Psychosocial safety climate, work conditions, and emotions in the workplace: A Malaysian population-based work stress study. *International Journal of Stress Management, 18*(4), 324–347. doi:10.1037/a0024849.

Idris, M. A., Dollard, M. F., Coward, J., & Dormann, C. (2012). Psychosocial safety climate: Conceptual distinctiveness and effect on job demands and worker psychological health. *Safety Science, 50*, 19–28. doi:10.1016/j.ssci.2011.06.005.

Idris, M. A., Dollard, M. F., & Tuckey, M. R. (2015). Psychosocial safety climate as a management tool for employee engagement and performance: A multilevel analysis. *International Journal of Stress Management, 22*(2), 183–206. doi:10.1037/a0038986.

Idris, M. A., Dollard, M. F., & Yulita, (2014). Psychosocial safety climate, emotional demands, burnout, and depression: A longitudinal multilevel study in the Malaysian private sector. *Journal of Occupational Health Psychology, 19*(3), 291–302. doi:10.1037/a0036599.

International Labour Organization. (2011). ILO introductory report: Global trends and challenges on occupational safety and health. In *Paper presented at the XIX World Congress on Safety and Health at Work*. Istanbul.

James, L. R., & Sells, S. B. (1981). Psychological climate: Theoretical perspectives and empirical research. In D. Magnusson (Ed.), *Toward a psychology of situations: An international perspective* (pp. 275–295). Hillsdale, NJ: Erlbaum.

Jiang, L., Yu, G., Li, Y., & Li, F. (2010). Perceived colleagues' safety knowledge/behavior and safety performance: Safety climate as a moderator in a multilevel study. *Accident Analysis and Prevention, 42*(5), 1468–1476. doi:10.1016/j.aap.2009.08.017.

Kozlowski, S. W. J., & Klein, K. J. (2000). A multilevel approach to theory and research in organizations: Contextual, temporal and emergent processes. In K. J. Klein & S. W. J. Kozlowski (Eds.), *Multilevel theory, research, and methods in organizations* (pp. 3–90). San Fransisco, CA: Jossey-Bass.

Kwan, S. S. M., Tuckey, M. R., & Dollard, M. F. (2014). The role of the psychosocial safety climate in coping with workplace bullying: A grounded theory and sequential tree analysis. *European Journal of Work and Organizational Psychology*,. doi:10.1080/1359432X.2014.982102.

Kath, L. M., Magley, V. J., & Marmet, M. (2010a). The role of organizational trust in safety climate's influence on organizational outcomes. *Accident Analysis and Prevention, 42*(5), 1488–1497. doi:10.1016/j.aap.2009.11.010.

Kath, L. M., Marks, K. M., & Ranney, J. (2010b). Safety climate dimensions, leader–member exchange, and organizational support as predictors of upward safety communication in a sample of rail industry workers. *Safety Science, 48*(5), 643–650. doi:10.1016/j.ssci.2010.01.016.

Katz-Navon, T., Naveh, E., & Stern, Z. (2005). Safety climate in health care organizations: A multidimensional approach. *Academy of Management Journal, 48*(6), 1075–1089. doi:10.5465/AMJ.2005.19573110.

Keren, N., Mills, T. R., Freeman, S. A., & Shelley, M. C. (2009). Can level of safety climate predict level of orientation toward safety in a decision making task? *Safety Science, 47*(10), 1312–1323. doi:10.1016/j.ssci.2009.01.009.

Khandan, M., Maghsoudipour, M., Vosoughi, S., & Kavousi, A. (2013). Safety climate and prediction of ergonomic behavior. *International Journal of Occupational Safety and Ergonomics, 19*(4), 523–530. doi:10.1080/10803548.2013.11077018.

Kwon, O. J., & Kim, Y. S. (2013). An analysis of safeness of work environment in Korean manufacturing: The "safety climate" perspective. *Safety Science, 53*, 233–239. doi:10.1016/j.ssci.2012.10.009.

Law, R., Dollard, M. F., Tuckey, M. R., & Dormann, C. (2011). Psychosocial safety climate as a lead indicator of workplace bullying and harassment, job resources, psychological health and employee engagement. *Accident Analysis and Prevention, 43*(5), 1782–1793. doi:10.1016/j.aap.2011.04.010.

Larsson, S., Pousette, A., & Törner, M. (2008). Psychological climate and safety in the construction industry-mediated influence on safety behaviour. *Safety Science, 46*(3), 405–412. doi:10.1016/j.ssci.2007.05.012.

Lee, J. J., & Ok, C. M. (2015). Drivers of work engagement: An examination of core self-evaluations and psychological climate among hotel employees. *International Journal of Hospitality Management, 44*, 84–98. doi:10.1016/j.ijhm.2014.10.008.

Lee, S., & Dalal, R. S. (2016). Climate as situational strength: Safety climate strength as a cross-level moderator of the relationship between conscientiousness and safety behaviour. *European Journal of Work and Organizational Psychology, 25*(1), 120–132. doi:10.1080/1359432X.2014.987231.

Lee, T. Z., Wu, C. H., & Hong, C. W. (2007). An empirical investigation of the influence of safety climate on organizational citizenship behavior in Taiwan's facilities. *International Journal of Occupational Safety and Ergonomics, 13*(3), 255–269. doi:10.1080/10803548.2007.11076726.

Leroy, H., Dierynck, B., Anseel, F., Simons, T., Halbesleben, J. R. B., McCaughey, D., et al. (2012). Behavioral integrity for safety, priority of safety, psychological safety, and patient safety: A team-level study. *Journal of Applied Psychology, 97*(6), 1273–1299. doi:10.1037/a0030076.

Lu, C. S., & Tsai, C. L. (2008). The effects of safety climate on vessel accidents in the container shipping context. *Accident Analysis and Prevention, 40*(2), 594–601. doi:10.1016/j.aap.2007.08.015.

Mathieu, J. E., Maynard, M. T., Taylor, S. R., Gilson, L. L., & Ruddy, T. M. (2007). An examination of the effects of organizational district and team contexts on team processes and performance: A meso-mediational model. *Journal of Organizational Behavior, 28*(7), 891–910. doi:10.1002/job.480.

Medibank Private Ltd. (2008). The cost of workplace stress in Australia.

Mark, B. A., Hughes, L. C., Belyea, M., Chang, Y., Hofmann, D., Jones, C. B., et al. (2007). Does safety climate moderate the influence of staffing adequacy and work conditions on nurse injuries? *Journal of Safety Research, 38*(4), 431–446. doi:10.1016/j.jsr.2007.04.004.

Martin, A. J., Jones, E. S., & Callan, V. J. (2005). The role of psychological climate in facilitating employee adjustment during organizational change. *European Journal of Work and Organizational Psychology, 14*(3), 263–289. doi:10.1080/13594320500141228.

Martin, C. A., & Bush, A. J. (2006). Psychological climate, empowerment, leadership style, and customer-oriented selling: An analysis of the sales manager-salesperson dyad. *Journal of the Academy of Marketing Science, 34*(3), 419–438. doi:10.1177/0092070306286205.

McCaughey, D., DelliFraine, J. L., McGhan, G., & Bruning, N. S. (2013). The negative effects of workplace injury and illness on workplace safety climate perceptions and health care worker outcomes. *Safety Science, 51*(1), 138–147. doi:10.1016/j.ssci.2012.06.004.

Mearns, K., Hope, L., Ford, M. T., & Tetrick, L. E. (2010). Investment in workforce health: Exploring the implications for workforce safety climate and commitment. *Accident Analysis and Prevention, 42*(5), 1445–1454. doi:10.1016/j.aap.2009.08.009.

Mearns, K., Whitaker, S. M., & Flin, R. (2003). Safety climate, safety management practice and safety performance in offshore environments. *Safety Science, 41*(8), 641–680. doi:10.1016/S0925-7535(02)00011-5.

Morrow, S. L., McGonagle, A. K., Dove-Steinkamp, M. L., Walker, C. T., Marmet, M., & Barnes-Farrell, J. L. (2010). Relationships between psychological safety climate facets and safety behavior in the rail industry: A dominance analysis. *Accident Analysis and Prevention, 42*(5), 1460–1467. doi:10.1016/j.aap.2009.08.011.

Naveh, E., Katz-Navon, T., & Stern, Z. (2005). Treatment errors in healthcare: A safety climate approach. *Management Science, 51*(6), 948–960. doi:10.1287/mnsc.1050.0372.

Neal, A., & Griffin, M. A. (2006). A study of the lagged relationships among safety climate, safety motivation, safety behavior, and accidents at the individual and group levels. *Journal of Applied Psychology, 91*(4), 946–953. doi:10.1037/0021-9010.91.4.946.

Nielsen, M. B., Mearns, K., Matthiesen, S. B., & Eid, J. (2011). Using the Job Demands-Resources model to investigate risk perception, safety climate and job satisfaction in safety critical organizations. *Scandinavian Journal of Psychology, 52*(5), 465–475. doi:10.1111/j.1467-9450.2011.00885.x.

Ostroff, C., Kinicki, A. J., & Tamkins, M. M. (2003). Organizational culture and climate. In W. C. Borman & D. R. Ilgen (Eds.), *Handbook of psychology: Industrial and organizational psychology* (Vol. 12, pp. 565–593). New York, NY: Wiley.

Payne, S. C., Bergman, M. E., Rodríguez, J. M., Beus, J. M., & Henning, J. B. (2010). Leading and lagging: Process safety climate-incident relationships at one year. *Journal of Loss Prevention in the Process Industries, 23*(6), 806–812. doi:10.1016/j.jlp.2010.06.004.

Probst, T. M. (2004). Safety and insecurity: Exploring the moderating effect of organizational safety climate. *Journal of Occupational Health Psychology, 9*(1), 3–10. doi:10.1037/1076-8998.9.1.3.

Probst, T. M., Brubaker, T. L., & Barsotti, A. (2008). Organizational injury rate underreporting: The moderating effect of organizational safety climate. *Journal of Applied Psychology, 93*(5), 1147–1154. doi:10.1037/0021-9010.93.5.1147.

Probst, T. M., & Estrada, A. X. (2010). Accident under-reporting among employees: Testing the moderating influence of psychological safety climate and supervisor enforcement of safety practices. *Accident Analysis and Prevention, 42*(5), 1438–1444. doi:10.1016/j.aap.2009.06.027.

Reichers, A. E., & Schneider, B. (1990). Climate and culture: An evolution of constructs. In B. Schneider (Ed.), *Organizational climate and culture* (pp. 5–39). San Fransisco: Jossey-Bass.

Rundmo, T. (2000). Safety climate, attitudes and risk perception in Norsk Hydro. *Safety Science, 34*(1), 47–59. doi:10.1016/S0925-7535(00)00006-0.

Siu, O. L., Phillips, D. R., & Leung, T. W. (2004). Safety climate and safety performance among construction workers in Hong Kong: The role of psychological strains as mediators. *Accident Analysis and Prevention, 36*(3), 359–366. doi:10.1016/S0001-4575(03)00016-2.

Smith, G. S., Huang, Y. H., Ho, M., & Chen, P. Y. (2006). The relationship between safety climate and injury rates across industries: The need to adjust for injury hazards. *Accident Analysis and Prevention, 38*(3), 556–562. doi:10.1016/j.aap.2005.11.013.

Tholén, S. L., Pousette, A., & Törner, M. (2013). Causal relations between psychosocial conditions, safety climate and safety behaviour: A multi-level investigation. *Safety Science, 55*, 62–69. doi:10.1016/j.ssci.2012.12.013.

Tomás, J. M., Cheyne, A., & Oliver, A. (2011). The relationship between safety attitudes and occupational accidents: The role of safety climate. *European Psychologist, 16*(3), 209–219. doi:10.1027/1016-9040/a000036.

Tordera, N., González-Romá, V., & Peiró, J. M. (2008). The moderator effect of psychological climate on the relationship between leader–member exchange (LMX) quality and role overload. *European Journal of Work and Organizational Psychology, 17*(1), 55–72. doi:10.1080/13594320701392059.

Varonen, U., & Mattila, M. (2000). The safety climate and its relationship to safety practices, safety of the work environment and occupational accidents in eight wood-processing companies. *Accident Analysis and Prevention, 32*(6), 761–769. doi:10.1016/S0001-4575(99)00129-3.

Vinodkumar, M. N., & Bhasi, M. (2009). Safety climate factors and its relationship with accidents and personal attributes in the chemical industry. *Safety Science, 47*(5), 659–667. doi:10.1016/j.ssci.2008.09.004.

Wallace, J. C., Popp, E., & Mondore, S. (2006). Safety climate as a mediator between foundation climates and occupational accidents: A group-level investigation. *Journal of Applied Psychology, 91*(3), 681–688. doi:10.1037/0021-9010.91.3.681.

Wang, J., Leung, K., & Zhou, F. (2014). A dispositional approach to psychological climate: Relationships between interpersonal harmony motives and psychological climate for communication safety. *Human Relations, 67*(4), 489–515. doi:10.1177/0018726713495423.

Wills, A. R., Watson, B., & Biggs, H. C. (2006). Comparing safety climate factors as predictors of work-related driving behavior. *Journal of Safety Research, 37*(4), 375–383. doi:10.1016/j.jsr.2006.05.008.

Wu, T. C., Chang, S. H., Shu, C. M., Chen, C. T., & Wang, C. P. (2011). Safety leadership and safety performance in petrochemical industries: The mediating role of safety climate. *Journal of Loss Prevention in the Process Industries, 24*(6), 716–721. doi:10.1016/j.jlp.2011.04.007.

Zohar, D. (2002). The effects of leadership dimensions, safety climate, and assigned priorities on minor injuries in work groups. *Journal of Organizational Behavior, 23*(1), 75–92. doi:10.1002/job.130.

Zohar, D., Huang, Y. H., Lee, J., & Robertson, M. (2014). A mediation model linking dispatcher leadership and work ownership with safety climate as predictors of truck driver safety performance. *Accident Analysis and Prevention, 62*, 17–25. doi:10.1016/j.aap.2013.09.005.

Zohar, D., & Polachek, T. (2014). Discourse-based intervention for modifying supervisory communication as leverage for safety climate and performance improvement: A randomized field study. *Journal of Applied Psychology, 99*(1), 113–124. doi:10.1037/a0034096.

Zhang, Z., Zyphur, M. J., & Preacher, K. J. (2009). Testing multilevel mediation using hierarchical linear models problems and solutions. *Organizational Research Methods, 12*(4), 695–719. doi:10.1177/1094428108327450.

Zohar, D. (1980). Safety climate in industrial organizations: Theoretical and applied implications. *Journal of Applied Psychology, 65*(1), 96–102. doi:10.1037/0021-9010.65.1.96.

Zohar, D. (2000). A group-level model of safety climate: Testing the effect of group climate on microaccidents in manufacturing jobs. *Journal of Applied Psychology, 85*(4), 587–596. doi:10.1037/0021-9010.85.4.587.

Zohar, D. (2010). Thirty years of safety climate research: Reflections and future directions. *Accident Analysis and Prevention, 42*, 1157–1522. doi:10.1016/j.aap.2009.12.019.

Zohar, D., & Luria, G. (2005). A multilevel model of safety climate: Cross-level relationships between organization and group-level climates. *Journal of Applied Psychology, 90*(4), 616–628. doi:10.1037/0021-9010.90.4.616.

Chapter 7
Designing Work that Works in the Contemporary World: Future Directions for Job Design Research

Sharon K. Parker and Fangfang Zhang

Abstract Much research shows that good work design has positive outcomes for individuals and organisations. After a brief review of two popular work design perspectives (designing motivating work; designing safe and healthy work), the primary goal of this chapter is to identify some important future research directions. This chapter highlights key areas that need more attention from researchers and practitioners: putting work design into context to consider the effects of rapid changes currently occurring in the workplace and the workforce; identifying the value of work design from a longer term and more strategic perspectives; paying more attention to employee-initiated forms of work design; giving greater attention to why poor work design continues; and investigating the effects of culture on work design and cross-cultural research on work design. This chapter concludes by advocating the collaboration of researchers and practitioners to take up the challenge of work design to achieve decent jobs for all.

Keywords Work design · Job characteristics · Proactivity · Job crafting · Future work

Introduction

Work design, which refers to 'the content and organization of one's work tasks, activities, relationships and responsibilities' (Parker 2014, p. 662), has been linked not only with positive individual outcomes, but also the effective functioning of organisations and even societies. For individuals, work design can affect their sense of meaning, health and well-being, creativity, development and more. At the same

S.K. Parker (✉) · F. Zhang
Management and Organisations, UWA Business School,
The University of Western Australia, Perth, Australia
e-mail: sharon.parker@uwa.edu.au

F. Zhang
e-mail: fangfang.zhang@research.uwa.edu.au

A. Shimazu et al. (eds.), *Psychosocial Factors at Work in the Asia Pacific*,
DOI 10.1007/978-3-319-44400-0_7

time, work design can also affect many significant goals in organisations, such as safety, performance and innovation. At the societal level, work design is also considered critical, as shown by the International Labor Organization's Decent Work Agenda that aims to not just secure work for all, but to ensure that work is of high quality.

In the past decades, researchers and practitioners have applied work design theories to understand workers' experiences and behaviours across an array of organisations. However, many important questions remain unsolved (Humphrey et al. 2007), especially in light of the global shifts in work organisation that give rise to new challenges. Work design theory and practice must develop in accordance with changes in the nature of work (e.g. service-oriented industries and increased popularity of virtual work) as well as changes in the nature of workforce (e.g. ageing, different generation cohorts and dual working parents).

The goal of this article is to identify some important future research directions. To set the scene, we begin by providing a brief overview of the most two popular approaches to work design. We then turn to the core of this chapter, which concerns future research avenues. Of the many different directions that can be identified, we argue for five aspects as especially important.

Existing Work Design Research and Theories

In this section, we provide a brief overview of the dominant approaches to work design research present within the field of industrial/organisational psychology. Our goal is not to thoroughly recount all of the literature since many other reviews (e.g., Torraco 2005; Parker 2014) and meta-analyses (e.g. Humphrey et al. 2007; Nahrgang et al. 2011) already achieve this goal. Rather, our aim is to give a flavour of what have been some of the key directions.

Designing Motivating Work

At the dawn of the Industrial Revolution, influenced by Smith's (1776) concept of the 'division of labor' as well as Taylor's (1911) notion of scientific management, job simplification became the mainstream of work design. Job simplification meant that managers carried out the 'mental' work such as decision-making, whilst operators' jobs composed only the 'manual' work.

However, the negative outcomes of job simplification (e.g. increased turnover and reduced mental health) prompted interest amongst some scholars and practitioners in redesigning work to improve and optimise employees' work experiences and organisational productivity. At the group level, researchers in the UK at the Tavistock Institute proposed sociotechnical systems (STS) theory, or the integrating of technical aspects and human relations aspects into the work system, rather than the prior sole focus on technical aspects (Trist and Bamforth 1951; Emery and Trist 1969). At the individual level, redesign efforts to increase the motivational quality of work included job rotation (rotating workers from one job to another job), job enlargement (expanding the content of jobs to include additional tasks) and job enrichment (e.g. increasing employees' autonomy over the planning and execution of their own work). These redesign ideas were ultimately consolidated into the Job Characteristics Model (JCM) (Hackman and Oldham 1976), which became a dominant theory of motivational work design.

The JCM proposes that work design should have five core job characteristics (skill variety, autonomy, feedback, task significance and task identity), which generate three critical psychological states (individuals' experiencing meaning, feeling responsible for their outcomes, and understanding the results of their efforts), thus enhancing employee motivation, job satisfaction, and performance and reducing turnover. Several meta-analyses and longitudinal and quasi-experimental studies have established that work characteristics affect attitudinal outcomes in ways largely consistent with the key principles of the JCM (Humphrey et al. 2007; Parker and Wall 1998). When it comes to performance and behavioural outcomes, although meta-analyses show links between work characteristics and subjective job performance, the effects of motivational work design on performance are rather more inconsistent in existing studies.

Although the JCM has been a dominant model of work design, it has been critiqued and its core elements have been extended. For example, Morgeson and Humphrey (2006) expanded the five core work characteristics into 21 job characteristics. These characteristics include: motivation characteristics (similar to those in the JCM), knowledge motivation characteristics (e.g. cognitive demands), social characteristics (e.g. task interdependence) and contextual characteristics (e.g. physical work conditions). Parker et al. (2001) proposed the Elaborated Job Characteristics Model, identifying a broader set of job characteristics (e.g. social work characteristics, such as interdependence, and different forms of autonomy, such as autonomy over working hours) as well as an expanded set of outcomes (e.g. customer satisfaction, work–home conflict, innovation) and additional moderators and mediators.

In recent times, two extensions to the traditional motivational approach include the proactive and relational perspectives on work design (Grant and Parker 2009). Proactive perspectives emerged because increasing uncertainty raises the value of using one's initiative and innovative behaviours amongst the workforce. Research thus considers how work design can promote more proactive attitudes and behaviours. For example, Parker et al. (2010) argued that work design (e.g., job autonomy) can promote three important motivational states ('can do', 'reason to', and 'energised to' motivation) that, in turn, lead to proactive behaviours. Tornau and Frese (2013) identified the importance of job control and social support in promoting proactive work behaviours.

In addition, whereas traditional work design theories assumed that managers took responsibility for structuring jobs for employees, with employees then passively accepting the tasks assigned to them, proactive perspectives recognise a more agentic role for employees in shaping their own work designs. Thus, proactive work design perspectives include the idea that proactive individuals can shape their own work designs, and the notion that work designs can shape individuals' motivation and opportunity to behave proactively at work (Grant and Parker 2009).

A further new perspective that has extended the traditional motivational view is the relational approach to work design. Changes in the social context of work, such as increases in the use of teams to complete work in most organisations, warrant this relationally oriented perspective. In particular, Grant (2007) argued that work can be designed so that employees interact, or connect in some way, with the beneficiaries of their work, which in turn affects their motivation, attitudes and job performance. In jobs where employees can connect with beneficiaries, employees are likely to empathise with these beneficiaries, and hence develop stronger affective commitment towards them, which will encourage employees' higher levels of effort, persistence and helping behaviours. Evidence is shown in several field experiments (Grant 2007, 2008). In contrast with the JCM work design theory that emphasises intrinsic motivation, the relational perspective is concerned with how work design can stimulate prosocial motivation, the desire to help others. This is a key contribution because when enriched types of work redesign are untenable for some reason, the relational work design might be considered to increase the meaning of work.

It is likely that different contexts will need different forms of relational work design. For example, for doctors who already had frequent contact with patients (that is, connections with beneficiaries were already high), providing social support to doctors was a powerful form of relational work design that resulted in improved work outcomes (Parker et al. 2013).

Designing Work that is Healthy and Safe

The link between work design and employee health has been of interest for many decades. Nevertheless, continued attention is needed for the design of healthy work today due to the increased complexity, demands and pressure in many jobs and heightened concerns about health issues in society.

The most dominant work design model relevant to designing healthy work is the job demands-control model of strain (Karasek 1979), which was extended to include social support (the demand-control-support model, Karasek and Theorell 1990). The model proposes that high job demands (e.g. high work load), low social support and low decision latitude (i.e. low job control and skill discretion), will lead to strain on employees, and stress-related physical symptoms such as heart disease. A particular twist of the model is that it also proposes that, if the high demands occur accompanied by high decision latitude, a so-called 'active job', then strain will not occur and there will be other benefits such as strengthened feelings of mastery and confidence, which help workers to deal with further job demands, and promote learning (Karasek and Theorell 1990).

A vast number of studies have tested the job demands-control model. There is clear evidence to show that excess job demands cause strain (De Lange et al. 2003). Other studies show that high job demands and low control affect cardiovascular disease, especially for men (Belkic et al. 2004). Excessive job demands can also reduce safety (Nahrgang et al. 2011). In terms of the effects of control on health, many cross-sectional studies show that a lack of perceived job control is associated with negative outcomes such as anxiety, depression, burnout, excess alcohol consumption, although the results are not quite as consistent in longitudinal studies, perhaps because of individual differences or contextual variables (Warr 2011). Finally, evidence for the buffering effects of job control on job demands is also rather mixed: the buffering effect is by and large supported in laboratory studies (e.g. Karasek 1979) but inconsistently supported in many field studies (e.g. De Lange et al. 2003).

Like the JCM, the job demands-control model has been critiqued and extended. Bakker and Demerouti (2007) proposed the job demands-resources model, which theorises a wider range of job resources beyond autonomy and skill discretion, such as career opportunities and participation in decision-making. Among the resources, evidence for the positive effects of social support is especially clear and consistent. Social support can not only fulfil basic needs for belongingness, but also promote the achievement of work goals, thus both results in motivational outcomes (e.g. engagement) and alleviates strain (Demerouti and Bakker 2011).

In further extension of the job demands-control model, scholars have divided demands into challenge demands and hindrance demands (LePine et al. 2005). Challenge demands create opportunities for development and achievement, such as job scope and responsibility, whereas hindrance demands are regarded as obstacles to achievement and growth, such as role ambiguity and job insecurity. Crawford et al. (2010) suggested that both types of demands are associated with strain, but hindrance demands are also associated with other negative outcomes such as turnover and withdrawal whilst challenge demands are positively related to motivation and performance. It is noticeable that even with challenge stressors, there might be a tipping point at which excess or sustained levels are damaging to individuals. Rather than investigating how to categorise demands into challenges and hindrances, it may be of value to integrate appraisal theory to consider how demands are appraised by the particular individual (Ohly and Fritz 2010). Appraisals also vary for individuals in different situations (Fisher et al. 2013).

Challenges and Future Directions

Whilst the above perspectives have been, and continue to be, important, there are also future directions to consider including theoretical development of the motivation model (e.g. Parker and Ohly 2009), of the demands-resources model (Bakker and Demerouti 2007), and of other models. Recommendations are also often made for methodological improvements, such as more longitudinal studies, better incorporation of levels issues or the consideration of configurations (for a summary of suggestions from recent reviews, see Parker et al. (in press)). Here, we focus on five directions that we consider most important.

Changing Theory in Light of a Changing Context

Although there have been rich advances in work design theory, researchers need to more thoroughly consider the effects of remarkable changes in work context over the past few decades, as well as forthcoming changes, and adapt work design theory and models accordingly (Grant and Parker 2009; Grant et al. 2010). All the changes in workplace and workforce give rise to important and rather neglected research issues. We illustrate this in relation to three example changes.

An Ageing Population in Many Countries

The workforce in most industrialised countries is ageing. Because of increasing life expectancies and changing welfare policies, many older people will need to continue to work for many years after standard retirement ages. Some individuals enjoy their work and will want to work longer, but others will not. Meanwhile, many organisations are interested in retaining older workers because of their accumulated knowledge, skills and experiences. From a societal perspective, retaining older workers is needed for an effective economy. Thus it is imperative to consider how work can be better designed to attract and retain older people (Zacher and Griffin 2015).

When individuals age, there are changes in their physical health and abilities, cognitive abilities and even their personality, across the lifespan. At the same time, older individuals often have accumulated job-based knowledge and greater crystallised intelligence. Thus it is important to consider what types of work design can promote healthy and engaging work which is more suitable for ageing people, especially in the context of changes occurring work in general (e.g. rising intellectual and technological demands). Ng and Feldman's (2010) meta-analysis found that older workers have more positive job attitudes in part because of their perceived time limitations. They have a greater interest in emotionally fulfilling activities, meaningful work and have more generative motives. These aspects should be integrated into productive work design. Future research should also take account of the interactions between individuals and the work. For example, Kooij (2015) argued that ageing workers can enact different types of proactive behaviours to improve their current and future person-job fit and job environment, and thus age more successfully.

Increasing Digitalisation of Work

Across all industries, jobs and roles are undergoing dramatic changes due to rapid advances in digital technology. Bradlow (2015: 45) foresaw that cognitive computing and digitalisation means that 'the nature of employment—the type of work humans do—is going to change dramatically in the coming few decades'. Computers and robots are increasingly replacing humans, resulting in some patterns and forms of work disappearing, leaving only high-skilled jobs with more cognitively complex activities and challenging analytical, problem-solving and decision-making tasks. Meanwhile, amongst the remaining jobs, characteristics of tasks and roles performed by workers are also being transformed by digital technology. Since work design is all about the tasks people do, it is important to consider how tasks can be allocated between people and computers. For example, in a study of a telecommunications company that adopted complex technologies to ensure standardised service, scholars (e Sá and de Sá 2015) indicated that frontline employees confronted conflicting demands between delivering highly consistent service and customising it to each customer. The authors concluded that more autonomy and feedback is needed in the job if employee and customer satisfaction are both to be enhanced.

In addition, new contexts such as virtual work have emerged because of advances in technology that enable transcending traditional barriers of time and location. Technology such as smart phones and other such devices have also blurred distinctions between work and nonwork (Olson-Buchanan and Boswell 2006). Work design theories need to answer questions about whether and how we should separate employees physically and temporally from their organisations. Research is then needed to investigate the effects of these new work situations have on the employees and the performance of the work. It is also important to design work to support effective collaboration since virtual teams can have difficulties in coordinating (Erez 2010).

Because of the advances of technology, many companies have adopted flexible working arrangements (e.g. reduced hours and remote working). Although this has provided more autonomy to workers, attention should be paid to potential unanticipated outcomes such as work intensification. Kelliher and Anderson (2009) identified three different types of work intensification resulting from flexible working: imposed intensification, influenced by the different work time arrangements of other employees; enabled intensification, such that flexible working employees increase their work time proactively; and intensification as an act of reciprocation or exchange. They argued that although no negative effects were found in their study, this interpretation should be taken cautiously, since longer term effects were not studied. Longitudinal research is needed to explore the effects of flexible working, and to compare different types of flexible working, such as comparing the traditional approach to allow flexible hours with contemporary experiments in (for example) results-only work environments (Perrow 2011).

Combating Sedentary Work

A further direction is to actively design work to better combat physical strains. These days, there is a shifting concern from physically demanding or risky occupations to sedentary occupations in which there is insufficient physical activity. People currently spend much time being sedentary, and are likely to spend more sedentary in the future because of increasing availability of technology. Existing research has suggested that sedentary behaviours are detrimental to health, such as being associated with obesity and related chronic diseases (Choi et al. 2010; Boyle et al. 2011). New paradigms are required to design work that protects or improves employees' physical health and capacity (Straker and Mathiassen 2009). For example, designing work with reasonable work hours, and with sufficient opportunity for walking breaks, is one way to help address the issues arising from increasingly sedentary jobs in many occupations.

Longer Term and More Strategic Perspectives on the Value of Work Design

Although motivational work design theory has been extended in various ways and can be extended further, Parker (2014) argued that designing work for motivation is not enough, especially given to the rapid changes in the nature of work and workforce. Rather than just adding extra dependent variables to empirical studies, we need to explore when, why and how work design can help to achieve different purposes. Besides the role of work design in facilitating motivation, performance, health and well-being, work can be designed to achieve at least two other key outcomes (Parker 2014).

First, work design can be a vehicle for learning and development. At the aggregate level, there is a great shortage of skills globally. At the individual level, employees require skills to be effective within a complex environment. It is important to consider how to design work that can promote employees' learning and development. For example, Parker (2014) argued that individuals' cognitive capabilities can be enhanced via good work design and, relatedly, that levels of cognitive decline (and even dementia) can be reduced. Likewise, good work can promote the development of values, motivations and identities that can, in turn, facilitate healthy ageing (Wu et al. 2015; Rodin 2014).

Second, increased environmental complexity and pressure to satisfy many stakeholders require scholars to consider how to design work that promotes more than one outcome at the same time, especially competing outcomes, for example, control and flexibility. Parker (2014) reviewed three forms of work design that are beneficial for reconciling the tension between control and flexibility-ambidexterity, enabling bureaucracy, and high-reliability organising. For example, work designs that empower employees to allocate their time to best address the conflicting demands of exploration and exploitation may be a beneficial element of ambidexterity (O'Reilly and Tushman 2008; Gibson and Birkinshaw 2004). In highly centralised contexts, enabling bureaucracy as a concept recognises that employees can be motivated by participation and high levels of accountability even though their job autonomy is low (Adler and Borys 1996; De Treville and Antonakis 2006). In high-reliability organisations (HROs), control and flexibility can be achieved through under-specification of structures, which allows the subordination of hierarchical authority during critical events (Weick et al. 2008). Overall, despite the relevance of these perspectives, they have rarely been considered from a work design point of view, and there is much more theoretical speculation than there is rigorous research.

The above outcomes of work design—learning and development, and achieving a balance between control and flexibility—have had significantly less attention in the literature relative to motivation and health outcomes. We hope that future research will develop these perspectives, so we can go beyond existing mainstream paradigms.

More Attention to Bottom-Up, Employee-Initiated Forms of Work Design

With global, economic and technological developments, there is increasing uncertainty and complexity in organisations as well as within employees' careers. Grant and Parker (2009) suggested that management in organisations should no longer design fixed and static jobs, but rather design flexible jobs to allow and motivate employees to behave adaptively and proactively in order to best manage the uncertainty and complexity they face. Such flexible jobs also allow individuals the chance to craft their work to achieving a good balance between work demands and resources (Tims et al. 2012). Indeed, scholars have suggested that even employees who occupy jobs characterised by low levels of autonomy can customise, or craft, their jobs to some degree to meet their individual needs and preferences (Wrzesniewski and Dutton 2001; Berg et al. 2010). Job crafting has been found to be significantly and positively related to the attitudinal outcomes (e.g. job satisfaction) and behavioural outcomes (e.g. in-role performance) of employees (Petrou et al. 2012; Tims and Bakker 2010). Job crafting, negotiating idiosyncratic deals (i-deals), and other forms of proactive agentic behaviour that shape one's tasks and responsibilities can be considered to be 'bottom up' forms of work design.

Although research on the topic has gathered pace in recent years, there is still relatively little research on bottom-up forms of work redesign like job crafting, including its different forms. Wrzesniewski and Dutton (2001) proposed three kinds of job crafting (cognitive crafting, task crafting and relational crafting), and Tims et al. (2012) developed a scale consisting of four types of job crafting that pertain to the job demands-resources framework (increasing social job resources, increasing structural job resources, increasing challenging job demands and decreasing hindering job demands). Slemp and Vella-Brodrick (2013) highlighted the role of cognitive crafting. More research is needed on when different forms of crafting arise, and their different drivers and outcomes. Likewise, the mechanisms underpinning job crafting need more attention. For example, Bakker et al. (2012) concluded that employees with proactive personality will actively change their work environment to ensure their job demands and resources are suitable for their own abilities and needs, thus facilitating engagement and performance. Slemp and Vella-Brodrick (2014) applied self-determination theory (SDT; see Gagné and Deci 2005) and argued that job crafting satisfies psychological needs and thereby can predict individuals' well-being.

Greater Attention to Why Poor Work Design Continues

There continues to be many low-wage, low-quality jobs in advanced and developing countries (Osterma and Shulman 2011) and indeed a widening gap between good and bad jobs in the US (Kalleberg 2011). Large-scale surveys, like the European Working Conditions Survey, also show evidence of poor work design. The version of this survey conducted in 2010, involving more than 44,000 participants across Europe, showed that more than 20 % of jobs have poor intrinsic quality. Poor work design is also witnessed in new jobs, such as weatherisation jobs (making houses more energy efficient) in the United States (Osterma and Shulman 2011).

Within the Asia Pacific region also, there is evidence of poor quality work. For example, Dollard et al. (2012) assessed more than 5000 employees in Australia and identified some industries (e.g. Transport and storage, accommodation, cafes and restaurants and Health and community services) as experiencing a high risk of poor psychological health as a result of their work. They also identified the problem of long working hours, with more than 40 % of participants working more than standard hours and 18 % working longer than 48 h per week. This phenomenon is also common in other countries, such as Japan, Korea, Taiwan and other regions of China: large numbers of employees are required to work long hours, which results in overworked, stressed individuals who experience physical and mental symptoms such as fatigue, musculoskeletal discomfort, sleeping disorders, depression and anxiety (Cheng 2015).

With abundant evidence of continuing poor work design, at the same time as evidence that poor work design is harmful to individuals and often to organisations, it is vital to understand the research of drivers or antecedents of work design. Parker (2014) identified several drivers of poor work design, including increased competitive pressure, national polices and institutions, changes such as outsourcing and IT, a lack of managerial awareness of the returns of good work design from relevant professionals, and difficulties and challenges in implementing work design in organisations. Morgeson et al. (2010) similarly called for researchers to explore the genesis of work design, and highlighted the role of occupational and organisational context on work design. In their review, they identified two distinct ways that context might influence work design: as a main effect on work design characteristics and as cross-level moderators that shape the relationship between work characteristics and outcomes of work design.

A related perspective comes from Dollard and Bakker (2010), who developed the psychosocial safety climate (PSC) model. PSC refers to policies, practices and procedures in an organisation that enable the protection of worker psychological health and safety. These authors identified PSC as causally affecting working conditions. Applying the job demands-resources (JD-R) framework, they regard PSC as an organisational resource that can influence both job resources and job demands. Building on previous work, Idris and Dollard (2014) focused on the effects of PSC on job demands that are divided into challenge demands and hindrance demands. They suggested that organisational PSC levels can predict levels of hindrance demands, so PSC should be regarded as an important factor when creating healthy and safe working environment.

Despite the recent interest in determinants of work design, overall, research on this topic is very limited. In order to understand why poor-designed jobs persist and to achieve better work design, we need more attention to the forces that create or sustain poor work designs.

Developing Culturally Appropriate Theories of Work Design

Culture was rarely regarded as a critical variable to explain organisational behaviours before Barrett and Bass's (1976) review of cross-cultural industrial and organisational psychology literature. However, because of increasing globalisation, there is a particular need for researchers and practitioners to pay more attention to the effects of culture on work design. Moreover, the adaption of work design theories evolved in Western cultural contexts might not be suitable and effective in other sociocultural contexts. Thus existing work design theories and constructs that have been developed in Western cultural contexts cannot be automatically assumed to apply to different cultural environments.

On this topic, Erez and Earley (1993) argued that national-level cultural values shape whether certain work designs enable employees to experience a sense of self-worth and well-being. Erez (2010) further analysed how culture influences work design by comparing three major work design models that emerged in three different cultures. For example, American values are known to shape and encourage people to be distinct from others to achieve a sense of self-worth and well-being (Brewer and Chen 2007; Markus and Kitayama 1991). The job enrichment work design (Hackman and Oldham 1980) is in accordance with American cultural values because it focuses on giving individuals opportunities to experience a sense of autonomy and personal responsibility, consistent with high individualism and low power distance values. Under this individualistic culture, it is not surprising that relational characteristics are less emphasised in the job enrichment model. Erez (2010) also suggested that culture moderates the relationships between certain work characteristics (autonomy and feedback) and their behavioural outcomes. For example, work autonomy and empowerment are regarded as important motivational factors in individualistic cultures. However, a study of Indian employees showed opposite results, with less satisfaction in employees who were empowered by their boss and higher satisfaction in those who were simply told what to do. This finding was attributed to the high power distance and collectivistic values in India (Robert et al. 2000), although as it is just a single study, such an interpretation needs further validation. As a further example, work family conflict (WFC) arising from poor work design varies in different cultural environments. Research suggested that the WFC of Chinese employees resulted more from work demands, whereas the WFC of American employees resulted more from family demands (Yang et al. 2000). In China there is also a greater gender-based division of WFC because of the culture: both work-to-family conflict and family-to-work conflict affect women's well-being because they are dually exposed to work and family demands (Li and Angerer 2014).

Cross-cultural research on how culture shapes work design, as well as how employees in different culture perceive certain job characteristics, will help enable good work design according to different cultural environments and values.

Conclusion

Work design is an important topic, and we have learned much about how to design work, the costs and benefits of different types of work design, and how and why work design leads to a diverse set of outcomes. Of course, there is always more to learn, and our chapter has highlighted five key areas for future research. We hope that researchers will take up some of these challenges, in close collaboration with practitioners, so that we can achieve the ILO's goal: 'to promote rights at work, encourage decent employment opportunities, enhance social protection and strengthen dialogue on work-related issues' (http://www.ilo.org/global/about-the-ilo/mission-and-objectives/lang-en/index.htm).

References

Adler, P. S., & Borys, B. (1996). Two types of bureaucracy: Enabling and coercive. *Administrative Science Quarterly, 41*(1), 61-89.

Bakker, A. B., & Demerouti, E. (2007). The job demands-resources model: State of the art. *Journal of Managerial Psychology, 22*(3), 309–328.

Bakker, A. B., Tims, M., & Derks, D. (2012). Proactive personality and job performance: The role of job crafting and work engagement. *Human Relations, 65*(10), 1359–1378.

Barrett, G. V., & Bass, B. M. (1976). Cross-cultural issues in industrial and organizational psychology. In M. Dunnette (Ed.), *Handbook of industrial and organizational psychology* (pp. 1639–1686). Chicago: Rand McNally.
Belkic, K. L., Landsbergin, P. A., Schnall, P. L., & Baker, D. (2004). Is job strain a major source of cardiovascular disease risk? *Scandinavian Journal of Work, Environment & Health, 30*, 85–128.
Berg, J. M., Wrzesniewski, A., & Dutton, J. E. (2010). Perceiving and responding to challenges in job crafting at different ranks: When proactivity requires adaptivity. *Journal of Organizational Behavior, 31*(2–3), 158–186.
Boyle, T., Fritschi, L., Heyworth, J., & Bull, F. (2011). Long-term sedentary work and the risk of subsite-specific colorectal cancer. *American Journal of Epidemiology, 173*(10), 1183–1191.
Bradlow, H. (2015) The impact of emerging technologies in the workforce of the future. In *Australia's future workforce?* (pp. 38–47). The Committee for Economic Development of Australia.
Brewer, M. B., & Chen, Y. (2007). Where (and who) are collectives in collectivism: Toward conceptual clarification of individualism and collectivism. *Psychological Review, 114*, 133–151.
Cheng, Y. (2015). Policy responses to work-related stress: Examining Taiwan's experiences from a welfare state regime perspective. *Safety Science, 78*, 111–116.
Choi, B., Schnall, P. L., Yang, H., Dobson, M., Landsbergis, P., Israel, L., et al. (2010). Sedentary work, low physical job demand, and obesity in US workers. *American Journal of Industrial Medicine, 53*(11), 1088–1101.
Crawford, E. R., LePine, J. A., & Rich, B. L. (2010). Linking job demands and resources to employee engagement and burnout: A theoretical extension and meta-analytic test. *Journal of Applied Psychology, 95*(5), 834.
De Lange, A. H., Taris, T. W., Kompier, M. A., Houtman, I. L., & Bongers, P. M. (2003). "The very best of the millennium": Longitudinal research and the demand-control-(support) model. *Journal of Occupational Health Psychology, 8*(4), 282–395.
Demerouti, E., & Bakker, A. B. (2011). The job demands-resources model: Challenges for future research. *SA Journal of Industrial Psychology, 37*(2), 01–09.
De Treville, S., & Antonakis, J. (2006). Could lean production job design be intrinsically motivating? Contextual, configurational, and levels-of-analysis issues. *Journal of Operations Management, 24*(2), 99–123.
Dollard, M. F., & Bakker, A. B. (2010). Psychosocial safety climate as a precursor to conducive work environments, psychological health problems, and employee engagement. *Journal of Occupational and Organizational Psychology, 83*(3), 579–599.
Dollard, M., Bailey, T., McLinton, S., Richards, P., McTernan, W., Taylor, A., et al. (2012). *The Australian workplace barometer: Report on psychosocial safety climate and worker health in Australia*. Safe Work Australia: Canberra.
Emery, F. E., & Trist, E. L. (1969). Sociotechnical systems. In F. E. Emery (Ed.), *Systems thinking* (pp. 281–296). London: Penguin Books.
Erez, M. (2010). Commentary Culture and job design. *Journal of Organizational Behaviour, 31*, 389–400.
Erez, M., & Earley, P. C. (1993). *Culture, self-identity, and work*. New York: Oxford University Press.
e Sá, P. M., & de Sá, A. C. P. (2015). Tensions raised by TQM demands upon work design in technologically controlled environments: The Case of a Call Centre. In M. Peris-Ortiz, J. Álvarez-García & C. R. Armengot (Eds.), *Achieving competitive advantage through quality management* (pp. 253–264). Springer.
Fisher, C. D., Minbashian, A., Beckmann, N., & Wood, R. E. (2013). Task appraisals, emotions, and performance goal orientation. *Journal of Applied Psychology, 98*(2), 364.
Gagné, M., & Deci, E. L. (2005). Self-determination theory and work motivation. *Journal of Organizational Behavior, 26*(4), 331–362.
Gibson, C. B., & Birkinshaw, J. (2004). The antecedents, consequences, and mediating role of organizational ambidexterity. *Academy of Management Journal, 47*(2), 209–226.

Grant, A. M. (2007). Relational job design and the motivation to make a prosocial difference. *Academy of Management Review, 32*(2), 393–417.
Grant, A. M. (2008). Employees without a cause: The motivational effects of prosocial impact in public service. *International Public Management Journal, 11*(1), 48–66.
Grant, A. M., & Parker, S. K. (2009). Redesigning work design theories: The rise of relational and proactive perspectives. *The Academy of Management Annals, 3*(1), 317–375.
Grant, A. M., Fried, Y., Parker, S. K., & Frese, M. (2010). Putting job design in context: Introduction to the special issue. *Journal of Organizational Behavior, 31*(2–3), 145–157.
Hackman, J. R., & Oldham, G. R. (1976). Motivation through the design of work: Test of a theory. *Organizational Behavior & Human Performance, 16*, 250–279.
Hackman, J. R., & Oldham, G. R. (1980). *Work redesign*. Reading, MA: Addison-Wesley.
Humphrey, S. E., Nahrgang, J. D., & Morgeson, F. P. (2007). Integrating motivational, social, and contextual work design features: A meta-analytic summary and theoretical extension of the work design literature. *Journal of Applied Psychology, 92*(5), 1332–1356.
Idris, M. A., & Dollard, M. F. (2014). A multi-level study of psychosocial safety climate, challenge and hindrance demands, employee exhaustion, engagement and physical health. In M. F. Dollard, A. Shimazu, R. B. Nordin, P .Brough, & M. R. Tuckey (Eds.), *Psychosocial factors at work in the Asia Pacific* (pp. 127–143). Springer Netherlands.
Kalleberg, A. L. (2011). *Good jobs, bad jobs: The rise of polarized and precarious employment systems in the United States, 1970s to 2000s*. New York: Russell Sage Found.
Karasek Jr, R. A. (1979). Job demands, job decision latitude, and mental strain: Implications for job redesign. *Administrative Science Quarterly, 24*(2), 285–308.
Karasek, R., & Theorell, T. (1990). Healthy work: Stress, productivity, and the reconstruction of working life. *The American Journal of Public Health, 80*, 1013–1014.
Kelliher, C., & Anderson, D. (2009). Doing more with less? Flexible working practices and the intensification of work. *Human Relations, 63*(1), 83–106.
Kooij, D. T. (2015). Successful aging at work: The active role of employees. *Work, Aging and Retirement, 1*(4), 309–319.
LePine, J. A., Podsakoff, N. P., & LePine, M. A. (2005). A meta-analytic test of the challenge stressor–hindrance stressor framework: An explanation for inconsistent relationships among stressors and performance. *Academy of Management Journal, 48*(5), 764–775.
Li, J., & Angerer, P. (2014). Work-family conflict and worker wellbeing in china. In M. F. Dollard, A. Shimazu, R. B. Nordin, P. Brough & M. R. Tuckey (Eds.), *Psychosocial factors at work in the Asia Pacific* (pp. 309–321). Springer Netherlands.
Markus, H. R., & Kitayama, S. (1991). Culture and self: Implications for cognition, emotion and motivation. *Psychological Review, 98*, 224–253.
Morgeson, F. P., & Humphrey, S. E. (2006). The work design questionnaire (WDQ): Developing and validating a comprehensive measure for assessing job design and the nature of work. *Journal of Applied Psychology, 91*, 1321–1339.
Morgeson, F. P., Dierdorff, E. C., & Hmurovic, J. L. (2010). Work design in situ: Understanding the role of occupational and organizational context. *Journal of Organizational Behavior, 31*(2–3), 351–360.
Nahrgang, J. D., Morgeson, F. P., & Hofmann, D. A. (2011). Safety at work: A meta-analytic investigation of the link between job demands, job resources, burnout, engagement, and safety outcomes. *Journal of Applied Psychology, 96*, 71–94.
Ng, T. W. H., & Feldman, D. C. (2010). The relationships of age with job attitudes: A meta-analysis. *Personnel Psychology, 63*, 677–718.
Ohly, S., & Fritz, C. (2010). Work characteristics, challenge appraisal, creativity, and proactive behavior: A multi-level study. *Journal of Organizational Behavior, 31*(4), 543–565.
Olson-Buchanan, J. B., & Boswell, W. (2006). Blurring boundaries: Correlates of integration and segmentation between work and non-work. *Journal of Vocational Behavior, 68*, 432–445.
O'Reilly, C., & Tushman, M. (2008). *Ambidexterity as a dynamic capability: Resolving the innovator's dilemma. Research in Organizational Behavior, 28*, 185-206.

Osterma, P., & Shulman, B. (2011). *Good jobs America: Making work better for everyone*. New York: Russell Sage Found.

Parker, S. K. (2014). Beyond motivation: Job and work design for development, health, ambidexterity, and more. *Annual Review of Psychology, 65*, 661–691.

Parker, S. K., & Ohly, S. (2009). Extending the reach of job design theory: Going beyond the job characteristics model. In A. Wilkinson, N. Bacon, T. Redman & S. Snell (Eds.), *The Sage handbook of human resource management* (pp. 269–286). London: Sage.

Parker, S. K., & Wall, T. (1998). *Job and work design: Organizing work to promote well-being and effectiveness*. London: Sage Publications.

Parker, S. K., Bindl, U. K., & Strauss, K. (2010). Making things happen: A model of proactive motivation. *Journal of Management, 36*, 827–856.

Parker, S. K., Morgeson, F. P., & Johns, G. (in press). Work design theory and research: Looking back over 100 years and looking forward to the future. *Journal of Applied Psychology*. Invited article, Special Centennial Issue.

Parker, S. K., Wall, T. D., & Cordery, J. L. (2001). Future work design research and practice: Towards an elaborated model of work design. *Journal of Occupational and Organizational Psychology, 74*(4), 413–440.

Parker, S. K., Johnson, A., Collins, C., & Nguyen, H. (2013). Making the most of structural support: Moderating influence of employees' clarity and negative affect. *Academy of Management Journal, 56*(3), 867–892.

Perrow, C. (2011). *Normal accidents: Living with high risk technologies*. Princeton: Princeton University Press.

Petrou, P., Demerouti, E., Peeters, M. C., Schaufeli, W. B., & Hetland, J. (2012). Crafting a job on a daily basis: Contextual correlates and the link to work engagement. *Journal of Organizational Behavior, 33*(8), 1120–1141.

Robert, C., Probst, T. M., Martocchio, J. J., Drasgow, F., & Lawler, J. J. (2000). Empowerment and continuous improvement in the United States, Mexico, Poland, and India: Predicting fit on the basis of the dimensions of power distance and individualism. *Journal of Applied Psychology, 85*(5), 643.

Rodin, J. (2014). Health, control, and aging. In M. M. Baltes & P.B. Baltes (Eds.), *The psychology of control and aging* (pp. 139–165). New York: Psychology Press.

Slemp, G. R., & Vella-Brodrick, D. A. (2013). The job crafting questionnaire: A new scale to measure the extent to which employees engage in job crafting. International Journal of Wellbeing, 3(2), 126–146.

Slemp, G. R., & Vella-Brodrick, D. A. (2014). Optimising employee mental health: the relationship between intrinsic need satisfaction, job crafting, and employee well-being. *Journal of Happiness Studies, 15*(4), 957–977.

Smith, A. (1776). *The wealth of nations*. London: W. Strahan and T. Cadell.

Straker, L., & Mathiassen, S. E. (2009). Increased physical workloads in modern work—A necessity for better health and performance? *Ergonomics, 52*(10), 1215–1225.

Taylor, F. W. (1911). *Scientific management*. New York, NY: Harper Row.

Tims, M., & Bakker, A. B. (2010). Job crafting: Towards a new model of individual job redesign. *SA Journal of Industrial Psychology, 36*(2), 1 9.

Tims, M., Bakker, A. B., & Derks, D. (2012). Development and validation of the job crafting scale. *Journal of Vocational Behavior, 80*(1), 173–186.

Torraco, R. J. (2005). Work design theory: A review and critique with implications for human resource development. *Human Resource Development Quarterly, 16*(1), 85–109.

Tornau, K., & Frese, M. (2013). Construct clean—up in proactivity research: A meta—analysis on the nomological net of work—related proactivity concepts and their incremental validities. *Applied Psychology, 62*(1), 44–96.

Trist, E. L., & Bamforth, K. W. (1951). Some social and psychological consequences of the Longwall method of coal-getting. *Human Relations, 4*, 3–38.

Warr, P. B. (2011). *Work, happiness, and unhappiness*. Hoboken: Taylor and Francis.

Weick, K. E., Sutcliffe, K. M., & Obstfeld, D. (2008). Organizing for high reliability: Processes of collective mindfulness. *Crisis Management, 3*, 81–123.

Wrzesniewski, A., & Dutton, J. E. (2001). Crafting a job: Revisioning employees as active crafters of their work. *Academy of Management Review, 26*(2), 179–201.

Wu, C. H., Griffin, M. A., & Parker, S. K. (2015). Developing agency through good work: Longitudinal effects of job autonomy and skill utilization on locus of control. *Journal of Vocational Behavior, 89*, 102–108.

Yang, N., Chen, C. C., Choi, J., & Zou, Y. (2000). Sources of work-family conflict: A Sino-U.S. comparison of the effects of work and family demands. *Academy of Management Journal, 43*, 113–123.

Zacher, H., & Griffin, B. (2015). Older workers' age as a moderator of the relationship between career adaptability and job satisfaction. *Work, Aging and Retirement, 1*(2), 227–236.

Chapter 8
Prevalence, Distribution, and Trends of Workplace Violence and Its Associated Health Problems: Findings from National Surveys of Taiwan

Yawen Cheng and Li-Chung Pien

Abstract Workplace violence is increasingly recognized as an important occupational health issue in Taiwan. This chapter provides an overview of the problem and policy debates concerning workplace violence in Taiwan, and presents empirical findings on its distributions, trends, antecedents, and associated health risks based on survey data of the general working population. Results showed that workplace violence in the forms of physical violence, verbal violence, psychological violence, and sexual harassment had increased markedly from 2010 to 2013. In general, women were more likely than men to experience workplace violence. In health care sectors, women had particularly higher prevalence rates of workplace violence than men, which may attribute to a greater gender inequality in health care settings. Results from multilevel analyses with adjustment of workers' actual experiences of workplace violence showed that neighborhood-level workplace violence was positively associated with mental health risks in women but not in men. This finding suggested that working in an environment where aggressive or abusive behaviors are more prevalent may entail a greater mental health risk to women. Research improvement should be made in many aspects, ranging from the measures for workplace violence, study designs to investigate the casual mechanisms of workplace violence and health consequences, to the strategies for effective prevention. Furthermore, as the nature of workplace violence are embedded in social context, researchers, and occupational health practitioners should pay attention to contextual factors that might influence societal tolerance of abusive work practices and workers' vulnerability to health impacts of workplace violence.

Keywords Workplace violence · Survey · Multi-level analysis · Mental health · Gender

Y. Cheng (✉) · L.-C. Pien
Institute of Health Policy and Management, College of Public Health, National Taiwan University, Taipei, Taiwan
e-mail: yawen617@gmail.com

A. Shimazu et al. (eds.), *Psychosocial Factors at Work in the Asia Pacific*,
DOI 10.1007/978-3-319-44400-0_8

Introduction

Workplace violence is recognized as a serious psychosocial work hazard in many countries. According to the International Labor Organization (ILO), workplace violence is defined as "incidents where staff are abused, threatened or assaulted in circumstances related to their work, including commuting to and from work, involving an explicit or implicit challenge to their safety, well-being or health." Violent incidents in the workplace can be physical or psychological, and the source may be from people outside the work organization, such as customers, clients or strangers, or from those within the work organization, including co-workers and supervisors (Martino 2002). In contrast to the term "workplace bullying," which refers specifically to repeated and regular mistreatment with escalating aggression, long duration, and power imbalance between the perpetrator and the victim, the term workplace violence refers to a wide spectrum of conditions, ranging from physical attacks, homicide, verbal abuse, threat, bullying, mobbing to harassment (Chappell and Di Martino 2006).

There have been numerous empirical studies from western countries examining the prevalence and the forms of workplace violence in general working populations (Harrell 2011; Parent-Thirion et al. 2012; Venema and Klauw 2012). For instance, results from the European Working Conditions Survey of 2010 showed that prevalence rates of workers who had been exposed to verbal violence, psychological bullying, physical violence and sexual harassment over the previous month were 11, 4, 2, and 1 %, respectively (Parent-Thirion et al. 2012). High risk occupations for workplace violence have been recognized including health care workers, policemen, correctional officers, teachers, social workers, taxi drivers, sales personnel, and workers who interact frequently with certain clients in stressful conditions (Harrell 2011; Langeland 2012; Parent-Thirion et al. 2012; Pedersen and Christiansen 2005: 235). Certain work characteristics prone to workplace violence have also been identified, such as night work, shift work (Camerino et al. 2008), work involving time pressure and heavy workloads (Estryn-Behar et al. 2008; Hills and Joyce 2013), employment insecurity, interpersonal conflicts within the work organization and low workplace justice (Hills and Joyce 2013; Mehdad et al. 2012; Pien et al. 2014; Roche et al. 2010). In addition to physical health harm, victims of workplace violence have been found to have greater mental health risks such as anxiety, depression, and stress-related problems such as sleep disorders, burnout, and sickness absence (Lallukka et al. 2011; Mayhew and Chappell 2007; Takaki et al. 2010). Negative impacts of workplace violence on work organizations have also been documented, including reduced work morale, deteriorated work performance, and increased costs associated with workers' compensation and corporate administrative expenses. However, studies on this topic have been largely conducted in western populations. Because workplace violence is likely to be perceived and responded to quite differently across different cultures and social circumstances, the prevalence, antecedents and health consequences might be experienced differently in East Asian populations.

This chapter begins with an overview of the problem of workplace violence in Taiwan, following by a brief review of analytical framework guiding epidemiologic studies on workplace violence and existing evidences from epidemiologic studies conducted in East Asian populations. In the second half of this chapter, we present empirical findings on the distributions, trends, antecedents, and health risks of workplace violence in the general working population of Taiwan.

Workplace Violence in Taiwan

In Taiwan, workplace violence has been a hot topic in recent years, as cases of workers being attacked or harassed by clients, supervisors or co-workers were increasingly reported by the media. The reported victims of workplace violence came from a wide range of occupations, including health care workers, social workers, security guards, salespersons and service workers, and the forms of workplace violence ranged from verbal abuses, sexual harassment to bodily attacks. Among these cases, increased attention has been on patient-to-staff violence in medical settings which appears to be on the rise since the early 2000s. In 2002, the Ministry of Health and Welfare promulgated a guideline for hospitals to strengthen security measures. The mostly publicized event in recent years occurred in December 2013, which involved a young female nurse who was slapped in the face by a township councilor because the latter's request to obtain medical information of her hospitalized father over the phone was refused. This event, after being publicized by the media, evoked a strong reaction from the nursing community, who had been for years protesting against prolonged working hours and inadequate labor rights protection. The public reacted sympathetically to the resentment from the nursing community, prompting the Ministry of Health and Welfare to amend the Medical Care Act. The amendment, passed by the Congress in January 2014, makes any violent act against medical personnel an indictable offense with a high level of punishment.

In response to growing public concerns regarding workplace violence, the Ministry of Labor of Taiwan had also amended the Occupational Safety and Health Act (OSHAct) in 2013 by introducing a new clause (Article 6, Paragraph 2), which stipulates that for enterprises with a workforce of 100 employees or more, "the employer shall properly plan and adopt necessary safety and health measures to prevent physical or mental harm caused by wrongful actions of others during the execution of job duties." The amended OSHAct has been formally implemented since July 2014. However, its feasibility has been challenged, due to the vague definition of "wrongful actions" and unclear directions for employers concerning the scope and content of "necessary safety and health measures."

Workplace Violence and Health Consequences

Analytical Framework of Psychosocial Work Hazards and Health

Workplace violence, defined as any form of aggressive or abusive behavior, is a type of psychosocial work hazard. A schematic framework linking psychosocial work hazards, reversible health responses and irreversible health outcomes is presented in Fig. 8.1 (Hurrell and McLaney 1988; Landsbergis 2009; Landsbergis et al. 2014).

In epidemiologic studies, workplace violence is often classified into the following four types: physical violence, verbal violence, psychological violence, and sexual harassment. It is known that how psychosocial work hazards are perceived and reacted could be greatly modified by personal factors, such as worker's personality, experience, work attitudes, work expectation, resources for coping and the co-existence of other stressors. It can also be expected that how aggressive behaviors are interpreted and responded are largely affected by surrounding cultural and social conditions. For instance, in a society or work organization where abusive behaviors are allowed or even encouraged, victims of workplace violence would be expected to tolerate the situation and to take on the consequences. The perception of workplace violence and workers' tolerance to workplace violence are expected to be greatly influenced by culture-specific factors as well as the presence and extent of labor protection policies. However, to our knowledge, the influences of

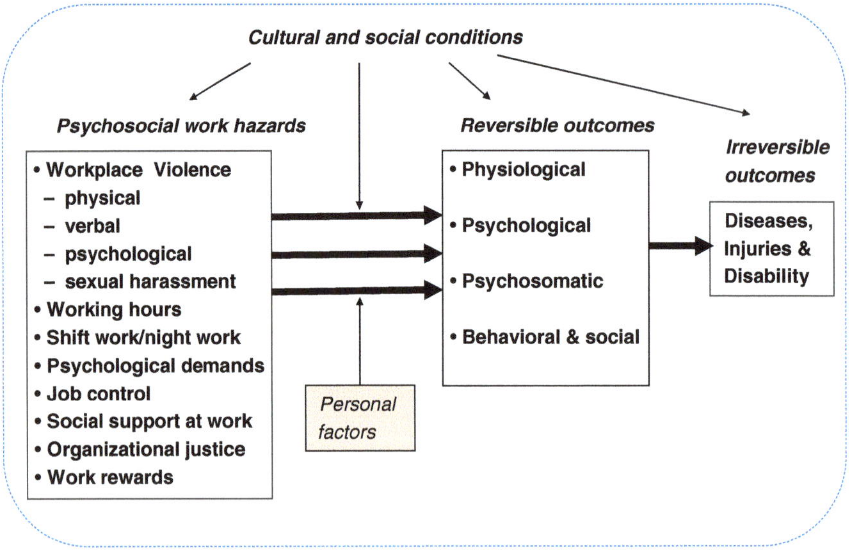

Fig. 8.1 Analytical framework of psychosocial work hazards and health

contextual factors on the perception of workplace violence and its impacts on workers' health and well-being have rarely been addressed in East Asian populations.

Medical Violence

In the East Asian countries, workplace violence has attracted considerable public attention and research interest, but most of the studies have focused on medical violence, especially patient-to-staff violence in physical nature (KOSHA 2012; Lee et al. 2014; Park 2013). In Taiwan, Chen et al. (2008) surveyed a total of 222 nursing workers at a psychiatric hospital, and reported very high one-year prevalence rates of verbal abuse, physical violence, bullying/mobbing and sexual harassment of 51, 35, 16, and 10 %, respectively. In another questionnaire survey of 521 nurses by Pai and Lee, the 1-year prevalence was 51 % for verbal abuse, 30 % for bullying/mobbing, 20 % for physical violence, and 13 % for sexual harassment (Pai and Lee 2011). These findings suggested that workplace violence in all forms are quite common in health care settings in Taiwan.

Workplace Bullying and Workplace Violence in the General Working Population

While workplace bullying and power harassment have been intensively studied in many western countries and in Japan, this issue has rarely been investigated in Taiwan. In Japan, a recent survey of 699 general workers who volunteered to answer a survey questionnaire in the Tokyo area revealed a prevalence of personally experienced workplace bullying of 15 % over the past 6 months (Naito 2013). Another study from Japan based on a representative sample of community-based working population showed that over the past month prior to the survey, 6 % of respondents had experienced workplace bullying (Tsuno et al. 2015). In a recent study from South Korea, Lee et al. utilized data from the 2011 Korean Working Conditions Survey of 29,171 employees and reported that the prevalence rates of verbal abuse, threats or humiliating behaviors and unwanted sexual attention over the past month were 4.8, 1.5, and 1.0 %, respectively (Lee et al. 2014). Studies from South Korea and Japan have consistently shown that temporary employees, workers with long working hours, night workers, shift workers, and workers with low socioeconomic status were at an increased risk of experiencing workplace bullying (Lee et al. 2014; Tsuno et al. 2015). In Taiwan, there have been growing interests in the problems of workplace bullying as well as various types of workplace violence in working people besides health care workers.

In the following section, we present empirical evidence of workplace violence in the general working population of Taiwan.

Prevalence, Distribution and Trends of Workplace Violence and Its Associated Health Problems in General Employees of Taiwan

Survey Methods

The Ministry of Labor of Taiwan has conducted nationwide cross-sectional surveys of the general working population every 3–5 years since 1994. In each round, a representative sample of employees in Taiwan was selected by a two-stage random sampling process. In the first stage, all districts and villages throughout Taiwan were grouped into 23 urbanization levels, and from each level, districts and villages were randomly selected. In the second stage, a random sample of households was selected within each district or village, and residents of the sampled households who were working at the time of the survey were identified and invited to participate in the survey.

A standardized self-administered questionnaire was delivered by a trained interviewer to the selected household, which was collected after one week by the same interviewer and onsite checking was performed to ensure its completeness. We utilized cross-sectional data from the surveys conducted in 2010 and 2013. The questionnaire included items which assessed the experiences of workplace violence encountered over the previous 12 months, including physical violence (such as beating, kicking, pushing, pinching, pulling), verbal violence (such as abusive language, verbal harassment, cynical comments), psychological violence (such as threats, intimidation, discrimination, exclusion, bullying, harassment), and sexual harassment (such as sexually suggestive and inappropriate behavior). Psychosocial work characteristics were assessed, which include five items for psychological job demands (work fast, work hectic, excessive work, no enough time, work required concentration), three items for job control (learn new thing, no repetitive work, own decision), 1 item for physical job demands, one item for job insecurity, and seven items for workplace justice (fair responsibility, fair work rewards, fair evaluation, respect, trust, transparency, reliable information). Items for psychosocial job demands and job control were adopted from the Chinese version of the Job Content Questionnaire (C-JCQ), which was based on Karasek's Job Strain model. This model postulates that a combination of high demands and low control causes high job strain and leads to negative health outcomes (Cheng et al. 2003; Karasek and Theorell 1990). Workplace justice is defined as the extent to which employees are treated fairly and with respect in the workplace (Colquitt 2001; Moorman 1991). The validity of the Chinese version of the 9-item scale can be found elsewhere (Cheng et al. 2011). Due to the constraint on the length of questionnaire, only selected items were included in the surveys. Responses of these items were all recorded on a four-point Likert scale. Self-rated health status, quality of sleep, mental health status and level of job satisfaction were also assessed.

The study population of the survey of 2010 consisted of 9509 male and 7777 female employees, and the study population of the survey of 2013, which was drawn independently, consisted of 9976 male and 8054 female employees.

Prevalence, Distributions, and Trends of Workplace Violence

The demographic characteristics and the prevalence of the four types of workplace violence and major health outcomes in the surveys of 2010 and 2013 are summarized in Table 8.1. Notable increases in the prevalence of all the four types of workplace violence were observed from 2010 to 2013.

In 2013, the percentages of employees who had experienced any type of workplace violence over the past year were 9.45 % in men and 10.62 % in women. Among male employees, security guards were found to have the highest prevalence of any workplace violence (16.71 %), following by low-skilled manual workers (11.54 %). Among female employees, high prevalence rates of workplace violence were found in health care workers (15.00 %) and workers in financial and business service sectors (13.88 %).

Among the four types of workplace violence, verbal violence was the most common, following by psychological violence, physical violence and sexual harassment. This finding was similar to that from other countries (Demir and Rodwell 2012; Lehto 2004; Lo et al. 2012; Parent-Thirion et al. 2012). Our findings also suggest that in general, women are more likely than men to suffer workplace violence in all forms except physical violence. However, in health care settings, women reported higher workplace violence in all forms: the one-year prevalence in men and women, respectively, was 6.10 and 11.49 % for verbal violence, 3.66 and 4.66 % for psychological violence, 2.44 and 2.48 % for physical violence, and 1.22 and 2.17 % for sexual harassment (Pien et al. 2014).

An examination across age groups revealed that younger employees were in general at higher risk for workplace violence, except for physical violence which was found to be more prevalent in men in the age range of 45–54 years. Furthermore, unfavorable work characteristics such as shift work, long working hours, heavy workloads, low and medium workplace justice and employment insecurity were found to be associated with higher risks for workplace violence (Table 8.2).

It is especially worth noticing that as compared to those who reported high workplace justice, male and female employees who reported low workplace justice had a 6.03- and 5.00-fold increased risks, respectively, for workplace violence (Table 8.3).

Table 8.1 Demographic characteristics, experiences of workplace violence over the past 12 months and health outcomes of participants in the 2010 and 2013 surveys

	Male				Female			
	2010 (*n* = 9509)		2013 (*n* = 9976)		2010 (*n* = 7777)		2013 (*n* = 8054)	
	n	%/SD	*n*	%/SD	*n*	%/SD	*n*	%/SD
Age (years): mean (SD)	40.89	10.01	40.54	11.26	39.32	9.69	38.86	10.89
15–24	–	–	641	6.43 %	–	–	688	8.54 %
25–34	3124	32.85 %	2821	28.28 %	3006	38.65 %	2555	31.72 %
35–44	2851	29.98 %	2781	27.88 %	2267	29.15 %	2223	27.60 %
45–54	2457	25.84 %	2484	24.90 %	1947	25.04 %	1827	22.68 %
55–65	1077	11.33 %	1175	11.78 %	557	7.16 %	732	9.09 %
66 above	–	–	74	0.74 %	–	–	29	0.36 %
Education level								
≤Junior high	1986	20.89 %	1962	19.67 %	1365	17.55 %	1352	16.79 %
Senior high	4805	50.53 %	4796	48.06 %	3900	50.15 %	3754	46.61 %
University and above	2718	28.58 %	3218	32.26 %	2512	32.30 %	2948	36.60 %
Any violence[a]	753	7.90 %	943	9.45 %	727	9.35 %	856	10.62 %
Physical	77	0.81 %	150	1.50 %	37	0.48 %	70	0.87 %
Verbal	647	6.80 %	805	8.07 %	582	7.48 %	695	8.63 %
Psychological	322	3.39 %	407	4.08 %	316	4.06 %	370	4.59 %
Sexual harassment	36	0.38 %	53	0.53 %	132	1.70 %	182	2.26 %
SRH (self-rated health)								
Good	6077	63.91 %	6361	63.76 %	4850	62.36 %	5100	63.32 %
Bad	3432	36.09 %	3615	36.24 %	2927	37.64 %	2954	36.68 %
Mental health by BSRS[b]	–	–	2.75	3.23	–	–	3.11	3.38
In normal range	–	–	8514	85.35 %	–	–	6645	82.55 %
Mild- severe	–	–	3938	39.47 %	–	–	3260	40.48 %
Data missing	–	–	1	0.01 %	–	–	4	0.05 %
Sleep problems								
No	7711	81.09 %	8873	88.94 %	5948	76.48 %	6893	85.58 %
Yes	1798	18.91 %	1103	11.06 %	1829	23.52 %	1161	14.42 %

[a]Numbers of the four types do not add up to "any violence" because some victims experienced multiple types of violence
[b]Brief Symptom Rating Scale

The fact that workers with disadvantaged social positions were at higher risks for workplace violence has been consistently documented in previous studies (Estryn-Behar et al. 2008; Hills and Joyce 2013; Kamchuchat et al. 2008; Lawoko et al. 2004; Mehdad et al. 2012; Pien et al. 2014; Roche et al. 2010; Venema and

Table 8.2 Prevalence of workplace violence by age, education level and work characteristics in men and women (based on the 2013 survey data)

Variable	*N*	Male									
		VV (*n* = 805)		PSV (*n* = 407)		PV (*n* = 150)		SH (*n* = 53)		Any violence (*n* = 943)	
		n	(%)	*n*	(%)	*n*	(%)	*n*	(%)	*n*	(%)
Age											
15–24	641	47	7.33	25	3.90	6	0.94	7	1.09	54	8.42
25–34	2821	246	8.72	132	4.68	39	1.38	14	0.50	287	10.17
35–44	2781	238	8.56	119	4.28	43	1.55	14	0.50	283	10.18
45–54	2484	186	7.49	92	3.70	47	1.89	9	0.36	220	8.86
55–65	1175	84	7.15	38	3.23	15	1.28	9	0.77	95	8.09
66 above	74	4	5.41	1	1.35	0	0	0	0	4	5.41
Education level											
≦Junior high	1962	158	8.05	65	3.31	33	1.68	14	0.71	184	9.38
Senior high	4796	393	8.19	195	4.07	88	1.83	24	0.50	460	9.59
University and above	3218	254	7.89	147	4.57	29	0.90	15	0.47	299	9.29
Work shift											
Fixed day shift	7611	511	6.71	256	3.36	71	0.93	35	0.46	601	7.90
Night/Rotated shift	2264	281	12.41	144	6.36	75	3.31	18	0.80	327	14.44
Missing	101	13	12.87	7	6.93	4	3.96	0	0	15	14.85
Work hours/week (h)											
≦48 h	8510	638	7.50	331	3.89	119	1.40	49	0.58	755	8.87
>48 h	1466	167	11.39	76	5.18	31	2.11	4	0.27	188	12.82
Job control(3 items)											

(continued)

Table 8.2 (continued)

Variable	N	Male									
		VV (n = 805)		PSV (n = 407)		PV (n = 150)		SH (n = 53)		Any violence (n = 943)	
		n	(%)	n	(%)	n	(%)	n	(%)	n	(%)
High	601	52	8.65	23	3.83	7	1.16	4	0.67	63	10.48
Medium	7573	575	7.59	288	3.80	115	1.52	42	0.55	664	8.77
Low	1802	178	9.88	96	5.33	28	1.55	7	0.39	216	11.99
Psychological demands (5 items)											
High	3077	426	13.84	219	7.12	56	1.82	13	0.42	489	15.89
Medium	4651	264	5.68	136	2.92	62	1.33	26	0.56	315	6.77
Low	2248	115	5.12	52	2.31	32	1.42	14	0.62	139	6.18
Missing	–	–	–	–	–	–	–	–	–	–	–
Workplace justice (7 items)											
High	781	33	4.23	18	2.30	8	1.02	4	0.51	37	4.74
Medium	8219	571	6.95	264	3.21	117	1.42	41	0.50	675	8.21
Low	894	200	22.37	122	13.65	25	2.80	8	0.89	228	25.50
Missing	82	1	1.22	3	3.66	0	0	0	0	3	3.66
Physically demanding											
Yes	5333	539	10.11	259	4.86	108	2.03	36	0.68	617	11.57
No	4634	265	5.72	147	3.17	41	0.88	17	0.37	324	6.99
Missing	9	1	11.11	1	11.11	1	11.11	0	0	2	11.11
Employment security											

(continued)

Table 8.2 (continued)

Variable	N	Male									
		VV (n = 805)		PSV (n = 407)		PV (n = 150)		SH (n = 53)		Any violence (n = 943)	
		n	(%)	n	(%)	n	(%)	n	(%)	n	(%)
Yes	4762	292	6.13	147	3.09	79	1.66	24	0.50	335	7.03
No	5207	513	9.85	260	4.99	71	1.36	29	0.56	608	11.68
Missing	7	0	0	0	0	0	0	0	0	0	0
Variable	N	Female									
		VV (n = 695)		PSV (n = 370)		PV (n = 70)		SH (n = 182)		Any violence (n = 856)	
		n	(%)	n	(%)	n	(%)	n	(%)	n	(%)
Age											
15–24	688	65	9.45	28	4.07	6	0.87	21	3.05	82	11.92
25–34	2555	262	10.25	139	5.44	25	0.98	74	2.90	319	12.49
35–44	2223	180	8.10	96	4.32	12	0.54	45	2.02	221	9.94
45–54	1827	128	7.01	82	4.49	14	0.77	29	1.59	161	8.81
55–65	732	57	7.79	23	3.14	11	1.5	12	1.64	69	9.43
66 above	29	3	10.34	2	6.90	2	6.9	1	3.45	4	13.79
Education level											
≤Junior high	1352	97	7.17	46	3.40	16	1.18	29	2.14	124	9.17
Senior high	3754	299	7.96	151	4.02	26	0.69	99	2.64	371	9.88
University and above	2948	299	10.14	173	5.87	28	0.95	54	1.83	361	12.25
Work shift											
Fixed day shift	6463	471	7.29	263	4.07	44	0.68	100	1.55	584	9.04
Night/Rotated shift	1525	220	14.43	106	6.95	25	1.64	81	5.31	268	17.57
Missing	66	4	6.06	1	1.52	1	1.52	1	1.52	4	6.06

(continued)

Table 8.2 (continued)

Variable	*N*	Female									
		VV ($n = 695$)		PSV ($n = 370$)		PV ($n = 70$)		SH ($n = 182$)		Any violence ($n = 856$)	
		n	(%)	*n*	(%)	*n*	(%)	*n*	(%)	*n*	(%)
Work hours/week (h)											
≦48 h	7118	574	8.06	308	4.33	60	0.84	156	2.19	716	10.06
>48 h	936	121	12.93	62	6.62	10	1.07	26	2.78	140	14.96
Job control (3 items)											
High	446	47	10.54	27	6.05	4	0.90	12	2.69	55	12.33
Medium	5923	471	7.95	244	4.12	52	0.88	124	2.09	581	9.81
Low	1685	177	10.50	99	5.88	14	0.83	46	2.73	220	13.06
Psychological demands (5 items)											
High	2482	394	15.87	212	2.26	30	1.21	78	3.14	471	18.98
Medium	3665	222	6.06	115	3.14	26	0.71	63	1.72	270	7.37
Low	1906	79	4.14	43	8.54	14	0.73	41	2.15	115	6.03
Missing	1	–	–	–	–	–	–	–	–	–	–
Workplace justice (7 items)											
High	640	37	5.78	13	2.03	4	0.63	6	0.94	41	6.41
Medium	6665	491	7.37	240	3.60	50	0.75	137	2.06	619	9.29
Low	689	165	23.95	114	16.55	16	2.32	38	5.52	193	28.01
Missing	60	2	3.33	3	5.00	0	0	1	1.67	3	5.00
Physically demanding											
Yes	3284	409	12.45	207	6.30	50	1.52	101	3.08	480	14.62
No	4763	286	6.00	163	3.42	20	0.42	81	1.70	376	7.89
Missing	7	0	0	0	0	0	0	0	0	0	0

(continued)

Table 8.2 (continued)

Variable	N	Female									
		VV (n = 695)		PSV (n = 370)		PV (n = 70)		SH (n = 182)		Any violence (n = 856)	
		n	(%)	n	(%)	n	(%)	n	(%)	n	(%)
Employment security											
Yes	3774	256	6.78	134	3.55	31	0.82	59	1.56	314	8.32
No	4264	437	10.25	236	5.53	39	0.91	122	2.86	539	12.64
Missing	16	2	12.50	0	0	0	0	1	6.25	3	18.75

Type of workplace violence: *PV* physical violence, *VV* verbal violence, *PSV* psychological violence, *SH* sexual harassment

Table 8.3 Logistic regression models of any workplace violence over the past 12 months in men and women (based on the 2013 survey data)

Variable	Male		Female	
	OR	(95 % CI)	OR	(95 % CI)
Age				
15–24	1.00		1.00	
25–34	1.21	(0.88, 1.66)	0.98	(0.75, 1.29)
35–44	1.20	(0.87, 1.64)	0.79	(0.60, 1.05)
45–54	1.12	(0.81, 1.55)	0.76	(0.57, 0.83)
55–65	1.14	(0.79, 1.63)	0.86	(0.61, 1.09)
66 above	0.96	(0.33, 2.77)	1.60	(0.53, 4.87)
Work shift				
Fixed day shift	1.00		1.00	
Night/rotated shift	1.69	(1.47, 1.93)***	1.66	(1.42, 1.94)***
Work hours/week (hrs)				
≤48 h	1.00		1.00	
>48 h	1.23	(1.03, 1.47)*	1.31	(1.07, 1.61)*
Job control (3 items)				
High	1.00		1.00	
Medium	0.87	(0.65, 1.16)	0.80	(0.59, 1.09)
Low	1.06	(0.77, 1.45)	1.00	(0.71, 1.40)
Psychological demands (5 items)				
Low	1.00		1.00	
Medium	1.07	(0.87, 1.32)	1.18	(0.93, 1.48)
High	2.50	(2.04, 3.06)***	3.10	(2.49, 3.86)***
Physically demanding				
No	1.00		1.00	
Yes	1.02	(1.00, 1.03)	1.00	(0.97, 1.03)
Employment security				
Yes	1.00		1.00	
No	0.99	(0.96, 1.02)	1.01	(0.99, 1.02)
Workplace justice (7 items)				
High	1.00		1.00	
Medium	1.81	(1.30, 2.53)***	1.57	(1.13, 2.17)**
Low	6.03	(4.21, 8.64)***	5.00	(3.48, 7.20)***

* $p < 0.05$; ** $p < 0.01$; *** $p < 0.001$

Klauw 2012). In our analyses, the prevalence of workplace violence was strongly associated with the level of perceived workplace justice. It suggests that the experiences of workplace violence may be closely embedded in the power structure within a work organization.

Health Consequences of Workplace Violence

Findings from multivariate analyses (see Table 8.4) showed that employees who had experienced any type of workplace violence were found to be at a higher risk for poor self-rated health status (OR men 2.10, women 2.37), poor mental health (OR men 3.16, women 3.05), and poor sleep quality (OR men 2.91, women 3.26), after adjustments for age and other work characteristics.

Among the four types of workplace violence, psychological violence appeared to have the strongest association with poor health and poor mental health. Studies from western populations also suggested that among all the four types of workplace violence, psychological type of workplace violence such as threat, intimidation, exclusion, and bullying seemed to carry the greatest health risks to affected workers (LeBlanc and Kelloway 2002; Mayhew and Chappell 2007; Pien et al. 2014). It could be explained by a closer link of psychological violence to an oppressive work culture or imbalanced power structure in the work organization, which is more likely to be a prolonged and collective phenomenon thus would have greater impacts on worker health and well-being. In contrast, the more explicit types of workplace violence such as physical violence may be more likely to be recognized and intervened thus may be less likely to lead to victim blaming.

Neighborhood Effects of Workplace Violence

Previous studies showed that residents living in a violent neighborhood were prone to mental disorders including depression and anxiety disorders (Clark et al. 2008). Dollard and her colleagues examined the interaction effects of environmental demands, reflected by the neighborhood levels of unemployment and public housing density, and personnel resources, measured at the work-station level, on police officer perceived distress and work morale; they concluded that organizational failure to adapt to the environmental context led to workers' distress and impaired work morale (Dollard et al. 2013). Similarly, one may expect working in a violent area or neighborhood where aggressive behaviors are more prevalent additional mental health risks, regardless of workers' experience of workplace violence. However, to our knowledge, little research has been conducted to examine the contextual effects of neighborhood characteristics on workers' mental health risks, independent from the effects of workers' actual experiences of workplace violence.

We analyzed data from the 2010 survey with a multilevel analytical approach to examine the associations of neighborhood-level workplace violence measured at the county/city level with individual-level mental distress status, after adjustment of individual level experience of workplace violence as well as other work characteristics. Subjects who did not complete items for the assessment of workplace conditions (n = 40) and subjects in the Penghu County (n = 137) were excluded.

Table 8.4 Multiple logistic regression models of health outcomes and job dissatisfaction in male and female employees (based on the 2013 survey data)

Variable	Male						Female					
	Poor SRH		Poor mental health		With sleep problems		Poor SRH		Poor mental health		With sleep problems	
	OR	(95 %CI)	OR	(95 %CI)	OR	(95 %CI)	OR	(95 %CI)	OR	(95 %CI)	OR	(95 %CI)
Any violence	2.10	(1.82, 2.42)***	3.16	(2.70, 3.69)***	2.91	(2.42, 3.45)***	2.37	(2.03, 2.76)***	3.05	(2.60, 3.59)***	3.26	(2.76, 3.85)***
Physical violence	2.11	(1.50, 2.96)***	3.27	(2.30, 4.66)***	2.95	(2.03, 4.29)***	2.57	(1.54, 4.29)***	3.46	(2.08, 5.77)***	3.82	(2.30, 6.33)***
Verbal violence	2.13	(1.83, 2.49)***	3.20	(2.71, 3.77)***	2.95	(2.47, 3.52)***	2.39	(2.02, 2.83)***	3.39	(2.85, 4.04)***	3.51	(2.93, 4.20)***
Psychological violence	2.20	(1.78, 2.73)***	4.15	(3.33, 5.15)***	3.99	(3.18, 4.99)***	2.85	(2.26, 3.59)***	3.83	(3.05, 4.81)***	4.17	(3.31, 5.24)***
Sexual harassment	0.97	(0.54, 1.73)	2.24	(1.18, 4.25)*	2.55	(1.30, 4.99)**	1.41	(1.04, 1.91)*	1.55	(1.10, 2.19)*	2.25	(1.60, 3.15)***

Regression model controlled for age, work shift, work hours, job control, psychological demands, physical demands, employment security, and organizational justice

* $p < 0.05$; ** $p < 0.01$; *** $p < 0.001$

The size of this subgroup was small and the Penghu County is a small offshore island where working conditions are dramatically different from those in Taiwan. This resulted in a final sample size at the individual level (level 1) of 17,109 employees (9393 males and 7716 females) and at the neighborhood level (level 2) of 22 counties/cities. Descriptive statistical analyses and individual-level logistic regression were performed with SAS 9.3, and two-level random-effect logistic regression analyses were performed using HLM software version 7.

Findings from gender-stratified analyses showed that neighborhood-level prevalence of workplace violence ranged from 4.7 to 14.7 % in men and from 6.1 to 14.8 % in women across 22 counties/cities. As shown in Table 8.5, the intra-class correlation coefficient (ICC, defined as the between-neighborhood variance divided by the within-neighborhood variance plus the between-neighborhood variance), were 3.5 % in the null model of male subgroup and 2.9 % in female subgroup, both reaching the level of statistical significance ($P < 0.001$). Individual experience of workplace violence was the most significant predictor for mental distress problems, with odds ratios of 3.294 and 2.945 for men and women, respectively. In addition, compared to those who live in counties with low level of workplace violence, female workers who lived in counties with high level of workplace violence had increased risks for mental distress problems (OR = 1.749 in women). However, neighborhood workplace violence was not associated with mental health risk in men (Table 8.5) (Pien et al. 2015).

Reasons for increased mental health risks among workers who are exposed to a violence-prone environment could be multiple. First, workers who witness or hear of workplace violence may also feel threatened, causing anxiety and stress-related health problems. Second, a high occurrence of workplace violence can be seen as an indicator of unsafe working environment, where abusive behaviors or violent acts are tolerated and safety and mental health well-being of employees are neglected. Third, areas characterized with a high prevalence of workplace violence may indicate a work culture in which workplace violence is deemed unavoidable, and as a consequence, social support systems to prevent it for occurring or to assist victims are more likely to be fragmented or non-existent. Findings from our study suggest that preventative strategies targeting workplace violence should also pay attention to neighborhood and social environmental factors that might influence societal tolerance to abusive work practices and workers' vulnerability to mental health impacts of workplace violence.

Challenges and Future Directions

Research interest on workplace violence and workplace bullying is still quite limited in Taiwan. Results from our analyses showed that as compared to Western countries, the prevalence of workplace violence in the general working population of Taiwan was lower. However, media attention on workplace violence has been increasing in recent years. Further investigation will be needed to understand to

Table 8.5 Individual-level and county-level predictors of emotional distress: individual-level and multilevel models (based on 2010 survey data)

	Male				Female			
	Model with compositional variables only		Model with compositional and contextual variables		Model with compositional variables only		Model with compositional and contextual variables	
	OR	(95 % CI)	OR	(95 % CI)	OR	(95 % CI)	OR	(95 % CI)
Level 1								
Intercept	0.110	(0.085, 0.141) ***	0.125	(0.097, 0.161) ***	0.264	(0.166, 0.418) ***	0.185	(0.121, 0.284) ***
Individual-level workplace violence (yes/no)	3.294	(2.792, 3.886) ***	3.311	(2.805, 3.908) ***	2.945	(2.400, 3.614) ***	2.921	(2.378, 3.588) ***
Age 25–34 (Ref.)		1		1	1			
Age 35–44	1.316	(1.209, 1.432) ***	1.318	(1.211, 1.434) ***	1.178	(1.027, 1.352) *	1.179	(1.027, 1.353) *
Age 45–54	1.395	(1.270, 1.532) ***	1.398	(1.273, 1.536) ***	0.970	(0.842, 1.117)	0.969	(0.840, 1.118)
Age 55–65	1.053	(0.838, 1.323)	1.055	(0.841, 1.324)	0.839	(0.631, 1.116)	0.841	(0.632, 1.119)
Shift work (yes/no)	1.138	(1.056, 1.226) ***	1.139	(1.057, 1.227) ***	1.155	(1.030, 1.296) *	1.155	(1.028, 1.297) *
Working hours >48 h (yes/no)	1.153	(0.999, 1.330)	1.151	(0.997, 1.328)	0.979	(0.736, 1.303)	0.978	(0.734, 1.304)
Job control (continuous)	1.088	(1.032, 1.148) **	1.089	(1.032, 1.148) **	1.096	(1.052, 1.142) ***	1.096	(1.052, 1.142) ***
Psychological work demands (continuous)	1.252	(1.214, 1.290) ***	1.252	(1.214, 1.290) ***	1.255	(1.216, 1.297) ***	1.256	(1.215, 1.297) ***
Employment insecurity (yes/no)	1.168	(1.004, 1.359) *	1.168	(1.003, 1.360) *	1.014	(0.904, 1.137)	1.015	(0.905, 1.138)
Physical job demands (yes/no)	0.894	(0.773, 1.034)	0.895	(0.775, 1.034)	1.012	(0.886, 1.155)	1.013	(0.887, 1.156)
Workplace justice (continuous)	0.930	(0.912, 0.948) ***	0.930	(0.912, 0.948) ***	0.930	(0.914, 0.946) ***	0.930	(0.914, 0.946) ***
Level 2								
Workplace violence low (Ref.)			1				1	
Workplace violence medium			0.961	(0.648, 1.426)			1.636	(1.276, 2.098) ***
Workplace violence high			0.705	(0.474, 1.050)			1.749	(1.270, 2.410) **
Variance component	0.151***	0.148***	0.108**	0.047**				
ICC	0.151/(0.151 + 3.29) = 0.044		0.148/ (0.148 + 3.29) = 0.043		0.108/ (0.108 + 3.29) = 0.032		0.047/(0.047 + 3.29) = 0.014	

* $p < 0.05$; ** $p < 0.01$; *** $p < 0.001$

Table cited from: Pien et al. (2015). Associations of neighborhood-level workplace violence with workers' mental distress problems: a multilevel analysis of Taiwanese employees. *Journal of Occupational Health, 57: 555–564*

what extent the observed increases in the prevalence of workplace violence from 2010 to 2013 reflect the changes in occurrence of workplace violence or to the increasing recognition of the existing reality of problematic workplace practices or behaviors which might have long been regarded as normal and tolerated.

Findings concerning high risk populations, correlated work characteristics and health consequences of workplace violence from our analyses are in general consistent with previous studies. However, it is noticed that in Taiwan, women were more susceptible than men to workplace violence. Health care workers were found to have relatively high prevalence rates of workplace violence and a noticeable gender inequality in the prevalence of all forms of workplace violence even with adjustment for major work characteristics. This phenomenon may be attributed to a greater gender inequality in the workplace of Taiwan. In-depth investigation is needed to understand the nature and the gender aspects of abusive or violent behaviors in general workplaces and in specific work settings. Our findings that level of workplace violence at the neighborhood-level influence workers' mental health status also deserve further exploration. To our knowledge, very few studies have been conducted to investigate how societal tolerance to abusive work practices affects workers' physical and mental health status even for bystanders.

There were several limitations in our surveys. First, the cross-sectional nature of the surveys restricted the causal interpretation of the observed associations. Reverse causations are possible. For instance, workers with existing mental health problems may have exaggerated the problems of workplace violence, and/or more easily become victims of workplace violence (Aquino and Bradfield 2000; Nielsen and Einarsen 2012). Future research should use a longitudinal study design to better understand the causal consequences of workplace violence on workers' health. The second limitation concerns the measure of workplace violence, which was based on self-report and contained no detailed information regarding the nature of workplace violence. Future research should assess the problems of workplace violence in a more objective manner and specify the sources, frequency, severity as well as relevant contextual factors such as attitude of others or responses from the work organization toward the workplace violence.

The labor authority of Taiwan has taken steps to respond to the growing public concerns of workplace violence, including adopting a preventive clause in the Occupational Safety and Health Act (OSHAct), establishing procedures specifically designed for the reporting and investigating of workplace violence, and strengthening labor inspection accordingly. However, it remains questionable if these measures could be effectively implemented. There has been a lot of discussion on these issues. A major issue concerns the definition of workplace violence, especially in the form of psychological violence. Employers' groups have raised criticisms regarding the new regulation, arguing that language and terminology used in legislation are ambiguous and the scope of employers' responsibility are poorly defined. On the other hand, labor rights groups have demanded the labor authority to establish a helpline to encourage reporting and to strengthen mechanisms for the protection of victims and, as well, whistle-blowers of workplace violence.

While the policy debate on workplace violence is evolving quickly in Taiwan as well as in many other countries, more research is urgently needed. Research improvements could be made in many aspects, ranging from the measures for workplace violence, study designs to investigate the casual mechanisms of workplace violence and health consequences, to the strategies for effective prevention of workplace violence. Researchers should also bear in mind that the nature of workplace violence is embedded in a social context, which can differ greatly across countries. Therefore, a comprehensive understanding of the local context is essential for developing effective policy actions to workplace violence.

References

Aquino, K., & Bradfield, M. (2000). Perceived victimization in the workplace: The role of situational factors and victim characteristics. *Organization Science, 11*(5), 525–537.

Camerino, D., Estryn-Behar, M., Conway, P. M., van Der Heijden, B. I., & Hasselhorn, H. M. (2008). Work-related factors and violence among nursing staff in the European NEXT study: A longitudinal cohort study. *International Journal of Nursing Studies, 45*(1), 35–50.

Chappell, D., & Di Martino, V. (2006). *Violence at work.* Geneva: International Labour Organization.

Chen, W. C., Hwu, H. G., Kung, S. M., Chiu, H. J., & Wang, J. D. (2008). Prevalence and determinants of workplace violence of health care workers in a psychiatric hospital in Taiwan. *Journal of Occupational Health, 50*(3), 288–293.

Cheng, Y., Luh, W. M., & Guo, Y. L. (2003). Reliability and validity of the Chinese version of the Job Content Questionnaire in Taiwanese workers. *International Journal of Behavioral Medicine, 10*(1), 15–30.

Cheng, Y., Huang, H. Y., Li, P. R., & Hsu, J. H. (2011). Employment insecurity, workplace justice and employees' burnout in Taiwanese employees: A validation study. *International Journal of Behavioral Medicine, 18*(4), 391–401.

Clark, C., Ryan, L., Kawachi, I., Canner, M. J., Berkman, L., & Wright, R. J. (2008). Witnessing community violence in residential neighborhoods: A mental health hazard for urban women. *Journal of Urban Health, 85*(1), 22–38.

Colquitt, J. (2001). On the dimensionality of organizational justice: A construct validation of a measure. *Journal of Applied Psychology, 86*, 386–400.

Demir, D., & Rodwell, J. (2012). Psychosocial antecedents and consequences of workplace aggression for hospital nurses. *Journal of Nursing Scholarship, 44*(4), 376–384.

Dollard, M. F., Osborne, K., & Manning, I. (2013). Organization–environment adaptation: A macro-level shift in modeling work distress and morale. *Journal of Organizational Behavior, 34*(5), 629–647.

Estryn-Behar, M., van der Heijden, B., Camerino, D., Fry, C., Le Nezet, O., Conway, P. M., et al. (2008). Violence risks in nursing—results from the European 'NEXT' Study. *Occupational Medicine (Lond), 58*(2), 107–114.

Harrell, E. (2011). Workplace violence, 1993–2009. *National crime victimization survey and the census of fatal occupational injuries.* Washington, DC: Bureau of Justice Statistics. www.bjs.gov/index.cfm?ty=pbdetail&iid=2377.

Hills, D. J., & Joyce, C. M. (2013). Personal, professional, and work factors associated with Australian clinical medical practitioners' experiences of workplace aggression. *Annals of Occupational Hygiene, 57*(7), 898–912.

Hurrell, J. J, Jr., & McLaney, M. A. (1988). Exposure to job stress—a new psychometric instrument. *Scandinavian Journal of Work, Environment & Health, 14*(Suppl 1), 27–28.

Kamchuchat, C., Chongsuvivatwong, V., Oncheunjit, S., Yip, T. W., & Sangthong, R. (2008). Workplace violence directed at nursing staff at a general hospital in southern Thailand. *Journal of Occupational Health, 50*(2), 201–207.

Karasek, R., & Theorell, T. (1990). *Healthy work. Stress, productively, and the reconstruction of working life*. New York: Basic Books.

Korean Occupational Safety and Health Administration. (2012). Working conditions in Korea: Survey highlights.

Lallukka, T., Rahkonen, O., & Lahelma, E. (2011). Workplace bullying and subsequent sleep problems—the Helsinki Health Study. *Scandinavian Journal of Work, Environment & Health, 37*(3), 204–212.

Landsbergis, P. A. (2009). *Interventions to reduce job stress and improve work organization and worker health. Unhealthy work: Causes, consequences, cures* (pp. 193–209). Amityville, NY: Baywood Publishing.

Landsbergis, P. A., Grzywacz, J. G., & LaMontagne, A. D. (2014). Work organization, job insecurity, and occupational health disparities. *American Journal of Industrial Medicine, 57*(5), 495–515.

Langeland, B. T. (2012). Positive trends in working conditions and occupational health. *European Working conditions observatory (EWCO)*, 12.

Lawoko, S., Soares, J. J., & Nolan, P. (2004). Violence towards psychiatric staff: A comparison of gender, job and environmental characteristics in England and Sweden. *Work & Stress, 18*(1), 39–55.

LeBlanc, M. M., & Kelloway, E. K. (2002). Predictors and outcomes of workplace violence and aggression. *Journal of Applied Psychology, 87*(3), 444.

Lee, H.-E., Kim, H.-R., & Park, J. S. (2014). Work-related risk factors for workplace violence among Korean employees. *Journal of Occupational Health, 56*(1), 12–20.

Lehto, A.-M. (2004). Violence, bullying and harassment in the workplace. *European Foundation for the improvement of living and working conditions, 2007*. http://www.eurofound.europa.eu/.

Lo, T. W., Chappell, D., Kwok, S. I., & Wu, J. (2012). Workplace violence in Hong Kong, China: Nature, impact, and preparedness. *International Journal of Offender Therapy and Comparative Criminology, 56*(6), 955–975.

Martino, V. D. (2002). *Workplace violence in the health sector: Country case studies: Brazil, Bulgaria, Lebanon, Portugal, South Africa, Thailand, and an Additional Australian Study*. Geneva: ILO/ICN/WHO/PSI Joint Programme on Workplace Violence in the Health Sector.

Mayhew, C., & Chappell, D. (2007). Workplace violence: An overview of patterns of risk and the emotional/stress consequences on targets. *International Journal of Law and Psychiatry, 30*(4–5), 327–339.

Mehdad, A., Tabakh, E. Y., & Mehdizadegan, I. (2012). Relationship between perceived organizational justice and workplace violence intervention. *New Findings in Psychology, 7* (23), 19–36.

Moorman, R. (1991). Relationship between organizational justice and organizational citizenship behaviors: Do fairness perceptions influence employee citizenship? *Journal of Applied Psychology, 76*, 845–855.

Naito, S. (2013). *Workplace bullying and harassment*. Japan Institute for Labour Policy and Training Report, no. 12 (pp. 113–133). http://www.jil.go.jp/english/reports/documents/jilpt-reports/no.12.pdf.

Nielsen, M. B., & Einarsen, S. (2012). Outcomes of exposure to workplace bullying: A meta-analytic review. *Work & Stress, 26*(4), 309–332.

Pai, H. C., & Lee, S. (2011). Risk factors for workplace violence in clinical registered nurses in Taiwan. *Journal of Clinical Nursing, 20*(9–10), 1405–1412.

Parent-Thirion, A., Vermeylen, G., van Houten, G., Lyly-Yrjänäinen, M., Biletta, I., & Cabrita, J. (2012). Fifth European working conditions survey—overview report (pp. 57–59).

Park, S. (2013). Workplace bullying and harassment *JILPT report, no. 12*, pp. 91–112.

Pedersen, H., & Christiansen, R. (2005). *Violence or harassment at work*. Centre for Alternative Social Analysis (CASA). http://www.eurofound.europa.eu/ewco/2005/09/DK0509NU03.htm.

Pien, L.-C., Cheng, Y.-W., Chen, I.-S., & Chen, C.-J. (2014). The prevalence of workplace violence and its Association with the health status of Taiwanese employees. *Taiwan Journal of Public Health, 33*(1), 36–50 (in Chinese).

Pien, L. C., Chen, D. R., Chen, C. J., Liang, K. M., & Cheng, Y. (2015). Associations of neighborhood-level workplace violence with workers' mental distress problems: A multilevel analysis of Taiwanese employees. *Journal of Occupational Health, 57*, 555–564.

Roche, M., Diers, D., Duffield, C., & Catling-Paull, C. (2010). Violence toward nurses, the work environment, and patient outcomes. *Journal of Nursing Scholarship, 42*(1), 13–22.

Takaki, J., Taniguchi, T., Fukuoka, E., Fujii, Y., Tsutsumi, A., Nakajima, K., et al. (2010). Workplace bullying could play important roles in the relationships between job strain and symptoms of depression and sleep disturbance. *Journal of Occupational Health, 52*(6), 367–374.

Tsuno, K., Kawakami, N., Tsutsumi, A., et al. (2015). Socioeconomic determinants of bullying in the workplace: A national representative sample in Japan. *PLoS One, 10*(3), e0119435.

Venema, A., & Klauw, M. V. D. (2012). *Impact of workplace violence on employees*. European Working Condictions Observatory, EWCO. http://eurofound.europa.eu/observatories/eurwork/articles/other/impact-of-workplace-violence-on-employees.

Chapter 9
Psychosocial Hazards and Musculoskeletal Disorders: Are There Different Roles for Workplace Factors Between Office Workers in Malaysia and Australia?

Jodi Oakman, Ismail Maakip and Tessa Keegel

Abstract Musculoskeletal disorders (MSDs) are considered to be a major occupational health problem contributing significantly to absenteeism, disability and loss of productivity. The majority of studies related to MSDs have been conducted in developed countries such as Australia, and it is proposed that contributing factors linked with MSD development might operate differently in developing countries like Malaysia, as a result of sociocultural differences. A key issue in the development of MSDs is the contribution of psychosocial factors; however, this is not reflected in current management practices which tend to focus predominately on physical factors. Malaysia and Australia have very different societal structures, which influence the way work is organised and the expectations of employees at their workplaces. Therefore, it is plausible that the contribution of workplace factors to MSD development might differ. This chapter will explore a range of issues in relation to the development of MSDs and use a population of office workers in Australia and Malaysia to explore different explanatory models. A survey tool was used to assess a range of workplace and personal factors, including: work–life balance, job satisfaction, physical hazards, coping strategies, and psychosocial hazards. Analysis was undertaken to assess relevant predictors for each population and then a comparison undertaken to identify key differences between the populations. The chapter will also discuss the results from a qualitative study of female Malaysian office workers who were asked about their coping strategies for persistent musculoskeletal pain. Despite similarities in the prevalence of musculoskeletal discomfort in both the Australian and Malaysian populations, differences were identified in the relative contribution of factors. The findings from this study provide insights into future policy development of management of MSDs. Malaysia is at a formative stage in term of risk management for MSDs and as such a different focus is needed to adequately address relevant workplace factors.

J. Oakman (✉) · I. Maakip · T. Keegel
Department of Public Health, Centre for Ergonomics and Human Factors, La Trobe University, Bundoora 3086, Australia
e-mail: j.oakman@latrobe.edu.au

A. Shimazu et al. (eds.), *Psychosocial Factors at Work in the Asia Pacific*,
DOI 10.1007/978-3-319-44400-0_9

Keywords Risk management · Musculoskeletal disorders · Psychsocial · Physical · Hazards

Background

The aetiology of musculoskeletal disorders (MSDs) is multifactorial as a range of physical, psychosocial and individual hazards contribute to the development and exacerbation of MSDs (Bongers et al. 2002; Janwantanakul et al. 2010; Oakman 2014). However, most research in the area of MSDs has been undertaken in developed countries and may not be applicable to industrially developing countries (IDC) such as Malaysia. Previous studies have reported that the prevalence of MSDs varies between countries (Madan et al. 2008; Punnett et al. 2005), while Coggon et al. (2013) demonstrated large variations in the occurrence of disabling musculoskeletal illness between countries among occupational groups. This was partially explained by personal demographic, physical and psychosocial risk factors. Such variations may be also due to differences in the sociocultural context between countries and influences at an international, national, state, and local level (Dollard et al. 2014). Differences in work practices and culture have been reported to influence the differences in the prevalence and risk factors associated with MSDs (Carter and Bannister 1994; Janwantanakul et al. 2010). Madan et al. (2008) and Coggon (2005) argue that variation in the prevalence and risk factors of MSDs among workers performing similar jobs might be due to the differences in the sociocultural context of individual's lives and work environments, as recent studies have demonstrated the importance of the sociocultural context affecting the risk factors associated with MSDs (Vargas-Prada et al. 2013; Farioli et al. 2014). It is estimated that the greatest increase in the prevalence of MSDs in the next decade will be in industrially developing countries (World Health Organization 2003).

Occupational Health and Safety Systems in Malaysia and Australia

Regulatory frameworks influence the development and utilisation of risk management systems in organisations. Malaysia and Australia both have health and safety legislation based on the British system (Johnstone 1997). However, the interpretation of legislation and workplace practices is highly influenced by the expectations of employer and employees and the acceptance of what constitutes an acceptable level of risk. Cultural differences are likely to strongly influence what is considered acceptable practice in workplaces. Malaysian society values hierarchy and deference to those in higher positions (Hofstede 2001). This is very different to Australia where a more open discussion is valued with contributions from everyone encouraged. In workplaces, employees are expected and encouraged to raise issues of concern so that appropriate risk management strategies can be undertaken.

To most effectively manage conditions such as MSDs, regular and open communication is needed between employers or supervisors and employees to develop the most appropriate workplace accommodations to assist with the maintenance of workplace productivity. Disclosure of personal conditions is always challenging as it can result in negative consequences. However, without disclosure of a condition employees are restricted in the type of accommodations (e.g., modifications to duties, changes to work hours) they can access, relying more on colleagues and individually based modifications rather than systemic or organisational level changes.

MSDs in the Asia Pacific Region

The Asia Pacific region is a very diverse region covering some of the richest and the poorest countries (ILO 2014). As a result work practices across the region vary with some countries mostly agriculturally based and others more industrially orientated. Accurate workplace data is challenging to obtain particularly where much work is undertaken in the informal sector and workers are not covered by formal compensation schemes. Estimates of those affected by MSDs are likely to underrepresent real figures. Analysis undertaken as part of the global burden of disease study (Driscoll et al. 2014) estimated that disability adjusted life years (DALYs), which is a measure of overall disease burden expressed in terms of the number of years lost due to ill-health, disability or early death for low back pain, were 331 in Australia compared to 482 in South East Asia, where a large reliance on physically demanding work contributes significantly to these differences. These figures do not include informal workers or cumulative exposures and so are considered indicative of risk rather than absolute figures. Further insights are required to understand why these differences occur and the role of work organisation in the development of MSDs.

Workplace Factors and MSDs in Office Workers

MSDs are a major problem among office employees (Frumkin 2005) and considered to be a leading cause of occupational illness, resulting in absenteeism (Bongers et al. 2006) and reduced productivity (Ranasinghe et al. 2011). Office workers are exposed to a range of factors associated with increased risk of MSD development including: individual (age and gender); physical (static postures, prolonged sitting and repetitive movements); and psychosocial factors (e.g. workload, time pressures and job control) (Huysmans et al. 2011; Klussmann et al. 2008).

Many theoretical models have been proposed which describe links between a range of factors, workplace and individual and the development of MSDs (Bongers et al. 1993; Feuerstein 1996; Sauter and Swanson 1996; National Research Council (NRC) 2001; Karsh 2006; Côté et al. 2008). A model developed by Sauter and Swanson (1996) almost 20 years ago specifically described MSD development in office workers proposing that work organisation, psychological strain and individual factors influence the relationship between biomechanical strain and MSDs, and the manner by which workers detect and respond to physical hazards. The development of symptoms may be influenced by both the social context and the individual's own experience and as such the prevalence rates and predictors associated with MSD may differ from one country to another (Madan et al. 2008) as the context of employment and expectations from employee groups is different. The Sauter and Swanson model, despite the extensive changes in office work, still provides a highly relevant framework to consider MSD development in a contemporary office environment. What is less clear is the relevance of MSD models based on theories and research undertaken in developed countries such as Australia, European countries and the United States, for industrially developing countries such as Malaysia.

As the Malaysian economy develops and employment in the knowledge sectors increases compared to more physically demanding roles it is important to improve understanding of the role of work organisation and psychosocial factors on health conditions such as MSDs.

The following case studies are taken from a body of work, which aimed to examine the prevalence and predictors associated with MSDs in office workers in two countries, Malaysia and Australia. The aim of first case study was to identify if the prevalence rate of self-reported MSD discomfort differs between Malaysian and Australian employees. Second, it aimed to identify differences in predictors associated with self-reported MSD discomfort in each country. The second case study aimed to explore potential coping strategies amongst female office workers who stay at work despite having musculoskeletal discomfort.

Case Study 1: Comparison of Predictors and Prevalence of MSDs Between Malaysia and Australian Office Workers

The aim of this study was to examine and compare the prevalence and predictors associated with musculoskeletal discomfort between both Malaysian and Australian office workers.

Method

The study population consisted of 1184 public sector office workers in Malaysia and Australia, with 417 Malaysian (response rate: 65.5 %) and 767 Australian (response rate: 54.2 %) respondents. The majority of participants in both samples were females, with 333 (79.8 %) in Malaysia and 559 (72.9 %) in Australia, compared to only 84 (20.2 %) males in Malaysia and 208 (27.1 %) in Australia. A survey tool (described in detail elsewhere, see Oakman et al. 2014) was used to measure a range of workplace and personal factors, including: work–life balance, job satisfaction, physical hazards, coping strategies and psychosocial hazards. The Malaysian version underwent an in-depth translation process (Maakip et al. 2015).

Job satisfaction was measured using the item "Overall, how happy or satisfied are you with your job here, as a whole taking everything into account?" whilst for work–life balance, the question was "How satisfied are you with the balance between your home life and your work—considering how much time and energy you have?" (Oakman et al. 2014). Single items, with five-point response scales were used to measure job satisfaction and work–life balance (1 = very dissatisfied, 2 = dissatisfied, 3 = neutral, 4 = satisfied, and 5 = highly satisfied).

Physical demands were assessed using a 12-item measure and a five-point response scale (1 = never or hardly ever, 2 = seldom, 3 = sometimes, 4 = often, 5 = almost all the time) to assess participants' exposure to workplace physical hazards.

Workplace psychosocial hazards were assessed using 26 items from the Work Organisation Assessment Questionnaire (WOAQ) (Griffiths et al. 2006) with responses on a five-point scale (5 = very good, 1 = major problem).

Musculoskeletal discomfort was assessed with the following question: "In the last 6 months, have you ever experienced discomfort or pain towards the end of your working day?" (yes or no). Respondents who reported discomfort were then asked further questions related to severity and frequency of MSD discomfort for five body regions: (1) neck and shoulder, (2) hand and fingers, (3) arms, (4) middle to lower back and (5) hips, bottom, legs and feet. Frequency was recorded on a scale of 0 = never, 1 almost never, 2 = sometimes, 3 = often, 4 = almost always and severity from 1 = mild, 2 = moderate, 3 = severe discomfort. An overall discomfort score was calculated by multiplying frequency and severity for each body region and then summing.

Results

Prevalence of Musculoskeletal Discomfort Between Malaysia and Australia

Prevalence of musculoskeletal discomfort in the last 6 months differed between the two countries with 92.8 % of Malaysian respondents reporting musculoskeletal discomfort compared to 71.2 % of Australian respondents; the difference was significant using a t-test ($p < 0.001$).

Predictors of Musculoskeletal Discomfort in Malaysia and Australia

Hierarchical multiple regression was conducted separately for Malaysia and Australia to examine predictors associated with musculoskeletal discomfort (See Table 9.1). For Malaysia, the overall regression model was significant (F (6,

Table 9.1 Comparison by country of hierarchical multiple regression on self-reported MSD discomfort

Step	Variable	β	t	p	R^2	ΔR^2	*F*
Malaysia (n = 387)							
1	Age	−0.03	−0.68	0.49	0.01	0.01	2.33
	Gender	0.10	2.10	0.03*			
2	Age	−0.00	−0.27	0.97	0.05	0.04	5.73**
	Gender	0.09	1.91	0.05*			
	Work–life balance	−0.15	−2.63	0.00**			
	Job satisfaction	−0.09	−1.51	0.13			
3	Age	0.02	0.57	0.56	0.22	0.16	17.35**
	Gender	0.14	3.13	0.00**			
	Work–life balance	−0.13	−2.50	0.01**			
	Job satisfaction	−0.02	−0.46	0.64			
	Physical hazards	0.38	8.24	0.00**			
	Psychosocial hazards	−0.10	−1.94	0.05*			
Australia (n = 546)							
1	Age	0.06	1.47	0.14	0.02	0.02	6.11**
	Gender	1.28	3.01	0.00			
2	Age	0.04	1.06	0.28	0.07	0.05	11.27**
	Gender	0.16	3.92	0.00**			
	Work–life balance	−0.12	−2.50	0.01*			
	Job satisfaction	−0.14	−3.00	0.00**			
3	Age	0.06	1.56	0.11	0.15	0.07	16.47**
	Gender	0.14	3.66	0.00**			
	Work–life balance	−0.05	−1.10	0.26			
	Job satisfaction	−0.03	−0.57	0.56			
	Physical hazards	0.24	5.78	0.00**			
	Psychosocial hazards	−0.17	−3.27	0.00**			

* $p < 0.05$; ** $p < 0.01$; β = Beta

370) = 17.35, $p < 0.001$). The model for the Malaysian sample showed that gender ($\beta = 0.14$, $p < 0.01$), work–life balance ($\beta = -0.13$, $p < 0.01$), physical ($\beta = 0.38$, $p < 0.01$) and psychosocial hazards ($\beta = -0.10$, $p < 0.05$) were significantly associated with musculoskeletal discomfort. For Australian respondents, the overall regression model was also significant (F [6, 539] = 16.47; $p < 0.001$). Gender ($\beta = 0.14$, $p < 0.01$), physical ($\beta = 0.24$, $p < 0.01$) and psychosocial hazards ($\beta = -0.17$, $p < 0.01$) were significantly associated with musculoskeletal discomfort for the Australian sample.

Gender differences were tested in both samples with no significant differences found. However, in the Australian population women reported higher levels of satisfaction with work–home balance than men. No differences were found in the Malaysian sample.

Implications

This study identified differences in the prevalence rate of musculoskeletal discomfort between Malaysia and Australia. Work organisation including the nature of work, workstations, tool and equipment design, policies and procedures have been identified as potential causal factors for MSD development (Smith and Carayon-Sainfort 1989), these are likely to differ between Australia and Malaysia and provide some explanation for the difference in prevalence rates. Another possible explanation for the different prevalence rates between the Australian and Malaysian workers relates to the recognition of MSDs as an important work-related problem. In Australia, significant efforts have been undertaken to mitigate hazards and risks associated with MSDs (Ireland 1995; Macdonald and Oakman 2015). However, this is not the case in Malaysia where MSDs have only recently been recognised as a work-related problem (Lee 2007) and preventive measures such as addressing hazards relating to the psychosocial work environment are still underdeveloped (Idris et al. 2010).

This study identified three predictors: gender, physical hazards and psychosocial hazards that were associated with self-reported MSD discomfort in both countries, consistent with previous research involving office workers (Griffiths et al. 2012; Paksaichol et al. 2012). Work–life balance was only associated with increased MSD discomfort in the Malaysian population. This might be partially explained by the changing roles for women within Malaysian society. The Malaysian government has actively encouraged women to participate in the labour market (Joseph 2014); however, infrastructure to support them in managing this has not followed. In comparison, Australia has a wide range of initiatives including flexible or part-time working arrangements, or the ability to work from home, which assist with reducing work–life conflict (Baird 2011).

Of note is the difference in the level of contribution of physical and psychosocial hazards to MSD risk. In Malaysia, physical hazards were more strongly associated with MSD risk than psychosocial factors. In comparison, in Australia the contribution of physical and psychosocial factors to MSD risk was similar. This suggests potential different expectations in relation to workplace factors between the two countries. Sociocultural values may explain these differences and expectations of employees from their workplaces in relation to the provision of a safe working environment.

In addition, other factors such as work organisation, work culture and practices may also contribute to the differences in the development and experience of MSDs that exist between cultures. Previous studies reported that work organisation influences physical demands and musculoskeletal outcomes (Amick et al. 1999) and also psychosocial features such as job demands (work pace) and low decision latitude (Punnett and Wegman 2004). The way work is organised is known to differ from one country to another (Erez 2010) and this might also influence the experience of MSDs. This needs to be considered in the development of effective risk management strategies.

Case Study 2: The Voice of Malaysian Women Working with Musculoskeletal Pain

Thirteen women were interviewed to explore the strategies employed by Malaysian female office workers with musculoskeletal pain (MSP) in order to maintain productive employment. Participants were part of the larger study reported in Case Study 1 and had expressed interest in being interviewed to discuss their experiences relating to working with musculoskeletal pain. Twenty-five female office workers with musculoskeletal pain expressed interest in being interviewed by providing contact details, but only 18 of these could be contacted, and of those 13 agreed to participate.

All interview transcriptions (in Malay) were read, verified and checked by the first author [IM] against the original audio for accuracy and grammar twice, first in Malay and then in English. The interview data were classified and coded into tentative emerging themes and a basic framework. Two interviews were coded independently by two of the authors, and an iterative discussion was used to further develop the emerging codes and modify the coding framework. A further stage of coding was undertaken to eliminate redundant codes and establish analytic connections between distinct themes (Braun and Clarke 2006).

Work was of high importance to the women in this study, and they reported a strong sense of responsibility in contributing to their family and society through their workforce participation. A range of challenges were reported by these women, in maintaining their workload despite their musculoskeletal pain, and many had developed a range of personal strategies to enable them to remain productively employed. Women were working in a range of roles, but a common theme was their low level of control in how their work was allocated, as well as limited opportunity for them to make decisions independently due to the hierarchical structure of the work organisation. A sample of quotes to support the findings is provided.

Workplace Support

Colleagues provided a range of support mechanisms to participants, from completing work so that medical appointments could be attended, or assisting with physical tasks/work when pain levels made these tasks difficult. Lack of support from supervisors led participants to manage their condition independently. Numerous strategies included the delegation of duties to colleagues, provision of therapies such as massage machines or exercise classes and reflexology, and the use of spirituality were employed to manage painful conditions.

> He gives the work. We are the ones who have to find the solution as we are the ones who have the knowledge. He enquires. If we have a problem we will not ask him. He is not involved in coding. He is the forefront of the diagram or flowchart. So the supervisor is of little help. (P2)

Personal Strategies

Numerous personal strategies were employed to manage pain at work and included medication and the use of distraction techniques. Both pharmaceutical and traditional medications were used with variable effect. A range of activities was used to minimise the impact of pain on work performance, such as focusing on workplace tasks, taking breaks and regular movement (e.g. stretching and exercising) which acted as distractors from the pain. Spiritual strategies were also used by some to provide distraction from musculoskeletal pain. These strategies included listening to recordings of the Quran to manage pain, the morning bath, and 'ruku' (bowing/prostration) during prayers.

> For my back pain I did ruku' (bowing/prostration). Praise be to God it worked. I went for a course in the Science of Solat. They said the way we move makes us healthy so after that I tried it. I had a back pain and I did that Praise be to God, it worked. (P1).

Implications

Despite the long-term nature of their condition, only four women reported informing their supervisors of their musculoskeletal pain, suggesting the difficulty most had communicating effectively with their manager or employer. In Malaysia, where a strong hierarchical structure is evident with a reluctance to discuss matters of a personal nature with those more senior, disclosure of musculoskeletal pain is unlikely. The patriarchal nature of Malaysian society (Noor 2006) is an additional disincentive for women, such as those in the current study, to report their condition and negotiate for appropriate workplace accommodations to support them in managing their work.

One possible reason women in this study did not disclose their condition to supervisors is influenced by the need to avoid the '*malu*' (ashamed/embarrassed) and '*segan*' (reluctant) personality which are akin to hypersensitivity to what other people are thinking about one's self (Goddard 1996) and has a strong influence of communication in Malaysian workplaces, particularly between superiors and subordinates (Abdullah 1992). In addition, Malaysian women and particularly those who are Malay, are generally less open, less expressive, more inhibited and timid than their western counterparts (Noor 1999). A strong culture of adherence to the rules and norms of society which respects the avoidance of criticism or disagreement is a likely contributor to a reluctance to disclose personal conditions to one's supervisor.

Without disclosure and organisational support, workplace accommodations need to be developed at an individual or peer-related level. Rather than rely on supervisory support, women were much more likely to manage their workplace situation by negotiating support from their colleagues. Support from colleagues included listening, helping to complete work to meet deadlines and undertaking extra duties when required. These supports demonstrate the collective nature of Malaysian society which values long-term commitment to the 'member' group and responsibility for fellow members of the group (Abdullah 1992). Prioritisation of group benefits over individual benefits has been identified as a characteristic of collective societies (Ahmad 2001). This collective culture is demonstrated by the actions of the women in this study, through their expectations of and acceptance of assistance from their fellow workers in preference to that of their supervisors.

Supervisors were approached for support regarding work-related matters, where decisions required senior input, but not for personal matters. In the context of group membership, supervisors were considered at a different level and expectations of support were different to that of colleagues. This is consistent with the hierarchical nature of Malaysian society which values distinct roles with a large power distance between those with and without power (e.g. the supervisor and the worker) (Carroll et al. 2010). Direct discussion or consultation with supervisors is neither expected nor valued, with employees more likely to confide in colleagues than those in more senior roles than themselves.

Furthermore, Malaysia is a patriarchal society, where males are more often in positions of leadership and women work in jobs with low control (Tan 1991). Participation of Malaysian females in the work force is high at 53.6 % (Malaysian Statistics Department 2015), and despite working full-time employed women are also expected to manage the majority of home duties, potentially exposing them to additional and different hazards and risks than their male peers (Noor 2006). Availability of organisational support or services such as flexible work hours or formal childcare, to assist with managing the demands of dual work and home roles is limited, a risk factor for taking time off work (Hooftman et al. 2008). This raises challenges for those at work with conditions such as MSDs and in particular women who are managing these dual roles. The creation of a supportive work environment where nonwork roles are valued and supported is important but will require managers to be skilled in area so that they can discuss and deal with a range of issues which influence employees working lives (Hassan et al. 2014).

Challenges and Future Directions

The prevention of musculoskeletal discomfort is challenging. MSDs are complex with a multifactorial aetiology. In practical terms, the findings of this research support intervention strategies to reduce the prevalence of MSDs and its consequences in the workplace that address both physical and psychosocial factors (Macdonald and Oakman 2015). In addition, the sociocultural context of the target population needs to be taken into account when developing interventions targeting musculoskeletal discomfort in the workplace. Women in this study had limited control over their work, which was an inherent feature of their jobs. Increased job control may assist with development of risk management strategies to reduce work–home balance issues and to manage MSDs at work. Future directions for workplaces risk management programs should incorporate the following:

1. Improving the identification of workplace hazards and risks—both physical and psychosocial should be made a priority. Psychosocial risks and work-related stress are still not well-understood and are not prioritised in developing countries (Kortum et al. 2010).
2. Improve workplace management of MSDs: a shift from a reliance on individual strategies to organisational strategies is required to reduce the level of workplace factors associated with MSD. This will require a significant shift in workplace practices for Malaysia, including the education of supervisors about the relevant hazards and risks that contribute to the development of MSDs and the importance of managing these ongoing issues.
3. Incorporate work–home balance issues in workplace risk management of MSDs: new policies are needed to actively support women managing their work and home life (Hassan et al. 2014). This study found that this was a significant issue and requires attention. These new policies could include improved availability of child care, leave options and flexible working hours.

Conclusion

This chapter highlighted the range of factors relevant in the development of musculoskeletal disorders in two Asia Pacific countries. The first case study presented a quantitative exploration of predictors of MSD in office workers based in Australia and Malaysia. The second study explored the voices of women working with musculoskeletal pain in Malaysia.

MSD prevalence rates were higher in Malaysia than Australia, and differences in predictors were identified. In the Malaysian context, psychosocial factors were not as strongly associated with MSD compared to Australia. The sociocultural context may explain these differences, as the working conditions and employee expectations are likely to influence the interpretation and subsequent assessment of the psychosocial work environment.

Significant challenges exist as the sociocultural context of each country strongly influences the working conditions and the subsequent beliefs and behaviours of individuals both in their experience and in their willingness to report musculoskeletal discomfort at work. Further work to examine the effects of culturally specific frameworks is warranted in a range of sectors including the public service, particularly as developing countries such as Malaysia continue to grow within in a global economy that has changing work practices. These case studies demonstrate that the country in which you work is likely to influence the importance of workplace factors, and as such the management of these needs to be culturally sensitive.

References

Abdullah, A. (1992). *Understanding the Malaysian workforce*. Kuala Lumpur: Malaysian Institute of Management.

Ahmad, K. (2001). Corporate leadership and workforce motivation in Malaysia. *International Journal of Commerce and Management, 11*, 82–101.

Amick III, B. C., Swanson, N. G., & Chang, H. (1999). Office technology and musculoskeletal disorders: Building an ecological model. *Occupational Medicine, 14*(1), 97–112.

Baird, M. (2011). The state, work and family in Australia. *International Journal of Human Resource Management, 22*(18), 3742–3754.

Bongers, P., de Winter, C., Kompier, M., & Hilderbrandt, V. (1993). Psychosocial factors at work and musculoskeletal disease. *Scandinavian Journal of Work, Environment & Health, 19*(5), 297–312.

Bongers, P. M., Ijmker, S., van den Huevel, S. G., & Blatter, B. M. (2006). Epidemiology of work related neck and upper limb problems: Psychosocial and personal risk factors (part I) and effective interventions from a bio behavioural perspective (part II). *Journal of Occupational Rehabilitation, 16*(3), 279–302.

Bongers, P. M., Kremer, A. M., & ter Laak, J. (2002). Are psychosocial factors, risk factor for symptoms and signs of the shoulder, elbow, or hand/wrist? A review of the epidemiological literature. *American Journal of Industrial Medicine, 41*(5), 315–342.

Braun, V., & Clarke, V. (2006). Using thematic analysis in psychology. *Qualitative Research in Psychology, 3*, 77–110.

Carroll, C., Rick, J., Pilgrim, H., Cameron, J., & Hillage, J. (2010). Workplace involvement improves return to work rates among employees with back pain on long-term sick leave: A systematic review of the effectiveness and cost-effectiveness of interventions. *Disability Rehabilitation, 32*, 607–621.

Carter, J., & Bannister, E. (1994). Musculoskeletal problems in VDT work: Review. *Ergonomics, 37*(10), 1623–1648.

Coggon, D. (2005). Occupational medicine at a turning point. *Journal of Occupational and Environmental Medicine, 62*(5), 281–283.

Coggon, D., Ntani, G., Palmer, K., Felli, V., Harari, R., Barrero, L., et al. (2013). Disabling musculoskeletal pain in working populations: Is it the job, the person, or the culture? *Pain, 154* (6), 856–863.

Côté, P., van der Velde, G., Cassidy, J., Carroll, L., Hogg-Johnson, S., Holm, L., et al. (2008). The burden and determinants of neck pain in workers. *Spine, 33*(S1), S60–S74.

Dollard, M. F., Shimazu, S., Nordin, R. B., & Brough, P. (2014). Chapter 1 The context of psychosocial factors at work in the Asia Pacific. In M. F. Dollard, A. Shimazu, R. B. Nordin, P. Brough, & M. R. Tuckey (Eds.), *psychosocial factors at work in the Asia Pacific* (pp. 3–27). Dordrecht, The Netherlands: Springer International Publishing.

Driscoll, T., Jacklyn, G., Orchard, J., Passmore, E., Vos, T., Freedman, G., et al. (2014). The global burden of occupationally related low back pain: Estimates from the Global Burden of Disease 2010 study. *Annals of the Rheumatic Diseases, 73*(6), 975–981.

Erez, M. (2010). Culture and job design. *Journal of Organizational Behaviour, 31*(2–3), 389–400.

Farioli, A., Mattioli, S., Quaglieri, A., Curti, S., Violante, F., & Coggon, D. (2014). Musculoskeletal pain in Europe: The role of personal, occupational, and social risk factors. *Scandinavian Journal of Work, Environment & Health, 40*(1), 36–46.

Feuerstein, M. (1996). Workstyle: Definition, empirical support, and implications for prevention, evaluation, and rehabilitation of occupational upper-extremity disorders. In S. D. Moon & S. L. Sauter (Eds.), *Beyond biomechanics: Psychosocial aspects of musculoskeletal disorders in office work* (pp. 177–206). London: Taylor & Francis.

Frumkin, H. (2005). *Environmental health: From global to local*. San Francisco, CA: Wiley.

Goddard, C. (1996). The 'social emotions' of Malay (Bahasa Melayu). *Ethos, 24*, 426–464.

Griffiths, A., Cox, T., Karanika, M., Khan, S., & Tomas, J. (2006). Work design and management in the manufacturing sector: Development and validation of the Work Organisation Assessment Questionnaire. *Journal of Occupational and Environmental Medicine, 63*(10), 669–675.

Griffiths, K. L., Mackey, M. G., Adamson, B. J., & Peper, K. L. (2012). Prevalence and risk factors for musculoskeletal symptoms with computer based work across occupations. *Work, 42*(4), 533–541.

Hassan, Z., Dollard, M. F., & Winefield, A. H. (2014). Chapter 15 Malaysian model of work-family interface: Similar or different from the West? In M. F. Dollard, A. Shimazu, R. B. Nordin, P. Brough, & M. R. Tuckey (Eds.), *Psychosocial factors at work in the Asia Pacific* (pp. 293–307). Dordrecht, The Netherlands: Springer International Publishing.

Hofstede, G. (2001). *Culture's consequences: Comparing values, behaviour, institutions, and organisations across nations*. Thousand Oaks, CA: Sage.

Hooftman, W. E., Westerman, M. J., van der Beek, A. J., Bongers, P. M., & van Mechelen, W. (2008). What makes men and women with musculoskeletal complaints decide they are too sick to work. *Scandinavian Journal of Work, Environment & Health, 34*, 107–112.

Huysmans, M., Ijmker, S., Blatter, B., Knol, D., van Mechelen, W., Bongers, P. M., et al. (2011). The relative contribution of work exposure, leisure time exposure, and individual characteristics in the onset of arm-wrist-hand and neck-shoulder symptoms among office workers. *International Archives of Occupational Environmental Health, 85*(6), 651–666.

Idris, M. A., Dollard, M. F., & Winefield, A. H. (2010). Lay theory explanation of occupational stress: The Malaysian context. *Cross Cultural Management: An International Journal, 17*(2), 135–153.

International Labour Organization. (2014). *World of work report: Developing with jobs*. http://www.ilo.org/global/research/global-reports/world-of-work/2014/WCMS_243961/lang–en/index.htm. Accessed 4 Jan 2016.

Ireland, D. C. (1995). Repetition strain injury: The Australian experience—1992 update. *Journal of Hand Surgery, 20*(3), S53–S56.

Janwantanakul, P., Pensri, P., Jiamjarasrangsi, W., & Sinsongsook, T. (2010). The relationship between upper extremity musculoskeletal symptoms attributed to work and risk factors in office workers. *International Archives of Occupational and Environmental Health, 83*(3), 273–281.

Johnstone, R. (1997). *Occupational health and safety law and policy*. Sydney: The Law Book Company.

Joseph, C. (2014). *Growing up female in multi-ethnic Malaysia*. Hoboken, NJ: Taylor & Francis.

Karsh, B. T. (2006). Theories of work-related musculoskeletal disorders: Implications for ergonomic interventions. *Theoretical Issues in Ergonomics Science, 7*(1), 71–88.

Klussmann, A., Gebhardt, H., Liebers, F., & Rieger, M. A. (2008). Musculoskeletal symptoms of the upper extremities and the neck: A cross-sectional study on prevalence and symptom-predicting factors at visual display terminal (VDT) workstations. *BMC Musculoskeletal Disorders, 9*, 96.

Kortum, E., Leka, S., & Cox, T. (2010). Psychosocial risk and work-related stress in developing countries: Health impact, priorities, barriers and solutions. *International Journal of Occupational Medicine and Environmental Health, 23*(3), 225–238.

Lee, L. T. (2007). Opening address of chairman, NIOSH Malaysia. In M. K. Halimahtun (Ed.), *Proceedings of the agriculture ergonomics development conference* (p. 6). Kuala Lumpur: IEA Press.

Maakip, I., Keegel, T., & Oakman, J. (2015). Prevalence and predictors for musculoskeletal discomfort in Malaysian office workers: Investigating explanatory factors for a developing country. *Applied Ergonomics,*. doi:10.1016/j.apergo.2015.10.008.

Macdonald, W., & Oakman, J. (2015). Requirements for more effective prevention of work-related musculoskeletal disorders. *BMC Musculoskeletal, 16*, 293.

Madan, I., Reading, I., Palmer, K. T., & Coggon, D. (2008). Cultural differences in musculoskeletal symptoms and disability. *International Journal of Epidemiology, 37*, 1181–1189.

Malaysian Statistics Department. (2015). *Labour force survey report 2014*. Kuala Lumpur: Jabaran Perangkaan Negara.

National Research Council and Institute of Medicine. (2001). Musculoskeletal disorders and the workplace: Low back and upper extremity. *Panel on musculoskeletal disorders and the workplace. Commission on behavioural and social sciences and education*. Washington, DC: National Academic Press.

Noor, N. M. (1999). Roles and women's well-being: Some preliminary findings from Malaysia. *Sex Roles, 41*, 123–145.

Noor, N. M. (2006). Malaysian women's state of well-being: Empirical validation of a conceptual model. *Journal of Social Psychology, 146*, 94–115.

Oakman, J. (2014). Chapter 13 Using evidence to improve the management of work-related musculoskeletal disorders. In M. F. Dollard, A. Shimazu, R. B. Nordin, P. Brough, & M. R. Tuckey (Eds.), *Psychosocial factors at work in the Asia Pacific* (pp. 255–275). Dordrecht, The Netherlands: Springer International Publishing.

Oakman, J., Macdonald, W., & Wells, Y. (2014). Developing a comprehensive approach to risk management of musculoskeletal disorder in non-nursing health care sector employees. *Applied Ergonomics, 45*(6), 1634–1640.

Paksaichol, A., Janwantanakul, P., Purepong, N., Pensri, P., & van der Beek, A. (2012). Office workers' risk factors for the development of non-specific neck pain: A systematic review of prospective cohort studies. *Occupational and Environmental Medicine, 69*(9), 610–618.

Punnett, L., Prüss-Üstün, A., Nelson, D. I., Fingerhut, M. A., Leigh, J., Tak, S. W., et al. (2005). Estimating the global burden of low back pain attributable to combined occupational exposures. *American Journal of Industrial Medicine, 48*(6), 459–469.

Punnett, L., & Wegman, D. (2004). Work-related musculoskeletal disorders: The epidemiologic evidence and the debate. *Journal of Electromyography and Kinesiology, 14*(1), 13–23.

Ranasinghe, P., Perera, Y., Lamabadusuriya, D., Kulatunga, S., Jayawardana, N., Rajapakse, S., et al. (2011). Work related complaints of neck, shoulder and arm among computer office workers: A cross-sectional evaluation of prevalence and risk factors in a developing country. *Environmental Health, 10*, 70.

Sauter, S., & Swanson, N. (1996). An ecological model of musculoskeletal disorders in office workers. In S. D. Sauter & S. L. Moon (Eds.), *Beyond biomechanics: Psychosocial aspect of musculoskeletal disorders in office work* (pp. 2–18). Bristol: Taylor and Francis.

Smith, M. J., & Carayon-Sainfort, P. (1989). A balance theory of job design for stress reduction. *International Journal of Industrial Ergonomics, 4*(1), 67–79.

Tan, P. C. (1991). *Female participation at higher management levels in the public sector. Status and role of Malaysian women in development and family welfare*. Kuala Lumpur: National Population and Family.

Vargas-Prada, S., Serra, C., Martinez, J. M., Ntani, G., Declos, G., Palmer, K. T., et al. (2013). Psychological and culturally-influenced risk factors for the incidence and persistence of low back pain and associated disability in Spanish workers: Findings from the CUPID study. *Journal of Occupational and Environmental Medicine, 70*(1), 57–62.

World Health Organization (WHO). (2003). The burden of musculoskeletal conditions at the start of the new millennium. *World health organization technical report series 919*. Geneva: WHO.

Chapter 10
Psychosocial Safety Climate from Two Different Cultural Perspectives in the Asia Pacific: Iran and Australia Hospitals

Ali Afsharian, Amy Zadow and Maureen F. Dollard

Abstract Psychosocial safety climate (PSC) may be conceptualised as the organisational practices, policies and procedures for the protection of worker psychological health and safety. To date PSC theory has not been investigated at the boundaries of the Asia Pacific, in Iran, a developing country in the heart of the Middle East. We investigated PSC levels in Iran, and tested the theoretical paths of the extended Job Demands-Resources Model (Dollard and Bakker in J Occup Organ Psychol 83(3):579–599, 2010). The PSC-12 and work environment, emotional exhaustion and engagement scales were translated into Farsi and administered amongst 33 work groups in an Iranian hospital (N = 257), then compared with an Australian sample of hospital employees (N = 239, across 21 work groups). The findings provide evidence that PSC is a climate construct that exists as a group phenomenon cross-culturally; PSC in Iran has group like properties with around 11 % (cf 15 % in Australia) of the variance in PSC due to group-level factors, with high levels of homogeneity of perceptions of PSC within groups (0.92 vs 0.94 Australia). Australian hospital employees reported higher levels of PSC, skill discretion and decision authority, and lower levels of emotional demands, compared to the Iranian sample. Evidence in support of the climate concept also came from the way it behaved in a nomological network of analyses. The major theoretical paths delineated in PSC theory were confirmed in the Iranian data. Multilevel analysis showed that as a between-group effect in Iran and Australia, team PSC was significantly negatively related to psychological demands, and emotional exhaustion and significantly positively related to job resources, decision authority and work engagement. In Australia, an additional significant positive relationship was found between team PSC and higher levels of the job resource, skill discretion. The results support the utility of PSC theory in Iran (at least among hospital workers). Given empirical support also from Australia and Malaysia, we argue that workplace

A. Afsharian (✉) · A. Zadow · M.F. Dollard
Asia Pacific Centre for Work Health and Safety, A World Health Organization Collaborative Centre for Occupational Health, University of South Australia, Adelaide, Australia
e-mail: ali.afsharian@mymail.unisa.edu.au

A. Shimazu et al. (eds.), *Psychosocial Factors at Work in the Asia Pacific*,
DOI 10.1007/978-3-319-44400-0_10

assessment of PSC maybe useful to guide the development of organisational systems to prevent workplace psychosocial risk factors across the Asia Pacific.

Keywords Psychosocial safety climate · Job demands-resources · Health and work engagement

Introduction

Workplace psychosocial risk factors have negative impacts on workers' mental health and well-being and consequently their productivity and work experience (Dollard et al. 2014). The problem of workplace stress and its costs affects many employees across a wide range of occupational groups in Iran (Barzideh et al. 2014; Lotfizadeh et al. 2013; Mosadeghrad 2013). Knowledge of how work stress theories operate in countries such as Iran is limited (Kang et al. 2008; Leka and Cox, 2008). Most theoretical models of stress, tools, items and scales have been developed in Western countries and have not been tested in populations in the Asia Pacific despite being the world's most populous region (Brough et al. 2014; Dollard et al. 2014; Shimazu et al. 2010).

Despite the prevalence of work-related stress in Iran, and the social and economic consequences, research has not yet examined how managers and organisations can structure workplaces to prevent the development of work-related psychological health problems among employees. It is particularly important to test theoretical models cross culturally as cultures think, feel and act differently in relation to issues they experience at work (Iwata 2014). The nature of the workforce in Iran differs from other countries in the Asia Pacific as a large proportion of the almost 80 million population are young (more than 70 % under 30 years of age), highly educated (79 % hold high school diplomas or higher degrees), influenced by a mixture of three different cultural perspectives including Ancient Persian culture, Islamic culture, and more recently Western culture, and the public sector controls 80 % of the country's economy either directly (through ownership), or indirectly (through state-affiliated institutions) (Namazie and Tayeb 2006). Iran is a collectivist country with moderately high-power distance relationships in workplaces however the greater number of foreign joint ventures and multinational companies entering the country are influencing these values (Namazie and Tayeb 2006).

Recently, work stress studies conducted in Iranian organisations have concentrated on organisational safety climate (e.g. Jahanian and Hosaini 2014) and organisational culture (Abbasi and Zamani-Miandashti 2013). Research has identified that organisational culture is related to work stress in hospital nurses but is not related to other mental health measures (Ghassemi-Pirbalouti et al. 2013). Using multilevel structural equation modelling in a sample of Iranian library staff, organisational climate predicted some psychosocial risks (i.e. job demands) and psychological health issues (Yaminfirooz et al. 2015). The difficulty with measures of organisational safety climate is that they generally measure perceptions of physical safety and do not specifically examine variables that relate to psychological health.

Psychosocial Safety Climate (PSC) (Dollard and Bakker 2010) is a construct that is distinct from other related climate measures (i.e. physical safety climate, team psychological safety, perceived organisational support) and is superior to other team-level climate measures in terms of its ability to predict psychosocial risk factors such as job demands and resources, and also psychological health outcomes (Idris et al. 2012). PSC theory has not been tested in an Iranian population. A recent study has found that the PSC main elements are negatively related to work place psychosocial risk factors (Amiri et al. 2015). PSC is anticipated to be a more effective predictor of psychosocial risk factors and psychological health in Iranian workplaces than previous general safety climate measures that are not specifically designed for psychological health.

Psychosocial Safety Climate in the Asia Pacific Region

Greater research attention towards understanding the nature and influence of psychosocial risks, and the role of PSC (Dollard and Bakker 2010) across differing sociocultural contexts is required. Using multilevel techniques the aim of this research is to compare PSC theory in two separate counties in the Asia Pacific region; Iran, to bring new understanding towards the role of the prevention of psychosocial risk in an unexplored area, and Australia, a neoliberal economy with a strong emphasis on profit and productivity (Kawakami et al. 2014). Testing PSC theory in the Iranian population will add to the growing body of literature about the role of PSC across the Asia Pacific region which has been predominantly tested in Australia and Malaysia (i.e. Dollard and Bailey 2014; Dollard and Bakker 2010; Idris and Dollard 2011, 2014b; Idris et al. 2012; Kwan et al. 2014) (see Chap. 6 cross). This cross-cultural research will build knowledge about how PSC theory applies to alternative socio-cultural contexts in the Asia Pacific Region.

Theoretical Framework of Psychosocial Safety Climate

Psychosocial Safety Climate (PSC) (Dollard and Bakker 2010) is defined as the managerial policies, procedures and practices to support employees' psychological health in work environments (Dollard and McTernan 2011; Radzaz and Bahari 2013). Theoretically, PSC extends the Job Demands-Resources (JD-R) model (Demerouti and Bakker 2011). According to the JD-R model, psychosocial work aspects can be categorised as job demands—what workers have to do, and job resources—factors that assist workers to achieve work goals. The PSC theoretical framework extends two important paths of the widely used JD-R theoretical model, the health and motivation pathways (Demerouti et al. 2001), by defining the managerial and organisational context preceding the work conditions (job demands and resources).

In the JD-R model the health pathway describes the negative effects of excessive job demands leading to poor psychological health, while the motivational pathway focuses on the role of high levels of resources improving levels of work engagement and well-being. PSC is antecedent to the job demands and resources articulated in the JD-R model, and refers the managerial and organisational conditions that prevent the development of high levels of job demands and insufficient job resources. Consequently, PSC as a higher level construct has been described as a main upstream element in the prevention of work stress and an effective target for intervention (Dollard and Bakker 2010; Dollard et al. 2014). Since PSC precedes job design, it is likely to predict the level of psychological health problems such as psychological distress and emotional exhaustion via its relationship with job demands, and work engagement through its relationships with job demands such as skill discretion.

Psychosocial health and safety is attracting attention at both national and international levels (Bailey et al. 2015; World Health Organization 2015). This is particularly because continuous exposure to these psychosocial risk factors has been shown to be a robust predictor of psychological and also physical health problems (Biron et al. 2012). Moreover, reducing the prevalence of workplace psychosocial risk factors can improve job performance and productivity (Dollard and Bakker 2010).

PSC is designed to protect workers through the prevention of exposure to damaging psychosocial risk factors (Bailey et al. 2015; Dollard and Bakker 2010; Zadow and Dollard 2015). To this end, PSC embraces four basic elements; (a) management commitment, (b) management priority, (c) organisational communication and (d) organisational participation (Dollard and Bakker 2010). Management commitment describes decisive and rapid management intervention to prevent and control occupational issues causing stress at work and support employees affected by the negative consequences. Management priority relates to the importance given by managers to employees' psychological health and well-being (Idris et al. 2015). Organisational communication concerns communication about issues affecting the psychological health of employees including policies and practices that facilitate a mutual interaction between employees and managers with the purpose of problem solving and stress prevention in work groups and organisations (Idris et al. 2012). Organisational participation and involvement is characterised by management consulting with employees about psychosocial risk factors at work and engaging employees and other stakeholders such as supervisors, managers, unions and work health and safety representatives in the development of practices to prevent psychosocial risks throughout all levels of the organisation. Participation is a critical preventive strategy for occupational stress (Dollard and Gordon 2014). These four domains of PSC are vital elements for organisations looking to prevent and address workplace stress (Biron and Karanika-Murray 2014).

Even though the PSC model is recent, it is nascent, with a considerable number of studies conducted (e.g. Dollard et al. 2012; Dollard and Bakker 2010; Idris and Dollard 2011) in different organisations and contexts. They have shown that PSC is negatively related to job demands and poor psychological health (the health erosion path), and positively related to job resources and work engagement (the motivation path). The PSC model was born in Australia and is progressively growing in Asia Pacific countries, with more empirical and longitudinal studies [e.g. Australian Workplace Barometer (AWB)] focusing on PSC aspects in work contexts. Key PSC findings include the moderating role of PSC as a buffer of the effects of job demands and bullying on psychological health (Bond et al. 2010; Dollard and Bakker 2010; Dollard et al. 2012; Law et al. 2011), multilevel effects where work group classification is responsible for around 24 % of the variance in PSC (Dollard et al. 2014), the application of the PSC model to different cultural contexts, for example, Australia and Malaysia (Idris et al. 2012; Kwan et al. 2014) and that levels of PSC and subsequent workforce health are influenced by country sociopolitical mechanisms such as national ideology, policy and power (e.g. union density) (Dollard and Neser 2013).

This study tested PSC theory in an Iranian population. PSC was examined as a predictor of job demands (e.g. psychological and emotional demands), job resources (skill discretion and decision authority), emotional exhaustion and work engagement (See Fig. 10.1). As one of the first PSC studies in the Middle East, this multilevel and multi-group investigation will expand the PSC boundaries to consider the role of cultural differences. Generally, investigating climate and

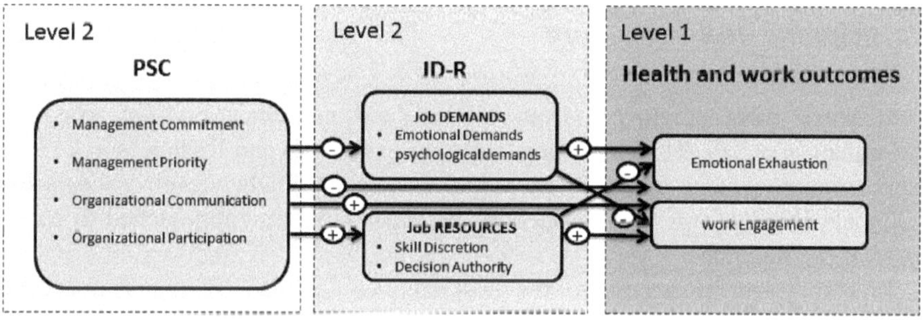

Fig. 10.1 PSC model

psychosocial risk factors in developing countries is challenging, complex and almost impossible (Kortum et al. 2010).

Given the worldwide impact of economic globalisation, technological advances, and the emergence of workplace psychosocial hazards (European Agency for Safety and Health at Work 2013) it is anticipated that workers in both Iran and Australia will report similar levels of PSC and work conditions. These psychosocial work factors are expected to impact upon workers in Iran and Australia despite their cultural differences. As work-related stress is acknowledged as a growing worldwide phenomenon affecting more than 40 million individuals across the European Union alone (World Health Organization 2008) it is anticipated that Iranian employees will report levels of emotional exhaustion and work engagement, consistent with European (European Agency for Safety and Health at Work 2013; World Health Organization 2008), Malaysian (Idris and Dollard 2014a, b; Idris et al. 2012) and Australian (e.g. Bailey et al. 2015; Dollard and Bailey 2014) samples. Accordingly we predict no net difference in organisational (PSC) and work conditions and reactions across Australia and Iran (Hypothesis 1).

Previous studies across public and private organisations (e.g. Dollard et al. 2012; Law et al. 2011; Zadow and Dollard 2015) and countries (e.g., Idris and Dollard 2014a) have shown that PSC is negatively related to job demands and emotional exhaustion, and is positively related to job resources and work engagement. Across Iran and Australia we expect that PSC at the team level predicts work conditions and outcomes (Hypothesis 2). Testing PSC theory in the Iranian population, and contrasting the results with an Australian sample will add to the growing body of the literature about the role of PSC and the management of psychosocial risk factors across the Asia Pacific region.

Method

This is a multi-group, multilevel, cross-sectional study.

Participants and Procedure

Participants were employees from clinical and non-clinical work groups in Australian (n = 239, 21 work groups, average size = 11) and Iranian (n = 257, 33 work groups, average size = 8) hospitals. To evaluate higher level concepts like PSC only work groups with an identifiable supervisor were approached to participate in the research.

In both countries access to the hospitals was granted by management but researchers could recruit the participants directly, with consideration to the work unit time schedule and priorities. In Australia participants completed the survey using hard copy or IPad surveys, and in Iran, hard copy only. In all cases data derived was given directly to the researchers (via letter, pick up, or electronically) with no organisational scrutiny. Ethics approval was given by the University of South Australia's ethics committee. All the participants were informed about the anonymity of the study and their participation was voluntary. Participants signed a written consent form in Iran.

Instruments

The instruments used in both countries were identical with the exception of language, English in Australia, and Farsi in Iran.

PSC

PSC-12 consists of four subscales each with three items; management commitment, management priority, organisational communication and organisational participation. The 12-item version was developed from the original scale that includes 26-item scale developed by Dollard and Kang (2007) as it has good validity and reliability (Cronbach's alphas of .81 or higher for all the subscales). The PSC-12 response list is ranged on a five-point Likert scale from 'strongly disagree' (one) to 'strongly agree' (five).

Job Demands

These were assessed using the Job Content Questionnaire (JCQ 2.0) (Job Content Questionnaire Centre 2012); psychological job demands (six items for the Australian sample and three items for the Iranian sample) and emotional demands (four items) were assessed on a four-point Likert scale from 'strongly disagree' (one) to 'strongly agree' (four) with reverse items recoded as required. The size of the psychological job demands scale was reduced for the Iranian sample to improve the reliability of the scale.

Job Resources

Job resources were assessed using the JCQ 2.0. In this study, skill discretion (six items) and decision authority (four items) were used to investigate job resources on a four-point Likert scale from 'strongly disagree' (one) to 'strongly agree' (four).

Health and Work Outcomes

Work Engagement

This consisted of vigour, dedication and absorption with three items measuring each aspect using the Utrecht Work Engagement Scale—Shortened Version (UWES-9) ($\alpha = 0.91$). A seven-point scale from 'never' (one) to 'every day' (seven) ranged the response list.

Emotional Exhaustion

This refers to psychological awareness of physical and emotional weakness triggered by work issues (Maslach and Jackson 1981). This was assessed using the five-item Maslach Burnout Inventory ($\alpha = 0.90$) (Maslach and Jackson 1996), with responses on a seven-point scale Likert scale from 'never' (one) to 'every day' (seven).

Statistical Analysis

Descriptive analysis and *t* tests were conducted using the Statistical Package for the Social Sciences (SPSS) (Version 22.0, 2013). Data from the individual level were nested within work unit, and to determine the functional relationships among nested workplace risk factors and phenomena, hierarchical linear modelling is recommended (Meade and Eby 2007). Hierarchical Linear Modeling (HLM 7) software (Bryk et al. 1996) was used for multilevel analysis. Face validity and consistency of the translated Iranian version of the scales were determined by five psychologists and psychiatrists' expert revisions. To confirm the psychometric properties of the research tool a pilot test–retest study on a small group of health care workers in Iran ($n = 15$) was conducted two times within a fortnight.

Results

The group-level properties of PSC were assessed using the intra-class coefficient (ICC [1]) which determines the proportion of variance due to the work group, the mean agreement index (r_{WG}) which represents homogeneity of variance within the work groups, and the ICC [2] which represents the reliability of the aggregated measure. The ICC [1] for PSC was 0.15 in Australia, and 0.11 in Iran, which indicates that approximately 15 % (Australia), and 11 % (Iran) of the variance in PSC is due to group-level random effects (see Table 10.1). The r_{WG} (median) = .94

Table 10.1 Means, standard deviations, Cronbach's alphas and correlations

	Australia				ICC	Iran				ICC	Correlations						
	N	*M*	SD	α	[1]	*N*	*M*	SD	α	[1]	1	2	3	4	5	6	7
1. PSC team level	227	3.30	0.92	0.97	0.151	257	3.09	0.80	0.94	0.105	1	−0.54**	−0.26**	0.40**	0.38**	−0.35**	0.41**
2. Psychological demands	239	2.84	0.47	0.71	0.139	257	2.80	0.48	0.67	0.040	−0.30**	1	0.41**	−0.08	−0.18**	0.48**	−0.33**
3. Emotional demands	239	2.74	0.62	0.86	0.252	257	2.97	0.59	0.80	0.063	−0.18**	0.48**	1	0.30**	−0.09	0.39**	−0.19**
4. Skill discretion	239	2.85	0.44	0.73	0.047	257	2.75	0.45	0.72	0.021	0.21**	−0.03	0.20**	1	0.45**	−0.08	0.29**
5. Decision authority	239	2.72	0.49	0.51	0.058	257	2.34	0.52	0.50	0.015	0.34**	−0.26**	−0.08	0.41**	1	−0.19**	0.27**
6. Emotional exhaustion	239	4.05	1.68	0.91	0.078	257	3.88	1.77	0.92	0.082	−0.39**	0.34**	0.26**	−0.25**	−0.27**	1	−0.37**
7. Work engagement	239	5.57	1.21	0.90	0.089	257	5.62	1.31	0.90	0.041	0.30**	−0.18**	−0.08	0.36**	0.26**	−0.54**	1

Correlations above the principal diagonal are from the Australian sample and below are from Iranian sample
$^*p < 0.05$, $^{**}p < 0.01$ (2-tailed)

for Australian sample and r_{WG} (median) = 0.92 for Iranian sample indicates that more than 90 % homogeneity of PSC perceptions within hospital workgroups in both contexts (James et al. 1984). PSC was also positively related to job resources and work engagement. The aggregated PSC measure was reliable as the ICC [2] was 0.97 and 0.94 for Australian and Iranian data respectively. These results provide justification for aggregating and assessing PSC at the group level.

Descriptives, means, standard deviations, Cronbach's alpha, and correlations between PSC team level and all the variables are presented in Table 10.1. Notably Cronbach's alpha for the variable, decision authority, demonstrated poor reliability and results involving this variable need to be interpreted with caution.

Hypothesis 1 proposed no differences between Australia and Iran on the work and health related measures. As shown in Table 10.2 using the *t* test there were no significant differences for psychological demands, emotional exhaustion and engagement supporting Hypothesis 1; but for PSC team level, emotional demands, skill discretion and decision authority of the hypothesis was not supported. Iranian workers reported lower levels of PSC, skill discretion and decision authority, and higher levels of emotional demands than their Australian counterparts.

Hypothesis 2 proposed that PSC team level predicts job demands, job resources, emotional exhaustion and work engagement. HLM analysis showed that the Iranian and Australian work teams reporting higher levels of PSC also reported lower levels of psychological demands, higher levels of decision authority and work engagement, and lower levels of emotional exhaustion. Australian work teams reporting high PSC also reported lower levels of higher levels of skill discretion (See Table 10.3).

Table 10.2 T-test differences between Iran and Australia on PSC, demands, resources, health and work outcomes

	Australia		Iran		95 % CI	*t*
	Mean	SD	Mean	SD		
PSC	3.30	0.92	3.09	0.84	0.08, 0.38	3.05**
Psychological demands	2.84	0.47	2.80	0.50	−0.05, 0.12	0.91
Emotional demands	2.74	0.62	2.97	0.61	−0.33, −0.11	−4.04**
Skill discretion	2.85	0.44	2.75	0.47	0.01, 0.17	2.33*
Decision authority	2.72	0.49	2.34	0.52	0.28, 0.46	8.36**
Emotional exhaustion	4.05	1.68	3.88	1.77	−0.15, 0.45	0.97
Work engagement	5.57	1.21	5.62	1.34	−0.24, 0.20	−0.19

N; Australia = 239, Iran = 257, $df = 510$. *CI* confidence interval
$^*p < 0.05$; $^{**}p < 0.01$ (2-tailed)

Table 10.3 Multi-level analysis of PSC team level (L2) as a predictor of level 1 factors

PSC	Psychological demands (Model 1)			Emotional demands (Model 2)			Skill discretion (Model 3)			Decision authority (Model 4)			Emotional exhaustion (Model 5)			Work engagement (Model 6)		
	$\beta 1$	S.E.	t	$\beta 1$	S.E.	t	$\beta 1$	S.E.	t	$\beta 1$	S.E.	t	$\beta 1$	S.E.	t	$\beta 1$	S.E.	t
Iran	−0.17**	0.04	−3.95	0.03	0.11	0.28	0.11	0.10	1.08	0.18**	0.06	3.04	−0.18**	0.06	−3.11	0.18*	0.07	2.48
Australia	−0.32**	0.07	−4.53	−0.14	0.11	−1.29	0.28*	0.12	2.40	0.20*	0.08	2.57	−0.25*	0.07	−3.60	0.13*	0.07	2.03

Note: Iran ($N = 257$, 33 work groups), Australia ($N = 239$, 21 work groups)
$\beta 1$, parameter estimate coefficient; S.E. Standard Error, t t-ratio
$^{*}p < 0.05$; $^{**}p < 0.01$

Discussion

Prior studies have not investigated PSC in Iran, a Muslim Middle Eastern country in the Asia Pacific. This study examines PSC, work conditions and psychological health amongst Iranian employees, and compares these results with an equivalent Australian sample, to examine similarities and differences between two Asian Pacific countries. This research is important as Iran has a unique large population of predominantly young, highly educated mainly public sector workers with a complex range of cultural influences, yet knowledge of how work stress theories operate in countries such as Iran is limited as most theoretical models of stress and measurement tools have been developed in Western countries (Brough et al. 2014; Dollard et al. 2014; Shimazu et al. 2010). Clearly it is critical to test theoretical models cross culturally across the Asia Pacific region as cultures react differently in relation to experiences at work (Iwata 2014). Measuring PSC in Iran enables the assessment of organisational system factors in the creation of the psychosocial work conditions that are a risk factor for work place stress, burnout, depression and anxiety, to develop and set priorities for policies and bench mark progress across the Asia Pacific.

In general, the study identified similarities and differences between the two Asian Pacific countries. Iranian employees reported lower levels of PSC, and the job resources, skill discretion and decision authority, and higher levels of emotional demands, than their Australian counterparts. Yet both the Iranian and Australian workers reported similar levels of psychological demands, emotional exhaustion and work engagement. Multilevel analysis identified that both Iranian and Australian work teams who report low PSC also experience higher levels of psychological job demands and emotional exhaustion and lower levels of decision authority and work engagement. The Australian work teams reporting lower levels of PSC also reported lower levels of skill discretion. These ground breaking research findings suggest that PSC theory as a predictor of workplace psychosocial risk factors can be applied to Middle Eastern countries such as Iran.

Strength, Limitations and Practical Implication

The strength of this study is the assessment of PSC theory in an unexplored area of the Asia Pacific, the Middle Eastern country of Iran. Translating the survey tool to Farsi and assessing psychosocial risk factors and psychological health amongst 33 work groups in an Iranian hospital represents a new frontier in work stress research. From a practical point of view the findings suggest that promoting high PSC in organisations in Iran will improve the psychological health of workers. Organisations in Iran can use the PSC framework to identify, measure, and monitor organisational psychosocial risk, target interventions, develop policies, benchmark progress and monitor trends to improve work conditions, productivity, work engagement and the psychological health of employees (Hall et al. 2010).

The complexity of undertaking this new research in Iran has restricted its scope. Future research should consider a larger sample size, including more organisational groups, and longitudinal methodology, as this study is underpowered and restricted in its ability to determine causality. A larger longitudinal sample will enable the examination of the mediated pathways through which PSC influences work conditions and psychological health conditions. The measurement of a wider range of job demands, including bullying and harassment, and job resources such as social support, would provide a stronger understanding of the work conditions that are most prevalent and influential in Iranian workplaces as predictors of workplace psychological health.

Collecting self-report data from different cultural contexts requires the development of trust and cultural sensitivity to respect social structures including morals, religion, politics and economic practices (Iwata 2014). To reduce misunderstanding and confusion about item meanings a combination of qualitative data collection and objective measurement would enrich the findings and shed light on cross-cultural differences in response styles including the use of styles such as acquiescence, extreme ratings, social desirability, or impression management (Iwata 2014). Triangulating evidence from a range of sources (e.g. injury rates, safety audit material or patient data), measuring PSC in alternative ways such as evidence of actual policies, practices and procedures for the protection of psychological health, and analysing how leadership styles and psychosocial safety-specific leadership training impact upon PSC levels would add to the evidence base about psychosocial risk in Iran (Zadow and Dollard 2015).

The present study adds to the literature as it provides support for PSC as a precursor to the work conditions that influence workplace psychological health. For the first time the propositions of the PSC model were shown in an Iranian sample broadening understanding of the assessment of psychosocial risk across the Middle East and supporting previous findings suggesting that the PSC theoretical framework can be applied cross culturally in both Western and Eastern contexts (e.g. Idris and Dollard 2011; Idris and Dollard 2012a, b; Idris et al. 2012). Building PSC in hospitals in Iran and Australia is required as we have a social, moral, economic and legal imperative to protect the psychological health of workers across the Asia Pacific region.

References

Abbasi, E., & Zamani-Miandashti, N. (2013). The role of transformational leadership, organizational culture and organizational learning in improving the performance of Iranian agricultural faculties. *Higher Education, 66*(4), 505–519. doi:10.1007/s10734-013-9618-8.

Amiri, D., Sann, L. M., Adon, M. Y., Mukhtar, F., Idris, K., Kuhn, K., et al. (2015). Relationship of psychosocial safety climate and workplace psychosocial risks: A randomized trail among personnel of an oil and gas company in Iran. *Asian Social Science, 11*(12), 69–83. doi:10.5539/ass.v11n12p69.

Bailey, T. S., Dollard, M. F., & Richards, P. A. (2015). A national standard for psychosocial safety climate (PSC): PSC 41 as the benchmark for low risk of job strain and depressive symptoms. *Journal of Occupational Health Psychology, 20*(1), 15–26. doi:10.1037/a0038166.

Barzideh, M., Choobineh, A., & Tabatabaee, H. (2014). Comparison of job stress dimensions in Iranian nurses with those from other countries based on the demand-control-support model. *Journal of Health Sciences and Surveillance System, 2*(2), 66–71.

Biron, C., Cooper, C. L., & Gibbs, P. (2012). Stress interventions versus positive interventions. In K. S. Cameron & G. M. Spreitzer (Eds.), *The Oxford handbook of positive organizational scholarship* (pp. 938–950). Oxford/New York: Oxford University Press.

Biron, C., & Karanika-Murray, M. (2014). Process evaluation for organizational stress and well-being interventions: Implications for theory, method, and practice. *International Journal of Stress Management, 21*(1), 85–111. doi:10.1037/a0033227.

Brough, P., Dollard, M. F., & Tuckey, M. R. (2014). Theory and methods to prevent and manage occupational stress: Innovations from around the globe. *International Journal of Stress Management, 21*(1), 1–6. doi:10.1037/a0035903.

Bryk, A. S., Raudenbush, S. W., & Congdon, R. T. (1996). *HLM: Hierarchical linear and nonlinear modeling with the HLM/2L and HLM/3L programs*. Willich: SSI Scientific Software International.

Demerouti, E., & Bakker, A. B. (2011). The job demands-resources model: Challenges for future research. *SA Journal of Industrial Psychology, 37*(2), 01–09.

Demerouti, E., Bakker, A. B., Nachreiner, F., & Schaufeli, W. B. (2001). The job demands-resources model of burnout. *Journal of Applied Psychology, 86*(3), 499–512.

Dollard, M. F., & Bailey, T. S. (2014). *The Australian workplace barometer: Psychosocial safety climate and working conditions in Australia*. Samford Valley: Australian Academic Press.

Dollard, M. F., & Bakker, A. B. (2010). Psychosocial safety climate as a precursor to conducive work environments, psychological health problems, and employee engagement. *Journal of Occupational and Organizational Psychology, 83*(3), 579–599.

Dollard, M. F., & Gordon, J. A. (2014). *Evaluation of a participatory risk management work stress intervention* (Vol. 21). Washington: Educational Publishing Foundation.

Dollard, M. F., & McTernan, W. (2011). Psychosocial safety climate: A multilevel theory of work stress in the health and community service sector. *Epidemiology and Psychiatric Sciences, 20* (04), 287–293.

Dollard, M. F., Shimazu, A., Nordin, R. B., Brough, P., & Tuckey, M. R. (2014). *The context of psychosocial factors at work in the Asia Pacific*. Berlin: Springer.

Ghassemi-Pirbalouti, M., Ahmadi, R., & Alavi, S. (2013). Association of organizational culture and job stress with mental health in nurses in Hajar and Kashani hospitals of Shahrekord city. *Journal of Clinical Nursing and Midwifery, 2*(3), 53–63.

Idris, M. A., & Dollard, M. F. (2011). Psychosocial safety climate, work conditions, and emotions in the workplace: A Malaysian population-based work stress study. *International Journal of Stress Management, 18*(4), 324–347.

Idris, M. A., & Dollard, M. F. (2014a). A multi-level study of psychosocial safety climate, challenge and hindrance demands, employee exhaustion, engagement and physical health. In *Psychosocial factors at work in the Asia Pacific* (pp. 127–143). Springer.

Idris, M. A., & Dollard, M. F. (2014b). Psychosocial safety climate, emotional demands, burnout, and depression: A longitudinal multilevel study in the Malaysian private sector. *Journal of Occupational Health Psychology, 19*(3), 291–302.

Idris, M. A., Dollard, M. F., Coward, J., & Dormann, C. (2012). Psychosocial safety climate: Conceptual distinctiveness and effect on job demands and worker psychological health. *Safety Science, 50*(1), 19–28.

Idris, M. A., Dollard, M. F., & Tuckey, M. R. (2015). Psychosocial safety climate as a management tool for employee engagement and performance: A multilevel analysis. *International Journal of Stress Management, 22*(2), 183–206. doi:10.1037/a0038986.

Iwata, N. (2014). Cultural distinctiveness in response bias. The context of psychosocial factors at work in the Asia Pacific. In M. F. Dollard, A. Shimazu, R. B. Nordin, P. Brough, & M.

R. Tuckey, (Eds.), *Psychosocial factors at work in the Asia Pacific* (pp. 3–27). Dordrecht, The Netherlands: Springer International Publishing.
Jahanian, R., & Hosaini, S. (2014). Orgnizational climate effects on employees' productivity. *Organizational Culture Management, 13*(4), 1135–1157.
James, L. R., Demaree, R. G., & Wolf, G. (1984). Estimating within-group interrater reliability with and without response bias. *Journal of Applied Psychology, 69*(1), 85–98.
Job Content Questionnaire Centre. (2012). The Job Content Questionnaire (JCQ). Department of Work Environment, University of Massachusetts. Retrieved 1 July 2014.
Kang, S., Staniford, A., Dollard, M. F., & Kompier, M. (2008). *Knowledge development and content in occupational health psychology: A systematic analysis of the journal of occupational health psychology, and work and stress 1996–2006*. Nottingham: Nottingham University Press.
Kortum, E., Leka, S., & Cox, T. (2010). Psychosocial risks and work-related stress in developing countries: Health impact, priorities, barriers and solutions. *International Journal of Occupational Medicine and Environmental Health, 23*(3), 225–238.
Kwan, S. S. M., Tuckey, M. R., & Dollard, M. F. (2014). The role of the psychosocial safety climate in coping with workplace bullying: A grounded theory and sequential tree analysis. *European Journal of Work and Organizational Psychology, 25*(1), 133–148.
Leka, S., & Cox, T. (Eds.). (2008). *PRIMA-EF. Guidance on the Euro-pean framework for psychosocial risk management*. Protecting Workers' Health Series no. 9. Geneva: WHO.
Lotfizadeh, M., Moazen, B., Habibi, E., & Hassim, N. (2013). Occupational stress among male employees of esfahan steel company, Iran: Prevalence and associated factors. *International Journal of Preventive Medicine, 4*(7), 803–808.
Maslach, C., & Jackson, S. E. (1981). The measurement of experienced burnout. *Journal of Occupational Behavior, 2*(2), 99–113.
Meade, A. W., & Eby, L. T. (2007). Using indices of group agreement in multilevel construct validation. *Organizational Research Methods, 10*(1), 75–96.
Mosadeghrad, A. M. (2013). Occupational stress and turnover intention: Implications for nursing management. *International Journal of Health Policy and Management, 1*(2), 169–176.
Namazie, P., & Tayeb, M. (2006). Human resource management in Iran. In K. M. Pawan & S. Budhwar (Eds.), *Managing Human Resources in The Middle East*, 20–39.
Radzaz, N., & Bahari, S. (2013). Psychosocial safety climate in organization: An overview of theoretical and empirical development. *Journal of Social and Development Sciences, 4*(9), 407–411.
Shimazu, A., Schaufeli, W. B., Miyanaka, D., & Iwata, N. (2010). Why Japanese workers show low work engagement: An item response theory analysis of the Utrecht Work Engagement scale. *BioPsychoSocial Medicine, 4*, 1–6.
World Health Organization and United Nations High Commissioner for Refugees. (2015). mhGAP Humanitarian Intervention Guide (mhGAP-HIG). Clinical management of mental, neurological and substance use conditions in humanitarian emergencies. Geneva: WHO.
Yaminfirooz, M., Nooshinfard, F., & Siamian, H. (2015). Structural equation model of organizational climate in Iranian academic libraries. *The Electronic Library, 33*(5), 943–958.
Zadow, A., & Dollard, M. F. (2015). Psychosocial safety climate. In P. S. Clarke, F. W. Guldenmund, & J. Passmore (Eds.), *The Wiley Blackwell handbook of the psychology of occupational safety and workplace health* (pp. 414–436). Routledge.

Part III
Practical Approach Towards Healthy Workplaces and Workers

Chapter 11
Organizational Tools for Psychosocial Risk Management: A Critical International Review

Rachael E. Potter, Alice Fattori and Maureen F. Dollard

Abstract The modern context of work has manifested complex and severe work-related psychosocial risks, generating various destructive social and economic outcomes. Yet numerous psychosocial risk management tools (e.g., national standard implementation guides) are publicly available, offering practical guidelines for organizations to readily adopt in order to decrease the impact of psychosocial risks. While psychosocial risk management tools include a process of risk assessment, there is an additional secondary focus on facilitating more practical means to reduce negative outcomes. This chapter functions as a resource that outlines and critiques all identified psychosocial risk management tools, providing individual summary sections for more in-depth analysis. Through clearly presenting each organizational-level psychosocial risk management tool, with key information and a deeper level of critique, this chapter operates as a valuable resource, and can assist with the transference of knowledge to all organizations regardless of geographical or resource-based constraints.

Keywords Psychosocial risk management tools · Risk assessment · Organizational-level

Introduction

The World Health Organization (WHO) recognizes that organizational toolkits are critical in providing frameworks and practical approaches to address fundamental health and safety issues in the workplace (WHO 2010). Psychosocial risk man-

R.E. Potter (✉) · M.F. Dollard
Asia Pacific Centre for Work Health and Safety,
The University of South Australia, Adelaide, Australia
e-mail: rachael.potter@mymail.unisa.edu.au

A. Fattori
Department of Clinical Services and Community Health,
The University of Milan, Milan, Italy

A. Shimazu et al. (eds.), *Psychosocial Factors at Work in the Asia Pacific*,
DOI 10.1007/978-3-319-44400-0_11

agement tools assist organizations establish practices that protect employee well-being, through processes relevant to the assessment and mitigation of specific risk factors. These organizational tools, designed to guide the practice of psychosocial risk management, differ in their broad composition and contextual-suitability, due to aspects such as psychosocial risks, quality of risk assessment and targeted enterprise size. The main objective of this chapter is twofold; (1) to provide a resource that identifies and critically evaluates existing psychosocial risk management toolkits, and therefore enables organizations to determine the most suitable tool for their needs; (2) to facilitate the distribution and transference of knowledge on these accessible organizational resources to all world regions, particularly the Asia Pacific region. A summary for each individual tool is provided, which is intended to provide an in-depth review of the tool's characteristics. Importantly, this task addresses an integral component of the WHO's Global Plan of Action (GPA) on Worker Health (2008–2017); initiated to develop and implement global preventative strategies that mitigate harmful psychosocial work-related factors, and invigorate policy development, infrastructure and partnerships to protect the health of all workers (WHO 2007a; 2013). Execution of the WHO GPA relies heavily on alliances between various international networks of academic departments and national institutes, nominated by WHO as collaborating centers, who offer support and resources in efforts to universally advocate for worker health. The following review aims to address an objective of the GPA, and responds to an appeal to identify, collect and disseminate tools (and resources) for the evaluation and improvement of personal health resources and global psychosocial work environments (WHO 2007a).

Organizational-Level Psychosocial Risk Management

At the organizational-level, the management of psychosocial risks involves a sequential and logical problem-solving process founded upon two distinct, yet intimately related, cycles of activity; risk assessment, and risk reduction (Cox et al. 2000). While tools may include a risk assessment process, there is an additional clear focus on practical means to lessen negative outcomes such as work-stress via risk reduction/management. The general paradigm for psychosocial risk management is based on a conceptual framework, proposed by Leka and Cox (2010), including stages of risk assessment, translation, intervention/risk reduction, and evaluation. It typically begins with the identification of issues, and an assessment of what these problems could inflict, with findings used to direct interventions that alleviate risks at the source. Figure 11.1 portrays the European Framework for Psychosocial Risk Management (PRIMA-EF); a well-regarded framework at both the organizational and policy level that serves as an exemplary model, outlining stages and providing accompanying guidance material with evidence-based best practice approaches (Leka and Cox 2008).

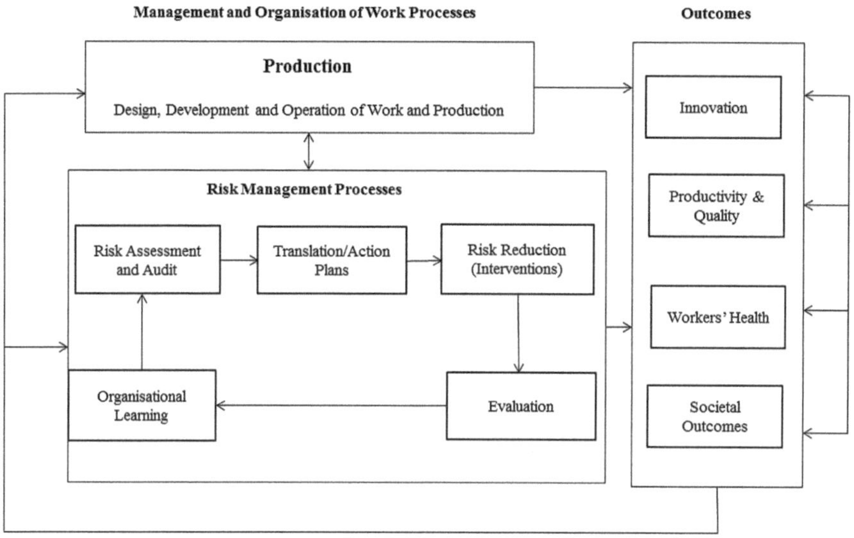

Fig. 11.1 PRIMA-EF model for the management of psychosocial risks at the enterprise level (adapted from Leka and Cox 2008)

The process of managing psychosocial risks requires a high degree of consideration for the social and organizational context. Tunnel-vision approaches are not appropriate due to the complex and context-dependent nature of psychosocial risks. Leka and Cox (2010) also suggest that psychosocial risk management entails a long-term outlook and a strong commitment by the employers and stakeholders, with equal participation of the workforce. Opposed to a once-off organizational intervention, psychosocial risk management is framed as a systematized and recurrent process that should be embedded into all organizational operations, as well as the broader work health and safety policy (Leka and Cox 2008). Findings from a study by Bergh et al. (2014) support the notion that organizations should include psychosocial risk indicators (and processes) in their current risk management system (in this case the PRIMA-EF processes). Through the development of a performance indicator for psychosocial risks in the oil and gas industry, this study gives valuable evidence regarding the importance of incorporating a proactive psychosocial risk management system into modern business strategy.

Psychosocial Risk Management in the Asia Pacific Region

Although international attention surrounding psychosocial risks has increased, psychosocial risk management interventions have been largely implemented in Europe and North America. Likewise a large proportion of the psychosocial risk management tools have been developed in response to macro-level legislation and/or policy initiatives within these countries. Specifically, considerable progress in Europe was achieved due to legal and institutional developments such as the Framework Directive 89/391/EEC (1989), the Framework Agreement of Stress (European Commission 2011), as well as increasing dissemination of scientific knowledge and publications that highlight the many social and economic benefits of psychosocial risk management for both workers and enterprise.

Yet countries within the Asia Pacific Region reflect a lesser degree of psychosocial risk management and tool development in comparison to Europe, in addition to less overall macro-level approaches and general occupational health psychology research evidence (Dollard et al. 2014; Kawakami et al. 2014). Whilst recognition of psychosocial factors and work-stress is growing across the Asia Pacific, strategies tend to be based on actions by a specific group or organization and there is not currently a great deal of macro-level psychosocial risk management. Some constructive developments include the 2008 XVIII World Congress on Safety and Health and Work in Seoul, entailing the signing of the Seoul declaration on Safety and Health at Work, which specifically asserts that it is a human right to have a safe and healthy work environment (WHO 2010). There are also other forms of guidelines and policy literature emerging in the Asia Pacific region with some mention to psychosocial risks, and their impact on wellbeing (Dollard et al. 2014).

There is a critical need to share knowledge and resources globally, particularly from Europe to the Asia Pacific region. It is important to disseminate information globally due to the regions' increasing recognition, prominence and reputation for worldwide leadership in a range of significant areas such as technology. For instance, the 10 states which comprise the Association of Southeast Asia Nations (2014) are committed to regional, economic, political and cultural integration in order to establish and maintain objectives that will advance Asia's position in the face of globalization. If current trends continue, the region will sustain development, which in turn provides greater exposure of risks to worker health. It is a logical humanitarian progression to share pre-existing knowledge and organizational tools as vital resources that can be considered by all organizations, regardless of geographical location, to reduce psychosocial risks and promote worker health. Importantly, within this movement it is essential to exercise a secondary focus on assisting small to medium enterprises that often lack the resources or systems for preventative approaches to psychosocial risks (WHO 2007b).

The Present Study

The aim of this chapter is to review organizational-level psychosocial risk management tools, and synthesize key points and principles for comparative purposes and knowledge transfer across global regions. An exhaustive search has been conducted to locate tools, using a mixed search strategy of online databases, snowballing, Internet-based search engine (Google Scholar), websites of stakeholder organizations in occupational health, as well as through macro-level initiatives/standards. It is important to note that there are many other health promotion initiatives, risk assessment tools and industry-specific tools available; however, the objective of this chapter was to only include tools that are readily usable by any organization for psychosocial risk management practice. Eleven tools were identified in total. It is not deemed appropriate to directly compare the tools or to make assumptions regarding superiority due to the high degree of uniqueness and different attributes. The tools canvas countries in the European Union, Canada and Australia. Best efforts have been exercised to locate tools regardless of language, yet it is acknowledge other tools may exist. Next, each tool is summarized individually.

The ILO Checkpoints (Geneva, 2012)

The ILO Checkpoints Stress Prevention Manual (ILO Checkpoints 2012), created by leading world experts in stress and work improvement, is highly focused on introducing simple and practical solutions for workplace stress. The tool is based on a checkpoint system of risk assessment, and provides complimentary information on risk management practices. The manual is stated as being suitable for any enterprise size and is a free resource. Within a small organization, the whole workplace can be checked; however, in the case of a larger organization, it is recommended that selected work areas of groups are defined and then checked separately.

The main focus is to use the checkpoint system for the discussion and exploration of certain psychosocial factors. Examples of these factors include leadership and justice and job demands. Each checkpoint item corresponds with an information section that outlines how and why it is important to improve these particular areas. Relevant illustrations are also presented next to checkpoint principles for further clarification. Whilst the checkpoint system is predominately considered a platform for assessment and discussion, the tool can also be used as a foundation for training workshops. Alternatively, the corresponding checkpoint information can function as information sheets for organization-wide distribution.

The initial part of the tool's composition provides brief instructions about preparatory work to conduct prior to the risk assessment. The checkpoints are then presented, and space is provided for the assessor's notes and to indicate whether the particular checkpoint requires action. The second half of the tool presents information pages, which suggest practical improvements relative to the checkpoint (psychosocial) areas. In total, there are 50 checkpoint items that are grouped under 10 core psychosocial aspects relevant to work stress. It is first recommended that organizations focus upon 20/30 checkpoints/aspects that are most important to their unique context. Using these checkpoints, an assessor conducts a worksite walk-through, and makes note of areas of improvement before executing focus groups with workers on these issues. Therefore, the checkpoints are predominantly for the use of the person conducting an assessment, rather than a survey distributed to all the workers. To ensure and improve validity and accuracy of the analysis, it is critical that discussions with employees about psychosocial risks occur alongside the walkthrough-based assessments. It is vital that focus groups are employed to discuss the findings to reduce any bias or observer subjectivity. The focus group also allows more in-depth information to be obtained, and is also an opportunity to confirm or refute any findings.

Pragmatically, this tool is most suitable for a person with some experience in human resources or occupational health and safety, due to the high degree of power and subjectivity that accompanies the walkthrough assessment. As such, it is imperative that the person has prior knowledge of the organization and about the nature and types of stress areas under inspection. The person must also be able to facilitate a group discussion about the findings and possible solutions. In addition, the checkpoints are somewhat ambiguous, suggesting general solutions that may require some more specialized input and training from persons with a health and safety background.

From a more critical perspective, the ILO checkpoints provide only a basic guide to psychosocial risks in the workplace. For this reason, it could be argued that the tool is not suitable for larger enterprises due to the overly simplified approach and lack of detail. While there are some suggested points for action, these are typically presented in vague way, without sufficient information for each of the processes or steps. Yet, for smaller enterprises, this lack of detail may generate some creative outcomes. For instance, without any prescriptive or clear instruction available, the enterprise is able to be more flexible and adaptive in their approach to mitigating stress and the contributing risks. Other issues of concern include the logistics of a worksite walkthrough and how this would work within a busy workplace.

Furthermore, the task of conducting a worksite assessment also evokes the issue of power imbalance and subjectivity between the assessor and employees, which may also lead to less accurate findings, particularly as there are no behavioral indicators linked with the assessment. Caution should also be exercised in the heavy use of group discussions, as in some cultures and organizational climates the practice of speaking out within a group may not be appropriate. Overall, the tool provides practical guidance on how to link workplace risk assessment with the process of stress prevention, and enables multifaceted action that can be adapted with respect to the unique organizational culture.

Managing the Causes of Work-Related Stress: A Step-by-Step Approach Using the Health and Safety Executives' Management Standards (Great Britain, 2007)

The step-by-step approach using the Management Standards (Health and Safety Executive 2007) was developed by the Health and Safety Executive (HSE) as a practical implementation guide for employers to meet specific management standards outlined by United Kingdom legislation. The document focuses on six key sources of work-stress: demands, control, support, relationships, roles and change, outlining the corresponding premium organizational conditions that foster high levels of health, wellbeing and performance. Through the inclusion of a simplified risk assessment process, such as surveys and focus groups, the tool helps employers initiate active discussion between managers and employees about practical improvements. Furthermore, advice and solutions relevant to the aforementioned areas of work design are also presented. The underlying objective of this step-by-step approach is to identify, and then close the gap between the organization's current condition and the ideal vision.

Following an introductory discussion on work-stress, the document defines each psychosocial aspect and states the optimal standard for each aspect. Within the document there is a focus on five steps to (1) identify the stress risk factors: understand the management standards; (2) decide who might be harmed: gather data; (3) evaluate the risks: exploring problems and developing solutions; (4) record findings: developing and implementing action plans; and (5) monitor and review action plans and assessment. At the end of each step, a checklist is provided to ensure sufficient completion of each phase. There are also additional sections regarding how to handle individual concerns, and further improvements after all steps are completed. Overall the tool is primarily aimed at organizations employing 50 or more people; however, smaller businesses may also find the approach helpful. The tool is written for management, human resource management staff, health and safety officers, trade union representatives or line managers.

A major strength of this tool is the amount of resources included. It includes a 35-item survey tool (HSE Management Standards Indicator tool), and provides questions about working conditions that corresponds with the six psychosocial factors outlined in the Management Standards. Results can be analyzed through an excel-based analysis tool on the CD. Yet, external forms of risk assessment may also be used. The tool also gives an example of a stress policy, an action-plan template, worked example, and a competency framework for line managers for managing stress at work.

In addition explanations and justifications regarding psychosocial risk management are provided and a strong business case is outlined and supported with macro-level evidence-based data. The tool also presents clear definitions of exactly what these key sources of stress look like, as well as a strong focus on implementing detailed preparatory work, and encompassing a comprehensive checkpoint system within each step. However, whilst there is a high level of information on what to do, there is not a lot of detail on practical approaches exploring *how* to conduct psychosocial risk reduction. Despite this, there is an overall favorable emphasis on organizational-level issues, reflecting a great deal of thought and discussion, and promotion of high levels of worker involvement.

Istas21 (CoPsoQ) Method (Version 2)—Trade Unions' Institute of Work, Environment and Health (Spain, 2014)

Istas21 CoPsoQ (Trade Unions' Institute of Work, Environment and Health 2014) is the Spanish version of the Copenhagen Psychosocial Questionnaire (CoPsoQ), and aims to provide a valid method of psychosocial risk assessment for the Spanish population. Version 1 was made in 2003, 1.5 in 2010 and 2 in 2014. Istas21 CoPsoQ enables the identification and evaluation of psychosocial risks through the voluntary active participation of employees.

As an evidence-based and validated tool, it is suitable for any type of work. Version 2 Istas21 CoPsoQ questionnaire consists of 109 questions on employment and working conditions (25 questions), exposure to psychosocial risk factors (69 questions) and health and wellbeing (15 questions); it is an individual, anonymous, confidential questionnaire which has two versions adapted to the size of the company: a version for organizations which employ 25 or more workers, and a short one for organizations with less than 25 workers. Employees should take active part in the process and the tool should not be modified.

To arrange and promote the risk management process, the methodology suggests creating a "Working Group" (WG) consisting of workers and employer's representatives, together with OSH professionals and technicians. The WG should schedule ongoing meetings, inform all employees of the evaluation process, and propose preventive actions suitable for the organizational context. A signed agreement about the intervention process between employee representatives and the management team is also suggested. To ensure active participation after the risk evaluation, the tool suggests implementing groups of workers (Prevention Circles) to identify preventive measures and monitor planned interventions. Guidelines and examples on conducting group discussions are provided. Istas21 CoPsoQ also provides an illustrated matrix to support users during the process, including preventive actions, timelines, the persons involved, the requested resources, and materials. Examples of suggested improvements include job rotation and enrichment, participatory role of employees, cooperation, organizational justice, promotion of team work, and flexible working hours.

The tool can be used by researchers, OSH technicians, occupational physicians and workers' delegates. The tool is public and free of charge, with the only limit being acceptance of the licenses terms. The English version of Istas21 CoPsoQ can be retrieved through contacting ISTAS via e-mail. Although the main focus of this method is the evaluation of risks, a thorough manual is included with descriptions pertaining to the risk management process that is founded on the basis of prevention-based action using a risk management paradigm. The methodology allows identification of improvement areas and promotes movement towards more healthy alternatives to work organization.

SME Vital (Switzerland, 2004)

This Swiss web-based tool was developed and tested by work health promotion practitioners and small and medium enterprises (SMEs), with the objective to produce a standardized toolkit that is central to the requirements of SMEs (KMU-*vital* 2014). The tool was created by researchers, practitioners, employer representatives, trade unions and governmental representatives, and has received national-level support through social dialog at its developmental stage. The program has ten modules that focus on psychosocial aspects in the work environment. The delivery of these modules is based on core principles such as employee participation, integration of all areas of the organization, and project management. Equal attention is given to both individual and environmental measures, consequently targeting the risks and resources to employee behavior and organizational structure. As the name implies, this tool has been designed for SMEs, although larger companies may still find it useful.

There are basic modules to establish workshops, and also implementation modules, which involve courses centered on health behavior (e.g., stress management), personnel development (e.g., team development) and organizational development (e.g., participatory job re-design). The first phase outlined in the tool is called Initiate Workplace Health Promotion, whereby an information brochure is distributed in the organization and the "starter workshop" is conducted with senior management to cultivate motivation, analyze the organization, set goals and to prepare an implementation plan for the modules to be delivered. The second phase is called Workplace Health Promotion Analysis, and involves administering surveys to both the employees and management to develop a dual action communication for health promotion. The management survey assesses the current state of work organization, personnel management practices and benefits to employees, whereas the employee survey measures the strengths and weakness of job tasks, work organization, participation, leadership, working climate, and commitment levels. In the third phase, health circles are utilized to implement the findings from the surveys. Both employees and management come together to discuss the results of the surveys and to problem-solve issues, establishing targets to workplace health promotion and an action-plan for the organization to adhere to. Then the action-plan is introduced, and may include a focus on (1) organizational development, (2) personnel development, (3) individual health behavior or (4) a variety of methods, depending on the context and needs of the organization. In the fourth stage, the results of the program are evaluated through the monitoring of change, derived from the results of the second wave of employee and management surveys, as well as using the specific company-based targets as benchmarks. The organization should engage in a continuous improvement cycle, and use health circles as a sustainable approach for health promotion.

A major strength of the SME Vital is that its processes, outcomes, and sustainability have been evaluated. It was piloted in ten SMEs and the last evaluation was conducted by independent and external persons. Benefits from the program include increased communication between employees and management and a better overall work climate, high levels of motivation and employee performance, and better competency in coping with demands and continual organizational change. However the tool has not been evaluated on economic value. Overall, this tool is claimed to be practical and easy to use as it provides clear guidelines and working materials. The standardized modules are also able to be adapted to the organization's requirements, which promote a sense of flexibility.

Instituto Nazional Per L'Assicurazione Contro Gli Infortuni Sul Lavoro (INAIL) (Italy, 2011)

The INAIL tool was developed with modularity and flexibility in mind, and permits the use of supporting tools to achieve a comprehensive risk assessment in line with the organizations' specific needs (INAIL 2011). It encompasses the HSE Management Standards 'Indicator tool' approach in the Italian context, and was formulated in compliance with the specific guidelines set by the European Framework Agreement on work-related stress (2004), the subsequent Italian Legislative Decree 81/2008, as well as the requirements by the Permanent Consultative Commission for Occupational Health and Safety in 2010.

The aim of the INAIL model is to provide organizations with a useful and sustainable two-step methodology that meets legislative risk assessment required in both public and private fields. The preliminary phase (Step 1), exclusively considers objective indicators of work-related stress divided in three areas: (1) objective information (e.g., injury rates, sick leave, turnover, procedures and sanctions, reports of occupational physicians and formal complaints), (2) work content factors (work environment and equipment, task planning, workloads, working hours and shifts), and (3) work context factors (organizational culture, role in the organization, decision-making autonomy and control, interpersonal conflicts at work, career development, communication, home-work balance). Step 3 is conducted by employers and OHS personnel, yet employees can be involved at the employers' discretion.

A value is assigned to each indicator (0 if decreased, 1 if unvaried and 4 if increased over the last 3 years) and the score of the three areas is then summed, providing the consequent risk level (low-medium-high). In case of medium or high risk levels, suitable or urgent corrective actions are required, and focus groups are suggested to identify proper corrective measures subsequent to risk identification. Furthermore, the INAIL methodology does not exclude the involvement of external professionals as well as the use of other validated tools.

The detailed phase, or 'in-depth assessment' (Step 2), occurs if corrective interventions are neither successful nor effective. This step requires the assessment of workers' subjective perceptions of psychosocial risk factors with the Indicator tool developed by HSE which assesses demands, control, support, relationships, role and change factors. The Indicator tool may be limited to homogenous groups of workers, relative to tasks or organizational sector. The tool may also be helpful for organizations which employ less than ten workers, by encouraging discussion through regular meeting, thus ensuring involvement of all employees. The INAIL methodology suggests communicating evaluation findings to the entire workforce, who should also be involved in monitoring the effectiveness of the measures taken. As a strength, the tools makes good reference to critical preparatory factors such as forming a steering group, developing training programs to inform employees about the process and ensuring scheduled deadlines are in place for the risk assessment plan.

Implementation Guide to the National Standard for Psychosocial Health and Safety in the Workplace (Canada, 2013)

Created by the Mental Health Commission of Canada (2014), the Implementation Guide is a detailed and comprehensive document, providing a voluntary set of guidelines, tools, and resources that are designed to accompany the Canadian National Standard for Psychosocial Health & Safety in the Workplace. This tool is a Psychological Health and Safety Management System (PHSMS) and, comparable to other management systems, it should be integrated within existing organizational policies and procedures. This tool provides exceptional descriptions and guidance surrounding each psychosocial issue with good use of inclusive language. Rather than acting as a prescriptive strategy, the tool gives an array of ideas and tips to choose from. The document is engaging, highly practical and clarifies terms into common language, which expands its target audience.

Overall, there is strong emphasis on assisting with the construction of an organizational system, rather than a singular initiative. A strong emphasis is placed upon looking at what is already in place, and then to enhance these pre-existing approaches. Examples of psychosocial risk factors addressed within the document include (but are not limited to) psychological support, organizational culture, psychological job demands, growth and development, recognition and reward, workload management, bullying and harassment, and protection of physical safety and other chronic stressors.

This tool is a lengthy document, which is superbly detailed and divided into a four piece framework, with each section including practical tools and techniques. Furthermore, prior to each chapter, a recap of the previous section is presented. Each section also includes an array of frequently asked questions and answers. The underlining ethos communicated by the Mental Health Commission is that organizations should focus on creating a flexible psychosocial risk management framework, which is built carefully and purposely over time and integrated into how the organizations' unique business is conducted. This tool is suitable for any organization, and it is difficult to pinpoint any weaknesses in its construction. Due to the well-written design and layout, any person (from employees to executives) would find this tool beneficial for improving knowledge about occupational health and safety matters.

The SOBANE Risk Management Strategy and the Déparis Method for the Participatory Screening of the Risks (Belgium, 2010)

The SOBANE Risk Management Strategy provides a highly systematic framework for risk management, and demonstrates exceptional level of consideration for each process (SOBANE 2010). Rather than a heavy focus on a simple recognition of risks, the strategy places a greater emphasis on instigating a solution-focused search. The document argues that many other psychosocial risk management methods have been developed in response to the European legislation, and that they are typically based on one inventory that provides only general or "stereotyped" recommendations. It criticizes less systematic tools, stating that they are not very effective, and often lack the right resources or instructions to guide the higher level screening and observation practices. SOBANE states that often the issues are resolved by experts rather than workers who are most knowledgeable in that area. Overall, SOBANE differentiates from wanting to be characterized as method, checklist, or even tool and aims to be a strategy that coordinates the efforts between the workers, technical staff, and the OHS practitioners. For this reason, there is not a large degree of flexibility in the methods.

The SOBANE strategy is built on the premise that the severity or difficulty of amending risk factors should correspond with decreasing knowledge from the employee to an expert. The strategy incorporates four levels of intervention (1) screening, (2) observation, (3) analysis, and (4) expertise. However, the tool does not state what (or who) is responsible for choosing the stage and facilitating the strategy implementation. It presents as a highly efficient framework, as different levels of the intervention strategy can be used at different times when necessary and also utilize different people. First, the initial screening phase uses the Déparis method; a screening tool guide consisting of a series of 18 tables, each with sub-headings relevant to that area. Screening is first carried out internally by those who are most familiar with the work. If the risks are not mitigated after this initial phase, then the second level (observation) occurs. In this phase, both employees and their local management collaborate with an internal OHS practitioner when available. If needed afterwards, a third level of intervention (analysis) can occur. This now requires the assistance of someone with the needed qualifications, tools and techniques. These people will often be OHS practitioners external to the company, intervening in close cooperation with those who conducted the screening and observation levels. For extreme or prominent issues, a fourth level of intervention—

expertise—is then conducted. The expertise level must be carried out by the same employees and OSH practitioners, with the additional assistance of highly specialized experts. This phase relates to particularly complex situations and often requires the use of more specialized measurements. At the end of any screening, the appropriate person should synthesize the results under the heading of the work situation and allocate a green, yellow, or red face to link with the state of that particular work situation, then, complete an inventory of the proposed improvement measures.

The strategy is suitable for all organization sizes. As a valuable component within the document, there is a section specifically dedicated to explaining risk management in the context of SMEs. Other valuable sections include acknowledgement of the Directive 89/391, the globality of the problems and quantification and qualification of risks. It also includes discussion of the role of the practitioner; an aspect that is commonly overlooked within other tools.

Overall, the strategy has a stronger focus on the prevention of physical risks. Psychosocial factors were purposefully positioned as the last aspect of risk prevention for two reasons. The first the organizations' general reluctance to address these issues and second, during these types of discussions, it is believed to be more appropriate to begin on more neutral technical subjects before approaching more sensitive topics such as psychosocial risks. Examples of the targeted risks include salary, information, and discrimination. Yet, under other headings, there are other factors that could be recognized as psychosocial risks: work organization, autonomy and personal responsibilities, work content, and time restraints.

The strength of this tool is that it really values worker involvement, yet justly recognizes the limitations of worker knowledge on how to solely mitigate risks. Another advantageous feature is that it promotes participative discussion about the issues (through the Déparis dialog meeting) and does not rely on quantitative survey answers. The document also includes a great deal of resources, such as a sample invitation for the Déparis screening, a list of the items discussed in the Déparis meeting, tables of the Déparis guide, which states areas to be discussed and what can be done in practice and when. Finally, there is a resource of a synthesis checklist of audit tools for the major risks (not to be used alone but in addition to the Déparis guide). In addition, there is a good inclusion of visual representations and tables to better communicate approaches. However, it does not include many practical suggestions and in some areas, there is a sense that the English version differs slightly from the German version. Overall, the SOBANE strategy reflects a detailed approach and in particular prompts consideration into how psychosocial risks are conceptualized, framing the issues from a deep-thinking and highly critical perspective.

The START Procedure for the Risk Assessment and Risk Management of Work-Related Stress (Germany, 2009)

The START procedure was established in response to the provisions of the German Labor Protection law and aligns with statutory requirements (Satzer and Gerey 2009). The tool has a stronger emphasis on risk assessment, rather than risk management and follows process-orientated logic. The START procedure for risk assessment uses basic analysis (screening) and suggests evaluating all available company data, using written questions for employees, as well as an external assessor to inspect workplaces and conduct interviews (using practical checklists).

The tool also uses a simple non-standard design survey tool (questionnaire), which is able to be contextualized to the organizations' unique culture. Within this questionnaire, some of the psychosocial risks include support from managers, training, working hours, and division of labor. However, the START procedure still considers the impact on the physical work environment (e.g., temperature) on mental stress. The START procedure also includes a focus on the risk management phase, outlining a dual design approach (i.e., stress-orientated and resource-related perspectives) and relevant stress reduction strategies.

The document incorporates a table that outlines the influential factors and characteristics at work on mental stress such as workflow and working climate. Then there is a description of the starting points, methods and tool beginning with a subsection on the central characteristics of the procedure and what to do before the risk assessment. There is also a section on how to determine mental stress through the START procedure (or the risk assessment phase), outlining the START questionnaire, and other aspects such as a description about the conception of the questionnaire. The tool provides an evaluation strategy for the risk assessment results, showing a number of graphs/pictures.

Overall, while the START procedure offers a good basis for psychosocial risk management, particularly the assessment process, it lacks a practical focus. In addition, the tool has a somewhat less clear structure than other tools, yet this may be attributable to the shortened translated English language version. A more thorough review of the original German handbook is recommended.

The Government of Western Australian Psychologically Safe and Healthy Workplaces: Risk Management Approach Toolkit (Australia, 2014)

This tool was developed by the Government of Western Australia–Department of Commerce (2014), and its construction is highly logical and easy-to-follow. First, the notion of psychologically healthy and safe workplaces is introduced, followed by risk factors and associated psychological symptoms and signs. Other discussed aspects include how to identify hazards, analyze workplace data, issues with direct observation, different type employee surveys, and ways of controlling risks. Some incorporated psychosocial risks include autonomy/control, support, role conflict/ambiguity, change, rewards and recognition, and organizational justice. There is also mention of physical stressors.

While this tools lacks some of the more detailed introductory material noted in other tools, it contains a high degree of practical resources. These include a workplace data analysis table, direct observation data, table of risk factors, risk management plan sample, employee survey measures, health self-report measures and leadership development tools. Unfortunately, it is recommended that information about psychosocial risk factors should be derived from observation, surveys and objective data, suggesting a low level of worker involvement and a high degree of subjectivity on behalf of the elected assessor.

For the risk management aspect, a plan is also provided, which allows elected personnel to develop an action plan, with space to elect a responsible person, specific dates and review comments. Another good aspect regarding the construction is that it clearly describes different types of risk factors, and provides tables that show different types (physical, cognitive, emotional, and behavioral) of associated signs and symptoms. This tool also provides great detail surrounding different types of workplace data and offers numerous examples. Within this section, there is also a table that displays various employee survey measure designs and the kinds of psychosocial risks that they include. Unlike other tools, there is also an inclusion of different forms of health surveys or assessment tools that measure health outcomes such as depression, psychological distress and coping skills. Yet overall, the construction or method of this tool is not very comprehensive, but rather acts as a starting point and may be useful in addition to other tools or as a means of commencing the psychosocial risk management process. Furthermore, the language of the document often positions workers as more passive actors, to be observed, rather as having an active part in the process.

Work Positive—A Stress Management Approach for SMEs—HEBS and HAS Joint Commission (Scotland cand Ireland, 2002)

For this chapter, this tool was unable to be retrieved which limits the ability to conduct a critical review. However, Work Positive is a tool for SME's that allows workplaces to manage stress through a five-step process, and is available in a resources pack that includes a benchmarking tool, a risk assessment survey, and guidance material, instructions for application, guidance on risk reduction and an analysis package (EU-OSHA 2002). Work Positive was established to address a substantial void regarding the availability and suitability of work health and safety tools for SMEs. The Health Education Board in Scotland (HEBS) and the Health and Safety Authority (HAS) in Ireland commissioned a consultancy enterprise, ENTEC UK to create this self-administered tool for small to medium businesses.

A secondary objective was to develop a tool that could be administered without the assistance of an external consultant. The findings from the tool then allow the organization to recognize supportive mechanisms, and act on the information that arose from using the tool. The tools have been validated and piloted in a range of organizations and organizational sectors. Risk assessment and benchmarking tools were piloted in 14 organizations.

There is a clear focus on organizational-level stressors as opposed to outcomes at an individual level. Stressors that are covered by the tool include management structure and style, human resource management (selection procedures, feedback pay, training, promotional opportunities, disciplinary procedures, interpersonal relations, and health and safety), work process (duration of work shift patterns, work/rest regime, workload, quality control, goal setting, training), job characteristics (skill variety, task identify task significance, autonomy, feedback), social/technical/ environmental design (team and group working, technological change, environmental design), and incidents (redundancy, organizational change, takeover).

Stresswise—Preventing Work-Related Stress. A Guide for Employers in the Public Sector (State Government of Victoria, Australia, 2007)

Worksafe Victoria's strategy for work-related stress incorporates practical advice and resources to assist with the prevention of health problems through psychosocial risks (Worksafe 2007). The document follows a logical format, with excellent attachments and surveys embedded within different steps. The overall process is succinctly presented, and incorporates descriptions about which resource/worksheet to complete at each stage. Key definitions are also provided to clarify different terms, and unlike many other tools there is distinction between hazards and risks.

Overall the visual presentation of the document is very clear. The tool's steps include first identifying potential work-related stress hazards, determining the work-related stress risks, controlling the hazards and risks and then implementing continuous improvement, with trials, reviews, and evaluation. At the first step (identifying potential work hazards) there are two attachments provided that: (1) gives information about how to examine and interrogate workplace data; and, (2) sample survey questions. This first step also includes the completion of an OHS work-related stress prevention worksheet to identify and record potential stress hazards. Lists of hazards are already included in this section.

The tool differentiates between three different arenas to hazards/risks—the social and physical environment, the systems of work and the management of work. Under social and physical work, the hazards include organizational culture, career development, home/work demands, physical work environment and equipment. Regarding systems of work, the psychosocial hazards are workload/pace, work schedule/working hours and participation and control. Finally, at the management of work level, the hazards include supervision and information, instruction and training. At the second step of the tools methodology (determining work-related stress risks) there is an attachment for the antecedents that potential for work-related stress. For this step, another worksheet needs to be completed.

Step 3 refers to the process of controlling work-related stress hazards and risk, whereby workgroup consultations are used to find the best measures or actions to introduce. Within this phase, the process occurs at three levels (with help from the attachment of the OHS work-related stress prevention worksheet): (1) to identify the hazards; (2) to determine the stress risks; and, (3) to then consider the measures/actions to control these risks. The fourth step proposes a continual implementation of improvement, suggesting to trial, review and evalaute the process. Action planning resources are also provided, with a case study example to assist with this action planning stage. The tool also acknowledges that some issues may need to be authorized and action taken at a higher level. An intervention modelled on Stresswise was conducted in an Australian public sector organization. It used a participatory risk management approach and capacity building workshops to develop and implement action plans to reduce work and organizational stress risk factors (e.g., job design, performance management, work quality, and organizational change) and stress outcomes (e.g., work stress, morale, and sickness absence duration) (Dollard and Gordon 2014). The intervention used an existing organizational development survey of work conditions and well-being as a risk assessment and evaluation tool. After 12 months of intervention, relative to control groups (n = 17 work units) the intervention group (n = 5) showed significant improvements in job design, training and development, and morale, and marginal effects for work quality and positive performance management. Organizational sickness absence duration decreased, consistent with an intervention effect. Top management commitment and support, worker participation, and action plan implementation were important components for intervention success.

Overall, the system is very clear and concisely written. It does not discriminate between enterprise sizes but it does state it is a guide for employers in the public sector. The document provides detail about legal obligations of Australian workplaces and clarifies legal terms and explanations for work-stress. A further strength is that it presents various ways of assessing risks, and promotes thinking about risks in a more all-encompassing way. For example, rather than just identifying risks, you should also consider the situation in which they occur, the frequency and duration, and the harmful precursors and/or outcomes experienced by the employees. There is also good consideration for issues such as privacy and confidentiality of personal information, and it also advocates process repetition at least annually or when employees change.

Conclusion, Challenges, and Future Directions

Due to enacted safety legislation, many countries now mandate organizations to conduct regular psychosocial risk assessments (Dollard et al. 2007), and then, to intervene to eliminate or reduce them through the necessary preventative or protective measures. The challenge now is to put existing policies and legal duties into practice, with the assistance of informative tools that offer guidance and support to organizations in providing constructive psychosocial risk management practices (Leka and Cox 2010). These tools are particularly integral to SMEs, as well as organizations in developing or emerging economies, which may lack the knowledge of an occupational health and safety professional or have restricted resources. Through identifying and reviewing each tool within this chapter, it is hoped that knowledge may be shared throughout the world regions, and that the relevant persons are able to make an educated decision in selecting which tool to be the most appropriate for the organizational context.

However, there is a general lack of scientific evidence regarding evaluation of the implementation psychosocial risk management processes outlined in the tools. Consequently, it is important that future research asserts scientific evidence on the effectiveness of these practical approaches to address this major gap within the literature. As a result of developing greater evidence, more organizations will be encouraged to include the psychosocial risk management processes in their own organizational policies and practices.

It is also apparent that psychosocial risk management has been mainly developed in Europe, North America, and Australia. At present, there is a particularly prominent gap of evidence-based policy guidance surrounding psychosocial risk management in the Asia Pacific Region, and the current policy lacks practical recommendations, with little substantive or purposeful guidance for organizational utilization. Therefore, areas in the Asia Pacific Region may benefit from adapting these tools to fit the cultural context, or develop methods based on the psychosocial risk management paradigm. It is imperative to employ more applied principles, such as those outlined within psychosocial risk management toolkits, to support the cultivation of healthy work environments. Overall, in a world fraught with ever-increasing globalization, shifting employment arrangements and work-intensification, organizations must implement practical approaches to manage the inevitable presence of psychosocial risks. These tools help guide organizational-level approaches that translate legislative requirements into practice, providing the necessary resources (e.g., action planning sheets) and information.

References

Association of South East Asian Nations. (2014). Retrieved from http://www.asean.org/asean/about-asean. Retrieved 21 December 2015.

Bergh, L. I. V., Hinna, S., Leka, S., & Jain, A. (2014). Developing a performance indicator for psychosocial risk in the oil and gas industry. *Safety Science, 62*, 98–102.

Cox, T., Griffiths, A., Barlow, C., Randall, R., Thomson, T., & Rial-González, E. (2000). *Organizational interventions for work stress: A risk management approach*. Sudbury: HSE Books.

Dollard, M. F., Shimazu, S., Bin Nordin, R., & Brough, P. (2014). Chapter 1 The context of psychosocial factors at work in the Asia Pacific. In M. F. Dollard, A. Shimazu, R. B. Nordin, P. Brough, & M. R. Tuckey (Eds.), *Psychosocial factors at work in the Asia Pacific*. Dordrecht: Springer.

Dollard, M., Skinner, N., Tuckey, M., & Bailey, T. (2007). National surveillance of psychosocial risk factors in the workplace: An international overview. *Work & Stress: An International Journal of Work, Health and Organizations, 21*(1), 1–29.

Dollard, M. F., & Bailey, T. S. (Eds.). (2014). *Australian workplace barometer: Psychosocial safety climate and working conditions in Australia*. Samford Valley, QLD: Australian Academic Press.

Dollard, M. F., & Gordon, J. A. (2014). Evaluation of a participatory risk management work stress intervention. *International Journal of Stress Management, 21*, 27–42.

EU-OSHA. (2002). Chapter 3 Improvements in the psychosocial working environment: "Work positive"—A stress management approach for SMEs—HEBs and HAS Joint Commission-Scotland and Ireland. In *Systems and programmes: How to tackle psychosocial issues and reduce work-related stress*. Luxembourg: Office for Official Publications of the European Communities.

European Commission. (2011). *Report on the implementation of the European social partners' Framework Agreement on Work-related Stress*. Retrieved from http://www.europarl.europa.eu/registre/docs_autres_institutions/commission_europeenne/sec/2011/0241/COM_SEC%282011%290241_EN.pdf.

Framework Directive 89/391/EEC-OSH. (1989). Retrieved from https://osha.europa.eu/en/legislation/directives/the-osh-framework-directive/1. Retrieved 8 August 2015.

Government of Western Australia Department of Commerce. (2014). *Psychologically safe and healthy workplaces: Risk management approach toolkit*. Retrieved from https://www.commerce.wa.gov.au/sites/default/files/atoms/files/psychologically-healthy-and-safe-workplace-risk-management-toolkit.pdf. Retrieved 7 September 2015.

Health and Safety Executive. (2007). *Managing the causes of work-related stress. A step-by-step approach using the Management Standards*. Retrieved from http://www.hse.gov.uk/pubns/priced/hsg218.pdf. http://apps.who.int/iris/bitstream/10665/44428/1/9789241500272_eng.pdf. Retrieved 4 May 2015.

INAIL. (2011). Valutazione e Gestione da stress lavoro correlate. Manuale ad uso delle aziende in attuazione del D.Lgs 81/08 e s.m.i. Milano: Tipografia INAIL. Retrieved from INAIL: http://85.18.194.67/focusstresslavorocorrelato/documenti/maulae.pdf. Retrieved 7 August 2015.

International Labour Office. (2012). *Stress prevention at work checkpoints. Practical improvements for stress prevention in the workplace*. Retrieved from http://www.ilo.org/wcmsp5/groups/public/—dgreports/—dcomm/—publ/documents/publication/wcms_168053.pdf. Retrieved 3 April 2015.

Kawakami, N., Park, J., Dollard, M. F., & Dai, J. (2014). Chapter 2 Psychosocial factors at work in Japan, Korea, Australia, and China. In M. F. Dollard, A. Shimazu, R. B. Nordin, P. Brough, & M. R. Tuckey (Eds.), *Psychosocial factors at work in the Asia Pacific*. Dordrecht: Springer.

KMU-*vital*. (2014). KMU-*vital*: Ein Programm von Gesundheitsförderung Schweiz. Retrieved from http://www.kmu-vital.ch/default2.asp?cat=-1. Retrieved 01 January 2015.

Leka, S., & Cox, T. (2008). *The European framework for psychosocial risk management PRIMA-EF*. Retrieved from http://www.prima-ef.org/uploads/1/1/0/2/11022736/prima-ef_ebook.pdf. Retrieved 6 June 15.

Leka, S., & Cox, T. (2010). Psychosocial risk management at the workplace level. In S. Leka & J. Houdmont (Eds.), *Occupational health psychology*. Chichester: Wiley.

Mental Health Commission of Canada. (2014). Assembling the pieces. An implementation guide to the national standard for psychological health and safety in the workplace. Retrieved from http://www.mentalhealthcommission.ca/English/issues/workplace/national-standard. Retrieved 4 May 2015.

Satzer, R., & Gerey, M. (2009). *Stress-mind-health, the START procedure for the risk assessment and risk management of work-related stress*. Düsseldorf: Hans-Böckler-Stiftung.

SOBANE. (2010). The SOBANE risk management strategy and the déparis method for the participatory screening of risks. FPS Employment, Labour and Social Dialogue. Retrieved from http://www.deparisnet.be/sobane/SOBANEeng.htm. Retrieved 8 September 2015.

Trade Unions' Institute of Work, Environment and Health (ISTAS). (2014). *ISTAS CoPsoQ (version 2)*. Retrieved from http://www.copsoq.istas21.net/index.asp?ra_id=31. Retrieved 6 July 2015.

Worksafe. (2007). Stresswise- preventing work-related stress. A guide for employers in the public sector (Ed. 2). Retrieved from https://www.worksafe.vic.gov.au/__data/assets/pdf_file/0007/9529/WSV1088.03.092C10WEBsmall.pdf. Retrieved 9 July 2015.

World Health Organization. (2007a). *Workers' health: Global plan of action. Sixtieth world health assembly*. Geneva: WHO Press.

World Health Organization. (2007b). *Raising awareness of stress at work in developing countries a modern hazard in a traditional working environment advice to employers and worker representatives*. Retrieved from http://www.who.int/occupational_health/publications/raisingawarenessofstress.pdf. Retrieved 4 May 2005.

World Health Organization. (2010). *WHO healthy workplace framework and model: Background and supporting literature and practices*. Geneva: WHO Press.

World Health Organization. (2013). *WHO global plan of action on workers' health (2008–2017): Baseline for implementation. Global country survey 2008/2009. Executive summary and survey findings*. Geneva: WHO Press.

Chapter 12
Development of the New Brief Job Stress Questionnaire

Akiomi Inoue, Norito Kawakami, Teruichi Shimomitsu, Akizumi Tsutsumi, Takashi Haratani, Toru Yoshikawa, Akihito Shimazu and Yuko Odagiri

Abstract The present study aimed to investigate the reliability and construct validity of a new version of the Brief Job Stress Questionnaire (New BJSQ), which measures an extended set of psychosocial factors at work by adding new scales/items to the current version of the BJSQ. Additional scales/items were extensively collected from theoretical models of job stress and similar questionnaires in several countries. Scales/items were field-tested and refined through a pilot Internet survey. Finally, an 84-item standard version questionnaire, a 63-item recommended set, and a 23-item short version (141, 120, and 80 items in total when combined with the current 57-item BJSQ) were developed. A nationally representative survey was administered to employees in Japan ($n = 1633$) in 2010/2011 to examine the reliability and construct validity. As a result, most scales showed acceptable levels of internal consistency (Cronbach's alpha) and test-retest reliability over one year. Principal component analyses showed that the first factor

A. Inoue (✉)
Department of Mental Health, Institute of Industrial Ecological Sciences,
University of Occupational and Environmental Health,
1-1 Iseigaoka, Yahatanishi-Ku, Kitakyushu 807-8555, Japan
e-mail: akiomi@med.uoeh-u.ac.jp

N. Kawakami · A. Shimazu
Department of Mental Health, Graduate School of Medicine,
The University of Tokyo, 7-3-1 Hongo, Bunkyo-Ku, Tokyo 113-0033, Japan

T. Shimomitsu
Japan Health Promotion and Fitness Foundation, 2-6-10 Higashishimbashi,
Minato-Ku, Tokyo 105-0021, Japan

T. Shimomitsu · Y. Odagiri
Department of Preventive Medicine and Public Health,
Tokyo Medical University, 6-1-1 Shinjuku, Shinjuku-Ku,
Tokyo 160-8402, Japan

A. Tsutsumi
Department of Public Health, Kitasato University School of
Medicine, 1-15-1 Kitasato, Minami-Ku, Sagamihara 252-0374, Japan

A. Shimazu et al. (eds.), *Psychosocial Factors at Work in the Asia Pacific*,
DOI 10.1007/978-3-319-44400-0_12

explained 50 % or greater proportion of the variance in most scales. A scale factor analysis and a correlation analysis showed that these scales fit the proposed theoretical framework. These findings provided a piece of evidence that the New BJSQ scales are reliable and valid. The New BJSQ can be a useful instrument to evaluate psychosocial work environment and positive mental health outcomes in the workplace.

Keywords New Brief Job Stress Questionnaire (New BJSQ) · Principal component analysis · Cronbach's alpha · Test-retest reliability · Scale factor analysis · Correlation analysis

Introduction

In Japan, the number of workers with mental health problems is increasing (Ministry of Health, Labour and Welfare, Japan 2013) and thus primary prevention of mental health problems is a high priority for both employers and employees. Previous studies have shown that "assessing and improving work environment" effectively reduces mental health problems (Kawakami 2002; Semmer 2006); thus, the Brief Job Stress Questionnaire (BJSQ) (Shimomitsu et al. 2000) and Job Stress Assessment Diagram (JSAD) (Kawakami et al. 2000) have been developed with an aim to assess and improve work environment in Japan. The BJSQ and JSAD have been widely used in research and practice in the field of mental health in the Japanese workplace (e.g., Kobayashi et al. 2008; Umanodan et al. 2009).

However, more than 10 years have passed since the development of these tools; and since then, the field of prevention of job stress and workplace mental health has developed rapidly. First, in addition to the traditional Job Demands-Control (JD-C) model (Karasek 1979), the Effort-Reward Imbalance (ERI) model has been proposed (Siegrist 1996) and found to be associated with various health problems, such as poor mental health and cardiovascular diseases (CVD) (Kivimäki et al. 2006; Siegrist 2010; Tsutsumi and Kawakami 2004; van Vegchel et al. 2005). Second, recent research in this field has focused on higher level organizational factors, such as organizational justice (i.e., the extent to which employees perceive workplace decision-making procedures and interactions to be fair) (Greenberg 1987) and workplace social capital (i.e., shared values, attitudes, and norms of trust and

T. Haratani
Occupational Stress Research Group,
National Institute of Occupational Safety and Health, 6-21-1 Nagao, Tama-Ku,
Kawasaki 214-8585, Japan

T. Yoshikawa
Research Center for Overwork-Related Disorders, National Institute of
Occupational Safety and Health, 6-21-1 Nagao, Tama-Ku, Kawasaki 214-8585, Japan

reciprocity as well as practices of collective action in their work unit) (Kawachi 1999). These organizational factors were also found to be associated with poor mental health and CVD (Fujishiro and Heaney 2009; Kivimäki et al. 2006; Murayama et al. 2012; Ndjaboué et al. 2012; Robbins et al. 2012). Third, advancing research on work–family interface has indicated that both negative and positive spillovers from work life to non-work life are important factors in mental health among workers (Shimada et al. 2010; Shimazu et al. 2010, 2011). Fourth, with the introduction of the positive psychology to this field, positive attitude at work, such as work engagement (Schaufeli et al. 2002), has received an increased attention as an alternative mental health and well-being outcome among workers. Finally, workplace bullying or harassment at work has become a prominent problem in occupational health (Einarsen et al. 2003; Leymann 1996). However, these newly proposed factors and outcomes cannot be measured by the current BJSQ; thus, they should be measured with a short questionnaire that would easily assess psychosocial work environment as well as their employee (i.e., health-related) and organizational (i.e., business-related) outcomes in the practice.

Such multidimensional and comprehensive assessment of these traditional and newly proposed psychosocial factors and outcomes complies with psychosocial risk management framework in European countries, such as the Psychosocial Risk Management-European Framework (PRIMA-EF) (Leka et al. 2008) and the UK Health and Safety Executive's (HSE) Management Standards for work-related stress (Cousins et al. 2004). PRIMA-EF is a part of the World Health Organization's Healthy Workplaces Framework (Burton 2010) which proposes the healthy workplace model: a comprehensive way of thinking and acting that addresses work-related physical and psychosocial risks; promotion and support of healthy behaviors; and broader social and environmental determinants. On the other hand, the UK HSE Management Standards cover six primary sources of stress at work, such as demands, control, support (managerial support and peer support), relationship (conflict and unacceptable behavior), role (role ambiguity and role conflict), and change (preparedness for organizational changes),which are associated with poor health and well-being, lower productivity, and increased sickness absence.

We thus developed a new version of the Brief Job Stress Questionnaire (New BJSQ), which can assess "job demands" (i.e., physical, social, or organizational job aspects that require sustained physical and/or psychological effort and are associated with certain physiological and/or psychological costs) and "job resources" (i.e., physical, psychological, social, or organizational job aspects that may be functional in achieving work-related goals; reduce job demands and the associated physiological and psychological costs; and stimulate personal growth and development) as well as employee and organizational "outcomes" multidimensionally and comprehensively by adding its scales/items to the current version of the BJSQ.

Methods

Development of an Item Pool

Review of the Current BJSQ Scales

First, we reviewed the current BJSQ scales to assess what scales should be newly added. The BJSQ is a 57-item questionnaire developed in Japan (Shimomitsu et al. 2000). The items of the scales are measured on a four-point Likert-type response option and assess a wide range of "psychosocial work environment", "stress reactions", and "buffering factors" based on the job stress model proposed by the group of researchers from the US National Institute for Occupational Safety and Health (NIOSH) (Hurrell and McLaney 1988). Regarding "psychosocial work environment", the BJSQ measures *quantitative job overload* (three items), *qualitative job overload* (three items), *physical demands* (one item), *interpersonal conflict* (three items), *poor physical environment* (one item), *job control* (three items), *suitable jobs* (one item), *skill (under)utilization* (one item), and *intrinsic reward* (one item). For "buffering factors", *supervisor support* (three items) and *coworker support* (three items) as well as *support from family and friends* (three items) are measured. An 18-item scale measures five aspects of *psychological stress reaction*: *vigor* (three items), *anger-irritability* (three items), *fatigue* (three items), *anxiety* (three items), and *depression* (six items). Another 11-item scale is prepared to measure *physical stress reaction*. The BJSQ also measures *job satisfaction* and *family life satisfaction* (one item for each). All of these scales have been proven to show acceptable or high levels of internal consistency reliability and factor-based validity (Shimomitsu et al. 2000). We concluded that the current BJSQ measured basic elements of task-level psychosocial work environment based on the JD-C and Demand-Control-Support (DCS) models (Johnson and Hall 1988; Karasek 1979) as well as psychological and physical health outcomes while it did not measure workgroup- or organizational-level factors or positive mental health outcomes.

Collection of Scales and Items Based on Recent Theories on Job Stress

We collected scales and items related to "job demands", "job resources", or "outcomes" and evaluated suitability of these for the New BJSQ based on three sources: recent theories of job stress, already-established questionnaires of job stress, and a series of meetings with stakeholders. We first reviewed the relevant literature to find recent theories on job stress and their measures that were developed in the last 10 years but not used in the current BJSQ. This work identified several theories, including the ERI model (Siegrist 1996), emotional demands (Hochschild 1979), bullying or mobbing (Einarsen et al. 2003; Leymann 1996), organizational justice (procedural justice and interactional justice) (Bies and Moag 1986; Leventhal 1980; Thibaut and Walker 1975), and workplace social capital (Kawachi 1999) as "job demands" or "job resources"; and work engagement (Schaufeli et al. 2002) as a potential "outcome". Although a large part of these scales and items have been reported for their reliability and validity, our original items were partly included in the item pool. The established scales for these constructs were also reviewed and their items were included in the item pool of the New BJSQ. Each "job resources" scale was classified into three levels, i.e., "task-level", "workgroup-level", and "organizational-level" in order to indicate targets of a relevant intervention. Some proposed scales were combined because of their conceptual overlap (e.g., role ambiguity and role clarity).

Collection of Scales and Items from Existing Questionnaires

We also reviewed questionnaires and/or published guidance of job stress and related variables, which have been used in practice. These included PRIMA-EF (Leka et al. 2008), which provides a list of a wide range of psychosocial work environment that can be related to workers' mental health. The UK HSE Management Standards for work-related stress (Cousins et al. 2004) developed a questionnaire to measure six aspects of work environment mentioned earlier: demands, control, support, relationship, role, and change. The second version of the Copenhagen Psychosocial Questionnaire (COPSOQ II) (Pejtersen et al. 2010) is designed to measure a wide range of psychosocial factors, but the instrument is particularly unique in that it measures emotional demands, predictability, possibilities for development, quality of leadership, social community at work and trust (as a part of workplace social capital), justice and respect, and family-work (im) balance. The Korean Occupational Stress Scale (KOSS) (Chang et al. 2005), developed in an Asian country, was also used as a reference. It measures eight dimensions of psychosocial work environment: physical environment, job demand, insufficient job control, interpersonal conflict, job insecurity, organizational system, lack of reward, and occupational climate. We compared the scales included in these questionnaires to cover all these concepts in the New BJSQ.

Proposal of Additional Scales from Stakeholder Meetings

We held a series of stakeholder meetings, which were held twice a year attended by researchers from five institutes/departments of occupational safety and health, occupational health staffs (physicians, nurses, and hygienists), and representatives of two employer associations and one employee association. Based on group discussions in the meetings, several new concepts of "job resources" were proposed. (1) *Workplace where people compliment each other* measures a workplace in which workers are appropriately appreciated and comprises items that may overlap with items of reward at work to some extent even though the reward scale did not specifically intend to measure this aspect of work. (2) *Workplace where mistakes are acceptable* assesses a workplace in which workers have a chance to recover even if they failed or made a mistake at work. (3) *Diversity* concerns worker diversity, particularly in terms of psychological differences by gender, age, and employment status. These aspects of organizational characteristics were added to the scale/item pool to create the New BJSQ.

Candidate Scales/Items for a Pilot Study

Through the process described above, we developed a trial version of the New BJSQ comprising 34 scales (129 items). These were *quantitative job overload, emotional demands, role conflict, work-self balance (negative)*, and *workplace harassment* classified as "job demands" (five scales, 14 items); *job control, meaningfulness of work, role clarity, career opportunity, novelty*, and *predictability* classified as "task-level job resources" (six scales, 19 items); *monetary/status reward, esteem reward, job security, leadership, interactional justice, workplace where people compliment each other, workplace where mistakes are acceptable, collective efficacy* (i.e., team members' belief that they can successfully organize and execute the courses of action required to accomplish given goals) (Bandura 1997), and *workplace social capital* classified as "workgroup-level job resources" (nine scales, 38 items); *trust with management, preparedness for change, procedural justice, respect for individuals, fair personnel evaluation, diversity, career development*, and *work-self balance (positive)* classified as "organizational-level job resources" (eight scales, 33 items); and *work engagement, performance of a duty, realization of creativity, active learning, job performance*, and *others* classified as "outcomes" (six scales, 25 items).

A Pilot Internet Survey

On March 17, 2010, Japanese employees aged 15 years or older who registered with Yahoo! Research monitors were invited to complete an anonymous Web-based self-administered questionnaire including the current BJSQ and the trial version of the New BJSQ. On the same day, the number of respondents reached 1000 (687 men and 313 women) and the survey was terminated. Based on the data from these 1000 respondents, we further reduced the number of items and developed a final standard version of the New BJSQ. We calculated Cronbach's alpha coefficient and item-total correlation coefficient (ITC) for each candidate scale, and if possible, limited the number of items to two or three, five at maximum, in reference to opinions of occupational health staffs (e.g., occupational physicians, occupational health nurses, and clinical psychologists).

Development of a Standard Version

We fixed the final standard version of the New BJSQ comprising 30 scales and 84 items (49 scales and 141 items in total when combined with the current 57-item BJSQ). All New BJSQ scales are available at http://www.jstress.net (only in Japanese language).

Development of a Recommended Set

Not all New BJSQ scales are always necessary to assess the work environment: Users can select needed scales in accordance with occupation or feature of their company. Therefore, from May 2010 to February 2011, occupational health staffs and personnel/labor staffs who participated in conferences on occupational health (e.g., the Annual Meeting of the Japan Society for Occupational Health) were invited to complete an anonymous Web-based self-administered questionnaire, which asked them to choose "important scale(s)" and "unnecessary or hard-to-use scale(s)" from the newly added scales (multiple answers were possible). Based on 103 valid responses, we selected higher priority scales from the standard version and confirmed a recommended set of the New BJSQ. The final recommended set of the New BJSQ comprised 23 scales (63 items in total). When they are combined with the current 57-item BJSQ, the total number of scales (items) are 42 (120).

Development of a Short Version

Since the New BJSQ comprises a large number of scales and items, it may be a problem for users to complete it. If we used the New BJSQ in addition to the current BJSQ, which has already 57 items, it would be burdensome to use it in practice. To cope with this dilemma, we developed a short version of the New BJSQ. This short version can assess each higher priority scale, which is included in the recommended set, by one or two item(s). The development of the short version was based on the COPSOQ II (Pejtersen et al. 2010), which are used mainly in Denmark and its short version can assess each dimension by one or two item(s).

For the 15 scales comprising three or more items, the selection of items for the short version was based on ITC calculated for each scale. One item with highest ITC was selected from each scale. There were few exceptions. For the *role clarity* scale, the ITC was lower for the selected item ("I know what my duties and responsibilities are") (0.478) than that for another item ("How much authority I have in my job is clear") (0.481) among men. However, the ITC was better for selected item (0.453) than that for the other item (0.380) among women. Thus, we selected the former item. For the *diversity* scale, the ITC was lower for the selected item ("In my workplace, all types of workers (regular full-time employees, non-regular employees, part-time workers, etc.) are respected equally as fellow members of the company or organization") (0.504) compared to another item ("My workplace provides a pleasant working environment for young people") (0.513). However, considering a current increasing concern about non-regular or precarious employment (Benach and Muntaner 2007; Inoue et al. 2010), we selected the former item. The average ITC for the new 15 single-item scales of the short version was 0.693, ranging from 0.478 to 0.882. For the *meaningfulness of work* scale, a three-item scale was constructed for the New BJSQ by adding two items to its one-item current BJSQ scale on *intrinsic reward*. However, for the short version, the one-item *intrinsic reward* scale was still used. For six of the seven two-item scales, i.e., *work-self balance (negative)*, *monetary/status reward*, *esteem reward*, *workplace where mistakes are acceptable*, *work-self balance (positive)*, and *workplace harassment*, one of the two items was selected for the short version based on a discussion among the authors, considering its content validity, representativeness of the items (i.e., applicable to most situations), and comprehensibility. We decided to keep two items to measure *work engagement* in the short version because the two items measure different dimensions of this concept (i.e., vigor and dedication).

Mapping Scales onto a Theoretical Framework

According to the discussions with and suggestions from the stakeholder meeting, we developed a new theoretical framework for a positive mental health at work, which is called the "*Kenko-Ikiiki (Healthy and Active) Workplace model*", as a new Japanese framework for prevention of job stress and promotion of positive mental health (Fig. 12.1). The model was based on the Job Demands-Resources (JD-R) model (Schaufeli and Bakker 2004), in which "job demands" predict negative emotional reactions (such as burnout) while "job resources", including "task-level", "workgroup-level", and "organizational-level", predict both negative and positive emotional reactions (such as work engagement). Based on an extensive discussion, we included each scale of the New BJSQ onto the "*Kenko-Ikiiki Workplace model*" (see Fig. 12.1). In this model, *workplace social capital* and *workplace harassment*, as well as *mental and physical health* (measured as *psychological and physiological stress reactions* by the current BJSQ) and *work engagement*, were included as "outcomes" of the "job demands" and "job resources". The decision was made because in the stakeholder meetings, a workplace with greater social capital and without workplace harassment was considered as one of current business goals of a company and also because the *workplace social capital* scale seemed to measure employees' evaluation of connectedness in a workplace, which was considered to be an "outcome" of social capital rather than of work environment (Kouvonen et al. 2006). However, it should be noted that the "*Kenko-Ikiiki Workplace model*" provides only a broader conceptual framework of relationships among its components, just like the US NIOSH job stress model (Hurrell and McLaney 1988).

In this model, *mental and physical health* and *work engagement* were included as "employee outcomes", and *workplace social capital* and *workplace harassment* were included as "organizational outcomes". The decision to add *workplace social capital* as "organizational outcomes" was made through an extensive discussion during the stakeholder meetings. *Workplace social capital* is an important psychosocial factor at work in a collective society like Japan; thus, it should be emphasized. It is similar to a concept of team work, which underlies the productivity of a workplace in Japan; hence, it can be an important intermediate outcome or goal of the organizational activity. While components of *workplace social capital*, such as trust and justice at workplace (Kouvonen et al. 2006), are measured separately in the New BJSQ, it would be useful to have an overall measure of perceived *workplace social capital* as a summary "outcome" of these "job resources", as indicated by items of the current *workplace social capital* scale. Perceived *Workplace social capital* may affect "employee outcomes", and vice versa, as shown in Fig. 12.1.

Scales and the number of items on the current BJSQ and New BJSQ are shown in Table 12.1.

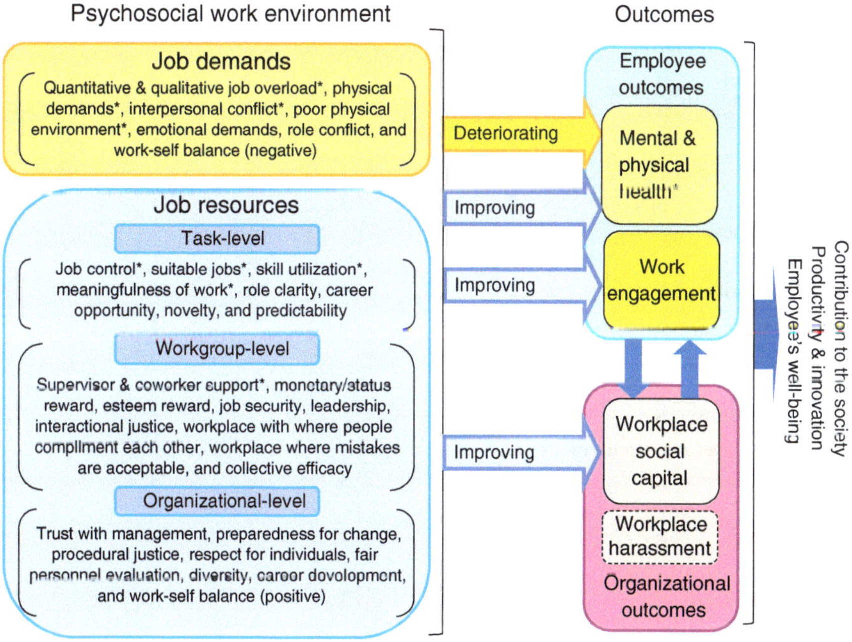

Fig. 12.1 A new framework of prevention of job stress and promotion of positive mental health in Japan, the "*Kenko-Ikiiki (Healthy and Active) Workplace model*", which incorporates the current BJSQ/New BJSQ scales. *Scales which are included in the current BJSQ

Table 12.1 Scales and the number of items on the current Brief Job Stress Questionnaire (BJSQ) and New BJSQ

Scales	Current BJSQ (B) or New BJSQ (N)	Number of items (BJSQ + New BJSQ standard version)	Number of items (BJSQ + New BJSQ recommended set)	Number of items (BJSQ + New BJSQ short version)
Job demands				
1. Quantitative job overload	B	3	3	3
2. Qualitative job overload	B	3	3	3
3. Physical demands	B	1	1	1
4. Interpersonal conflict	B	3	3	3
5. Poor physical environment	B	1	1	1
6. Emotional demands	N	3	3	1
7. Role conflict	N	3	3	1
8. Work-self balance (negative)	N	2	2	1
Task-level job resources				
9. Job control	B	3	3	3
10. Suitable jobs	B	1	1	1
11. Skill utilization	B	1	1	1
12. Meaningfulness of work	B/N[b]	3	3	1
13. Role clarity	N	3	3	1
14. Career opportunity	N	3	3	1
15. Novelty	N	3	–	–
16. Predictability	N	3	–	–
Workgroup-level job resources				
17. Supervisor support	B	3	3	3
18. Coworker support	B	3	3	3
19. Support from family and friends[a]	B	3	3	3

(continued)

Table 12.1 (continued)

Scales	Current BJSQ (B) or New BJSQ (N)	Number of items (BJSQ + New BJSQ standard version)	Number of items (BJSQ + New BJSQ recommended set)	Number of items (BJSQ + New BJSQ short version)
20. Monetary/status reward	N	2	2	1
21. Esteem reward	N	2	2	1
22. Job security	N	3	3	1
23. Leadership	N	3	3	1
24. Interactional justice	N	3	3	1
25. Workplace where people compliment each other	N	3	3	1
26. Workplace where mistakes are acceptable	N	2	2	1
27. Collective efficacy	N	3	–	–
Organizational-level job resources				
28. Trust with management	N	3	3	1
29. Preparedness for change	N	3	3	1
30. Procedural justice	N	3	–	–
31. Respect for individuals	N	3	3	1
32. Fair personnel evaluation	N	3	3	1
33. Diversity	N	3	3	1
34. Career development	N	5	5	1
35. Work-self balance (positive)	N	2	2	1
Outcomes				
36. Vigor	B	3	3	3
37. Anger-irritability	B	3	3	3
38. Fatigue	B	3	3	3

(continued)

Table 12.1 (continued)

Scales	Current BJSQ (B) or New BJSQ (N)	Number of items (BJSQ + New BJSQ standard version)	Number of items (BJSQ + New BJSQ recommended set)	Number of items (BJSQ + New BJSQ short version)
39. Anxiety	B	3	3	3
40. Depression	B	6	6	6
41. Physical stress reaction	B	11	11	11
42. Job satisfaction	B	1	1	1
43. Family life satisfaction[a]	B	1	1	1
44. Workplace harassment	N	2	2	1
45. Workplace social capital	N	3	3	1
46. Work engagement	N	2	2	2
47. Performance of a duty	N	3	–	–
48. Realization of creativity	N	3	–	–
49. Active learning	N	3	–	–
Total number of items		141	120	80

– No scale
[a]Non-work environment or outcome
[b]A three-item scale was constructed for the New BJSQ by adding two items to its one-item BJSQ scale on intrinsic reward. However, for the short version of New BJSQ, the one-item intrinsic reward scale was still used

Evaluation of Reliability, Validity, and Normative Scores of the New BJSQ

Participants

To evaluate reliability and validity and obtain normative scores of the New BJSQ, we conducted cross-sectional and one-year prospective studies of a nationally representative sample of workers in Japan. In November 2010, a self-administered questionnaire was mailed to 5000 Japanese people aged 20–60 years selected by a two-stage random sampling. More specifically, we first selected 100 municipalities randomly by considering the population size and then selected 50 residents randomly from each municipality using the population registry. If the selected municipality did not allow us to access population registry, we randomly selected another municipality. By February 2011, we received 2400 completed questionnaires, of which 2384 were valid (response rate, 47.7 %). Among the respondents, 1633 respondents (847 men and 786 women) were classified as being employed. Out of these 1633 employed respondents, 479 agreed to participate in a follow-up survey. In November 2011, the same questionnaires were sent to these participants and 417 questionnaires (202 men and 215 women) were returned by December 2011 (response rate, 87.1 %). Research Ethics Committee of the Graduate School of Medicine and Faculty of Medicine, The University of Tokyo reviewed and approved aims, designs, and procedures of the Internet-based pilot study, the cross-sectional and prospective studies, as well as the aforementioned pilot Internet survey (No. 2953).

Measures

The self-administered questionnaires at baseline and a follow-up included all scales of the current BJSQ and New BJSQ.

Statistical Analysis

Based on the baseline cross-sectional data (1633 employees), a national average and standard deviation of each scale of the current BJSQ and New BJSQ were calculated for the total sample. Unlike calculating a scale score as a sum of the item scores, in this analysis, a scale score was calculated as an average item score (i.e., a sum of the item scores divided by the number of items) ranging from 1 to 4 for all the scales of current BJSQ and New BJSQ after converting all item scores so that higher scores indicated better status (e.g., higher scores of "job demands" scales mean lower job demands and a higher score of *psychological stress reaction* means lower level of psychological distress; on the other hand, higher scores of "job resources" scales mean higher job resources; for the *novelty* scale, the score was transformed that the higher score means greater frequency of encountering new things at work). This procedure allowed us to standardize averages and ranges of scores across scales and to interpret scale scores easier, making the comparison of the scale scores more convenient.

Cronbach's alpha coefficient for each scale was calculated to evaluate internal consistency reliability. A proportion of variance explained by the first factor was calculated for scales with more than one item to examine their factor-based validity. Polychoric correlation coefficients between scales (or items) of the short version and scales of the standard version were calculated to evaluate validity of the short version. Furthermore, based on the data from 417 respondents who completed the one-year follow-up, Pearson's correlation coefficients were calculated to evaluate one-year test-retest reliability. For these analyses, a pair-wise deletion of cases rather than list-wise deletion was used when items had a missing response.

Using 1442 respondents who completed all the 34 "psychosocial work environment" scales (excluding the *support from family and friends* scale because of non-work environment), exploratory and confirmatory factor analyses were conducted for 34 scales to see whether the factor structure fit the JD-R model (Schaufeli and Bakker 2004), in which "psychosocial work environment" can be classified into "job demands" and "task-", "workgroup-", and "organizational-level job resources". For the exploratory factor analysis, the principal factor method with Oblimin rotation was used to extract the number of factors based on the scree test criterion. The scree test involves plotting the eigenvalues in descending order of their magnitude against their factor numbers and determining where they level off. The break between steep slope and leveling off indicates the number of meaningful factors. For the confirmatory factor analysis, model fit was assessed using fit indices including the goodness of fit index (GFI), adjusted goodness of fit index (AGFI), comparative fit index (CFI), and root mean square error of approximation (RMSEA) estimated by the maximum likelihood method. To examine whether the data fit the JD-R model (Schaufeli and Bakker 2004), in which "job demands" predict negative emotional reactions (such as burnout) while "job resources", including "task-level", "workgroup-level", and "organizational-level", predict both negative and positive emotional reactions (such as work engagement), polychoric correlation coefficients were calculated between 35 scales (including the *support from family and friends* scale) of "psychosocial work environment" and selected "outcomes" scales (i.e., *psychological stress reaction, physical stress reaction, work engagement, workplace social capital*, and *workplace harassment*) using 1398 respondents who completed all scales.

All the analyses were conducted using the IBM SPSS Statistics and Amos version 19.

Results

National Average of the New BJSQ

For the nationally representative sample of 1633 employees, average scores for most scales of the current BJSQ and New BJSQ fell between 2.0 and 3.0, with an average of 2.6. The average score was higher for *workplace harassment* (3.58), *depression* (3.27), and *physical stress reaction* (3.22) and lower for *work-self balance (positive), respect for individuals, quantitative job overload*, and *fair personnel evaluation* (2.10–2.15). The pattern was similar for the short version scales. More detailed information about the national average scores by gender, occupation, employment type, and industry is available at http://www.jstress.net (only in Japanese language).

Reliability of the New BJSQ

Almost all scales showed high internal consistency reliability (Cronbach's $\alpha \geq 0.70$). The Cronbach's alpha coefficients were moderate for *interpersonal conflict*, *role clarity*, *predictability*, *job security*, and *diversity* ($0.60 < r < 0.70$). Furthermore, among 417 workers who completed one-year follow-up, one-year test-retest reliability as measured by Pearson's correlation coefficient was high ($r \geq 0.50$) for most scales. Concerning the standard version, Pearson's correlation coefficient was slightly lower for *skill utilization*, *role clarity*, *predictability*, *workplace harassment*, and *performance of a duty*. Regarding the short version, the correlation was lower for *role clarity*, *preparedness for change*, and *workplace harassment* ($0.34 < r < 0.50$).

Factor-Based Validity of the New BJSQ

For most scales, the variance explained by the first factor in the principal component analysis exceeded 50 %. The variance explained was lower (30–50 %) for the *psychological stress reaction* and *physical stress reaction* scales of the current BJSQ.

Validity of the Short Version

Polychoric correlation analyses showed that all scales (or items) in the short version correlated highly with scales of the standard version ($r > 0.80$).

Scale Factor Analysis

We created a scree plot for the exploratory factor analysis of 34 scales of the current BJSQ and New BJSQ, which measure "psychosocial work environment". According to the scree test criterion, three-factor structure was thought to be meaningful because the break between the steep slope and leveling off was between factor number three and four.

When we assumed the three-factor structure, most "organizational-level job resources" scales showed high loadings on Factor 1 (> 0.70). Most scales from "workgroup-level job resources" also showed moderate factor loadings (> 0.50) on this factor. Factor 1 could be interpreted as "workgroup- and organizational-level job resources". Most "job demands" scales showed higher factor loading on Factor 2, possibly representing a "job demands" dimension. Three out of eight scales of "task-level job resources" showed high loadings on Factor 3. *Skill utilization* and *role clarity* did not load on any factor (< 0.50) while highest factor loadings were shown in Factor 3. Therefore, Factor 3 could be interpreted as "task-level job resources". The inter-factor correlation between Factors 1 and 2 was 0.20; between Factors 1 and 3 was 0.56; and between Factors 2 and 3 was 0.09, respectively.

In the confirmatory factor analysis, assuming that there were four factors (i.e., "job demands" and "task-", "workgroup-", and "organizational-level job resources"), fit indices were 0.79, 0.76, 0.78, and 0.08 for GFI, AGFI, CFI, and RMSEA, respectively. Factor loading for each scale was all significant ($p < 0.01$). When we conducted the same analysis assuming that there were three factors, based on the result of the exploratory factor analysis, these indices were 0.77, 0.74, 0.75, and 0.09, respectively. An additional analysis to compare the four-factor structure and the three-factor structure based on the result of the exploratory factor analysis indicated that the expected cross-validation index (ECVI) was 3.94 for the former model and 4.41 for the latter model, showing the former model had better fit.

Correlations with "Outcomes"

Polychoric correlation coefficients between "psychosocial work environment" scales and "outcomes" scales were calculated using the data from 1398 respondents who completed all scales (Table 12.2). In general, "job demands" scales correlated strongly with *psychological and physical stress reactions* but modestly with *work engagement* and *workplace social capital.* "Job resources" scales correlated with *psychological and physical stress reactions* to a similar extent. However, these scales, particularly "workgroup-" and "organizational-level job resources" scales, correlated with *work engagement* and *workplace social capital* more strongly than did "job demands" scales. These findings are consistent with the theoretical framework of the JD-R model (Schaufeli and Bakker 2004) in which "job demands" predict negative emotional reactions (such as burnout) while "job resources" predict both negative and positive emotional reactions (such as work engagement).

Discussion

In the present study, we developed the New BJSQ, which can assess an extensive set of "job demands", "job resources", and "outcomes", by adding items/scales to the current version of the BJSQ. Most scales of the New BJSQ as well as the current BJSQ showed acceptable levels of internal consistency and test-retest reliability over one year. Principal component analyses of scale items showed that the first factor explained 50 % or more of variance for most scales, suggesting factor-based validity of these scales. Correlation analyses also showed a certain level of validity

Table 12.2 Polychoric correlation coefficients between psychosocial work environment (i.e., job demands and job resources) and outcomes measured by using the current BJSQ and New BJSQ scales: a national representative sample of employees of Japan in 2010/2011

Scales	Psychological stress reaction	Physical stress reaction	Work engagement	Workplace social capital	Workplace harassment
Job demands					
1. Quantitative job overload	0.361**	0.251**	−0.050	0.072**	0.207**
2. Qualitative job overload	0.240**	0.174**	−0.241**	−0.056*	0.147**
3. Physical demands	0.142**	0.103**	−0.110**	0.022	0.126**
4. Interpersonal conflict	0.494**	0.282**	0.305**	0.570**	0.531**
5. Poor physical environment	0.268**	0.179**	0.259**	0.337**	0.240**
6. Emotional demands[a]	0.583**/ 0.530**	0.384**/ 0.331**	0.172**/ 0.164**	0.251**/ 0.200**	0.419**/ 0.379**
7. Role conflict[a]	0.505**/ 0.448**	0.319**/ 0.286**	0.236**/ 0.195**	0.410**/ 0.376**	0.431**/ 0.420**
8. Work-self balance (negative)[a]	0.499**/ 0.503**	0.317**/ 0.305**	0.160**/ 0.167**	0.220**/ 0.226**	0.275**/ 0.298**
Task-level job resources					
9. Job control	0.329**	0.190**	0.290**	0.241**	0.219**
10. Suitable jobs	0.411**	0.171**	0.610**	0.361**	0.254**
11. Skill utilization	0.142**	0.092**	0.326**	0.193**	0.157**
12. Meaningfulness of work[a]	0.331**/ 0.386**	0.142**/ 0.166**	0.738**/ 0.742**	0.455**/ 0.479**	0.183**/ 0.220**
13. Role clarity[a]	0.245**/ 0.156**	0.103**/ 0.047	0.328**/ 0.329**	0.394**/ 0.278**	0.153**/ 0.130**
14. Career opportunity[a]	0.300**/ 0.329**	0.150**/ 0.162**	0.578**/ 0.594**	0.425**/ 0.402**	0.162**/ 0.158**
15. Novelty	−0.141**	−0.096**	0.151**	0.017	- 0.098**
16. Predictability	0.208**	0.124**	0.229**	0.220**	0.091**
Workgroup-level job resources					
17. Supervisor support	0.360**	0.209**	0.395**	0.409**	0.314**
18. Coworker support	0.305**	0.180**	0.321**	0.459**	0.264**
19. Support from family and friends[b]	0.196**	0.105**	0.175**	0.210**	0.164**
20. Monetary/status reward[a]	0.337**/ 0.317**	0.241**/ 0.243**	0.331**/ 0.264**	0.427**/ 0.378**	0.223**/ 0.173**
21. Esteem reward[a]	0.390**/ 0.370**	0.237**/ 0.224**	0.438**/ 0.429**	0.511**/ 0.454**	0.341**/ 0.302**
22. Job security[a]	0.361**/ 0.237**	0.248**/ 0.154**	0.306**/ 0.181**	0.332**/ 0.239**	0.326**/ 0.215**

(continued)

Table 12.2 (continued)

Scales	Psychological stress reaction	Physical stress reaction	Work engagement	Workplace social capital	Workplace harassment
23. Leadership[a]	0.299**/ 0.293**	0.170**/ 0.149**	0.429**/ 0.449**	0.461**/ 0.471**	0.184**/ 0.222**
24. Interactional justice[a]	0.376**/ 0.375**	0.211**/ 0.209**	0.420**/ 0.423**	0.503**/ 0.484**	0.362**/ 0.340**
25. Workplace where people compliment each other[a]	0.342**/ 0.326**	0.189**/ 0.189**	0.434**/ 0.429**	0.454**/ 0.437**	0.302**/ 0.301**
26. Workplace where mistakes are acceptable[a]	0.322**/ 0.314**	0.177**/ 0.180**	0.480**/ 0.413**	0.458**/ 0.414**	0.240**/ 0.256**
27. Collective efficacy	0.320**	0.165**	0.482**	0.518**	0.188**
Organizational-level job resources					
28. Trust with management[a]	0.366**/ 0.358**	0.200**/ 0.207**	0.421**/ 0.391**	0.547**/ 0.517**	0.329**/ 0.314**
29. Preparedness for change[a]	0.341**/ 0.292**	0.159**/ 0.153**	0.393**/ 0.365**	0.501**/ 0.465**	0.247**/ 0.207**
30. Procedural justice	0.303**	0.209**	0.354**	0.477**	0.245**
31. Respect for individuals[a]	0.373**/ 0.377**	0.246**/ 0.237**	0.514**/ 0.506**	0.510**/ 0.536**	0.235**/ 0.275**
32. Fair personnel evaluation[a]	0.307**/ 0.291**	0.193**/ 0.194**	0.396**/ 0.359**	0.505**/ 0.444**	0.205**/ 0.196**
33. Diversity[a]	0.285**/ 0.269**	0.156**/ 0.142**	0.342**/ 0.353**	0.447**/ 0.414**	0.222**/ 0.207**
34. Career development[a]	0.302**/ 0.301**	0.181**/ 0.176**	0.477**/ 0.489**	0.545**/ 0.513**	0.211**/ 0.194**
35. Work-self balance (positive)[a]	0.435**/ 0.486**	0.244**/ 0.259**	0.662**/ 0.677**	0.417**/ 0.435**	0.190**/ 0.204**

Based on data from 1398 respondents who completed all the scales. Note that all scale scores were converted so that higher scores indicate a better status. See text for more detail

*$p < 0.05$; **$p < 0.01$. No asterisk means $p > 0.05$

[a]Correlations between the standard version scale and outcomes are shown before the slash; correlations between the short version item and outcomes are shown after the slash

[b]Non-work environment

of the short version. Exploratory factor analysis of the current BJSQ/New BJSQ scales of "psychosocial work environment" indicated that the three-factor structure (i.e., "job demands", "task-level job resources", and combined factor for "work-group- and organizational-level job resources") is meaningful while confirmatory factor analysis showed better mode fit for the firstly assumed four-factor structure rather than the three-factor structure based on the result of the exploratory factor analysis. A correlation analysis showed that "job demands" and "job resources" scales were associated with *psychological and physical stress reactions* while "job resources" scales were also associated with positive "outcomes" scales, such as *work engagement* and *workplace social capital*, as predicted by the JD-R model (Schaufeli and Bakker 2004). These findings provided evidence that the New BJSQ scales are reliable and valid and fit a theoretical framework of the "*Kenko-Ikiiki Workplace model*" based on the JD-R model.

As introduced earlier, the principal aim of the New BJSQ is to assess "psychosocial workplace environment" and their employee (i.e., health-related) and organizational (i.e., business-related) "outcomes" in an extensive way. By using the national average scores as well as information about their distributions by gender, occupation, employment type, and industry, as norms, the New BJSQ scales can be used to assess "psychosocial work environment" and related "outcomes" to prevent stress at work and promote positive mental health at work. Newly added scales can be used to assess "psychosocial work environment" with a broader range of theoretical models of job stress, such as ERI (i.e., *monetary/status reward*, *esteem reward*, and *job security*) and organizational justice (i.e., *interactional justice* and *procedural justice*), and a boarder range of "outcomes", such as *work engagement*, *workplace social capital*, and *workplace harassment*. The New BJSQ followed the tradition of the current BJSQ, assessing "psychosocial work environment" and "outcomes" simultaneously, which is also used in the PRIMA-EF approach (Cousins et al. 2004). An additional unique feature of the New BJSQ is that it includes the scale of *workplace social capital* as an "organizational outcome" summarizing influence of psychosocial "job resources". This approach may have some merits. While "outcomes" are a primary indicator of the need for an intervention, measuring "psychosocial work environment" could provide information on components of work environment, which should be a target of the intervention. The information provided by this approach on the association between "psychosocial work environment" and "outcomes", which may vary depending on workplace, occupation, and industry, could be also useful for planning an intervention. Furthermore, "outcomes" assessed by the New BJSQ are supposed to predict further distal "employee outcomes", such as satisfaction and well-being, and "organizational outcomes", such as productivity and innovation, which need to be addressed in the future research.

Another important feature of the New BJSQ is that it has the standard version, the recommended set, and the short version, which can assess work environment by fewer items. Especially for the recommended set, users can assess recommended "psychosocial work environment" and "outcomes" of which scales/items were selected based on the opinions of occupational health staffs and personnel/labor staffs. However, if users have interest in "psychosocial work environment" or "outcomes", which are not included in the recommended set, they can add them freely to the recommended set. Furthermore, for the short version, users can assess the recommended set of "psychosocial work environment" and "outcomes" by only 80 items if combined with the current 57-item BJSQ, which may be easy-to-use in practice. On the other hand, because the short version may not have sufficient measurement accuracy, it may not be suitable for scientific research. The standard version may be more desirable for use in scientific research rather than the short version.

The present study has some limitations that should be considered. First, the response rate in the present study was only 47.7 %. In addition, out of these respondents ($n = 1633$), only 479 participated in the follow-up survey. Although we calculated national average of each scale of the current BJSQ and New BJSQ using these 1633 respondents, it should be noted that the national average scores of the present study is only preliminary and may be affected by a selection bias to some extent. Further research using larger sample with higher response rate should be conducted to calculate more precise national average scores. Second, we exhaustively reviewed the relevant literature to find recent theories on job stress and their measures. Accordingly, we selected new scales/items according to the questionnaires and/or published job stress and related variables used in foreign studies, which may provide a piece of content validity of the New BJSQ. However, a more detailed content validity could not be examined. Similarly, the present study provided a partial support for construct validity of the New BJSQ by calculating a proportion of variance explained by the first factor and conducting factor analyses and correlation analyses between "psychosocial work environment" and "outcomes". However, convergent and discriminant validities using other reliable and valid measurements (e.g., Job Content Questionnaire [JCQ] (Karasek 1985), General Health Questionnaire [GHQ] (Goldberg 1972), Center for Epidemiologic Studies Depression [CES-D] Scale (Radloff 1977), World Health Organization Health and Work Performance Questionnaire [WHO-HPQ] (Kessler et al. 2003), etc.) could not be examined. Thus, more detailed content and construct validities should be examined in a future study. Third, a few scales of the New BJSQ showed only modest internal consistency and test-retest reliability, particularly for the *role clarity* scale. Further review of these items is needed to achieve higher measurement accuracy. Fourth, since the confirmatory factor analysis did not reach the recommended acceptable level for model fit (i.e., GFI, AGFI, and CFI > 0.90 and RMSEA < 0.05) (Hu and Bentler 1999), further study on factor structure of the New BJSQ is needed. Finally, as mentioned earlier, the standard version has 141 items in total when combined with the current 57-item BJSQ, which may be hard-to-use in practice due to large number of items. However, the recommended set and the short versions were also developed. Future study should use item response theory (IRT) to further reduce the number of items.

Conclusion

Although the New BJSQ remains a matter of further revisions, it can assess a broader set of psychosocial factors at work compared to the current BJSQ in accordance with a proposed Japanese framework of prevention of job stress, the "*Kenko-Ikiiki Workplace model*".

References

Bandura, A. (1997). *Self efficacy: The exercise of control*. New York: W. H. Freeman and Company.

Benach, J., & Muntaner, C. (2007). Precarious employment and health: Developing a research agenda. *Journal of Epidemiology and Community Health, 61*, 276–277.

Bies, R. J., & Moag, J. S. (1986). Interactional justice: Communication criteria of fairness. In R. J. Lewicki, B. H. Sheppard & M. H. Bazerman (Eds.), *Research on negotiation in organizations* (Vol. 1, pp. 43–55). Greenwich: JAI Press.

Burton, J. (2010). *WHO healthy workplace framework and model: Background and supporting literature and practices*. Geneva: World Health Organization.

Chang, S. J., Koh, S. B., Kang, D., Kim, S. A., Kang, M. G., Lee, C. G., et al. (2005). Developing an occupational stress scale for Korean employees. *Korean Journal of Occupational and Environmental Medicine, 17*, 297–317.

Cousins, R., Mackay, C. J., Clarke, S. D., Kelly, C., Kelly, P. J., & McCaig, R. H. (2004). 'Management Standards' and work-related stress in the UK: Practical development. *Work & Stress, 18*, 113–136.

Einarsen, S., Hoel, H., Zapf, D., & Cooper, C. L. (2003). The concept of bullying at work: The European tradition. In S. Einarsen, H. Hoel, D. Zapf & C. L. Cooper (Eds.), *Bullying and emotional abuse in the workplace: International perspectives in research and practice* (pp. 3–30). London: Taylor & Francis.

Fujishiro, K., & Heaney, C. A. (2009). Justice at work, job stress, and employee health. *Health Education & Behavior, 36*, 487–504.

Goldberg, D. (1972). *The detection of psychiatric illness by questionnaire: A technique for the identification and assessment of non-psychotic psychiatric illness*. London: Oxford University Press.

Greenberg, J. (1987). A taxonomy of organizational justice theories. *Academy of Management Review, 12*, 9–22.

Hochschild, A. R. (1979). Emotion work, feeling rules, and social structure. *American Journal of Sociology, 85*, 551–575.

Hu, L., & Bentler, P. M. (1999). Cutoff criteria for fit indexes in covariance structure analysis: Conventional criteria versus new alternatives. *Structural Equation Modeling, 6*, 1–55.

Hurrell, J. J. Jr., & McLaney, M. A. (1988). Exposure to job stress—A new psychometric instrument. *Scandinavian Journal of Work, Environment & Health, 14*(Suppl. 1), 27–28.

Inoue, A., Kawakami, N., Tsuchiya, M., Sakurai, K., & Hashimoto, H. (2010). Association of occupation, employment contract, and company size with mental health in a national representative sample of employees in Japan. *Journal of Occupational Health, 52*, 227–240.

Johnson, J. V., & Hall, E. M. (1988). Job strain, work place social support, and cardiovascular disease: A cross-sectional study of a random sample of the Swedish working population. *American Journal of Public Health, 78*, 1336–1342.

Karasek, R. A. (1979). Job demands, job decision latitude and mental strain: Implications for job redesign. *Administrative Science Quarterly, 24*, 285–308.

Karasek, R. (1985). *Job Content Questionnaire and user's guide*. Lowell: University of Massachusetts at Lowell.

Kawachi, I. (1999). Social capital and community effects on population and individual health. *Annals of the New York Academy of Sciences, 896*, 120–130.

Kawakami, N. (2002). Improvement of work environment. *Sangyo Eiseigaku Zasshi, 44*, 95–99. (in Japanese).

Kawakami, N., Miyazaki, S., Tanaka, M., Hiro, H., Nagami, M., Inaba, R., et al. (2000). The Final development of the Job Stress Assessment Diagram and investigation of its usefulness in practice. In M. Kato (Ed.), *Ministry of Labor sponsored grant for the prevention of work-related illness: The 1999 report* (pp. 12–26). Tokyo: Tokyo Medical University (in Japanese).

Kessler, R. C., Barber, C., Beck, A., Berglund, P., Cleary, P. D., McKenas, D., et al. (2003). The World Health Organization Health and Work Performance Questionnaire (HPQ). *Journal of Occupational and Environmental Medicine, 45*, 156–174.

Kivimäki, M., Virtanen, M., Elovainio, M., Kouvonen, A., Väänänen, A., & Vahtera, J. (2006). Work stress in the etiology of coronary heart disease—A meta-analysis. *Scandinavian Journal of Work, Environment & Health, 32*, 431–442.

Kobayashi, Y., Kaneyoshi, A., Yokota, A., & Kawakami, N. (2008). Effects of a worker participatory program for improving work environments on job stressors and mental health among workers: A controlled trial. *Journal of Occupational Health, 50*, 455–470.

Kouvonen, A., Kivimäki, M., Vahtera, J., Oksanen, T., Elovainio, M., Cox, T., et al. (2006). Psychometric evaluation of a short measure of social capital at work. *BMC Public Health, 6*, 251.

Leka, S., Cox, T., & Zwetsloot, G. (2008). The European framework for psychosocial risk management (PRIMA-EF). In S. Leka & T. Cox (Eds.), *The European framework for psychosocial risk management: PRIMA-EF* (pp. 1–16). Nottingham: I-WHO Publications.

Leventhal, G. S. (1980). What should be done with equity theory? New approaches to the study of fairness in social relationships. In K. Gergen, M. Greenberg & R. Willis (Eds.), *Social exchange: Advances in theory and research* (pp. 27–55). New York: Plenum Press.

Leymann, H. (1996). The content and development of mobbing at work. *European Journal of Work & Organizational Psychology, 5*, 165–184.

Ministry of Health, Labour and Welfare, Japan. (2013). *Survey on state of employees' health 2012*. Tokyo: Ministry of Health, Labour and Welfare, Japan (in Japanese).

Murayama, H., Fujiwara, Y., & Kawachi, I. (2012). Social capital and health: A review of prospective multilevel studies. *Journal of Epidemiology, 22*, 179–187.

Ndjaboué, R., Brisson, C., & Vézina, M. (2012). Organisational justice and mental health: A systematic review of prospective studies. *Occupational and Environmental Medicine, 69*, 694–700.

Pejtersen, J. H., Kristensen, T. S., Borg, V., & Bjørner, J. B. (2010). The second version of Copenhagen Psychosocial Questionnaire (COPSOQII). *Scandinavian Journal of Public Health, 38*(Suppl. 3), 8–24.

Radloff, L. S. (1977). The CES-D scale: A self-report depression scale for research in the general population. *Applied Psychological Measurement, 1*, 385–401.

Robbins, J. M., Ford, M. T., & Tetrick, L. E. (2012). Perceived unfairness and employee health: A meta-analytic integration. *Journal of Applied Psychology, 97*, 235–272.

Schaufeli, W. B., & Bakker, A. B. (2004). Job demands, job resources, and their relationship with burnout and engagement: A multi-sample study. *Journal of Organizational Behavior, 25*, 293–315.

Schaufeli, W. B., Salanova, M., González-Romá, V., & Bakker, A. B. (2002). The measurement of engagement and burnout: A confirmative analytic approach. *Journal of Happiness Studies, 3*, 71–92.

Semmer, N. K. (2006). Job stress interventions and the organization of work. *Scandinavian Journal of Work, Environment & Health, 32*, 515–527.

Shimada, K., Shimazu, A., Bakker, A. B., Demerouti, E., & Kawakami, N. (2010). Work-family spillover among Japanese dual-earner couples: A large community-based study. *Journal of Occupational Health, 52*, 335–343.

Shimazu, A., Bakker, A. B., Demerouti, E., & Peeters, M. C. (2010). Work-family conflict in Japan: How job and home demands affect psychological distress. *Industrial Health, 48*, 766–774.

Shimazu, A., Demerouti, E., Bakker, A. B., Shimada, K., & Kawakami, N. (2011). Workaholism and well-being among Japanese dual-earner couples: A spillover-crossover perspective. *Social Science & Medicine, 73*, 399–409.

Shimomitsu, T., Haratani, T., Nakamura, K., Kawakami, N., Hayashi, T., Hiro, H., et al. (2000). The Final development of the Brief Job Stress Questionnaire mainly used for assessment of the individuals. In M. Kato (Ed.), *Ministry of Labor sponsored grant for the prevention of work-related illness: The 1999 report* (pp. 126–164). Tokyo: Tokyo Medical University (in Japanese).

Siegrist, J. (1996). Adverse health effects of high-effort/low-reward conditions. *Journal of Occupational Health Psychology, 1*, 27–41.
Siegrist, J. (2010). Effort-reward imbalance at work and cardiovascular diseases. *International Journal of Occupational Medicine and Environmental Health, 23*, 279–285.
Thibaut, J., & Walker, L. (1975). *Procedural justice: A psychological analysis*. Hillsdale: Erlbaum.
Tsutsumi, A., & Kawakami, N. (2004). A review of empirical studies on the model of effort-reward imbalance at work: Reducing occupational stress by implementing a new theory. *Social Science & Medicine, 59*, 2335–2359.
Umanodan, R., Kobayashi, Y., Nakamura, M., Kitaoka-Higashiguchi, K., Kawakami, N., & Shimazu, A. (2009). Effects of a worksite stress management training program with six short-hour sessions: A controlled trial among Japanese employees. *Journal of Occupational Health, 51*, 294–302.
van Vegchel, N., de Jonge, J., Bosma, H., & Schaufeli, W. (2005). Reviewing the effort-reward imbalance model: Drawing up the balance of 45 empirical studies. *Social Science & Medicine, 60*, 1117–1131.

Chapter 13
Occupational Stress and Coping Strategies Among Malaysian Employees: Where Is the Role of Organizations?

Rusli Bin Nordin and Cindy Biding Ahin

Abstract Occupational stress affects employees in different ways, such as dysfunctional behaviors, and contribute toward poor physical and mental health. Research have shown that coping strategies play important roles in alleviating psychological distress at work. Since appropriate coping strategies are effective in controlling the psychosocial stressors and may be the only measures available in most organizations, therefore, organizations are encouraged to promote more coping skills training among their employees as part of their legal and corporate responsibility. In Malaysia, the Occupational Safety and Health Act (OSHA) 1994 clearly spells out the responsibility of employers (organizations) in providing a safe and healthy work environment for employees. This study is to review the available research findings in selected industries in Malaysia in order to identify and highlight potential sources of occupational stress and ways of managing the stress. Results indicate that significant occupational stressors were unrealistic objectives, incompetent boss, time pressure and deadlines, work pressure, home-work interface, performance pressure, excessive workload, long working hours, insufficient number of staff, competition in career development and progression, and role ambiguity in addition to lack of support from coworkers and supervisors, depression, anxiety and use of avoidance coping strategies. Various coping strategies were adopted by employees in different industries in Malaysia to address their work related stress: "divert thinking and disregarding" (by doing something fun), networking and learning more effective ways of communication, positive reframing, and emotional support. Cognitive, social, and emotional coping strategies, especially the former, was also found to positively influence occupational stress among managers in electronic firms; in Japan, sociocultural beliefs related to coping strategies and the computerized cognitive behavioral therapy (CCBT) and Internet-based CBT (iCBT) show great promises. However, the benefits of coping strategies and resilience on lowering the level of workplace stress among working mothers and working females have not gained much support from Malaysian organizations. Further

R.B. Nordin (✉) · C.B. Ahin
Jeffrey Cheah School of Medicine and Health Sciences, Monash University Malaysia, No. 8 Jalan Masjid Abu Bakar, 80100 Johor Bahru, Johor, Malaysia
e-mail: rusli.nordin@monash.edu

A. Shimazu et al. (eds.), *Psychosocial Factors at Work in the Asia Pacific*,
DOI 10.1007/978-3-319-44400-0_13

research should examine the effectiveness of the psychosocial safety climate (PSC) framework, if adopted, in preventing and reducing occupational stress and to involve managers. Organizations need to incorporate effective coping strategies into their intervention programs and to provide regular training and monitoring of their employees' well-being.

Keywords Coping strategies · Occupational stress · OSHA act (1994) · Psychosocial safety climate (PSC)

Introduction

As workplaces become more dynamic and issues of employee engagement dominate the workplace agenda, occupational stress becomes one of the most prominent issues in today's organizations. Stress affects different people in different ways, such as dysfunctional behaviors, and contribute toward poor physical and mental health (Ahsan et al. 2009). Occupational stress may be the cause of burnout, illnesses, high labor turnover, absenteeism, poor morale, reduced efficiency and performance. Recent research on occupational stress highlights the positive and negative effects of workplace stressors on work-related outcome and strains (especially psychological distress) (Umanodan et al. 2009; Edwards et al. 2014). Thus, coping plays an important role in alleviating strains, especially in psychological distress, when no other interventive measures are available (Edwards et al. 2014). Appropriate coping strategies are effective in controlling the stressors and may be the only measures available in most organizations (Morimoto and Shimada 2015).

However, more importantly, organizations must take responsibility in providing a safe and conducive working environment in order to prevent and mitigate the physical and psychosocial risks that are inherent in all organizations. This responsibility is embodied in the official law of many countries and is often cited as the principle on which the whole aspect of safety and health aspects of employees' well-being rests. An example is the Malaysian Occupational Safety and Health Act (OSHA) 1994 that clearly spells out the responsibility of employers (organizations) in providing a safe and healthy work environment for employees. Under part IV general duties of employers and self-employed persons, Section 15. General duties of employers and self-employed persons to their employees, it is stated that Ahsan et al. (2009) *It shall be the duty of every employer and every self-employed person to ensure, so far as is practicable, the safety, health and welfare at work of all his employees* (OSHA 1994).

Generally, organizations are more receptive to providing the physical environment aspect as noncompliance would be easily detected upon inspection and audit. However, providing a safe and healthy psychosocial environment requires a very strong commitment from organizations because these aspects are not easily measured and may require ongoing surveillance in order to determine the level of psychosocial safety in organizations. The *Australian Workplace Barometer: Psychosocial Safety Climate and Working Conditions in Australia* is one such example of an effort to address the paucity of information and procedures surrounding the psychosocial safety climate (PSC) and working conditions in an Australian setting that could be applied in other countries, especially those in the Asia Pacific region such as Malaysia (Dollard and Bailey 2014). The many challenges in the workplace including increased work targets, threats of job loss, organizational change, continuous technological development, and conflicting demands from stakeholders are just some of the diverse contributors to occupational stress that organizations must accept and take responsibility. Finally, the combined organizational and employees' responsibility in ensuring an optimal PSC may be the remedy in addressing the long standing issues in managing psychosocial stress in the workplace.

Study Objective

This study is to review the available research findings of researches in selected industries in Malaysia in order to identify and highlight potential sources of occupational stress and ways of managing the stress, especially if there are organizational intervention apart from the usual coping and counseling strategies under the Employee Assistance Program (EAP). As such, the findings are not comprehensive enough to cover all aspects of work stress and management in Malaysia. This study looked at research carried out on several different groups of workers and professionals in several industries. These included the furniture, electronic and construction industries, academia, entrepreneurs in small medium enterprises (SMEs), employees in private sectors, workers and correctional officers in public services. Nevertheless, this brief review will highlight many of the issues identified above and whether there are efforts, both by organizations and employees, in addressing occupational stress in the Malaysian setting.

Results and Discussion

The studies found that there were several factors contributing toward occupational stress. The significant occupational stressors were unrealistic objectives, incompetent boss, time pressure and deadlines (Salleh et al. 2008), work pressure, home–work interface, performance pressure (Ahsan et al. 2009), excessive workload, long working hours, insufficient number of staff, competition in career development and progression (Mohd Zukri and Noor Hassim 2010), and role ambiguity (Syed Ismail et al. 2014; Lloyd 2014). It was further stated that lack of support from coworkers and supervisors, depression, anxiety and use of avoidance coping were also found to be the sources of stress (Mukosolu et al. 2015).

Various coping strategies were adopted by employees in different industries in Malaysia to address their work related stress. These coping strategies were found to be effective and positively influence occupational stress. However, there is very little in the way of organizational intervention to address the long list of workplace stressors identified above apart from the EAP. For example, issues of time pressure and deadlines, performance pressure, excessive workload, long working hours, insufficient number of staff, and role ambiguity are perfectly within the domain of organizations to intervene. There should be continuing organizational efforts in addressing these potentially serious and deleterious psychosocial risks so that workers do not suffer from serious complications (physical and psychosocial) in the long run that could be costly in terms of industrial compensation and reduced productivity.

One of the coping strategies to overcome occupational stress was "divert thinking and disregarding" (by doing something fun), networking, and learning more effective ways of communication (Ahmad and Xavier 2010; Kumaresan et al. 2015). Other coping strategies that were found to have significant effect in reducing occupational stress were positive reframing and emotional support (Mohd Zukri and Noor Hassim 2010). Facing the problem at hand and working to resolve the problem was a much preferred way of addressing stress rather than trying to evade from the problem (Lloyd 2014). Organizations could have provided a less stressful work environment by developing a more flexible work routine, mentor–mentee program between junior and senior staff members, and providing regular and effective training in communication (Lloyd 2014).

Cognitive coping provides positive adaptation outcome for managers in the electronics industry (Lazarus 2006). Cognitive coping have been widely researched. The cognitive-stress coping resource (problem-focused or task-oriented) is indicative of one's ability to maintain a positive outlook towards others, sense of self-worth, and optimism about life in general (Edwards et al. 2014). Social coping method was also found to positively influence occupational stress (Umanodan et al. 2009). The social coping resource is indicative of the availability of social networks that can provide support in times of stress. Seeking support from others and gaining social support from personal social networks are useful methods for decreasing stress (Idris et al. 2010). It remains whether organizations are willing to spend money on most of these training programs that could only be effective and beneficial if conducted on a regular basis by competent trainers and regularly monitored to indicate effectiveness across time. A recent development in the area of cognitive behavioral therapy (CBT) in Japan looks at the great potential of introducing computerized CBT (CCBT) and Internet-based CBT (i-CBT) in the workplace in preventing mental disorders, especially major depressive episodes, among working populations (see Chap. 15 by Imamura et al. for a comprehensive discussion on this issue). It would be interesting to note whether organizations are ready to embrace these novel approaches that address psychosocial risks using computerized and Internet-based solutions since, if proven cost-effective, should be adopted by organizations that are concerned about the mental health state of their employees.

It is interesting to note that in Malaysia, although most workers perceived that individual factors play an important role in occupational stress, organizational factors seem to be the dominant factor that has been identified as contributors to occupational stress (Lian and Tam 2014). One example is the effects of coping strategies and resilience on the level of workplace stress among working mothers and working females. Much of the research have focused on working mothers and working females in general but their circumstances are very different and need to be examined separately. Despite the presence of social policies that support working females and especially working mothers, these social policies have not been fully adopted by the majority of organizations. The provision of a more female-friendly and also mother-friendly work environment will go a long way towards improving work engagement and productivity among working mothers.

There is a correlation between work stressors and the adopted coping strategies although there is a wide variation depending on the type of problems being dealt with, the personality profile of employees, and the interplay between the employees and the organizational demand (Sathasivam and Kumaraswamy 2014). An interesting finding from the study was that most of the managers were not aware of any coping methods associated with the stressors and personality traits of an individual. It was also found out that in spite of employers promoting work life balance for employees, there were no programs made available to manage individual managers suffering from job stress (Sathasivam and Kumaraswamy 2014). Cognitive coping method appears to be a very effective and prevalent method among managers experiencing job stress across genders. Electronics managers also employ social and emotional coping methods to cope with job stress. These coping strategies could easily be incorporated into regular training programs and workshops for managers so that the best coping method is tailored to individual managers.

Regardless of the type of coping strategies, whether it is problem-focused, emotion-focused or avoidant coping, greater use of coping strategies presumed to be in line with socio-cultural beliefs was related to lower psychological distress for task stressors (Morimoto and Shimada 2015). A study in Japan have shown that, regardless of the type of coping strategy, greater use of coping strategies presumed to be in line with sociocultural beliefs was related to lower psychological distress for task stressors compared to interpersonal stressors (Morimoto and Shimada 2015). This additional evidence on the efficacy of coping strategies should prompt organizations to incorporate these strategies into their corporate interventions to reduce workplace stress.

Future Research Directions

Organizations need to examine their PSC constructs on a regular basis in order to fully comprehend the nature and severity of occupational stressors in their workplaces. PSC is conceived as a climate that is present in each type of organization, as it reflects management commitment, organizational communication, management priority, and organizational participation in relation to employees' psychosocial health. Helping managers to understand the importance of psychological health and PSC will help to provide better support to employees, and create better working conditions (Idris and Dollard 2014). Hence, the way forward is to move to the next level in addressing occupational stress by involving the management through the PSC framework.

It is assumed that poor psychosocial well-being and stressors lead to depression, anxiety, absenteeism, stress, and poor performance. However, it is also possible that an employee's state of physical health and attitude also contributes toward self-perceived distress and negative perception of the work environment. Either way, addressing this issue from the organizational level through workplace health promotion programs, which not only address physical health but more importantly psychosocial well-being which is the cause of occupational stress, can set the path for positive change in the workplace. Successful workplace health promotion programs which offer organizational leadership, health risk screening, individually tailored programs, and a supportive workplace culture can be considered for implementation at the organizational level.

Studies on emerging psychosocial risks in developing countries (Malaysia is a developing country) indicated that occupational health and safety priorities have changed during the last decade and point to the need for a comprehensive framework for action, for monitoring psychosocial risks and addressing work-related stress, violence, harassment, and unhealthy behaviors. There is a suggestion that a more comprehensive, multilevel intervention framework is necessary in order to address psychosocial risk factors and work-related stress in developing countries (Kortum and Leka 2014).

As there is very little research in addressing occupational stress at the organizational level, particularly in Malaysia, it is suggested that organizations at the managerial level look into involving managers to understand the need for the prevention and mitigation of occupational stress and intervention strategies in anticipation of the problems and once problems have been identified.

Conclusion

It is important for organizations to understand the psychosocial well-being and needs of their human resources. Employees are valuable assets to the organization and therefore it is imperative to take into account the nature of their job as well as the work environment and the stress that can come along. There is a need for individuals to learn new skills and lifelong learning must take place in the form of continuous training and development of human resources. Organizations also need to provide training on how to cope with stress and adapt to the changing work environment through job redesigning, rotation, and appropriate intervention to correct the person–environment misfit (Ahsan et al. 2009).

References

Ahmad, S. Z., & Xavier, S. R. (2010). Stress and coping style of entrepreneurs: A Malaysian survey. *International Journal of Entrepreneurship, 14*, 25–36.

Ahsan, N., Abdullah, Z., Yong, G. F. D., & Alam, S. S. (2009). A study of job stress on job satisfaction among university staff in Malaysia: An empirical study. *European Journal of Social Sciences, 8*(1), 121–131.

Dollard, M. F., & Bailey, T. S. (Eds.). (2014). *Australian workplace barometer: Psychosocial safety climate and working conditions in Australia*. Samford Valley, QLD: Australian Academic Press.

Edwards, B. D., Franco-Watkins, A. M., Cullen, K. L., Howell, J. W., & Acuff, R. E. Jr. (2014). Unifying the challenge-hindrance and sociocognitive models of stress. *International Journal of Stress Management, 21*(2), 162–185.

Idris, M. A., & Dollard, M. F. (2014). Psychosocial safety climate. Emotional demands, burnout, and depression: A longitudinal multilevel study in the Malaysian private sector. *Journal of Occupational Health Psychology, 19*(3), 291–302.

Idris, M. A., Dollard, M. F., & Winefield, A. H. (2010). Lay theory explanations of occupational stress: The Malaysian context. *Cross Cultural Management: An International Journal, 17*(2), 135–153.

Kortum, E., & Leka, S. (2014). Tackling psychosocial risks and work-related stress in developing countries: The need for a multilevel intervention framework. *International Journal of Stress Management, 21*(1), 7–26.

Kumaresan, V. S., Malek, M. D. A., & Abdullah, A. F. (2015). Job stress among Malaysian managers: The moderating role of coping methods. *International Journal of Social Sciences Studies,*. doi:10.11114/ijsss.v3i3.742.

Lazarus, R. S. (2006). Emotions and interpersonal relationships: Toward a person centred conceptualization of emotions and coping. *Journal of Personality, 74*(1), 9–46.

Lian, S. Y., & Tam, C. L. (2014). Work stress, coping strategies and resilience: A study among working females. *Asian Social Science, 10*(12), 41–52.

Lloyd, I. I. (2014). Emotional intelligence and stress coping in high stress occupations (North Central University). *Ph.D. Dissertation*. http://gradworks.umi.com/36/65/3665230.html.

Mohd Zukri, I., & Noor Hassim, I. (2010). A study of occupational stress and coping strategies among correctional officers in Kedah, Malaysia. *Jurnal Kesihatan Masyarakat, 16*(2), 66–74.

Morimoto, H., & Shimada, H. (2015). The relationship between psychological distress and coping strategies: Their perceived acceptability within a socio-cultural context of employment, and the motivation behind their choices. *International Journal of Stress Management, 22*(2), 159–182.

Mukosolu, O., Ibrahim, F., Rampal, L., & Ibrahim, N. (2015). Prevalence of job stress and its associated factors among Universiti Putra Malaysia staff. *Malaysian Journal of Medicine and Health Sciences, 11*(1), 27–38.

OSHA. (1994). *Laws of Malaysia. Act 514: Occupational safety and health act 1994*. Kuala Lumpur: Government of Malaysia.

Salleh, A. L., Bakar, R. A., & Keong, W. K. (2008). How detrimental is job stress: A case study of executives in the Malaysian furniture industry. *International Review of Business Research Papers, 4*(5), 64–73.

Sathasivam, K., & Kumaraswamy, N. (2014). Coping strategies of job stress among managers of electronics industries in Malaysia. *Journal of Asian Scientific Research, 4*(10), 534–540.

Syed Ismail, S. I., Abdullah, M. M., Khan, N., & Hong, Y. H. (2014). An investigation on level, sources of occupational stress and coping strategies among civil engineers in Malaysia's construction industry. *Australian Journal of Basic Applied and Sciences, 8*(17), 257–264.

Umanodan, R., Kobayashi, Y., Nakamura, M., Kitaoka-Higashiguchi, K., Kawakami, N., & Shimazu, A. (2009). Effects of a worksite stress management training program with six short hour sessions: A controlled trial among Japanese employees. *Journal of Occupational Health, 51*, 294–302.

Chapter 14
Effects of Internet-Based Cognitive Behavioral Therapy (iCBT) Among Healthy Workers: Current Research Evidence

Kotaro Imamura, Norito Kawakami and Akihito Shimazu

Abstract Previous research has shown that cognitive behavioral therapy (CBT) is effective in reducing work-related stress, preventing the onset of major depressive episodes, and increasing positive mental health among workers. An innovative way to deliver CBT-based treatment widely is by using computerized CBT (CCBT) and CCBT via the internet (iCBT). In this part, we will review and introduce the recent iCBT studies, and discuss the possibility of utilization of iCBT program in workplace.

Keywords Depression · Internet-based cognitive behavioral therapy · Prevention · Work engagement · Workers

Introduction

Recently, Internet-based cognitive behavioral therapy (iCBT) has been the focus of constant attention on improving symptoms or preventing onset of mental disorders. Internet-based cognitive behavioral therapy has the special features of high anonymity and high accessibility. In terms of anonymity, iCBT is suitable for addressing psychological problems because it can enable users to avoid the stigma associated with seeing a therapist (Gega et al. 2004). In terms of accessibility, iCBT provides users with the opportunity to obtain treatment at any time and at any place, such as in the workplace or at home, and study the content as much as they want (Spek et al. 2007). Furthermore, iCBT would have merit since it can provide a viable alternate mental health resource for people who have geographical, physical, psychological, and/or financial barriers to seeking traditional, face-to-face care (Ruwaard et al. 2007).

K. Imamura (✉) · N. Kawakami · A. Shimazu
Department of Mental Health, Graduate School of Medicine,
The University of Tokyo, Tokyo, Japan
e-mail: kouima-tky@umin.ac.jp

A. Shimazu et al. (eds.), *Psychosocial Factors at Work in the Asia Pacific*,
DOI 10.1007/978-3-319-44400-0_14

Previous studies have shown a significant positive treatment effect of iCBT programs on common mental disorders, especially depression and anxiety in the clinical setting (Andrews et al. 2010; Arnberg et al. 2014). A meta-analysis of randomized controlled trials (RCTs) reported that iCBT can improve symptoms of patients who have major depressive disorder (Hedges' g = 0.56–0.99) and anxiety disorders (Hedges' g values were 0.92 for social phobia, 0.83 for panic disorder, and 1.12 for generalized anxiety disorder) more effectively compared with treatment as usual or waiting list (Andrews et al. 2010). Another meta-analysis showed that iCBT can improve mild to moderate depression (Cohen's d = 0.83) and social phobia (Cohen's d = 0.85) more effectively compared with waiting list (Arnberg et al. 2014). Thus, iCBT would be a viable treatment option for depression and anxiety disorders.

Only a few studies reported on effects of iCBT on relapse prevention of depression. One RCT and its follow-up study showed iCBT significantly prevented the relapse of depression (hazard ratio 0.16) after 2-year follow-up (Hollandare et al. 2011, 2013). Thus, iCBT shows promise for preventing relapse of partially remitted depression. Further study is needed to examine whether iCBT could prevent relapse of depression or other common mental disorders among large samples.

Some studies examined the effect of iCBT programs on preventing depression. Using self-reported symptoms of depression as an outcome, one study of adolescents reported a significant prevention effect of iCBT programs, though it included only male participants (Calear et al. 2009). In addition, one study of university students (Lintvedt et al. 2013) and one community-based study (Christensen et al. 2004) reported a significant effect of iCBT programs on improving depressive symptoms in non-clinical settings. However, a search of the literature revealed only one previous RCT (conducted by the authors) (Imamura et al. 2015a), which investigated the effect of an iCBT program on reducing the risk of major depressive episodes (MDEs) diagnosed according to the Diagnostic and Statistical Manual of Mental Disorders, 4th Edition, (DSM-IV) diagnostic criteria (American Psychiatric Association 2000). The evidence for the effect of an iCBT on reducing risk of MDE is limited.

Despite a number of benefits of using iCBT, studies in the workplace are still very few. Besides our RCT, two RCTs were conducted in the workplace. One study reported an intervention that consisted of one group session of CBT (150 min) and web-based CBT homework for 1 month significantly improved psychological distress among workers with higher psychological distress (Mori et al. 2014). However, the other RCT reported that an iCBT program failed to show a significant effect on improving psychological outcomes compared with information websites about general mental health (Phillips et al. 2014). A further RCT should be conducted to examine whether an iCBT program can be effective in a larger sample of workers with diverse characteristics. In this chapter, we introduce our original iCBT program for workers and previous RCTs examined to improve subthreshold depressive symptoms, to prevent the onset of MDE, and to increase work engagement among healthy workers.

Procedure of Development of the New iCBT Program for Workers

A new iCBT program was developed by authors during January to August in 2011. First, the structure and concept of the iCBT program were discussed, especially in terms of the number of lessons, their contents, participants' workload per lesson, homework assignment, and components of CBT. To develop the iCBT program for workers, the contents of the iCBT program must fit their usual work situation. The CBT components in this program also need to be adapted to be useful at work. The contents of this iCBT program were presented in the form of a cartoon story that showed a worker(s) learning how to cope more effectively with stress using a CBT with the help of a clinical psychologist. On making the contents of each component of the iCBT program, the author, who practiced CBT as a clinical psychologist in a clinical setting, wrote each script with professional help. After that, based on the scripts, the storyboards of every single scene were made by another clinical psychologist who was trained in CBT. Referring to the storyboards, the author developed each of the contents.

Overview of New iCBT Program for Workers

The iCBT program called "Internet CBT Program: Useful Mental Health Solutions Series for Business" is a 6-week web-based training course that provides CBT-based stress management skills (see Table 14.1; Fig. 14.1) (Imamura et al. 2014). This program is structured in six lessons, with one lesson per week. About 30 min are needed for each lesson, including the homework. This program can be used anywhere the internet is available. One of the unique features of the program is that training is provided along with a Manga (Japanese comic) story of a psychologist and a client to facilitate the understanding of the participants. Several merits of using a comic story with Manga characters have been acknowledged in research on education in school. First, it helps motivate participants to stay in the program (Hutchinson 1949). Second, it facilitates easy learning. A program with text combined with comic stories is easier for learners to understand compared with a text-only program (Hutchinson 1949; Sones 1944). Third, using a comic story fosters learners' interest in the program (Sones 1944). These merits might be applicable to education in the workplace because most Japanese people of working age are familiar with comics. The CBT skill components included in the program are: self-monitoring, cognitive restructuring, assertiveness, problem-solving, and relaxation. At the end of each lesson, participants will be asked to submit homework on a voluntary basis, and will receive feedback from trained staff (e.g., clinical psychologists) to facilitate their understanding. Feedback will be sent to the participants within 2 days after their submission.

Table 14.1 Contents of the iCBT program

Lesson no.	Title	Contents
1	Learning about stress	Learning about psychological stress model modified for this iCBT program. A guiding character, clinical psychologist Miss Rino, speaks about the relationship between stressors and stress reactions
2	Knack for self-case formulation based on a CB model	Learning about cognitive behavioral model and how to do self-monitoring based on CBT. Miss Rino introduces a five-part CB model using a vignette of a worker with a work-related problem
3	Try cognitive restructuring part 1	Learning about cognitive restructuring. Miss Rino gives a lecture on a cognitive ABC model by Beck AT (Activating/Actual event, Belief, and Consequence) and on identifying the automatic thoughts that cause a negative mood
4	Try cognitive restructuring part 2	Learning about cognitive restructuring and relaxation using breathing method. Miss Rino teaches participants how to change an automatic negative thought into an actual thought
5	Knack for communication	Learning about active listening and assertiveness. Miss Rino also teaches active listening and assertiveness skills based on the DESC (Describe, Express, Specify, and Choose or Consequence) script
6	How to solve your problem effectively	Learning about problem-solving methods. Miss Rino teaches participants how to sort out the problem and make a list of solutions using problem-solving methods

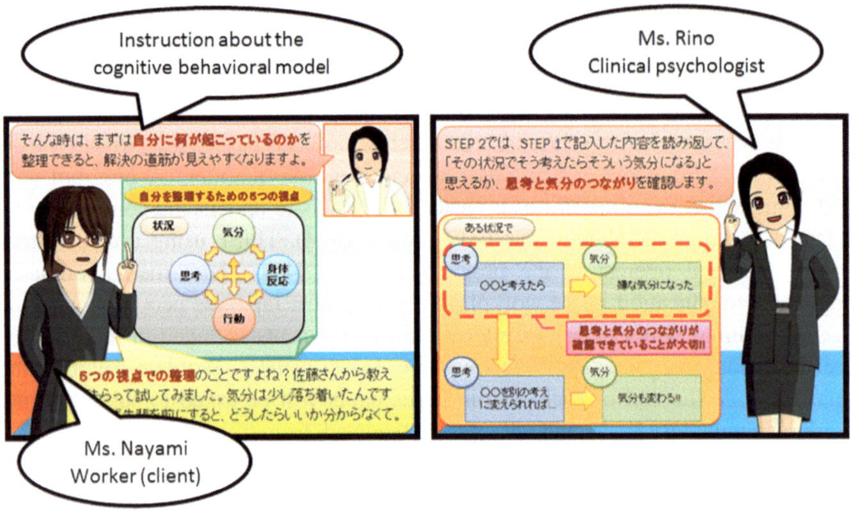

Fig. 14.1 A snapshot of an Internet-based cognitive behavioral therapy (iCBT) program developed in Manga (the Japanese comic)

Study 1: The Effects of the iCBT Program on Improving Subthreshold Depressive Symptoms Among Healthy Workers

The purpose of this study was to develop a new Internet-based computerized cognitive behavioral therapy (iCBT) program in Manga format for workers and to examine the effects of the iCBT program on improving subthreshold depression using a randomized controlled trial (RCT) design among workers employed in private companies in Japan (Imamura et al. 2014).

All workers in a company ($n = 290$) and all workers in three departments ($n = 1500$) at the headquarters of another large company were recruited by an invitation e-mail. Participants who fulfilled the inclusion criteria were randomly allocated to intervention or control groups ($N = 381$ for each group). The intervention group studied the iCBT program at a frequency of one lesson per week. Depression (Beck Depression Inventory II; BDI-II) was assessed as a primary outcome at baseline, and 3- and 6-month follow-ups for both intervention and control groups were performed.

As a result (see Table 14.2), the iCBT program showed a significant intervention effect on BDI-II ($t = -1.99$, $p < 0.05$) with small effect sizes (Cohen's d −0.16, 95 % confidence interval −0.32 to −0.004, at 6-month follow-up). This study first demonstrated that a computerized cognitive behavioral therapy delivered via the Internet is effective in improving depression in the general working population. It seems critical to improve program involvement of participants in order to enhance the effect size of an iCBT program.

Table 14.2 Effect of the Internet-based computerized cognitive behavioral therapy (iCBT) program on outcome variables ($N = 381$ in each group)

	Estimates of fixed effects[a]				Cohen's d[b]			
	Effect	(SE)	t	p	T2–T1	(95 % CI)	T3–T1	(95 % CI)
Depressive symptoms (BDI-II)	−0.51	(0.26)	−1.99	0.047	−0.14	(−0.30 to 0.02)	−0.16	(−0.32 to −0.004)
Psychological distress (K6)	−0.29	(0.17)	−1.72	0.09	−0.01	(−0.17 to 0.15)	−0.14	(−0.30 to 0.02)
Dysfunctional attitude (DAS)	−1.69	(0.69)	−2.43	0.02	−0.11	(−0.27 to 0.05)	−0.20	(−0.36 to −0.04)
Work engagement (UWES)	0.07	(0.03)	2.03	0.04	0.11	(−0.05 to 0.27)	0.16	(0.0007 to 0.32)
Work performance (HPQ)	0.00	(0.08)	0.04	0.97	0.04	(−0.12 to 0.20)	0.00	(−0.16 to 0.17)
Sick leave days	−0.32	(0.17)	1.84	0.07	−0.16	(−0.32 to 0.0003)	−0.14	(−0.30 to 0.02)

BDI-II Beck Depression Inventory II, *K6* Kessler's psychological distress scale, *DAS* Japanese version of the Dysfunctional Attitude Scale 24, *UWES* Utrecht Work Engagement Scale, *HPQ* Health and Work Performance Questionnaire, *T1* baseline, *T2* 3-month follow-up, *T3* 6-month follow-up

[a] A mixed-model for repeated measures conditional growth model analyses was conducted

[b] Cohen's *d* only among those who completed the questionnaire at baseline and at follow-up

Study 2: The Effects of the iCBT Program on Preventing the Onset of MDE Among Workers

The aim of this study was to investigate whether an iCBT program already shown to improve depressive symptoms at 6-month follow-up among workers (Imamura et al. 2014) could decrease the risk of DSM-IV major depressive episode (MDE) through 12 months, including the original 6-month follow-up of the trial plus an extended 6-month follow-up (Imamura et al. 2015a). After the 6-month follow-up (i.e., the end of the RCT), participants assigned to the control group were provided a chance to study the same iCBT program. Because the extension of the follow-up period was decided after the start of this study, we provided the iCBT program to the participants in the control group after the 6-month follow-up according to the original protocol. All participants were followed up at 12 months after the baseline survey. The primary outcome was a new onset of DSM-IV-TR MDE during the 12-month follow-up, as assessed by means of the web version of the WHO Composite International Diagnostic Interview (CIDI), version 3.0 depression section.

As a result (see Fig. 14.2), the intervention group had a significantly lower incidence of MDE at the 12-month follow-up than the control group (Log-rank $\chi^2 = 7.04$, $p < 0.01$). The hazard ratio for the intervention group was 0.22 (95 % confidence interval 0.06–0.75), when estimated by the Cox proportional hazard model. This study demonstrates that an iCBT program is effective in preventing MDE in the working population. However, it should be noted that MDE was measured by self-report, while the CIDI can measure the episodes more strictly following DSM-IV criteria.

Study 3: The Effects of the iCBT Program on Increasing Work Engagement Among Healthy Workers

This study reported on an RCT of the effectiveness of the iCBT program on work engagement (Imamura et al. 2015b). Data for this study were collected as secondary outcomes of an RCT primarily examining the effects of the iCBT intervention on improving subthreshold depressive symptoms among healthy workers (Imamura et al. 2014).

As a result (see Table 14.2), the iCBT program showed a significant intervention effect on work engagement ($p = 0.04$) with small effect sizes (Cohen's $d = 0.16$) at 6-month follow-up. On the other hand, mediation analysis showed that a change in depression marginally significantly mediated the effect on work engagement, which explained 26–31 % of the total effect. Improved depression by the iCBT program might contribute to improvement of work engagement to some extent. The iCBT program may be effective in improving work engagement among workers with the universal approach (i.e., targeting the whole working population). A mechanism with which a CBT program could improve work engagement should be investigated further in a future study.

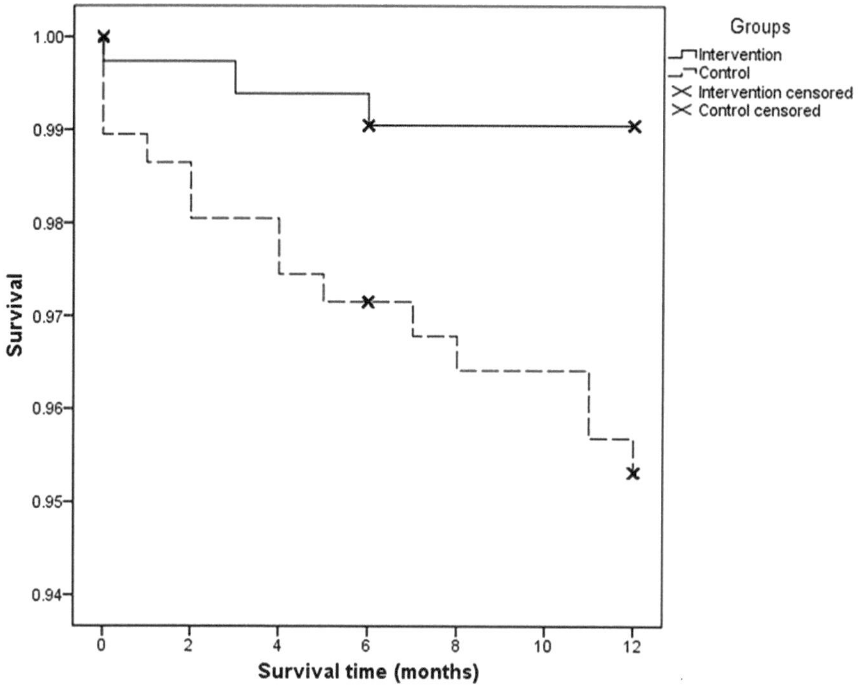

Fig. 14.2 Kaplan-Meier survival curves for not having major depressive episode (MDE) in the intervention and control groups during 12-month follow-up: Log-rank significance test for the group difference and hazard ratio (HR) and 95 % confidence interval (CI) by using Cox proportional hazard regression analysis

The Prospect and Challenge of iCBT Research in the Workplace

As noted above, the iCBT program could be effective on improving depressive symptoms, preventing the onset of MDE, and increasing work engagement among healthy workers. Preventing the onset of MDE would contribute to the primary prevention of depressive disorder in the workplace. Even though the effect size on depressive symptoms and work engagement is small, the public health impact may be still meaningful, if the great accessibility and minimal cost of this kind of program are considered. However, there are several challenges in further iCBT study in the workplace. First, the evidence for the effect of iCBT on any outcomes among healthy workers is still very limited. Only a few studies of iCBT in the workplace have been conducted and the iCBT programs for workers are very few. Further, larger-scale RCTs are needed to examine whether a CBT intervention could improve depressive symptoms, prevent the onset of MDE, and increase work engagement and work performance.

Conclusion

Previous studies show that an iCBT program would be effective on improving depressive symptoms, preventing the onset of MDE, and increasing work engagement in a general working population. These findings indicate a possible large public health impact of applying an iCBT program in improving mental health among workers.

Acknowledgments This study is supported by the Grant-in-Aid for Young Scientists (B) 2014 (Grant Number 26860433) from the Japan Society for the Promotion of Science.

References

American Psychiatric Association. (2000). *Diagnostic and statistical manual of mental disorders: DSM-IV-TR®*. American Psychiatric Pub.

Andrews, G., Cuijpers, P., Craske, M. G., McEvoy, P., & Titov, N. (2010). Computer therapy for the anxiety and depressive disorders is effective, acceptable and practical health care: A meta-analysis. *PLoS ONE, 5*(10), e13196. doi:10.1371/journal.pone.0013196.

Arnberg, F. K., Linton, S. J., Hultcrantz, M., Heintz, E., & Jonsson, U. (2014). Internet-delivered psychological treatments for mood and anxiety disorders: A systematic review of their efficacy, safety, and cost-effectiveness. *PLoS ONE, 9*(5), e98118. doi:10.1371/journal.pone.0098118.

Calear, A. L., Christensen, H., Mackinnon, A., Griffiths, K. M., & O'Kearney, R. (2009). The YouthMood project: A cluster randomized controlled trial of an online cognitive behavioral program with adolescents. *Journal of Consulting and Clinical Psychology, 77*(6), 1021–1032. doi:10.1037/a0017391.

Christensen, H., Griffiths, K. M., & Jorm, A. F. (2004). Delivering interventions for depression by using the internet: Randomised controlled trial. *British Medical Journal, 328*(7434), 265–268A. doi:10.1136/bmj.37945.566632.EE.

Gega, L., Marks, I., & Mataix-Cols, D. (2004). Computer-aided CBT self-help for anxiety and depressive disorders: Experience of a London clinic and future directions. *Journal of Clinical Psychology, 60*(2), 147–157. doi:10.1002/jclp.10241.

Hollandare, F., Anthony, S. A., Randestad, M., Tillfors, M., Carlbring, P., Andersson, G., et al. (2013). Two-year outcome of internet-based relapse prevention for partially remitted depression. *Behaviour Research and Therapy, 51*(11), 719–722. doi:10.1016/j.brat.2013.08.002.

Hollandare, F., Johnsson, S., Randestad, M., Tillfors, M., Carlbring, P., Andersson, G., et al. (2011). Randomized trial of Internet-based relapse prevention for partially remitted depression. *Acta Psychiatrica Scandinavica, 124*(4), 285–294. doi:10.1111/j.1600-0447.2011.01698.x.

Hutchinson, K. H. (1949). An experiment in the use of comics as instructional material. *Journal of Educational Sociology, 23*(4), 236–245. doi:10.2307/2264559.

Imamura, K., Kawakami, N., Furukawa, T. A., Matsuyama, Y., Shimazu, A., Umanodan, R., et al. (2014). Effects of an Internet-based cognitive behavioral therapy (iCBT) program in Manga format on improving subthreshold depressive symptoms among healthy workers: A randomized controlled trial. *PLoS ONE, 9*(5), e97167. doi:10.1371/journal.pone.0097167.

Imamura, K., Kawakami, N., Furukawa, T. A., Matsuyama, Y., Shimazu, A., Umanodan, R., et al. (2015a). Does Internet-based cognitive behavioral therapy (iCBT) prevent major depressive episode for workers? A 12-month follow-up of a randomized controlled trial. *Psychological Medicine, 45*, 1907–1917.

Imamura, K., Kawakami, N., Furukawa, T. A., Matsuyama, Y., Shimazu, A., Umanodan, R., et al. (2015b). Effects of an internet-based cognitive behavioral therapy intervention on improving work engagement and other work-related outcomes: An analysis of secondary outcomes of a randomized controlled trial. *Journal of Occupational and Environmental Medicine, 57*(5), 578–584. doi:10.1097/JOM.0000000000000411.

Lintvedt, O. K., Griffiths, K. M., Sorensen, K., Ostvik, A. R., Wang, C. E., Eisemann, M., et al. (2013). Evaluating the effectiveness and efficacy of unguided internet-based self-help intervention for the prevention of depression: A randomized controlled trial. *Clinical Psychology & Psychotherapy, 20*(1), 10–27. doi:10.1002/cpp.770.

Mori, M., Tajima, M., Kimura, R., Sasaki, N., Somemura, H., Ito, Y., et al. (2014). A Web-based training program using cognitive behavioral therapy to alleviate psychological distress among employees: Randomized controlled pilot trial. *JMIR Research Protocols, 3*(4):e70. Published online 2014 Dec 2. doi:10.2196/resprot.3629

Phillips, R., Schneider, J., Molosankwe, I., Leese, M., Foroushani, P. S., Grime, P., et al. (2014). Randomized controlled trial of computerized cognitive behavioural therapy for depressive symptoms: Effectiveness and costs of a workplace intervention. *Psychological Medicine, 44*(4), 741–752. doi:10.1017/S0033291713001323.

Ruwaard, J., Lange, A., Bouwman, M., Broeksteeg, J., & Schrieken, B. (2007). E-mailed standardized cognitive behavioural treatment of work-related stress: A randomized controlled trial. *Cognitive Behaviour Therapy, 36*(3), 179–192. doi:10.1080/16506070701381863.

Sones, W. W. D. (1944). The comics and instructional method. *Journal of Educational Sociology, 18*(4), 232–240. doi:10.2307/2262696.

Spek, V., Cuijpers, P., Nyklicek, I., Riper, H., Keyzer, J., & Pop, V. (2007). Internet-based cognitive behaviour therapy for symptoms of depression and anxiety: A meta-analysis. *Psychological Medicine, 37*(3), 319–328. doi:10.1017/S0033291706008944.

Chapter 15
Organizational Support for Mental Health, Stigmatization of Employees with Depression and Performance Appraisal: A Management Simulation Study

Angela Martin, Elizabeth Hobman, Emma Howarth and Kyla McDonald

Abstract There is a high prevalence of depression in working adults (lifetime prevalence estimates are one in five people or greater). This presents significant social and economic issues for organizations. Effective workplace management of employee depression and factors that influence these processes has been identified as an important area for research. This quasi-experimental simulation examined how attitudes toward employees with depression (affective, cognitive and behavioral forms of stigma) are influenced by contextual cues reflecting an organization's support for mental health and how these attitudes and context are associated with performance ratings of a fictional depressed employee. Participants (N = 348) in the experiment assumed the role of a call center manager with an employee suffering from depression and were randomly assigned to a group where cues were provided to them that reflected an organizational context that was either supportive or unsupportive toward mental health. Hierarchical regression analyses revealed that participants in the 'unsupportive' condition reported higher levels of cognitive stigma toward an employee with depression ($B = 0.126$; SE = 0.133; $p < 0.05$) and that the supportive or unsupportive nature of the cues participants received also moderated the relationship between an identified predisposing individual characteristic, help-seeking reticence, and cognitive stigma ($B = 0.416$; SE = 0.122;

A. Martin (✉)
Tasmanian School of Business and Economics, University of Tasmania,
Hobart, Australia
e-mail: Angela.Martin@utas.edu.au

E. Hobman
Commonwealth Scientific and Industrial Research Organisation,
Canberra, Australia
e-mail: Liz.Hobman@csiro.au

E. Howarth · K. McDonald
School of Psychology, The University of Queensland, Brisbane, Australia

A. Shimazu et al. (eds.), *Psychosocial Factors at Work in the Asia Pacific*,
DOI 10.1007/978-3-319-44400-0_15

$p < 0.01$). Affective stigma was associated with participants rating the performance of a depressed employee more negatively ($B = -0.189$; SE = 0.025; $p < 0.01$). These results provide impetus for organizations to develop work environments that signal support for employee mental health, strategies to reduce depression stigma among managers and appropriate mechanisms for dealing with employee depression in performance appraisal and performance management processes.

Keywords Workplace · Employee depression · Stigma · Mental health · Managers

Introduction

Depression is a common mental disorder that is characterized by depressed mood, loss of interest or pleasure, feelings of guilt or low self-worth, disturbed sleep or appetite, low energy, and poor concentration. It is the leading cause of disability and the second biggest contributor to the global burden of disease. One in five people experiences depression at some stage in their life and the majority of those affected are working adults (WHO 2009). This represents a significant problem for organizations, with impacts including an average of 3–4 days off work per month for those diagnosed with depression, impaired job performance while attending work (presenteeism), and a greater vulnerability in the employee to other illnesses (Cocker et al. 2011; Haslam et al. 2005; Murphy et al. 2006; Caruso and Myette 2008).

These impacts can be reduced by effective treatment. Unfortunately, approximately 60 % of those with depression do not seek the help that is critical to recovery and management of their condition (Avey 2005). In the workplace, managers are well positioned to provide both task-related and emotional support to employees with depression. However, research shows that depressed employees are not likely to seek help from managers for fear of stigmatization and that those who do disclose their condition can experience a lack of understanding and support (Haslam et al. 2005). The stigma of mental illness is a major barrier to achieving effective management of mental health issues in workplaces (Szeto and Dobson 2010). In particular, stigmatizing attitudes among managers may limit the degree to which they engage in supportive behavior such as promoting help-seeking, negotiating job accommodations, and facilitating effective return to work following mental health-related absences. These issues are particularly complex, considering that depression can be considered an 'invisible disability' and the dynamics of disclosure and privacy are important (Martin and Fisher 2014). There is also significant potential for stigma to result in bias and discrimination in processes associated with performance appraisal and career development (Perez and Wilkerson 1998).

Despite a growing body of literature on mental health and the workplace, the critical role of managers in developing effective responses to the problems outlined above requires further research (Martin et al. 2015). In order to help inform more effective management training and organizational development strategies (Szeto and Dobson 2010), we investigate antecedents and outcomes of depression stigma, with a particular focus on the role of contextual cues in a simulated work environment, in relation to how an employee with depression is perceived.

Managers' Stigmatizing Attitudes Toward Depressed Employees

Stigma broadly refers to "beliefs, attitudes, and behaviors that result in social rejection" (van Dorn et al. 2005, p. 153). In relation to mental illness, stigma can decrease the likelihood of workplace support (Barney et al. 2006). Martin (2010) examined managers' stigma toward employees with depression, finding three forms of stigma: affective (emotional distance or a dislike toward them), cognitive (negative beliefs about them), and behavioral (intentions to behave in a discriminatory way toward them). She found that both individual and contextual factors were associated with managers' self-reports of these forms of stigmatizing attitudes. Although there are implications of these results regarding individual manager characteristics for organizational support and training, the influence of contextual characteristics was noted as a priority area for broader, more pervasive organizational development. To date, how these prejudicial attitudes relate to managerial decision-making processes influencing performance appraisal and promotion decisions is yet to be examined empirically.

The current study continues investigation of the influence of individual characteristics upon stigma, and extends empirical investigation to investigation of the relationship between stigma and performance appraisal. Furthermore, the study improves on prior literature by examining the influence of the contextual environment on these relationships with an alternative methodology to the cross-sectional surveys that typify this area of research. We provide a brief theoretical rationale for a series of testable hypotheses below.

Organizational Support for Mental Health

Workplaces can foster effective mental health management strategies through the development and maintenance of a supportive organizational environment. In Martin's (2010) study, an important aspect of organizational context associated with managers' stigmatizing attitudes toward depressed employees was the presence of a mental health strategy (the extent to which the organization has mental health policies, procedures, and training programs). While mental health literacy programs show evidence that they can decrease stigmatizing attitudes among the working population (Kitchener and Jorm 2004) the broader influence of organizational contextual factors on the stigmatizing attitudes of managers toward depressed employees and their associated decision-making processes reflects a significant deficit in the literature.

The construct of organizational climate represents fertile ground for examining how context relates to attitudes toward employee mental health. Organizational climate reflects 'shared understandings' about priorities, procedures, and practices within an organization either generally or in relation to a specific 'facet' (Schneider 1990). In field studies, climate is usually operationalized as a high level of agreement among work group members about the facet of interest. Although it was an exploratory first attempt to study the phenomenon of interest, Martin's (2010) study utilized a cross-sectional survey design and was thus subject to a potential validity threat related to common method variance (Podsakoff et al. 2003). Contextual characteristics that were termed "indicators of a mental health climate" were self-reported and reflected participants' individual perceptions of varied organizational environments (managers from more than 200 different organizations). To address these limitations and extend theoretical development in this important new area of research, we employ a management simulation that allows context to be manipulated as an experimental variable and separate it from the measurement of other self-reported variables, allowing for potential causal processes concerned with context and individual attitudes and decision-making to be examined. However, as this does not allow us to examine climate as the 'shared' understanding of organizational members and as such, we herewith refer to the contextual variable in this study as Organizational Support for Mental Health (OSMH). Our approach aims to build evidence about whether organizations' attempts to signal support for mental health by communicating elements of a strategy designed to proactively deal with mental health and well-being of their employee, may lead to a reduction in stigmatizing attitudes toward employees with depression among its managers.

Hypothesis 1 Individuals who receive contextual cues that their organization is unsupportive toward mental health will report higher levels of affective, cognitive, and behavioral stigma toward a depressed employee, than those who receive cues that their organization is supportive toward mental health.

Martin (2010) provided an extensive rationale for the relationships between individual differences and managers' attitudes toward employee depression. Her study showed that less depression experience, an internal locus of control, higher levels of stress, and greater reticence to seek help for personal problems were associated with a greater propensity among managers to stigmatize depressed employees. She suggested that depression experience (gained either through their own experiences of depression or through contact with an employee or significant other), increases empathy and knowledge, resulting in lower stigma. Managers with an internal locus of control were seen as more likely to 'blame' the employee for their condition and those reporting higher stress may see employees with depression as an additional burden, causing them further problems. Managers who feel uncomfortable seeking help for personal issues often have stoic beliefs that one should cope with their problems without involving others and keep mental health issues to themselves, thereby judging others with mental health issues more harshly.

Hypothesis 2 Individuals who have less experience with depression, an internal locus of control, higher levels of stress, and greater help-seeking reticence will report higher levels of affective, cognitive, and behavioral stigma toward a depressed employee.

Martin (2010) encouraged researchers to help build theory in this area through systematic investigation. For example, she suggested examining the way individual and organizational characteristics might interact to influence the expression of such attitudes. The experimental design employed in the present study also allows further contribution to theoretical advances in our knowledge of depression stigma, by allowing an examination of mental health climate as a moderating situational factor rather than a simple direct effect variable. By examining the combined-interactive influence of individual characteristics and mental health climate on stigma, we apply an interactionist perspective (Terborg 1981). Hence, while a manager may be predisposed to have negative attitudes toward depressed employees because of a range of personal characteristics, the presence of a strong social context that is supportive of employee mental health may diminish the strength of these relationships and ultimately alter attitude–behavior relations.

Hypothesis 3 Organizational support for mental health (OSMH) will moderate the relationships between individual characteristics and managers' stigma, such that the associations between these individual characteristics and stigma will be reduced when OSMH is supportive.

Depression Stigma and Performance Appraisal

Another area for research development identified by Martin (2010) was in relation to the criterion validity of the measure of managers' stigmatizing attitudes such as whether outcomes of importance to individuals and organizations vary with the different dimensions of stigma. She suggested that managers with high levels of stigma might be more prone to exhibiting bias in processes such as performance appraisal resulting in lower performance appraisals of depressed employees. While empirical evidence on this is lacking, stereotype biases have been demonstrated in numerous other areas. Examples include age (Rupp et al. 2006), pregnancy (Halpert et al. 2006), and gender biases (Lyness and Heilman 2006), where supervisors rate employees more poorly based on these personal characteristics. It has also been observed that supervisors who hold prejudiced attitudes toward an employee give less weight to work behaviors than to personal characteristics in decision-making (Favero and Ilgen 1989). Fiske (1998) suggests that supervisors halt their search for performance-related information when presented with findings that confirm their expectations or stereotypes. For example, knowing that an employee is depressed may lead a supervisor to focus on situations in which performance has been poor, rather than considering all available performance and contextual information. This can lead to negative performance appraisals that are inconsistent with all available information, or do not take into consideration other factors that may be impacting on performance, such as the availability of resources needed to complete the job. Managers may make internal attributions for poor performance (e.g., because the individual is depressed) and external attributions for good performance (e.g., depressed individuals must have gained help from others). Such justifications and attributional biases may contribute to more negative appraisals of depressed employees (Martin and Fisher 2014).

Hypothesis 4 Stigma toward a depressed employee will be negatively associated with performance ratings, such that individuals who exhibit higher levels of affective, cognitive, and behavioral stigma will report lower performance ratings of a depressed employee than individuals with lower levels of stigma.

Context is also an important factor impacting performance ratings. Crandall and Eshleman (2009) model of prejudice proposes that individuals will express prejudicial responses when they feel that these responses are justified. Brief et al. (2000) showed this effect with black job applicants. Participants who received a business justification for discriminating against black job applicants were less likely to select black applicants, indicating that the presence of a justification is a significant predictor of prejudice. Similarly, we expect that a low OSMH context may further activate the influence of depression stigma on performance ratings, reducing the potential for leniency that may be associated with a more supportive or benevolent environment.

Hypothesis 5 Organizational support for mental health (OSMH) will moderate relationships between stigma and performance ratings, such that the associations between stigma and poorer performance ratings will be stronger when OSMH is lower.

Method

Participants

Three hundred and forty-eight undergraduate psychology students were recruited from an Australian university. The mean age of participants was 21.00 years (SD = 4.16, range 17–49 years). 71.2 % were female, 52.5 % were currently employed, and 33.2 % had previous management experience. Participants were self-selected and were remunerated with $10 (80.7 % of sample) or course credit (19.3 % of sample). There were no exclusion criteria and the recruitment method does not allow comparison of participants and nonparticipants.

Procedure

Participants entered the room and provided with an experiment code (e.g., 1, 2, 3) randomly allocating them to one of two conditions (organization = supportive or unsupportive, n = 174 in each group). The experimenter explained that the aim of the study was to investigate how managers make decisions, and that they were required to assume the role of a call center manager and complete three managerial tasks. All participants signed a consent form stating that the study had ethical clearance, participation was voluntary, responses were anonymous and participants could withdraw at any time.

Participants completed a pre-study questionnaire containing items regarding demographic information and measures of the independent variables in the study (personal characteristics). After participants completed the pre-study questionnaire, they received a document entitled 'Job Description,' and an accompanying instructional booklet of three managerial tasks, entitled 'Job 1: Rating Job Applicants,' 'Job 2: Responding to a Memorandum,' and 'Job 3: Performance Appraisals.' These tasks comprised a work sample of managerial jobs and served three purposes. First, it helped enhance the realism of the experiment as participants became immersed in realistic job activities. Second, it enabled the manipulation of the contextual cues to reflect OSMH. Finally, it enabled the assessment of mental health stigma toward an 'employee' within the 'company' and the assessment of their 'performance.' Participants were asked to assume the role of a manager and told that their documents contained all of the necessary information about the 'company,' their job history/responsibilities and the three tasks to be completed. Approximately 40 min were allocated to task completion. Self-pacing was encouraged as it would be consistent with the way a real manager would complete such jobs at work.

The first job, 'Job 1: Rating Job Applicants,' required participants to read résumés of three job applicants and rate the applicants' employment suitability. This task was unrelated to the experiment other than to prime the participant into thinking about themselves as managers in the simulated context.

OSMH was manipulated in the second managerial job, 'Job 2: Reading and Responding to a Memorandum.' Participants read an interoffice memorandum received from the CEO, describing either that the company was performing well or badly in supporting the mental health and well-being of employees. To increase perceived objectivity, accuracy, and representativeness of the information, the CEO relayed summary results from an employee survey. In both conditions, the memorandum began by describing some of the positive results from the survey.

OSMH was manipulated in the subsequent paragraphs of the memorandum. These paragraphs relayed additional survey results that reflected employee perceptions that the company was either supportive or unsupportive toward mental health and well-being. In the supportive condition, employee opinion survey results showed strong agreement on a series of statements relevant to mental health in the organization (e.g., reflecting various high levels of agreement such as 85, 90, and 95 %). These statements were based on elements of employee welfare, mental health strategy and depression disclosure norms (Martin 2010), and reflected themes including how much the organization cares for employees, the clarity of procedures and supports available, how confident employees are discussing mental health issues with their supervisors, and how confident supervisors were in their mental health management skills (extracts of study materials are available upon request). In the unsupportive condition, the memorandum described the results of the survey as being negative in relation to these themes, with low levels of endorsement of those same statements (e.g., 15, 10, and 5 % agreement).

Additional information was then given to participants to further enhance OSMH manipulation. The statement in the supportive condition read "*The results of the employee survey do not surprise you. At Aussie Mobile it is considered quite appropriate to discuss mental health problems like depression.*" The corresponding statement in the unsupportive condition read "*The results of the employee survey do not surprise you. At Aussie Mobile it is not considered appropriate to discuss mental health problems like depression.*" Participants were then asked to summarize the memorandum in preparation for a future staff meeting, as a way of ensuring that they had read and thoroughly processed it.

The third job, 'Job 3: Conducting Performance Appraisals,' required participants to read short performance descriptions of three current employees, rate several aspects of their performance on a four-point scale, and write a summary of each employee's performance. One of the employees, 'John,' was described as an employee who had been "recently diagnosed with depression." This description was a modified version of a vignette used by Wolkenstein and Meyer (2008). After participants completed the third job, a post-study questionnaire was administered to gather manipulation and realism check data and they were debriefed.

Measures

OSMH Manipulation

Mental health strategy. The statements used to evaluate the success of the manipulation of mental health strategy were adapted from Martin (2010). Seven statements were rated on a scale from one (*disagree strongly*) to seven (*agree strongly*). An example statement is "Managers at Aussie Mobile would know what to do if an employee has a problem with depression." The items made a reliable scale ($\alpha = 0.93$).

Depression disclosure norms. The statements used to evaluate the success of the depression disclosure norms manipulation were adapted from Martin (2010). Eight statements were evaluated on a scale from one (*disagree strongly*) to seven (*agree strongly*). An example statement is "Employee depression is generally considered a suitable topic for discussion at Aussie Mobile." The items made a reliable scale ($\alpha = 0.91$).

Welfare dimension. The check for the welfare manipulation was adapted from the welfare subscale of Patterson et al. (2005) organizational climate measure. Participants rated four statements on a seven point scale, from one (*disagree strongly*) to seven (*agree strongly*) e.g., "Aussie Mobile cares about its employees." The items made a reliable scale ($\alpha = 0.90$).

Measures of experiment realism. Six items were developed by the study authors to measure the realism of the experiment. An example item is "I really felt as though I was a contact centre manager for Aussie Mobile." The items made a reliable scale ($\alpha = 0.82$).

Individual Characteristics

Depression experience. The items measuring experience with depression were developed by Martin (2010). One item measured personal experience with depression ("Have you ever been diagnosed with depression?"). Two items measured experience with a significant other experiencing depression ("Have any of your close friends or family ever been diagnosed with depression" and "Have you ever managed or supervised an employee who disclosed that they had been diagnosed with depression or who you seriously believed was suffering from depression?"). All three items were scored using the response options, yes (1) or no (0). Scores were coded as a dichotomous variable, indicating either no experience or some experience with depression.

Symptoms of stress were assessed with the 7-item stress subscale of the brief version of the Depression Anxiety and Stress Scale (Henry and Crawford 2005). The items used a scale ranging from one = "did not apply to me at all," through to four = "applied to me most of the time" to assess the presence of symptoms such as "I find it difficult to relax." The items made a reliable scale ($\alpha = 0.85$).

Locus of control was assessed with the Valecha and Ostrom (1974) 11 item scale in which paired items are presented and one point is allocated for each item reflecting an internal locus of control, e.g., "people who can't get others to like them don't understand how to get along with others." The scale was only marginally reliable ($\alpha = 0.65$).

Help-seeking reticence. The measure for help-seeking reticence was based on the attitudes toward seeking professional help scale (Fischer and Turner 1970). Participants evaluated four items on a scale from one (*disagree strongly*) to seven (*agree strongly*). A sample item was "I find it difficult to talk about personal affairs with people such as doctors, teachers and clergymen." The scale was only marginally reliable ($\alpha = 0.66$).

Stigma

Martin's (2010) measurement of managers' affective, cognitive, and behavioral stigma was adapted so that participants rated their attitudes toward a specific employee, named John. Items were rated on a scale from one (*disagree strongly*) to seven (*agree strongly*). Sample items were: "It would make me feel awkward working alongside John" (affective); "It is John's own fault that he is suffering from depression" (cognitive); and "I would be prepared to make temporary changes to the job to help John's recovery process" (behavioral). All stigma scales had an acceptable level of reliability ($\alpha = 0.71$; 0.83; 0.70, respectively).

Performance Rating

Participants rated the performance of all employees including 'John' using 5 items developed specifically for the current study based on an examination of call center industry performance evaluation standards such as "Meets benchmarks for call handling time." Each of these competencies was rated on a scale where one = Must improve, and five = Exceptional. A composite performance appraisal score was created by taking the mean of these items. The items formed a reliable scale ($a = 0.84$).

Results

Preliminary Checks for Manipulation and Experimental Realism

Manipulation checks were performed on the data to determine if the manipulation of OSMH was successful. Independent groups t tests revealed a statistically significant difference between the supportive ($M = 5.78$, SD = 0.82) and unsupportive conditions ($M = 3.08$, SD = 1.26) on the mental health strategy check, $t(221) = 18.96$, $p < 0.001$. Similarly, there was a significant difference between the supportive ($M = 5.64$, SD = 0.82) and unsupportive conditions ($M = 3.20$, SD = 1.00) on the depression disclosure norm check, $t(221) = 19.83$, $p < 0.001$. The welfare norm manipulation check was also successful, $t(221) = 13.22$,

$p < 0.001$, with those in the supportive condition ($M = 6.05$, SD = 0.79) scoring the organization higher on employee welfare than the unsupportive condition ($M = 4.32$, SD = 1.13). Participants agreed the experiment was realistic ($M = 5.21$, SD = 0.98). Participants in the supportive ($M = 5.17$, SD = 1.04) and unsupportive conditions ($M = 5.24$, SD = 0.92) found the experiment to be equally realistic, $t(221) = -0.57$, $p = 0.567$.

Data Analysis

Next, data were prepared for analysis and examined to ensure the statistical assumptions for regression were met. No violations of the assumptions were found. Descriptive statistics for the study variables are provided in Table 15.1. A review of the Pearson's correlations indicated acceptable collinearity (<0.9) between the variables and only moderate correlations among the dependent variables indicating the discriminant validity and utility of separate regressions for the three dimensions of stigma. Prior to calculation of the product terms, all independent variables were centered (as recommended by Aitken and West 1991). According to our power calculations, the sample size was adequate for testing the proposed models (Tabachnick and Fidell 2007). There were no statistically significant differences in any of the study variables for the two experimental groups.

Moderated multiple regression analyses were conducted with a hierarchical model in which control variables were entered (age and gender) along with the independent variables in the first block, and the cross products, or interaction effects were entered in the second block. To test Hypotheses 1, 2, and 3 the independent variables (personal characteristics and OSMH condition) and interactions among them were regressed on the 3 types of stigma. To test Hypotheses 4 and 5, the independent variables (3 stigma types and OSMH condition) and interactions among them were regressed on the performance ratings (Table 15.2).

The first regression model explained approximately 9 % of the variance in participants' affective stigma toward the employee with depression. The results showed that age was significantly associated with affective stigma, with older participants reporting higher levels of affective stigma. Locus of control was also associated with affective stigma, with participants scoring higher on internal locus of control more likely to report stigmatizing attitudes. OSMH was not significantly associated with affective stigma. While an interaction between OSMH and depression experience explained an additional 2 % of the variance in affective stigma and showed a significant Beta, the second step of the model was not associated with a significant F change and was therefore not able to be interpreted.

Table 15.1 Descriptive statistics and intercorrelations of the study variables

	M	SD	1	2	3	4	5	6	7	8	9	10
1. Organizational support for mental health (OSMH)	–	–	1	−0.019	0.031	−0.011	0.088	0.025	0.002	−0.046	0.139	0.062
2. Age	20.95	5.059	−0.019	1	−0.028	0.255**	0.007	−0.094	0.033	−0.149	0.029	0.071
3. Sex	–	–	0.031	−0.028	1	.046	−0.057	−0.052	0.077	−0.017	−0.167	−0.168
4. Depression experience	0.802	0.765	−0.011	0.255**	0.046	1	−0.009	−0.055**	0.224	−0.050	−0.169**	−0.122
5. Locus of control	3.401	0.509	0.088	0.007	−0.057	−0.009	1	−0.090	−0.077	0.007	0.135	−0.051
6. Help-seeking reticence	3.567	1.098	0.025	−0.094	−0.052	−0.055	−0.090	1	0.015	0.194	0.208	0.222
7. Stress	0.667	0.593	0.002	0.033	0.077	0.224**	−0.077	0.015	1	0.077	0.040	−0.006
8. Affective stigma	4.456	1.034	−0.046	−0.149**	−0.017	−0.050	0.007	0.194**	0.077	1	0.124**	0.103
9. Cognitive stigma	2.69	1.325	0.139**	0.029	−0.167**	−0.169**	0.135**	0.208	0.040**	0.124**	1	0.350**
10. Behavioral stigma	2.001	0.905	0.062	0.071	−0.168**	−0.122*	−0.051	0.222	−0.006**	0.103	0.350	1**

Two tailed correlations; 1 = male, 2 = female; OSMH: 1 = supportive, 2 = unsupportive; *$p < 0.05$; **$p < 0.01$; ***$p < 0.001$

Table 15.2 Hierarchical regression results for stigma: standardized beta (std error)

Step 1: Main effects	Affective stigma	Cognitive stigma	Behavioral stigma
	$R^2 = 0.07$; F (7) = 3.4**	$R^2 = 0.14$; F (7) = 8.1***	$R^2 = 0.11$; F (7) = 5.7***
Standardized beta (std. error)			
Age	−0.130 (0.011)*	0.092 (0.014)#	0.124 (0.010)*
Sex	−0.013 (0.119)	−0.149 (0.147)**	−0.154 (0.102)**
Stress	0.089 (0.094)	0.099 (0.116)#	0.026 (0.081)
Locus of control	0.036 (0.108)**	0.139 (0.132)**	−0.047 (0.092)
Help-seeking reticence	0.183 (0.050)	0.206 (0.061)***	0.211 (0.043)***
Depression experience	−0.027 (0.75)	−0.193 (0.092)***	−0.141 (0.064)*
Organizational support for mental health	−0.056 (109)	0.126 (0.133)*	0.066 (0.093)
Step 2: Interactions	Affective stigma	Cognitive stigma	Behavioral stigma
	$R^2 = 0.09$; F (11) = 3.3*** change in $R^2 = 0.02$; F (4) = 2.3#	$R^2 = 0.17$; F (11) = 6.4*** change in $R^2 = 0.03$; F (4) = 3.0*	$R^2 = 0.12$; F (11) = 4.1*** change in $R^2 = 0.01$; F (4) = 1.1 (n.s.)
Standardized beta (std. error)			
Stress × organizational support for mental health	0.165 (0.190)	−0.052 (0.231)	0.065 (0.163)
Locus of control × organizational support for mental health	0.177 (0.216)	−0.310 (0.263)#	−0.109 (0.186)
Help-seeking reticence × organizational support for mental health	−0.114 (0.100)	0.416 (0.122)**	0.239 (0.086)
Depression experience × organizational support for mental health	−0.419 (0.146)*	0.069 (0.178)	−0.197 (0.126)

1 = male, 2 = female; OSMH: 1 = supportive 2 = unsupportive; *$p < 0.05$; **$p < 0.01$; ***$p < 0.001$; #$p < 0.10$

The second regression model explained approximately 17 % of the variance in managers' cognitive stigma toward the employee with depression. Sex was associated with cognitive stigma with women reporting lower levels of cognitive stigma than men. Main effects of locus of control, depression experience, help-seeking reticence, and mental health climate were observed, all in the hypothesized directions. A significant interaction between OSMH and help-seeking reticence was observed. The presence of this moderation effect was indicated by a significant change in r^2 as a result of the addition of the interaction term in the regression equation (3 %). Simple slopes analyses plotted in Fig. 15.1 enabled this effect to be interpreted. The slope was significant for the unsupportive OSMH condition with higher help-seeking reticence associated with more cognitive stigma, but the

Fig. 15.1 Slope test results for help-seeking reticence, cognitive stigma and organizational support for mental health

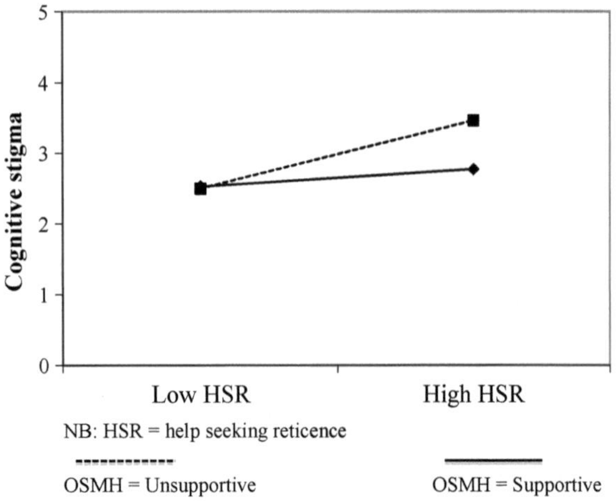

relationship between help-seeking reticence and cognitive stigma was not significant in the supportive condition.

The third regression model explained approximately 12 % of the variance in behavioral stigma toward the employee with depression. Age and sex were positively associated with stigma, with women and younger people reporting lower levels of stigma. Main effects of depression experience and help-seeking reticence were observed in the direction hypothesized. OSMH, nor the interaction between the condition and any of the personal characteristics, were significant.

As shown in Table 15.3, the fourth regression model explained approximately 8 % of the variance in participants' performance ratings of a depressed employee. Age was negatively associated with performance ratings, indicating that older participants rated the performance of the depressed employee more negatively. Affective

Table 15.3 Hierarchical regression results for performance appraisal

	Standardized beta	SE
Step 1: $R^2 = 0.06$; $F(6) = 3.7$***		
Age	0.031	0.005
Sex	−0.131*	0.056
Organizational support for mental health	0.066	0.050
Affective stigma	−0.189**	0.025
Cognitive stigma	0.014	0.020
Behavioral stigma	−0.051	0.030
Step 2: $R^2 = 0.08$; $F(9) = 3.3$*** change in $R^2 = 0.02$; $F(9) = 2.3$ (n.s.)		
Affective stigma × organizational support for mental health	0.381*	0.049
Cognitive stigma × organizational support for mental health	−0.054	0.041
Behavioral stigma × organizational support for mental health	−0.269	0.061

1 = male, 2 = female; OSMH: 1 = supportive, 2 = unsupportive; *$p < 0.05$; **$p < 0.01$; ***$p < 0.001$

stigma was significantly negatively associated with performance ratings but cognitive and behavioral stigma was not. While an interaction between OSMH and affective stigma explained an additional 2 % of the variance in performance and showed a significant Beta, the second step of the model was not associated with a significant F change and was therefore not able to be interpreted.

Discussion

This study primarily aimed to provide a controlled examination of the effects of organizational context on relationships of interest regarding managerial stigmatizing of employees with depression. Partial support for four of the five hypotheses was found in the study. In relation to the first hypothesis, there was some evidence that OSMH was associated with cognitive stigma. This result highlights the importance of communicating OSMH to managers, for the positive benefits it has on reducing cognitive stigma toward depressed employees. The lack of an effect on the other stigma types was unexpected. As differences between the two OSMH conditions were only observed for cognitive stigma, it suggests that such signals may encourage beliefs about employees with depression to be modified, but not emotional reactions or behavioral intentions.

Some support was found for the second hypothesis regarding the relationships between individual characteristics and stigma. It was expected that depression experience would be negatively associated with stigma. The results showed a relationship between depression experience and cognitive and behavioral stigma, echoing Martin's (2010) results for these same dimensions. This is consistent with the idea of gaining understanding about depression through 'contact' with someone who has direct experience of the condition, suggesting that it may be useful to design workplace training in ways that simulates this 'experience.' Also as predicted, individuals higher in help-seeking reticence reported more cognitive and behavioral stigma. Martin (2010) also found such an association for behavioral and cognitive stigma. These results suggest that those with a willingness seek help themselves may have more accurate thoughts about depression, and hence be more accepting, less judgemental, and more open to providing help to an employee with depression. Hence, normalizing help-seeking among managers may be an important mental health promotion strategy.

Hypothesis 3 predicted that OSMH would moderate the association between individual characteristics and affective, cognitive, and behavioral stigma, such that the individual predisposing characteristics would not be as strongly associated with stigma in the high OSMH condition. The results show partial support for this aspect of the third hypothesis regarding the moderating role of OSMH in the relationship between the participant characteristic of help-seeking reticence and their levels of cognitive stigma. This means that when OSMH was high, the extent to which participants were reticent to seek help for personal concerns was not associated with cognitive stigma. Conversely, when OSMH was low, managers' personal characteristics played a role in influencing their beliefs about employees with depression. The failure to detect similar moderating effects for affective and behavioral stigma was unexpected and inconsistent with organization behavior theories that suggest that organizational climate has a moderating effect in relation to the relationship between individual characterizes and attitudes/behavior (Parker et al. 2003).

The cognitive stigma measure was more strongly associated with the other study variables. This finding mirrors Martin's (2010) results showing that managers whose organizations had a clear mental health strategy reported lower levels of stigma but only for the cognitive dimension. Given our study aimed to provide a more stringent test of this relationship, we can have increased confidence in the importance of organizational context for the beliefs people hold about employees with depression. Behavioral stigma may be less likely to be reported in organizations given legal frameworks around discrimination, and hence there is less variance in this measure. Affective stigma may be more difficult to understand and target given the often subconscious nature of emotions and the fact that there is less research on affective stigma to draw upon. In general, the affective domain of attitudes has received far less attention in the research literature than the cognitive domain because it has been difficult to define and difficult to measure (Bolin et al. 2005).

In relation to the fourth hypothesis, there was some evidence that affective stigma was associated with lower performance ratings of the depressed employee. Research suggesting the role of affect and positive interpersonal relationships in performance appraisals (Lefkowitz 2000) may be one explanation for why affective stigma was found to be associated with performance ratings. The lack of a finding for the impact of cognitive and behavioral stigma on performance ratings was surprising given that previous research indicates that managers rate employees performance based on perceived negative personal characteristics (Halpert et al. 2006; Lyness and Heilman 2006; Rupp et al. 2006). No support was found for the fifth hypothesis, as OSMH, nor an interaction between it and the stigma types was associated with performance ratings. This finding is inconsistent with our theoretical predictions.

Implications for Workplace Mental Health Promotion

The findings highlight the importance of both individual characteristics and contextual factors in understanding stigma toward depressed employees and suggest that organizations need to be targeting both aspects in any mental health promotion interventions. In relation to individual differences, it was found that experience of depression is associated with less stigmatization of individuals with the illness. Watson and Corrigan (2005) suggest that while contact with persons who have experienced depression may be one of the best ways of reducing stigma, its implementation may prove more difficult than a widespread education program. There are ways however, to implement contact more easily in workplace training. For example, Crisp and Turner (2009) suggest that imagined contact is sufficient to reduce negative attitudes and Cameron and Rutland (2006) suggest that reading stories about disability can be helpful form of simulating 'contact.' Research evaluating the impact of different intervention strategies on the three types of stigma explored in the present study will be vital in ensuring research continues to inform practice.

The reluctance of participants to seek help for psychological issues was associated with how they perceived employees with depression. Consequently, if the willingness of managers to seek help was increased, this might lessen the stigma attached to employees with depression. This could be done through manager training on how to seek help, and realize that as a manager, it is acceptable (and indeed advantageous) for them to be seen by employees to seek help.

Another pertinent aspect of the findings is that OSMH was an important factor influencing cognitive stigma in both a direct and indirect manner. Organizations should aim to specifically to communicate this support by developing an integrated approach to mental health issues that includes prevention strategies (LaMontagne et al. 2014), assistance programs, mental health awareness training, and normalizing discussion of mental health issues. The importance of strong leadership of such initiatives is also critical and this has been recognized recently as central to creating 'psychosocial safety climate' (Dollard and Bakker 2010), a construct that is similar to our focus on OSMH.

Although not explicitly part of the hypotheses tested, participant age and gender included as control variables, displayed significant associations with components of stigma. Specifically, females reported less cognitive and behavioral stigma than did males and younger participants reported less affective and behavioral stigma than did older participants. This trend is consistent with previous research investigating depression stigma (Griffiths et al. 2008; Jorm et al. 1999; Martin 2010). These effects may have important implications in the workplace. Specifically, male or older managers may need more stigma reduction focussed training. The age and gender of the manager could also interact with the age and gender of the employee with depression. In the current study, the employee with depression was male, but stigma may differ if a female employee was described. For example, research has noted that male manager/male employee teams elicit more frustration than a female manager/male employee combination (McColl-Kennedy and Anderson 2005). In regard to depressed employees, this frustration may manifest through more stigmatizing attitudes.

Finally, the influence of affective stigma on performance ratings might indicate that this relatively unexplored form of stigma might be important to counter by better supporting managers in how to deal with performance issues among employees with depression (Martin et al. 2015). The complexity of factors influencing performance judgements is only further complicated by the presence of a mental health condition with known performance impacts (Haslam et al. 2005).

Limitations and Directions for Future Research

There are limitations to the study that need to be discussed. Although the quasi-experimental methodology was a strength in relation to theoretical development, it does limit the external generalizability of the findings. Although laboratory studies are common in organizational behavior and the simulation was designed to be as close to a manager's role as possible to counteract threats to ecological validity, there are several limitations and potential problems with the methodology we employed. First, while the significant differences between the conditions in terms of the manipulation checks suggest the conditions were distinct, some of the ratings in the unsupportive climate condition are still close to or above the median point in the scale, and rather than a clearly dichotomous supportive versus unsupportive condition, the manipulation could be considered to have manipulated highly supportive versus neutral. There is also a possibility that the manipulation introduced cognitive priming or a mood induction rather than a true manipulation of context. An experimentally simulated contextual manipulation shares some similarity with the concept of mood induction where participants are exposed to various types of media, feedback, or instruction to imagine affective states and a manipulation check measuring the mood in question is used to determine the success of the mood induction (Polivy 1981). However, our manipulation of OSMH was not intended to induce mood. Rather we presented factual information regarding survey results that simulate environmental information participants could use to form cognitive impressions about what it would be like to work in this organization. This approach is similar to that used by Ziegert and Hanges (2005), who utilized a presidential memo as method of manipulating organizational context for racial bias. Our stimulus materials attempted to clearly signify very low levels of OSMH using very low percentage agreement figures for survey results in the memo.

Although the use of vignettes has a long tradition in social attitude research (Burstin et al. 1980), the organizational information we presented in the vignette was by no means identical to the long-term nature of an organizational environment, nor the relationships between managers and subordinates. In addition, conducting performance ratings for 'paper people' raises issues of generalizability given real performance is rated on many, many samples of behavior over a long period of time. In particular, the vignette used to prompt the assessment of depression stigma, the target employee was described as depressed and a number of symptoms associated with the condition were presented (including a drop in work performance). This vignette was based on a previously validated vignette about depression (Wolkenstein and Meyer 2008) and as such it was framed as a stigma study and not a performance appraisal study. Results may have been different if an employee with depression was described as maintaining strong performance—although the literature around presenteeism and depression tells us that reduced performance is a common outcome of depression and accounts for most of the economic costs borne by employers (Cocker et al. 2011).

Sample characteristics must also be noted. As the sample contained psychology students, it may be that lower levels of mental health stigma than in the general population may have contributed to the results. However, studies have shown that even qualified mental health professionals are not immune to holding stigmatizing attitudes (Jorm et al. 1999). Approximately 33 % had management experience and 52 % were employed. For those that were not experienced managers, we argue that vicarious experience offered through workplace, family, and community social learning opportunities would provide sufficient experience to help them ‘assume’ the role of a manager. Nonetheless, one should exercise caution in generalizing the findings to the workplace.

A minor limitation was the failure of two of the scales to reach acceptable levels of reliability (Locus of control and Help-seeking reticence were both marginally below 0.70). More substantive limitations relate to the research design itself.

Future research is urgently needed exploring the links between employee depression and performance appraisal/performance management. Examining the role of justification, or ‘excuses,’ for performance appraisal decisions may also be illuminating. Justifications for racial bias that have been studied are ‘even innocuous’ past mistakes (Knight et al. 2003) and ‘business justifications’ regarding racial homogeneity of customers and staff (Brief et al. 2000). Such justifications may interact with personal biases to contribute to more negative appraisals of depressed employees.

While our results provide some indication that OSMH may lead to a reduction in cognitive stigma, it should be recognized that to completely evaluate a causal relationship, a longitudinal panel-designed intervention-based field study is required. Such a study would allow for the reverse causal relationship (i.e., widespread stigma can cause poor OSMH) also to be evaluated.

Multi-level studies examining the variables of interest at the level of employees, managers and organizations would be a useful future research objective. In this type of investigation, it would be possible to obtain measures of OSMH from groups of employees to examine the extent to which these perceptions are shared. Managerial stigma could also be measured from the perspective of employees. Research could also examine any variation in employee outcomes associated with the different types of stigma such as perceived discrimination, relationship quality, and career advancement. Similarly, at the organizational level, various facets of climate could be associated with mental health attitudes and relevant outcomes.

Finally, regarding our findings on age, gender, and stigma, we suggest future research could counterbalance vignettes with a male and a female with depression to investigate such an interaction effect. Similarly, different age combinations in managers and subordinates could also be important given research on age discrimination. The assessment of depression experience could also be further improved by including more information about how and when this ‘experience’ was gained (e.g., current, recent, treatment history, etc.).

Despite the evidence that our attempt to manipulate of the extent to which an organization was supportive of mental health was successful and realistic, future research should attempt to confirm these findings in the field. We suggest that building theory from both experimental and field studies incrementally will allow us to systematically explore this novel research agenda.

Conclusion

Employee depression has many challenges and costs, some of which are amplified if the work environment is not supportive. It is vital that we understand the antecedents of depression stigma in the workplace so that better support can be provided to employees with depression and barriers to effective treatment, employee retention, and productivity can be reduced. The quasi-experimental design of the study afforded examination of a potentially causal relationship between the level of organizational support for mental health and stigma. The results of this study have implications for workplace depression awareness training and organization development strategies that foster a work environment that emphasizes supportive management of employee mental health problems.

References

Aitken, L. S., & West, R. R. (1991). *Multiple regression: Testing and interpreting interactions*. Newbury Park, CA: Sage.

Avey, S. G. (2005). Challenges facing employers in the treatment of depression. *Journal of Managed Care Pharmacy, 11*, S3–S4.

Barney, L., Griffiths, K., Jorm, A., & Christensen, H. (2006). Stigma about depression and its impact on help-seeking intentions. *Australia New Zealand Journal of Psychiatry, 40*, 51–54.

Bolin, A. U., Khramtsova, I., & Saarnio, D. (2005). Using student journals to stimulate authentic learning: Balancing bloom's cognitive and affective domains. *Teaching Psychology, 32*, 154–159.

Brief, A. P., Dietz, J., & Cohen, R. R. (2000). Just doing business: Modern racism and obedience to authority as explanations of employment discrimination. *Organizational Behavior and Human Decision Processes, 81*(1), 72–97.

Burstin, K., Doughtie, E. B., & Raphaeli, A. (1980). Contrastive vignette technique: An indirect methodology designed to address reactive social attitude measurement. *Journal of Applied Social Psychology, 10*(2), 147–165.

Cameron, L., & Rutland, A. (2006). Extended contact through story reading in school: Reducing children's prejudice towards the disabled. *Journal of Social Issues, 62*(3), 469–488.

Caruso, G. M., & Myette, T. L. (2008). Introduction: the ACOEM depression in the workplace project. *Journal of Occupational and Environmental Medicine, 50*(4), 379–380.

Cocker, F., Martin, A. J., Scott, J., Venn, A., Otthal, P., & Sanderson, K. (2011). Factors associated with presenteeism amongst employed Australian adults reporting lifetime major depression with 12 month symptoms. *Journal of Affective Disorders, 135*(1–3), 231–240.

Crandall, C. S., & Eshleman, A. (2009). A justification-suppression model of the expression and experience of prejudice. *Psychological Bulletin, 129*(3), 414–446.

Crisp, R., & Turner, R. (2009). Can imagined interactions produce positive perceptions? Reduced prejudice through simulated contact. *American Psychologist, 64*, 213–240.

Dollard, M., & Bakker, A. (2010). Psychosocial safety climate as a precursor to conducive work environments, psychological health problems, and employee engagement. *Journal of Occupational and Organizational Psychology, 83*(3), 579–599.

Favero, J. L., & Ilgen, D. R. (1989). The effects of ratee prototypicality on rater observation and accuracy. *Journal of Applied Social Psychology, 19*(11), 932–946.

Fischer, E., & Turner, J. (1970). Orientations to seeking professional help: Development and research utility of an attitude scale. *Journal of Consulting and Clinical Psychology, 35*, 79–90.

Fiske, S. T. (1998). Stereotyping, prejudice, and discrimination. In D. T. Gilbert, S. T. Fiske, & G. Lindzey (Eds.), *The handbook of social psychology* (pp. 357–411). New York: McGraw-Hill.

Griffiths, K. M., Christensen, H., & Jorm, A. F. (2008). Predictors of depression stigma. *BMC Psychiatry, 8*(25), 1–12.

Halpert, J. A., Wilson, M. L., & Hickman, J. L. (2006). Pregnancy as a source of bias in performance appraisals. *Journal of Organizational Behavior, 14*(7), 649–663.

Haslam, C., Atkinson, S., Brown, S. S., & Haslam, R. A. (2005). Anxiety and depression in the workplace: Effects on the individual and organization (a focus group investigation). *Journal of Affective Disorders, 88*(2), 209–215.

Henry, J. D., & Crawford, J. R. (2005). The short-form version of the Depression Anxiety Stress Scales (DASS-21): Construct validity and normative data in a large non-clinical sample. *British Journal of Clinical Psychology, 44*, 227–239.

Jorm, A. F., Korten, A. E., Jacomb, P. A., Christensen, H., & Henderson, S. (1999). Attitudes towards people with a mental disorder: A survey of the Australian public and health professionals. *Australian and New Zealand Journal of Psychiatry, 33*, 77–83.

Kitchener, B. A., & Jorm, A. F. (2004). Mental health first aid training in a workplace setting: A randomized controlled trial. *BMC Psychiatry, 4*(23), 1–8.

Knight, J. L., Hebl, M. R., Foster, J. B., & Mannix, L. M. (2003). Out of role? Out of luck: The influence of race and leadership status on performance appraisals. *The Journal of Leadership and Organizational Studies, 9*(3), 85–93.

LaMontagne, A. D, Martin, A., Page, K., Reavley, N. J., Noblet, A. J., Milner, A. J., et al. (2014). Workplace mental health: Developing an integrated intervention approach. *BMC Psychiatry, 14*(131). doi:10.1186/1471-244X-14-131.

Lefkowitz, J. (2000). The role of interpersonal affective regard in supervisory performance ratings: A literature review and proposed causal model. *Journal of Occupational and Organizational Psychology, 73*(1), 67–85.

Lyness, K. S., & Heilman, M. E. (2006). When fit is fundamental: Performance evaluations and promotions of upper-level female and male managers. *Journal of Applied Psychology, 91*, 777–785.

Martin, A. (2010). Individual and contextual correlates of managers' attitudes toward depressed employees. *Human Resource Management, 49*(4), 647–666.

Martin, A., & Fisher, C. (2014). *Understanding and improving managers' responses to employee depression*. Industrial and Organizational Psychology: Perspectives on Science and Practice. doi:10.1111/iops.12147.

Martin, A., Woods, M., & Dawkins, S. (2015). Managing employees with mental health issues: Identification of conceptual and procedural knowledge for development within management education curricula. *Academy of Management Learning and Education, 14*(1):50–68. doi:10.5465/amle.2012.028.

McColl-Kennedy, J. R., & Anderson, R. D. (2005). Subordinate-manager gender combination and perceived leadership style influence on emotions, self-esteem and organizational commitment. *Journal of Business Research, 58*, 115–125.

Murphy, S. A., Duxbury, L., & Higgins, C. (2006). The individual and organizational consequences of stress, anxiety and depression in the workplace: A case study. *Canadian Journal of Community Mental Health, 25*(2), 143–157.

Parker, C. P., Baltes, B. B., Young, S. A., Huff, J. W., Altmann, R. A., Lacost, H. A., et al. (2003). Relationships between psychological climate perceptions and work outcomes: A meta-analytic review. *Journal of Organizational Behavior, 24*, 389–416.

Patterson, M. G., West, M. A., Shackleton, V. J., Dawson, J. F., Lawthom, R., Maitlis, S., et al. (2005). Validating the organizational climate measure: Links to managerial practices, productivity and innovation. *Journal of Organizational Behavior, 26*, 379–408.
Perez, E., & Wilkerson, B. (1998). *Mindsets, mental health: The ultimate productivity weapon*. Guelph: The Homewood Centre for Organizational Health at Riverslea.
Podsakoff, P. M., MacKenzie, S. B., Lee, J. Y., & Podsakoff, N. P. (2003). Common method biases in behavioral research: A critical review of the literature and recommended remedies. *Journal of Applied Psychology, 88*(5), 879–903.
Polivy, J. (1981). On the induction of emotion in the laboratory: Discrete moods or multiple affect states? *Journal of Personality and Social Psychology, 41*, 803–817.
Rupp, D. E., Vodanovich, S. J., & Crede, M. (2006). Age bias in the workplace: The impact of ageism and causal attributions. *Journal of Applied Social Psychology, 36*(6), 1337–1364.
Schneider, B. (1990). The climate for service: An application of the climate construct. In B. Schneider (Ed.), *Organizational climate and culture* (pp. 383–412). San Francisco, CA: Jossey-Bass.
Szeto, A. C. H., & Dobson, K. S. (2010). Reducing the stigma of mental disorders at work: A review of current workplace anti-stigma intervention programs. *Applied and Preventive Psychology, 14*, 41–56.
Tabachnick, B., & Fidell, L. (2007). *Using multivariate statistics* (5th ed.). Boston: Pearson.
Terborg, J. R. (1981). Interactional psychology and research on human behavior in organizations. *Academy of Management Review, 6*, 569–576.
Valecha, G. K., & Ostrom, T. M. (1974). An abbreviated measure of internal-external locus of control. *Journal of Personality Assessment, 38*, 369–376.
van Dorn, R. A., Swanson, J. W., Elbogen, E. B., & Swartz, M. S. (2005). A comparison of stigmatizing attitudes toward persons with schizophrenia in four stakeholder groups: Perceived likelihood of violence and desire for social distance. *Psychiatry, 68*(2), 152–163.
Watson, A. C., & Corrigan, P. W. (2005). Challenging public stigma: A target approach. In P. W. Corrigan (Ed.), *On the stigma of mental illness: Practical strategies for research and social change* (pp. 281–295). Washington, DC: American Psychological Association.
Wolkenstein, L., & Meyer, T. D. (2008). Attitudes of young people towards depression and mania. *Psychology and Psychotherapy: Theory, Research and Practice, 81*, 15–31.
World Health Organization. (2009). *Depression: What is depression?* Retrieved May 5, 2009, from http://www.who.int/mental_health/management/depression/definition/en/.
Ziegert, J. C., & Hanges, P. J. (2005). Employment discrimination: The role of implicit attitudes, motivation, and a climate for racial bias. *Journal of Applied Psychology, 90*(3), 553–562.

Part IV
Practical Approach in Specific Conditions

Chapter 16
Improving Psychosocial Factors in Small-Scale Enterprises in Japan and the Asia-Pacific Region

Jiro Moriguchi, Sonoko Sakuragi and Masayuki Ikeda

Abstract The Ministry of Health, Labour and Welfare of Japan has reported that smaller enterprises are less active in mental health promotion. Yet few studies exist on mental health activities in small-scale enterprises (with 10–49 employees) and in micro-scale enterprises (with fewer than 10 employees) in Japan. In a review of the literature on preventive occupational health and safety in these enterprises, the employer is the dominant player for any changes which need to be made to promote mental health. This study aimed to clarify the demands facing employers in micro-scale enterprises and small-scale enterprises regarding mental health activities and to establish measures for improving the existing situation in Japan. In 2012, a questionnaire survey was conducted on mental health with 1041 employers, including 367 micro-scale enterprises and 419 small-scale enterprises. The survey included questions about enterprise scales, types of industries, attitude of employers on mental health, annual budgets for mental health activities, future plans for mental health activities, and expectations for external occupational health specialists. The main expectation for external occupational health specialists was counseling for employees. Education for employers themselves was second highest (10.4 %) among the requests from employers in micro-scale enterprises. The median amount budgeted for mental health activities in micro-scale enterprises was 80 US dollars per year, with 37 % of micro-scale enterprises reporting nothing budgeted for it. Therefore, a brochure and video tools on mental health at an affordable price for employers in micro-scale enterprises were developed. Interviews about these tools were implemented in 11 micro-scale enterprises and 18 small-scale enterprises. An analysis of interviews with the employers revealed that most answered, "the brochure and the video tools are easy to understand" (73 % in micro-scale enterprises and 98 % in small-scale enterprises). After additional minor revisions, these tools have been distributed to help improve the mental health situation of these enterprises in Japan.

Keywords Small-scale enterprise · Micro-scale enterprise · Mental health · Employer · Educational tool

J. Moriguchi (✉) · S. Sakuragi · M. Ikeda
Kyoto Industrial Health Association, Kyoto, Japan
e-mail: moriguchi@hokenkai.jp

A. Shimazu et al. (eds.), *Psychosocial Factors at Work in the Asia Pacific*,
DOI 10.1007/978-3-319-44400-0_16

Introduction

Occupational health service activities for small-scale enterprises and micro-scale enterprises are often insufficient in many countries (Bradshaw et al. 2001; Park et al. 2002; Houtman et al. 2007) as they have limited access to human, economic, and technical resources (Champoux and Brun 2003). Thus, workers employed in small-scale enterprises usually have lower quality occupational health service, and sometimes poorer health conditions when compared to their counterpart workers in large-scale enterprises (Furuki et al. 2006; Kubo et al. 2006). Because good occupational health service requires the support of competent occupational health professionals (Nicholson 2004), it could be difficult to provide sufficient occupational health service in small-scale enterprises and micro-scale enterprises which have less access to competent occupational health professionals.

In Japan, the Industrial Safety and Health law stipulates that under the occupational health service provision it is an employer's duty to protect employee health irrespective of enterprise size, and that companies employing 50 or more workers must establish a health and safety committee and appoint an occupational physician (the number of occupational physicians varies as a function of employee numbers; Ministry of Health, Labour and Welfare, Japan 1972). Enterprises with fewer than 50 employees are regarded as small-scale enterprises, and the Japanese government has recently made several efforts to improve occupational health service in small-scale enterprises; for example, Regional Occupational Health Centers have been established to support occupational health service in small-scale enterprises.

The Basic Survey on Industrial Safety and Health (Ministry of Health, Labour and Welfare, Japan 2010) revealed that 87.0 % of enterprises with more than 50 workers had occupational physicians (either with a full-time or part-time contract). As expected, the percentage was higher (99.8 %) for enterprises with more than 1000 workers and lower (80.9 %) for enterprises with 50–99 workers. The percentage for even smaller enterprises was unknown as there was no legal stipulation for small-scale enterprises and micro-scale enterprises regarding contracting occupational physicians. The Survey on the State of Employees' Health (Ministry of Health, Labour and Welfare, Japan 2012) showed that the percentage of enterprises implementing mental health care was low (47.2 %) in Japan. Similar to the appointment of occupational physicians, the percentage was higher (99.1 %) for enterprises with more than 5000 workers and lower (38.9 %) for enterprises with 10–29 workers.

The World Health Organization (Houtman et al. 2007) has also reported that more than 80 % of the workforce was employed in small- and medium-scale enterprises. It is estimated that the percentage would be even higher in developing countries. Small- and medium-scale enterprises, in particular, as well as the informal sector have poor access to occupational health service and other external support. They often lack knowledge about occupational health in general. The occupational health situation in small-scale enterprises and micro-scale enterprises, including in the Asia-Pacific region, has been reported by several authors (Wang et al. 2009; Kaewboonchoo et al. 2011; Hannerz et al. 2012; Cocker et al. 2013; Lai et al. 2015), but most were limited to cross-sectional studies. Previous research has shown the beneficial effects of interventions designed to reduce occupational stress, such as cognitive behavior improvement (van der Klink et al. 2001; Kimura et al. 2015), supervisor training (Kawakami et al. 2006), and organization-focused intervention (Kobayashi et al. 2008; Tsutsumi et al. 2009). However, most studies have been on middle- and large-scale enterprises, and intervention studies implemented in small-scale enterprises and micro-scale enterprises have been scarce (Kristensen 2005; Merrill 2013). Given that such a large proportion of the workforce globally is employed in small- or micro-scale enterprises, further intervention study in small-scale enterprises and micro-scale enterprises is necessary. Study 1 clarified the attitudes of employers and the situation regarding mental health activities in small-scale enterprises and micro-scale enterprises, and established measures to improve the situation in Japan. Study 2 developed educational tools for improving mental health condition in micro-scale enterprises and small-scale enterprises there.

Study 1: Questionnaire Survey for Employers in Small-Scale Enterprises

Purpose

The study purposes were to clarify the attitudes of employers and the situation regarding mental health activities in small-scale enterprises and micro-scale enterprises, and to establish measures to improve the situation in Japan.

Method

In 2012, a mental health questionnaire was sent to 2603 employers in 10 selected prefectures (Hokkaido, Miyagi, Nigata, Tokyo, Shizuoka, Aichi, Kyoto, Osaka, Okayama, Fukuoka) in Japan. Completed questionnaires were obtained from 1041 employers in enterprises including 367 micro-scale enterprises and 419 small-scale enterprises. The response rate of the questionnaire was 40.0 %.

The questionnaires included items regarding enterprise scales, types of industries, current situations for mental health activities, annual budgets for mental health activities, cooperation with external specialists, future plans for mental health activities, and expectation for external occupational health specialists.

A normal distribution of the data was assumed, and the arithmetic mean and arithmetic standard deviation of the data were calculated. For evaluation of statistical significance, $p < 0.05$ was employed as the cut off. A Kruskal–Wallis test was used to detect possible differences in annual budgets for the mental health activities between enterprise sizes. A Cochran–Armitage trend test was used to detect the possible difference in the expectation for external occupational health specialists between enterprise sizes and other similar parameters. The data were processed using SPSS version 20.0 or Excel 2013.

Results 1: Mental Health Activities of Small- and Micro-Scale Enterprises

Table 16.1 shows employer knowledge on governmental mental health policy by enterprise scale. The percentage of "Yes, I know" answers regarding each mental health policy decreased significantly with the scale of the enterprise ($p < 0.01$ for each policy). For the question on knowledge of depression (i.e., Do you have a good knowledge of depression?), the ratio of the answer "knowing very well" also decreased with the scale of the enterprise ($p < 0.01$, data not shown).

Mental health measures implemented in each enterprise size are shown in Table 16.2. The percentage of measures implemented decreased with the scale of the enterprise ($p < 0.01$), except for employer education.

Results 2: Employer Expectations for Occupational Health Specialists and Annual Budget for Mental Health Activities of Small- and Micro-Scale Enterprises

The main employer expectation for external occupational health specialists was counseling for employees irrespective of enterprise size (Fig. 16.1). Education for employers themselves was the second highest request among employers in micro-scale enterprises. The expectation of employer education increased with the scale of the enterprise, although the difference was statistically insignificant ($p > 0.05$).

Table 16.3 shows the annual budget for mental health activities by enterprise size. A total of 629 enterprises out of 1041 (60.4 %) did not answer the question. Mean budget for mental health activities decreased significantly with the scale of the enterprise ($p < 0.01$, Kruskal–Wallis test). The ratio of the answer "None" increased with the scale of the enterprise as well ($p < 0.01$, Cochran–Armitage trend test). The median of the budget in micro-scale enterprises was 80 US dollars per year and 36.5 % of micro-scale enterprises answered that the budget was none.

Table 16.1 Employers' knowledge on governmental MH policy

	Enterprise scale by number of employees									
	2–9		10–49		50–299		300 and over		Total	
	No. of answers "Yes, I know"	%[a]	No. of answers "Yes, I know"	%[a]	No. of answers "Yes, I know"	%[a]	No. of answers "Yes, I know"	%[a]	No. of answers "Yes, I know"	%[a]
Guidelines on employees' MH promotion	44	12.0	102	24.3	52	40.0	59	47.2	257	24.7
Guidelines on return-to-work of employees with MH disorder	50	13.6	90	21.5	40	30.8	52	41.6	232	22.3
MH portal website	20	5.4	39	9.3	24	18.5	36	28.8	119	11.4
Measures against ill health from overwork	46	12.5	103	24.6	62	47.7	82	65.6	293	28.1

MH Mental health

[a]Calculated by total number of enterprises in each scale (2–9: 367, 10–49: 419, 50–299: 130, 300 and over: 125)

Table 16.2 MH measures implemented in enterprises

	Enterprise scale by number of employees									
	2–9		10–49		50–299		300 and over		Total	
	No. of answers	%[a]	No. of answers	%[a]	No. of answers	%[a]	No. of answers	%[a]	No. of answers	%[a]
Counseling for employees	7	1.9	31	7.4	25	19.2	54	43.2	117	11.2
Education for employees	28	7.6	61	14.6	38	29.2	51	40.8	178	17.1
Education for employers	26	7.1	39	9.3	10	7.7	13	10.4	88	8.5
Provision of MH brochures	11	3.0	37	8.8	19	14.6	26	20.8	93	8.9

MH Mental health

[a]Calculated by total number of enterprises in each scale (2–9: 367, 10–49: 419, 50–299: 130, 300 and over: 125)

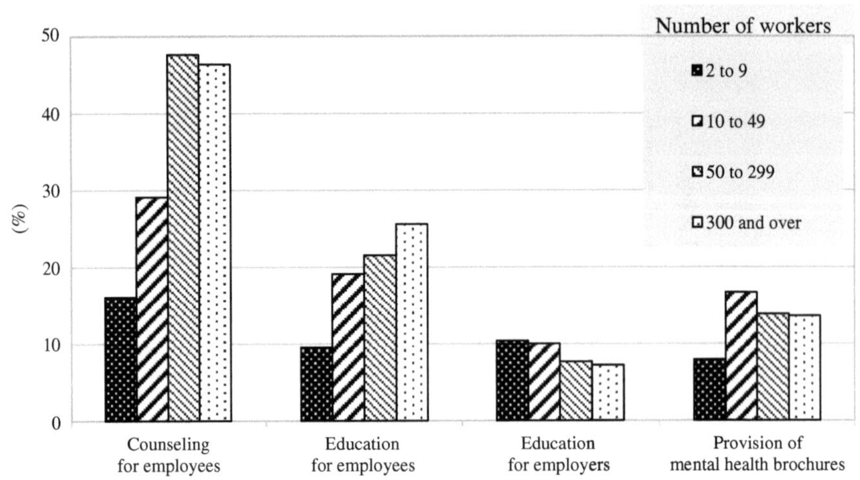

Fig. 16.1 Employers' expectations for occupational health specialists

Discussion

The results of Study 1 show that employer knowledge of mental health problems and mental health measures are insufficient in micro-scale and small-scale enterprises. Although employers in micro-scale enterprises request counseling for

Table 16.3 Annual budget for MH activities in enterprises

	Enterprise scale by number of employees				
	2–9	10–49	50–299	300 and over	Total
No.[a] of answers	189	153	43	27	412
Budget (1000 yen/year)					
Average	34	68	296	4120	342
Minimum	0	0	0	0	0
Median	10	30	100	1000	30
Maximum	1000	500	3000	26,000	26,000
No.[a] of answers as "None"	69	34	5	1	109
%	36.5	22.2	11.6	3.7	26.5

MH Mental health
[a]No.: number 100 Japanese yen was equivalent to 0.8 US dollars

employees and education for themselves (the employers), the budgets for mental health activities were significantly lower than they were for larger enterprises.

In this survey, completed questionnaires were obtained from 1041 employers in enterprises, including 367 micro-scale enterprises and 419 small-scale enterprises. Only a few surveys targeted at micro-scale enterprises and small-scale enterprises have been reported on previously in Japan (Ikeda et al. 2002, Tsuda et al. 2011, Hirata et al. 1999). These surveys were limited to one prefecture and the number of questionnaires obtained was less than 800. Therefore, the present survey was the largest ever nationwide survey for micro-scale enterprises and small-scale enterprises in Japan.

Mean budget for mental health activities decreased with the scale of the enterprise. The ratio of "None" for budget was 37 % in micro-scale enterprises. Moreover, nearly half of employers in micro scale enterprises (178 of 367 enterprises) did not answer the question. Potentially, employers who have a very low budget for mental health activities might feel hesitant about this question. Therefore, it can be estimated that most micro-scale enterprises cannot spend sufficient money on mental health activities. In this study, counseling for employees was the highest expectation of employers for occupational health specialists. Because counseling cannot generally be offered for free, the study group did not choose counseling as the main solution for improvement of mental health activities in micro-scale enterprises.

Education for employers themselves was the second highest request of micro-scale enterprise employers to occupational health specialists. This survey showed a lack of knowledge of mental health by employers in micro-scale enterprises and insufficient mental health activities in micro-scale enterprises as well. In a review of the literature on preventive occupational health and safety in small enterprises, Hasle and Limborg (2006) summarized that the owner (the employer in a small business is often the owner-manager) is the dominant actor regarding any changes made in small-scale enterprises, and that the personal values and priorities of the owner are determinants of the culture, social relations, and attitude of the enterprises. Thus, the owner is indeed the key person for occupational health in micro-scale enterprises and small-scale enterprises. Previous reports by Lamm (1997), Nicholson (2004), and Linnan and Birken (2006) corresponded with this.

Based on the results of Study 1, the study group decided to develop a brochure and video tools on mental health for employers in micro-scale enterprises and small-scale enterprises at an affordable price. The results of this are described in Study 2.

Study 2: Development of Educational Tools for Employers in Micro- and Small-Scale Enterprises in Japan to Improve Mental Health Activities

Purpose

The study purpose was to develop educational tools for improvement of mental health in micro-scale enterprises and small-scale enterprises in Japan.

Method 1: Development Process of Tools

Video tools and a brochure on mental health were developed in 2013 for employers in small-scale and micro-scale enterprises. The contents of the tools were decided based on the results of Study 1 and discussion with study group members. The study group selected several major contents regarding manager education in medium- and large-scale enterprises, such as the meaning of mental health issues and how to cope with mental health problems, early detection of employees with mental health problems and their management, and risk regarding violations of the law. An analysis of the questionnaire responses revealed that the main mental health activity of employers was daily communication with employees in micro-scale enterprises (52 %) and small-scale enterprises (64 %). Therefore, the tool includes four sections: "1. Stressors and stress reactions," "2. Communication," "3. Early detection," and "4. Prevention of law violation risk."

The "Stressor and stress reaction" section includes the cause of the stress reaction, and typical symptom and stressors/buffers of the National Institute for Occupational Safety and Health (NIOSH) model. The "Communication" section includes the basis and points of communication, points of active listening, and stress coping. The "Early detection" section includes early detection of employees with mental health problems, and work burden reduction. "Prevention of law violation risk" includes the worth of mental health measures in enterprises from the viewpoint of legislation and corporate social responsibility, such as cost needed for absent workers, responsibility of employers for damages, and preventive activities against disadvantage to enterprises.

We developed both a brochure and videos on mental health to educate employers. The video tools included four films of presentations by members of the study group. The brochure was 20 pages in total. Each video tool took 5–8 min to watch. The brochure and the videos tools contained essentially the same information.

Method 2: Tool Evaluation by Employers

The study group conducted interviews with employers on these tools in 11 micro-scale enterprises and 18 small-scale enterprises. In the questionnaire survey in Study 1, we included a question "Would you allow us to interview yon on your mental health activities?" We visited the employers who answered yes for acceptance.

The study group sent the brochure and the videos to 29 employers several weeks before the interview. A member of the study group visited each employer at his/her office. During the interview, the employers could browse the videos and read the brochure (Fig. 16.2). The interviewer asked about the brochure as a whole and about each section of the videos. The employers evaluated the tools using four choices—"easy to understand," "somewhat easy to understand," "relatively difficult to understand," and "difficult to understand,"—and gave concrete opinions if they wished. Each interview took between 30 and 60 min. Information from interviews was analyzed to help revise the tools.

For an evaluation of statistical significance, $p < 0.05$ was used as the cut off. A Chi-square test was used to detect possible differences of the understanding regarding the tools between small-scale enterprises and micro-scale enterprises. The data were processed using Excel 2013.

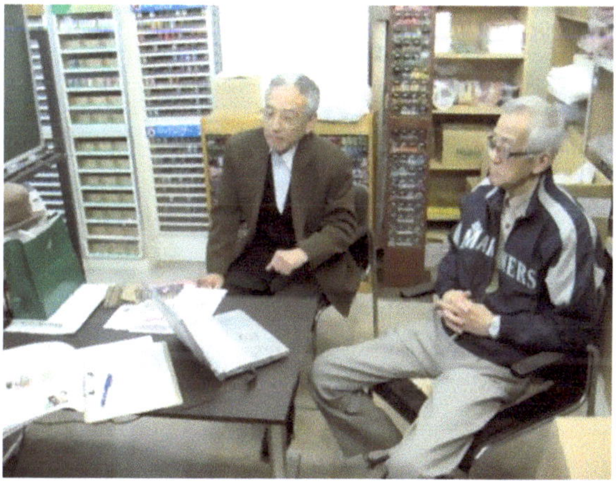

Fig. 16.2 Pictured are two employers being interviewed about the tool

Results

All employers completed the interview (n = 29). Evaluation of the tools by employers is shown in Table 16.4. Most employers in micro-scale enterprises and small-scale enterprises answered that the brochure and the videos were "easy to understand" or "relatively easy to understand." The "easy to understand" response was more dominant in the brochure and video 1 in small-scale enterprises (easy to understand vs. others = 88.9 vs. 11.1 %) compared to the micro-scale enterprises (45.5 vs. 54.5 %; $p < 0.05$ by Chi-square test).

Employers' major opinions were as follows: "both brochure and video tools are informative for understanding the importance of mental health" (e.g., if an employer missed some content in the videos, the content could be found in the brochure, either immediately or later), "information on regional occupational health centers should be more detailed," "practical examples should be given," and "we should listen more to our employees."

Based on the opinions of the employers, the tools were revised. The major revisions were as follows: "the usefulness of regional occupational health centers was emphasized," "an explanation of the regional occupational health center staff's confidentiality obligation was added," and "practical examples were added." For example, one of the practical examples added was a case of cooperation between social security attorneys and employers for support of a mental health case in micro-scale enterprises.

Table 16.4 Tool evaluation by employers

	Answer			
	Easy	Relatively easy	Relatively difficult	Difficult
MSE				
Brochure	5	3	2	1
Video 1	5	4	1	1
Video 2	6	2	2	1
Video 3	7	1	2	1
Video 4	4	3	3	1
SSE				
Brochure	16	2	0	0
Video 1	16	2	0	0
Video 2	13	4	1	0
Video 3	13	5	0	0
Video 4	12	5	1	0

The topic of the Video 1 was "Stressor and stress reaction."
The topic of the Video 2 was "Communication."
The topic of the Video 3 was "Early detection."
The topic of the Video 4 was "Prevention of law violation risk."
MSE Micro-scale enterprise, *SSE* Small-scale enterprise

After these revisions, distribution of these tools commenced in January 2015 with expectations that they would help the mental health situation in micro-scale enterprises and small-scale enterprises. The price of the tool (a brochure and video set) was about 7 US dollars. More than 3000 sets have been sold as of the end of August 2015.

Discussion

In Study 2, educational tools for employers regarding mental health were developed. Most employers in small-scale enterprises and micro-scale enterprises who accepted the interview by a study group member evaluated the brochure and videos positively.

In communication with an employer, the documents to be submitted to him/her should be short (Brosseau et al. 2007), easy to interpret (Walker and Tait 2004), industry subgroup-specific (Mayhew 2000) and have practical applications (Mayhew 1997) and good practice examples (Russell et al. 1998). Brosseau and Li (2005) stressed the importance of demonstrating the positive effects of occupational health service on employee health. Using the information as a reference, the study group made the tools short, including the practical examples. Because two types of the tool (the video and the brochure) can be used by the employers in various ways as they wish, the tools may be convenient for them. The employers were suspicious that occupational health specialists would force ideal and unrealistic measures on them in the questionnaire survey of Study 1; therefore, the study group tried to give realistic and concrete measures in the tools. However, in Video 4, "prevention of law violation risk," the study group gave a court precedent of a large enterprise to assist understanding. Because a precedent of a large enterprise could be unrealistic for the employers in micro-scale enterprises and small-scale enterprises, the rating was relatively lower here compared to the other tools. Therefore, the study group changed the precedent to one which was more suitable for small-scale enterprises and micro-scale enterprises in the revised version of the tools.

The regional occupational health centers are public occupational health centers in Japan, which can be used by employers and employees in enterprises with fewer than 50 employees. There were 325 regional occupational health centers in Japan in 2013, offering services at no charges, including health guidance for employers or employees based on the results of their health check-ups, health guidance for employees with mental health problems, health guidance for employees to solve overwork problems, and advice regarding the provision of work environment improvements based on worksite visits. Several issues still need to be solved, such as the low utilization rate and shortage in labor. The Survey on the State of Employees' Health (Ministry of Health, Labour and Welfare, Japan 2012) revealed that the rate of mental health activities with regional occupational health centers were only 3.9 % in enterprises with 10–29 employees and 7.5 % in enterprises with

30–49 employees. In the present study, nearly 90 % of the employers answered that they have never contacted their regional occupational health centers (data not shown in this chapter) while many commented that regional occupational health centers might be useful and more should be known about them. Therefore, we provided a description of the regional occupational health centers in further detail in the revised version of the tools.

Some employers were afraid that if the staff of regional occupational health centers recognized insufficient mental health activities of their enterprises, the staff might submit a report to the Labour Standards Inspection Office, whose main role is to check whether employers adhere to labor legislation. In the event an employer does not adhere to the legislation, the Labour Standards Inspection Office staff give the employer administrative guidance. These employers might have associated the regional occupational health center services with punishment by the Labour Standards Inspection Office. To assuage employers' concerns, an explanation of the regional occupational health center staff's confidentiality obligation was added to the tools.

The video tools were used for the education of employers in the present study. Several reports exist on the effectiveness of video tools. Brown et al. (2013) reported that a DVD for education of cancer patients and facilitation of workplace communication was seen favorably by cancer patients. E-learning material of stress management for small-scale enterprises was developed by the Miyazaki Occupational Health Promotion Center in Japan (Koiwaya and Tomiie 2005). They reported that this e-learning improved the occupational stress indicator. They also reported that the appearance of employees of the enterprise in the film and the included business specific contents of the enterprise in the film were effective in attracting their employees' interest. The study group considered that video tools, such as animations or TV dramas, could be more attractive than videos of presentations in this study. However, because of budget shortages, this idea did not materialize. It might be necessary to investigate the effects and cost-effectiveness of these kinds of tools in the future.

Psychosocial Factors in Small-Scale Enterprises in the Asia-Pacific Region

Although there is a general lack of studies on psychosocial factors in small-scale enterprises, of the extant studies there are several reports from the Asia-Pacific region. However, most were limited to be cross-sectional studies. Wang et al. (2009) in Taiwan reported that fatigue of employees was associated with a lack of physical exercise, more shift work, higher depression score, and less social support in small-scale enterprises. In Thailand, the workability index of employees in small-scale enterprises was associated with better mental health, higher social support at work, lower depression score, and lower age (Kaewboonchoo et al. 2011). They concluded that job stress reduction programs should be considered to improve workers' workability indices. An intervention program implemented in small-scale enterprises and micro-scale enterprises was found in the United States. Merrill (2013) reported that a worksite wellness program, including stress management activities, effectively improved health behaviors, health perceptions, and life satisfaction in small- and medium-scale enterprises. Further investigations for improvement of work-related psychosocial factors in small-scale enterprises and micro-scale enterprises in the Asia-Pacific region are expected in the near future.

Relevant Theoretical Frameworks

Participatory occupational risk reduction programs are gaining importance in small-scale enterprises (Kogi 2006). Such employee participatory programs are also effective for improvement of psychosocial factors in workplaces (Yoshikawa et al. 2007; Kobayashi et al. 2008; Tsutsumi et al. 2009). Common characteristics of improvements implemented in small workplaces are shown as "covering multiple technical areas," "mostly simple and low-cost types of improvements in each technical areas," "voluntarily selected by means of joint walkthroughs and small group discussions," and "implemented rapidly." (Kogi 2006).

It could also be important to involve employers in such occupational risk reduction programs. It has been reported that the employer is a dominant actor in relation to any changes made in small-scale enterprises (Hasle and Limborg 2006). The World Health Organization also has stated that employers and worker representatives must be aware and be able to prevent work-related stress in workers (Houtman et al. 2007). Cocker et al. (2013) reported that the owners in small and medium-scale enterprises with high psychological distress were aware of loss in their productivity. Maintenance of employer physical and mental health is essential for sustainable business of small-scale enterprises and micro-scale enterprises. Therefore, provision of support programs and educational tools for employers should be reasonable not only for employees' health but also employers' health and their business. The advantage of occupational health specialists in small-scale enterprises is that occupational physicians may have better opportunities to educate the employer not only through the activities such as attendance at the occupational health service committee but by direct conversation with the employer.

Houtman et al. (2007) proposed a stepwise approach on work-related stress management in developing countries. This approach could be applied to small-scale and medium-scale enterprises. The approach consists of five steps: Step 1. Detecting signs of work-related stress and taking preparatory actions, Step 2. Analyzing risk factors and risk groups, Step 3. Designing an action plan, Step 4. Implementing an action plan, and Step 5. Evaluating the interventions.

Challenges and Future Directions

Implementation of the Job Stress Questionnaire for employees has become a legal obligation for enterprises in Japan since 2015 (Ministry of Health, Labour and Welfare, Japan 2015). Employers are expected to use the questionnaire results for primary prevention, such as the participatory intervention for workplace improvement. Although primary prevention is not a legal obligation for employers so far, the authors completed a pilot study last year of the participatory intervention for workplace improvement in an enterprise employing eight employees (Kawakami et al. 2015). Participatory occupational risk reduction programs in small enterprises have already accomplished excellent results in several countries (Kogi 2006). Such programs are expected to spread further in the Asia-Pacific region.

The International Social Security Association has developed the "Guide for Risk Assessment in Small and Medium Enterprises." This addresses small- and medium-scale enterprises as a simple tool for hazard identification, including mental workload and risk assessment in workplaces (International Social Security Association 2010). When implementing the participatory occupational risk reduction programs, use of such risk assessment tools could make the program easier for occupational health specialists, employers, and employees in small-scale enterprises and micro-scale enterprises.

Conclusion

Employer education regarding mental health is important, especially in micro-scale enterprises. Most employers in small-scale enterprises and micro-scale enterprises appreciated our brochures and videos. After minor revisions, we have distributed these tools to help improve the mental health situation in micro-scale enterprises and small-scale enterprises.

Employee participatory programs for improvement of psychosocial factors in workplaces should be applied more to micro-scale enterprises and small-scale enterprises in the Asia-Pacific region.

Acknowledgments This study was supported by the Japan Foundation for Promoting Welfare of Independent Entrepreneurs and The Occupational Health Promotion Foundation, Japan.

References

Bradshaw, L. M., Curran, A. D., Eskin, F., & Fishwick, D. (2001). Provision and perception of occupational health in small and medium-sized enterprises in Sheffield, UK. *Occupational Medicine, 51*, 39–44.

Brosseau, L. M., Fredrickson, A. L., & Casey, M. A. (2007). Small business owners' opinions about written health and safety information. *Industrial Health, 45*, 209–216.

Brosseau, L. M., & Li, S. Y. (2005). Small business owners' health and safety intensions: A cross-sectional survey. *Environmental Health: A Global Access Science, 4*, 23.
Brown, R. F., Owens, M., & Bradley, C. (2013). Employee to employer communication skills: Balancing cancer treatment and employment. *Psychooncology, 22*, 426–433.
Champoux, D., & Brun, J. (2003). Occupational health and safety management in small size enterprises; An overview of the situation and avenues for intervention and research. *Safety Science, 41*, 301–318.
Cocker, F., Martin, A., Scott, J., Venn, A., & Sanderson, K. (2013). Psychological distress, related work attendance, and productivity loss in small-to-medium enterprise owner/managers. *International Journal of Environmental Research and Public Health, 10*, 5062–5082.
Furuki, K., Hirata, M., & Kage, A. (2006). Nationwide survey of occupational health activities in small-scale enterprises in Japan. *Industrial Health, 44*, 150–154.
Hannerz, H., Ferm, L., Poulsen, O. M., Pedersen, B. H., & Andersen, L. L. (2012). Enterprise size and return to work after stroke. *Journal of Occupational Rehabilitation, 22*, 456–461.
Hasle, P., & Limborg, H. J. (2006). A review of the literature on preventive occupational health and safety activities in small enterprises. *Industrial Health, 44*, 6–12.
Hirata, M., Kumagai, S., Tabuchi, T., Tainaka, H., Andoh, K., & Oda, H. (1999). Actual conditions of occupational health activities in small-scale enterprises in Japan: System for occupational health, health management and demands by small-scale enterprises. *Sangyo Eiseigaku Zasshi, 41*, 190–201. (Japanese).
Houtman, I., Jettinghoff, K., & Cedillo, L. (2007). *Raising awareness of stress at work in developing countries: A modern hazard in a traditional working environment: Advice to employers and worker representatives.* World Health Organization. http://www.who.int/occupational_health/publications/raisingawarenessofstress.pdf.
Ikeda, T., Nakata, K., Kobori, S., Hojo, M., & Sugishita, C. (2002). Willingness to implement mental health measures among small-scale enterprise employers in Ohta ward, Tokyo, Japan. *Sangyo Eiseigaku Zasshi, 44*, 200–207. (Japanese).
International Social Security Association. (2010). *Guide for risk assessment in small and medium enterprises*. International Social Security Association. https://www.issa.int/ja/details?uuid=451b4c81-ac0c-4272-92f8-b8fe9fe1e0bb.
Kaewboonchoo, O., Saleekul, S., & Usathaporn, S. (2011). Factors related to work ability among Thai workers. *Southeast Asian Journal of Tropical Medicine and Public Health, 42*, 225–230.
Kawakami, N., Takao, S., Kobayashi, Y., & Tsutsumi, A. (2006). Effects of web-based supervisor training on job stressors and psychological distress among workers. A workplace-based randomized controlled trial. *Journal of Occupational Health, 48*, 28–34.
Kawakami, N., Tsutsumi, A., Haratani, T., Shimazu, A., Odagiri, Y., Yoshikawa, T., et al. (2015). *Development of risk assessment tools for mental health measures in enterprises*. Study report of Ministry of Health, Labour and Welfare, Japan (pp. 98–121). (**Japanese**).
Kimura, R., Mori, M., Tajima, M., Somemura, H., Sasaki, N., Yamamoto, M., et al. (2015). Effect of a brief training program based on cognitive behavioral therapy in improving work performance: A randomized controlled trial. *Journal of Occupational Health, 57*, 169–178.
Kobayashi, Y., Kaneyoshi, A., Yokota, A., & Kawakami, N. (2008). Effects of a worker participatory program for improving work environments on job stressors. *Journal of Occupational Health, 50*, 455–470.
Kogi, K. (2006). Advances in participatory occupational health aimed at good practices in small enterprises and the informal sector. *Industrial Health, 44*, 31–34.
Koiwaya, Y., & Tomiie, T. (2005). *Stress management using e-learning system.* Study report of Miyazaki occupational health promotion center. (**Japanese**).
Kristensen, T. S. (2005). Intervention studies in occupational epidemiology. *Occupational and Environmental Medicine, 62*, 205–210.
Kubo, N., Usami, T., Haruyama, Y., Muto, T., Kimura, K., Yukawa, S., et al. (2006). Characteristics of lifestyle and health status of workers in small-scale enterprises in Japan. *Industrial Health, 44*, 161–165.

Lai, Y., Saridakis, G., & Blackburn, R. (2015). Job stress in the United Kingdom: Are Small and medium-sized enterprises and large enterprises different? *Stress and Health, 31*, 222–235.

Lamm, F. (1997). Small businesses and OH&S advisors. *Safety Science, 25*, 153–161.

Linnan, L. A., & Birken, B. E. (2006). Small businesses, worksite wellness, and public health: A time for action. *North Caroline Medical Journal, 67*, 433–437.

Mayhew, C. (1997). Small business occupational health and safety information provision. *Journal of Occupational Health Safety: Australia and New Zealand, 13*, 361–373.

Mayhew, C. (2000). OHS in Australian "micro" small business: Evidence from nine research studies. *Journal of Occupational Health Safety: Australia and New Zealand, 16*, 297–305.

Merrill, R. M. (2013). A small business worksite wellness model for improving health behaviors. *Journal of Occupational and Environmental Medicine, 55*, 895–900.

Ministry of Health, Labour and Welfare, Japan. (1972). *Industrial Safety and Health law*. Ministry of Health, Labour and Welfare, Japan. http://law.e-gov.go.jp/htmldata/S47/S47HO057.html. [Japanese]

Ministry of Health, Labour and Welfare, Japan. (2010). *Basic Survey on Industrial Safety and Health.* Ministry of Health, Labour and Welfare, Japan. http://www.mhlw.go.jp/toukei/list/dl/49-22_4.pdf.

Ministry of Health, Labour and Welfare, Japan. (2012). *Survey on State of Employees' Health.* Ministry of Health, Labour and Welfare, Japan. http://www.mhlw.go.jp/toukei/list/dl/h24-46-50_01.pdf.

Ministry of Health, Labour and Welfare, Japan. (2015). *Summary of stress check system based on amended Industrial Safety and Health Law*. Ministry of Health, Labour and Welfare, Japan. http://www.mhlw.go.jp/file/05-Shingikai-11201000-Roudoukijunkyoku-Soumuka/0000057447.pdf.

Nicholson, P. J. (2004). Occupational health services in the UK—Challenges and opportunities. *Occupational Medicine, 54*, 147–152.

Park, H., Ha, E., Kim, J., Jung, H., & Paek, D. (2002). Occupational health services for small-scale enterprises in Korea. *Industrial Health, 40*, 1–6.

Russell, R. M., Maidment, S. C., Brooke, I., & Topping, M. D. (1998). An introduction to UK schemes to help small firms control health risks from chemicals. *The Annals of Occupational Hygiene, 68*, 699–704.

Tsuda, Y., Tsukahara, T., Uchida, M., Washizuka, S., & Nomiyama, T. (2011). Present status of mental health management in small-scale enterprises in Nagano prefecture, Japan. *The Shinshu Medical Journal, 59*, 163–168. (Japanese).

Tsutsumi, A., Nagami, M., Yoshikawa, T., Kogi, K., & Kawakami, N. (2009). Participatory intervention for workplace improvements on mental health and job performance among blue-collar workers: A cluster randomized controlled trial. *Journal of Occupational and Environmental Medicine, 51*, 554–563.

van der Klink, J. J., Blonk, R. W., Schene, A. H., & van Dijk, F. J. (2001). The benefits of interventions for work-related stress. *American Journal of Public Health, 91*, 270–276.

Walker, D., & Tait, R. (2004). Health and safety management in small enterprises; An effective low cost approach. *Safety Science, 42*, 69–83.

Wang, F. W., Chiu, Y. W., Tu, M. S., Chou, M. Y., Wang, C. L., & Chuang, H. Y. (2009). Chronic fatigue of the small enterprise workers participating in an occupational health checkup center in southern Taiwan. *International Archives of Occupational and Environmental Health, 82*, 819–825.

Yoshikawa, T., Kawakami, N., Kogi, K., Tsutsumi, A., Shimazu, M., Nagami, M., et al. (2007). Development of a mental health action checklist for improving workplace environment as means of job stress prevention. *Sangyo Eiseigaku Zasshi, 49*, 127–142. (Japanese).

Chapter 17
Health Issues of Workers Engaged in Operations Related to the Accident at the Fukushima Daiichi Nuclear Power Plant

Koji Mori, Seiichiro Tateishi and Koh Hiraoka

Abstract A nuclear accident occurred in northern Japan at the Fukushima Daiichi Nuclear Power Plant of the Tokyo Electric Power Company (TEPCO) following a mega-earthquake and subsequent tsunami in March 2011. A large number of workers were engaged in the related works, which has shifted from emergency response to cooling of the fuel bars, stabilization of nuclear reactors by establishing cooling systems, and decommissioning of the nuclear reactors. In addition, a lot of workers were also engaged in rehabilitation of contaminated areas. Various health issues occurred among the workers. An emergency-care system for workers, including transportation to hospitals, has been one of the highest concerns, and an occupational health system did not function well. It took a few months to establish the systems. The workers were exposed to multiple health hazards, such as radiation, heat stress and psychological stress, and there were trade-offs among the hazards. Outbreak of infectious diseases and fitness for duties of temporary workers were also significant concerns from expert viewpoints. Experts in occupational health, emergency medicine, and other specialties did their best to manage the situations in cooperate with the Japanese government and TEPCO. There are several lessons learned from the experiences. Emergency response plans at national, local, and company levels should be reviewed and be improved for disasters in the future.

Keywords Decommision work · Decontamination work · Emergency work · Fukushima Daiichi Nuclear Power Plant · Nuclear disaster

---

K. Mori (✉)
Department of Occupational Health Practice and Management, Institute of Industrial Ecological Sciences, University of Occupational and Environmental Health, Kitakyushu, Japan
e-mail: kmori@med.uoeh-u.ac.jp

S. Tateishi · K. Hiraoka
Occupational Health Training Center, University of Occupational and Environmental Health, Kitakyushu, Japan

A. Shimazu et al. (eds.), *Psychosocial Factors at Work in the Asia Pacific*,
DOI 10.1007/978-3-319-44400-0_17

Introduction

A nuclear accident occurred in northern Japan at the Fukushima Daiichi Nuclear Power Plant (NPP) of the Tokyo Electric Power Company (TEPCO) following a mega-earthquake and subsequent tsunami in March 2011. Several types of operations related to the accident were performed as a result.

Since the accident, work in the NPP has shifted from emergency response to cooling of the fuel bars, stabilization of nuclear reactors by establishing cooling systems, and decommissioning of the nuclear reactors. A large number of TEPCO workers, manufacturers of nuclear reactors, construction companies and their contractors were engaged in the work and were consequently exposed to various health risks. TEPCO contracted various tasks to more than 20 companies (primary contractors), and each of them outsourced parts of tasks to multiple layers of subcontractors. This complex structure hindered consistent implementation of occupational health rules and programs that protected workers' health. In addition, for rehabilitation of contaminated areas following the accident, the Japanese government undertook decontamination work and management of the waste resulting from decontamination and contaminated goods. This work was assigned to private companies by central or local governments.

An emergency-care system for workers, including transportation to hospitals, has been one of the highest concerns among health-related issues at the Fukushima Daiichi NPP since the accident occurred. In addition, there were several occupational health issues, such as radiation exposure, heat stress, psychological stress, concern over the outbreak of infectious diseases, and fitness for work of temporary workers. In this complex situation, the participation of occupational health experts was essential in managing the issues.

In the chapter, we review the health issues occurred among the workers and describe the actions taken to solve them. And then, we summarize the lessons learned from the experience for the disasters in the future.

Establishment of Emergency Medical System for Workers

The radiation emergency medical system had consisted of the off-site center and radiation emergency hospitals on three levels (primary, secondary, tertiary), but it became nonfunctional just after the disaster.

On March 12, 2011, the off-site center (local response headquarters) had to be evacuated because everywhere within a 10-km radius of the Nuclear Power Plant (NPP) was designated an evacuation zone by government order; three of five of the initial hospitals had to be evacuated when the evacuation zone was expanded to a 20-km radius from the plant. The earthquake also damaged the essential facilities of Fukushima Prefecture Medical University Hospital (FMUH), a secondary radiation emergency hospital. The Japanese government and Fukushima Prefecture made every effort to reestablish the system in cooperation with the Tokyo Electric Power Company (TEPCO) and medical societies (Yasui 2014), such as the Japanese Association for Acute Medicine (JAAM) (Morimura et al. 2013), University of Occupational and Environmental Health, Japan (UOEH) (Mori et al. 2013).

The emergency medical system was reestablished gradually (Ojino and Ishii 2014). On March 13, the Fukushima Prefecture Radiation Emergency Medical Coordination Council was established and it was voluntarily organized by members who were familiar with radiation emergency medicine. On March 14, the Fukushima Medical University Hospital (FMUH), a designated secondary emergency hospital, started accepting radiation emergency patients. It takes 2.5 h by car or 15 min by helicopter to travel from the NPP. Although there were other hospitals nearer to NPP, they were not equipped to provide radiation emergency care. At 11:00 on the same day, a hydrogen explosion occurred in Unit 3 of the NPP, injuring 11 people, FMUH accepted 4 of them. On April 2, a facility for initial radiation emergency medicine was established in J-Village. J-Village is a sports training center located 20 km from the NPP that was used as a support base for the accident (Fig. 17.1). A total of 8 hospitals in Fukushima prefectures were prepared to provide general medical care for non-contaminated patients from April 2 to June 23. At this point in the reestablishment process, patients with high-dose exposure or heavy contamination were transported to the designated radiation emergency hospital, whereas patients in a severe condition with moderate, minor, or no exposure were transported to other hospitals.

TEPCO had basically have responsibilities for first-aid services. They made efforts to station a physician every daytime at the early stage of the accident, but it became difficult for them to secure it. UOEH was requested by TEPCO and the Nuclear and Industrial Safety Agency, and it dispatched physicians for on-site first-aid services to a quake-proof building at the NPP (Fig. 17.2). In addition, the

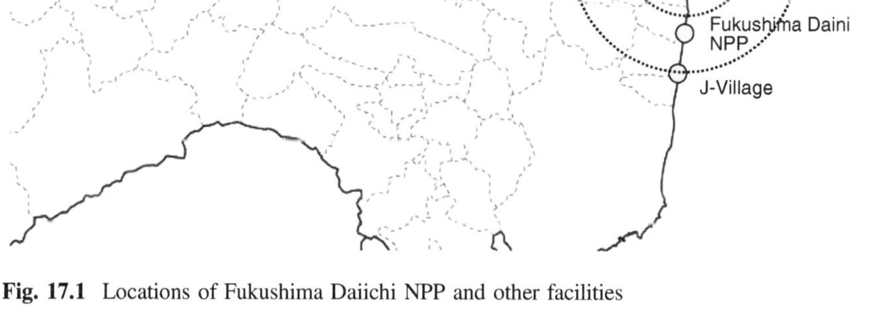

Fig. 17.1 Locations of Fukushima Daiichi NPP and other facilities

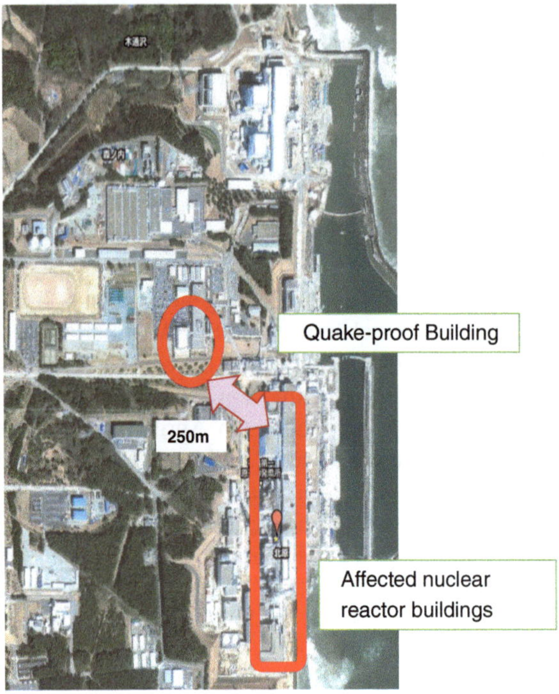

Fig. 17.2 Locations of affected nuclear reactor buildings and quake-proof building

government decided to establish 24-h system in cooperation with UOEH and the Japan Labor Health and Welfare Organization (Yasui 2014). The medical facility, so-called 5/6ER, was established in the service building of 5/6 nuclear reactors, and TEPCO reorganized an in-plant emergency medical system network to enhance preventive medicine and emergency medicine.

To facilitate the emergency medical system network, the TEPCO Fukushima Daiichi NPP Emergency Medical System Network was established, and network meetings were held periodically. Daily web meetings led by FMUH held for communication among the off-site center, on-site clinic, and the institutes concerned (Mori et al. 2013).

Establishment of Occupational Health System

A large number of workers belonging to various companies including the Tokyo Electric Power Company (TEPCO) were engaged in operations to stabilize the plant. The potential radiation exposure of these workers was the foremost concern. Some were exposed to more than 250 mSv of radiation during the initial response phase. However, their radiation exposures were carefully monitored and controlled thereafter. All of the workers at the plant were required to wear a standardized set of

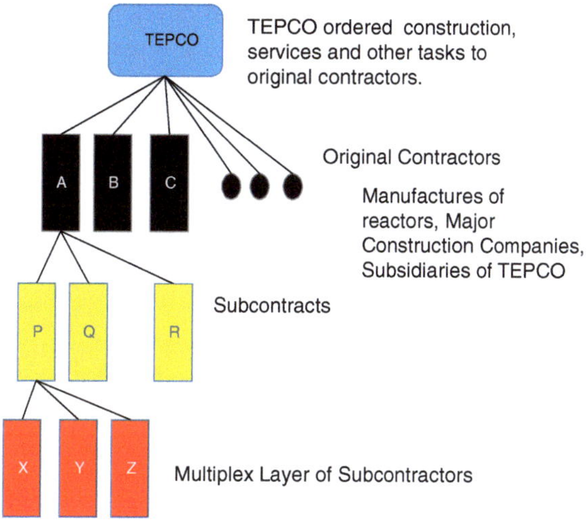

Fig. 17.3 Relationship among Companies Involved

personal protection equipment, i.e., chemical protection clothing made of polyolefin materials, a full-face respirator equipped with both dust and charcoal filters, double sets of gloves and shoe covers. Despite the relatively cool climate in the Fukushima area, a few cases of mild heat illness among the workers at the plant were reported between the end of March and early April, 2011.

With respect to the companies involved in the nuclear power plant (NPP) accident, TEPCO at the early stage contracted the services of over 20 primary contractors, each of which outsourced groups of workers to subcontractors in multiple layers (Fig. 17.3). The number of primary contractors increased thereafter. TEPCO's and the primary contractors' legal responsibilities to the subcontractors' heath care were limited. However, it was essential to establish an occupational health management system, in which TEPCO and the primary contractors had broader responsibilities to protect the health of all individuals involved in the serious conditions during the early phase of the work. However, TEPCO had no effective systems for managing the other occupational health risks, and few occupational health professionals contributed to health risk management. Under these circumstances, the potential for cases of fatal heat illness resulting from increased temperatures became a great concern.

One month after the accident, TEPCO requested University of Occupational and Environmental Health, Japan (UOEH) to dispatch physicians for first-aid services to a quake-proof building, as mentioned before. However, it was not expected to give professional advice about managing occupational health risks. Moreover, little time was left before the onset of the high temperature and humidity season. UOEH regarded the support opportunity as the entrance of professional support on occupational health, and decided to dispatch physicians. Then, UOEH took a three-step strategic approach to contribute to protecting workers from existing health hazards (Mori et al. 2013).

The objective of step 1 was to develop trustful relationships with the staff of TEPCO and outside contractors by providing sincere services for first-aid and health check-ups at the plant. The objective of step 2 was to develop and recommend practical occupational health programs based on our understanding of the real situation at the plant. UOEH requested every dispatched physician to report the work conditions at the plant and the services they provided. In addition, UOEH established a private study group to discuss necessary occupational health programs with UOEH graduates who were involved in the operations, mainly as occupational physicians of TEPCO or major primary contractors. UOEH then developed practical recommendations about the occupational health systems and programs specific to prevention of heat illness that should be implemented at the plant and presented them to the government and TEPCO. Based on our recommendation, the Ministry of Health, Labour, and Welfare (MHLW) issued guidelines on occupational safety and health at the plant for summer 2011 to TEPCO and the contractors on June 10. The objective of step 3 was to provide the necessary technical materials and advice on occupational health. UOEH provided training materials on heat stress, checklists on necessary occupational health practices at the plant for contractors, and so on. UOEH also implemented fitness for duty assessment programs and provided advice to workers who were beginning response or recovery operations at the plant.

Although severe heat illness was successfully prevented in summer 2011, the management system did not include a method by which to evaluate how each contractor implemented the occupational health programs, making continuous improvement difficult. TEPCO and the primary contractors had held weekly safety liaison meetings in the NPP in which they mainly discussed work processes and safety-related issues. One occupational health expert of TEPCO or UOEH attended the meeting every week and gave input from the viewpoint of occupational health in the discussion in August 2011.

TEPCO and the government announced that the nuclear reactors of the plant reached cold shutdown on December 16, 2011. The work phase moved from stabilization to decommissioning. This phase was expected to continue for more than 30 years. Therefore, an occupational health management system based on this condition should have been established. In this system, each company involved should have taken basic responsibilities to protect their own workers' health, and the occupational health experts should have provided technical support. A new liaison meeting with the primary contractors in charge of occupational health was held in October 2012 and was repeated once every 3 months. Occupational health issues in each season and work phase were discussed in each meeting. Occupational health experts from UOEH also attended each meeting and provided technical education and information. Because the contractors in charge of occupational health often changed, these efforts were made repetitively (Mori et al. 2014).

Challenge for Managing Multiple Health Risks

Workers in the nuclear power plant (NPP) were exposed multiple health hazards, such as radiation exposure, heat stress, psychological stress, concern over the outbreak of infectious diseases, and fitness for work of temporary workers. In addition, trade-offs were sometimes made among risks associated with the health hazards. The main health hazards were categorized into radiation, heat stress, psychosocial factors, biological agents, and fitness for workers' duties.

Radiation Exposure

The Japanese government increased the dose limit from 100 to 250 mSv exclusively for the emergency work performed at the affected NPP on March 14, 2011. Application of that emergency dose limit was abolished on December 16, 2011—except for specialists that were highly trained and experienced in operating and maintaining the facilities. During that period of emergency work, the effective dose of 172 workers exceeded 100 mSv, and that of six workers exceeded 250 mSv; the maximum dose was 678.8 mSv (Table 17.1). There are two ways of radiation exposure, internal exposure, i.e., intake of radioactive material orally or through airway, and external exposure. Internal exposure was the most significant influence on high doses (Yasui 2015). Significant leakage of air to the Tokyo Electric Power Company (TEPCO) employees was observed (average of 17.4 %) while testing of the fitness of the full-face respirators with dust filters and charcoal filters in September 2011. Internal exposure would have been prevented if the respirators had been properly fitted and the workers had followed respiratory protection usage guidelines for respirators (National Institute of Occupational Safety and Health, Japan 2011).

Table 17.1 Radiation exposure at the early phase

mSv	TEPCO	Contractors	Total
>250	6	0	6
200–250	1	2	3
150–200	24	2	26
100–150	117	20	137
50–100	398	298	696
20–50	645	2160	2805
10–20	484	2716	3200
<10	1615	11,104	12,719
Total	3290	16,302	19,592
Max (mSv)	678.8	238.4	678.8
Av. (mSv)	24.82	9.63	12.18

Total dose distribution among respond worker between March and December 31, 2011 (reevaluated in April 2013)

On March 24, 2011, several incidents of beta-ray exposure to the feet occurred during the emergency work when workers stepped into 30-cm-deep contaminated water. Investigation revealed that the workers did not monitor the ambient dose immediately before the work, did not wear long protective boots, and continued to work after a personal alarm dosimeter had sounded. Several other problems on the control and management of radiation exposure for emergency workers were observed: they included inappropriate exposure monitoring through a shortage of personal dosimeters, inappropriate dosimeter use and insufficient implementation of exposure control, and delayed internal exposure monitoring. The Ministry of Health, Labour and Welfare (MHLW) issued a series of compulsory directives and provided administrative guidance to TEPCO (Yasui 2013).

The possibility of radioactive material inhalation was considered to be low with the exception of some specific areas after announcement of the cold shutdown in December 2011. There were trade-offs associated with the risks, and countermeasures against radiation exposure increase the risk of heat illness (Fig. 17.4). The rules regarding respirator use, such as the use of half-face respirators, should have been eased in early 2012. However, workers were still concerned about radiation exposure, and they tended to continue using the full set of personal protective equipment after the rule was eased. Education and risk communication about radiation became important again. Nevertheless, it was expected that working in a high-dose environment would be necessary again when the decommissioning work progressed. Radiation protection measures should have been reviewed after June 2013 (Mori et al. 2014).

The MHLW published guidelines about long-term health care for emergency workers in October 2011[1]. The following is an overview of the guidelines: (1) establish a scheme of health management at each workplace according to its scale and conduct appropriate medical examinations; (2) conduct the following

Fig. 17.4 Trade-offs between radiation protection and other hazards

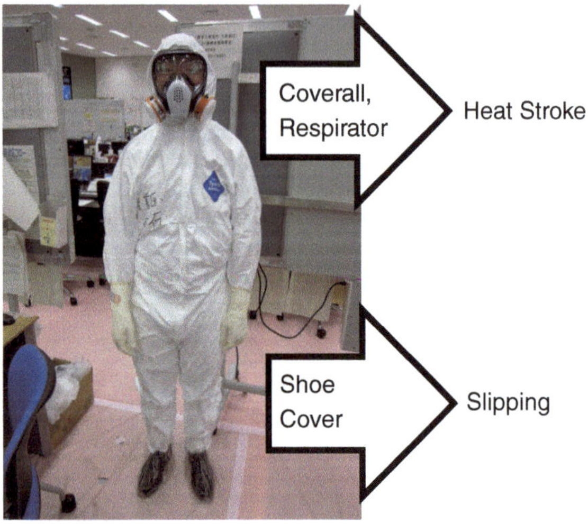

once a year for individuals who participated in emergency work—eye examination for cataracts with a slit-lamp in people with an exposure dose (effective dose) above 50 mSv, cancer screening, and thyroid tests for individuals with an effective dose of over 100 mSv; (3) provide health guidance for emergency workers.

The MHLW published a report written by a committee of experts, which included a long-term epidemiological study with a database for emergency staff who worked from March 14 to December 16, 2011 (Ministry of Health, Labour and Welfare 2014a). The exposure dose level of emergency workers was registered in the MHLW database, and they were periodically surveyed. The report stated that based on previous studies, the health effects were expected to include solid cancers, leukemia, noncancer diseases, and psychological distress.

Heat Stress

Heat illness was one of the major health risks for workers at the NPP in summer. All plant workers were required to wear standardized personal protection equipment to prevent radiation exposure and contamination. The equipment comprised chemical protective clothing made of polyolefin materials, a full-face respirator equipped with dust and charcoal filters, and a double set of gloves. This equipment obviously increased the risk of heat illness.

As mentioned in establishment of occupational health system, some cases of heat stress were reported at the end of March and beginning of April 2011, when the temperature was relatively cool in the Fukushima area. However, there were few concerns then about risks other than those associated with radiation. The MHLW issued an administrative guidance for preventing heat illness, which recommended the following: (1) since previous outbreaks of heat illness were concentrated at 14:00–17:00, discontinue work during that time; (2) begin work early in the morning; (3) set a limit on the number of consecutive working hours; (4) implement health checks before work; (5) provide workers with air-conditioned rest places where they can remove respiratory masks; (6) conduct education on preventing heat illness; (7) establish medical systems to treat heat illness patients (Yasui 2014).

TEPCO undertook measures following the MHLW instructions in cooperation with occupational health specialists from UOEH (Mori et al. 2013). At daily meetings held in the quake-proof building at 9:00 and 18:00, executives emphasized the importance of preventing heat illness. An air-conditioned rest room was installed near the operation site for the workers. For personal protection, workers wore a cool vest under a coverall and were required to drink an oral rehydration solution before the shift and after each 1-h shift. Workers at the site were allowed to do several shifts, with 1 h's work and a 40-min break. The latter involved removing protective clothing after checking for radioactive contamination, resting, and donning protective clothing again before work (Wada et al. 2012a, b). As a result, 43 cases of heat illness were reported between the end of March and early October 2011 (Fig. 17.5), but no severe heat illness was observed (Mori et al. 2013).

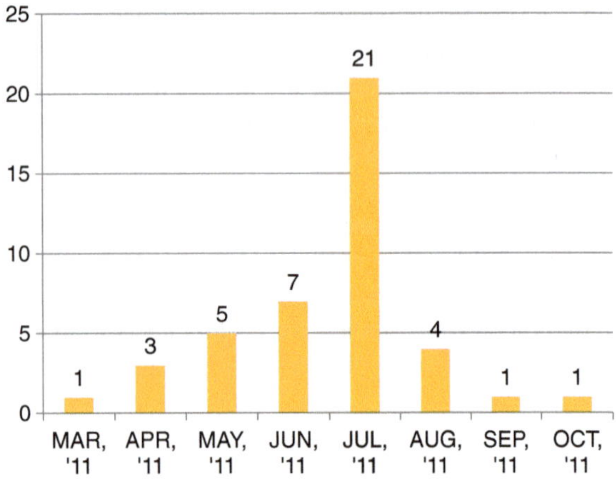

Fig. 17.5 Heat stroke occurrences in summer 2011

The program established in summer 2011 was enhanced and implemented in 2012 and 2013. For summer 2012, the program was prepared in March and implemented in early May. The program was further improved in 2013. Consequently, 23 and 17 cases of heat illness occurred in 2012 and 2013, respectively (Mori et al. 2014).

Psychosocial Factors

Psychological distress was one of major health hazards for the NPP workers, especially TEPCO employees. Some psychiatrists voluntarily provided counseling services for the TEPCO workers in the NPP at their lodging spaces in the Fukushima Daini NPP. Then, the National Defense Medical College began dispatching teams of critical incident stress specialists on July 10, 2011; they provided mental health services on a monthly basis (Sano et al. 2012). For contracted workers, occupational physicians provided healthcare services, including mental health support; the MHLW also offered toll-free telephone mental health services for all workers (Wada et al. 2012a, b).

Various psychological effects and the factors that affected them were reported by the psychiatrists. They examined general psychological distress, peritraumatic distress, and posttraumatic stress response (PTSR) in NPP workers in May and June 2011 (Shigemura et al. 2012). The subjects were full-time workers from Daiichi and Daini NPPs and reported that Daiichi workers were more often exposed to disaster-related stressors than Daini workers. The results for experiencing discrimination or slurs showed no statistically significant difference between the groups. Daiichi workers showed significantly higher rates of psychological distress and PTSR. For both groups, discrimination or slurs were associated with high psychological distress and high PTSR. Other significant associations in the two groups included tsunami evacuation and major property loss with psychological distress, and preexisting illness and major property loss with PTSR. They also developed a path model for the PTSR with the same data and peritraumatic distress of TEPCO employees (Shigemura et al. 2014).

Biological Agents

There were high risks of infectious disease outbreaks because many workers shared limited spaces for lodging and resting. Implementation of measures against influenza and norovirus infection was considered for winter 2011 (Mori et al. 2014). TEPCO provided free vaccination to all workers, including contractors. Additionally, it placed bottles of alcohol-based sterilization liquid extensively around Daiichi, Daini, and J-Village and put up posters to encourage workers to use the bottles. This program was continued almost unchanged in 2012. For November 2011 to May 2012 and November–May 2012, 182 and 195 influenza cases, respectively, were diagnosed at the NPP emergency clinic and other TEPCO-operated clinics.

With respect to norovirus infection countermeasures, TEPCO encouraged workers to wash their hands; it created a kit and a manual to deal with floors or other surfaces becoming contaminated by vomit or feces. UOEH developed and distributed a checklist to TEPCO and contractors to help them evaluate current practices and encouraged them to make improvements. An outbreak of norovirus affected 52 employees of the same primary contractor in December 2011. Excluding that outbreak, from November 2011 to March 2012 and November 2012 to March 2013, nine and 37 norovirus cases, respectively, were reported. No other outbreak was reported.

Tuberculosis was also a concern. The driver of a transportation bus for workers was diagnosed with tuberculosis in June 2011. Fortunately, tuberculosis was not transmitted to other workers. To prevent food poisoning, TEPCO provided refrigerators in resting spaces when it and contractors arranged lunch boxes for the workers in summer 2012; TEPCO enhanced refrigerators when workers were allowed to bring their own food in summer 2013.

Fitness for Duties of Workers

Nuclear power plant (NPP) workers were requested to work with multiple layers of personal protection equipment under stressful conditions. It took several hours to transport a sick person to a secondary or tertiary emergency hospital. Therefore, a higher fitness level was required of plant workers. However, workers were temporarily hired by contractors nationwide, and many began operations without judgment of their fitness for work.

The Tokyo Electric Power Company (TEPCO) understood the importance of fitness for the workers' duties. However, they hesitated to implement an assessment program because they were concerned that the limitations of the workers and the complicated procedures would affect their efforts to secure enough manpower. A procedure in which new plant workers were required to be judged "fit for duty" by a doctor was recommendable. Instead, however, the following procedure was implemented in October 2011. New workers completed a checklist regarding their own health condition, and doctors confirmed the details for workers with poorly controlled illnesses. However, this protocol was not effective enough to detect ill workers. The procedure was improved in April 2012, and the primary contractors were requested to confirm whether each new worker was judged "fit for duty" by a doctor according to pre-employment or recent periodic health check-ups. TEPCO provided these services in the J-Village clinic for small contractors that could not find an appropriate doctor at the time. TEPCO terminated these services in October 2012 because they determined that all of the contractors had secured doctors (Mori et al. 2014).

Though not a direct indicator, the effectiveness of assessment of fitness for duties was reflected in the number of reported deaths due to illness and that of ill workers transported to hospital by air ambulance. The numbers of reported deaths due to illness among the workers were one from March to June 2011, two from July to December 2011, one from January to June 2012, one from July to December 2012, and one from January to June 2013. Three of six cases were diagnosed as acute myocardial infarction. The numbers of ill workers transported to hospitals by air ambulances were four, zero, one, one, and zero for each period, respectively (Mori et al. 2014).

However, the cases of transportation to hospitals have increased since end of 2013 due to increase double of workers in the NPP. University of Occupational and Environmental Health, Japan (UOEH) developed guidelines on judgement of fitness for duty assessment and advised contractors of TEPCO to communicate with doctors who perform the judgement.

Workers Engaged in Decontamination and Other Related Works

The Japanese government decided to conduct decontamination work for the rehabilitation of contaminated areas. The decontamination work produced huge amounts of contaminated soil and waste. Existing government regulations did not consider situations where radiation sources were dispersed and workers dealt with radioactive materials outdoors ("existing exposure situations"). Therefore, the Ministry of Health, Labour and Welfare (MHLW) established new regulations—Ordinance on Prevention of Ionizing Radiation Hazards at Works to Decontaminate Soil and Wastes Contaminated by Radioactive Materials Resulting from the Great

Table 17.2 Selection criteria for personal protective equipment according to the level of ambient dust and radioactivity of the contaminated materials for decontamination work involving radioactive fallout

Concentration of ambient dust	Radioactivity concentration of contaminated materials	
	Over 50,000 kBq/kg	50,000 Bq/kg or below
Over 10 mg/m^3	Respiratory protective equipment with a filtration efficiency of 95 % or more, HAZMAT suits over long-sleeved shirts, rubber gloves, and rubber boots	Respiratory protective equipment with a filtration efficiency of 80 % or more, long-sleeved shirts, rubber gloves, and rubber boots
10 mg/m^3 or below	Respiratory protective equipment with a filtration efficiency of 80 % or more, long-sleeved shirts, rubber gloves, and rubber boots	Respiratory mask made with non-woven textiles, long-sleeved shirts, cotton gloves, and rubber boots

East Japan Earthquake and Related Works—which provided occupational radiological protection in existing exposure situations. In addition, the MHLW created new regulations for the protection of waste-disposal workers by amending the Ordinance on Prevention of Ionizing Radiation Hazards. The ordinances consisted of structure-based standards, exposure limits, and selection of appropriate personal protective equipment for the risk of internal exposure (Tables 17.2 and 17.3).

The decontamination workers were at risk of being exposed to radiation and other health hazards, such as heat stress in summer, coldness in winter, insect bites, and handling heavy materials (Wada et al. 2012a, b). The results of internal

Table 17.3 Selection criteria for personal protective equipment according to the level of ambient dust and radioactivity of the contaminated materials for work involving radioactive fallout-disposal of contaminated soil and wastes

Concentration of ambient dust	Radioactivity concentration of contaminated materials		
	Over 2000 kBq/kg	Over 500 kBq/kg 2000 kBq/kg or below	500 kBq/kg or below
Over 10 mg/m^3	Respiratory protective equipment with a filtration efficiency of 99.9 % or more, 2 layers of splash-tight HAZMAT suits over long-sleeved shirts, 2 layers of rubber gloves, and rubber boots	Respiratory protective equipment with a filtration efficiency of 95 % or more, splash-tight HAZMAT suits over long-sleeved shirts, rubber gloves, and rubber boots	Respiratory protective equipment with a filtration efficiency of 80 % or more, long-sleeved shirts, cotton gloves, and rubber boots 10 mg/m^3 or below
10 mg/m^3 or below	Respiratory protective equipment with a filtration efficiency of 95 % or more, long sleeved shirts, rubber gloves, and rubber boots	Respiratory protective equipment with a filtration efficiency of 80 % or more, long-sleeved shirts, rubber gloves, and rubber boots	Respiratory mask made with non-woven textiles, long-sleeved shirts, cotton gloves, and rubber boots

exposure monitoring among decontamination workers who had not been living in Fukushima Prefecture at the time of the incident was reported (Tsubokura et al. 2013). Their cesium exposure levels were below detection limits, but seven workers stated that they did not always wear masks during decontamination work. In a mail survey, more than half of respondents had experienced heat illness symptoms during decontamination work. However, there were few reports published on the situation regarding exposure or health effects on workers presently engaged in decontamination work and waste-disposal workers.

The MHLW reported the results of employer inspections related to decontamination work: 108 of 242 employers were in violation of applicable laws, such as the Labour Standards Act and Industrial Safety and Health Act, as of December 31 2012 (Ministry of Health, Labour and Welfare 2014b); 264 of 388 for January–June 2013 (Ministry of Health, Labour and Welfare 2013); 709 of 1784 for July–December 2013 (Ministry of Health, Labour and Welfare 2014c); and 181 of 313 for January–June 2014 (Ministry of Health, Labour and Welfare 2014d). In its early report, the MHLW described two examples of violation regarding methods for measuring external exposure dose through decontamination. (1) Workers whose total external exposure doses at workplaces were considered average values were selected to wear dosimeters; their measurement results were used as the external exposure doses for all workers at similar workplaces. However, the workers wearing dosimeters left dosimeters left their workplaces even though other workers were still working at the site, and their exposure doses were not measured accurately. (2) Workers are supposed to wear dosimeters on their chest or abdomen, but they put the dosimeters in their pants' pockets.

Lesson Learned from the Experience

The nuclear accident at the Fukushima Daiichi Nuclear Power Plant (NPP) following a mega-earthquake gave rise to an emergency. Though they lacked proper experience, many workers became engaged in difficult tasks. The system for safeguarding their health gradually developed through an ongoing trial-and-error process. There are a lot of lessons learned from our experiences for disasters in future.

The operators were responsible for emergency medical care at the NPP as part of Japan's National Response Plan—Bosai Kihon Keikaku (Cabinet Office, Government Japan 2014). However, it was difficult for function an emergency-care system. In the system, TEPCO basically had responsibility for on-site medical care, but they could not secure physicians at the NPP. The government thus supported to reestablish emergency-care system. In the event of a large-scale nuclear accident, the government needs to lead operations of the system and to assist by dispatching medical staff to affected plants.

The contractors assigned by the Tokyo Electric Power Company (TEPCO) were basically responsible for their workers' safety and health. Under a complex chain of order, however, it was difficult for occupational safety and health measures to disseminate throughout the entire work organization. In addition, trade-offs were sometimes made related to the risks associated with radiation exposure: countermeasures against one particular hazard periodically affected work schedules and increased the chance of other risks. The various countermeasures were implemented under the administrative guidance of the government and included the suspension of work in the afternoon at the early stage of emergency work. If major disasters occur, on-site occupational health involvement by the government is essential in protecting the health of workers engaged in response and recovery actions. According to occupational health experts, it was clear that thorough measures to deal with radiation exposure, heat stress, infectious diseases, psychological stress, and fitness for work were necessary from the early phase of the accident. However, it took a long time for occupational health experts, who were not included in the response plan, to gain a position and influence preventive health measures at the sites. When disasters occur, many workers and volunteers belonging to various organizations become engaged in response and recovery operations. They are often exposed to multiple health hazards, and there are sometimes trade-offs in the associated risks. The involvement of occupational health experts is essential to protect workers' health and lives. It is necessary to review current emergency response plans at national, local, and company levels and to secure their involvement in an emergency response organization.

Many workers engaged in operations at the NPP belonged to companies with insufficient occupational health resources. In the decontamination work, there was a high rate of heat illness symptoms and reported violation of applicable labor laws. It was reported that radiation protection of municipal employees who helped in evacuation and temporary return of residents was much poorer than among employees in public institutions under central government control. In the September 11 attacks on the World Trade Center (WTC) in 2001, a cloud of toxic particles generated by the burning and collapse of the buildings spread over Lower Manhattan and parts of neighboring districts. Rescue workers and community members exposed to those materials developed chronic physical illness and psychological trauma. It was reported that WTC volunteer responders without formal affiliation with a rescue organization had a higher rate of WTC-related accidents, physical illness, and mental illness than affiliated responders (Crane et al. 2014). They can be called a "vulnerable subgroup." It is to be expected of companies and other organizations that they should protect their workers' health—even in disasters. However, it is clear that many workers in the vulnerable subgroups did not receive appropriate support. The protection of workers should be enhanced in the emergency response plan including National Response Plan.

Except for cases of beta-ray burns, no evident adverse effects of radiation exposures have thus far been reported. However, various problems on the control and management of radiation exposure have been identified. The inappropriate fitness of respirators was a major cause of internal exposure exceeding the dose limit. It should be noted that the preparedness and training for dealing with emergency situations were insufficient. Future preparation for disasters, such as training and stocking equipment, should be designed to protect workers' health based on detailed scenarios.

If a major disaster occurs, the workers engaged in recovery operations may become victims. They may also become targets of criticism and discrimination because they are working for a company that is responsible for the accident. TEPCO employees were under such conditions, and psychological care was provided for them. The government opened toll-free telephone services for mental health. Considering that many workers were involved in recovery operations under a complex organization with multiple layers, it cannot be said that the system or services were sufficient. It is necessary to secure adequate numbers of specialists who are able to provide mental health support.

After a large disaster, there are various trade-offs between health risks and other factors. After the Fukushima incident, personal protection against radiation exposure and contamination increased the risk of heat illness and accidents. TEPCO was concerned that implementing a fitness-for-work evaluation program might result in manpower shortage and other issues. However, it is difficult to manage such issues when different departments or organizations share responsibility in a disaster situation. When the necessity for trade-offs becomes clear following a disaster, the departments or organizations concerned need to communicate positively with one another toward making the appropriate decisions.

Conclusion

As the result of nuclear accidents at the Fukushima Daiichi Nuclear Power Plant, we faced to unexpected sever conditions. A lot of workers were engaged in the related works and they were exposed to various health hazards. Experts in occupational health, emergency medicine, and other specialties did their best to manage the situations in cooperate with the Japanese government and the Tokyo Electric Power Company. In the article, we shared several lessons learned from the experiences for disasters in the future.

References

Cabinet Office, Government Japan. (2014). *Bosai Kihon Keikaku*. http://www.bousai.go.jp/taisaku/keikaku/pdf/kihon_basic_plan141128.pdf. Accessed 01 May 2015.

Crane, M. A., Cho, H. G., & Landrigan, P. J. (2014). Implications of the World Trade Center Health Program (WTCHP) for the public health response to the Great East Japan Earthquake. *Industrial Health, 52*, 5–12.

Ministry of Health, Labour and Welfare. (2013). *Results of supervision/instructions to employers of decontamination works (January–June, 2013) and request to the employers*. http://www.mhlw.go.jp/english/topics/2011eq/workers/dr/dr/pr_130724.html. Accessed 01 May 2015.

Ministry of Health, Labour and Welfare. (2014a). *A report of experts committee on the way of epidemiological studies for the workers engaged in emergency work in the TEPCO Fukushima Daiichi nuclear power plant.* http://www.mhlw.go.jp/stf/houdou/0000047387.html. Accessed 01 May 2015.

Ministry of Health, Labour and Welfare. (2014b). *Response and action taken by the Ministry of Health, Labour and Welfare of Japan on radiation protection for workers involved in the TEPCO Fukushima Daiichi Nuclear Power Plant accident.* http://www.mhlw.go.jp/english/topics/2011eq/workers/tepco/rp/irpw.pdf. Accessed 01 May 2015.

Ministry of Health, Labour and Welfare. (2014c). *Results of supervision/instructions to employers of decontamination works.* http://www.mhlw.go.jp/english/topics/2011eq/workers/dr/dr/pr_140312.html. Accessed 01 May 2015.

Ministry of Health, Labour and Welfare. (2014d). *Results of supervision/instructions to employers of decontamination works (January–June 2014).* http://www.mhlw.go.jp/english/topics/2011eq/workers/dr/dr/pr_140807.html. Accessed 01 May 2015.

Mori, K., Tateishi, S., Hiraoka, K., Kubo, T., Okazaki, R., Suzuki, K., et al. (2013). How occupational health can contribute in a disaster and what we should prepare for the future—Lessons learned through support activities of a medical school at the Fukushima Daiichi Nuclear Power Plant in Summer 2011. *Journal of Occupational Health, 55*, 6–10.

Mori, K., Tateishi, S., Kubo, T., Okazaki, R., Suzuki, K., Kobayashi, Y., et al. (2014). Transition of occupational health issues associated with stabilization and decommissioning of the nuclear reactors in the Fukushima Daiichi Nuclear Power Plant through 2013. *Journal of Occupational and Environmental Medicine, 56*, 1145–1152.

Morimura, N., Asari, Y., Yamaguchi, Y., Asanuma, K., Tase, C., Sakamoto, T., et al. (2013). Members of the Japanese Association for Acute Medicine, Emergency, Task Force on the Fukushima Nuclear Power Plant Accident (JAAM-TF-FNPPA). Emergency/disaster medical support in the restoration project for the Fukushima nuclear power plant accident. *Emergency Medicine Journal, 30*, 997–1002.

National Institute of Occupational Safety and Health, Japan. (2011). *A report of investigation on fitness of respirators in the TEPCO Fukushima Daiichi Stabilization Center (J-village).* http://www.mhlw.go.jp/stf/houdou/2r9852000001ri1k-att/2r9852000001ri6e.pdf. Accessed 01 May 2015.

Ojino, M., & Ishii, M. (2014). Reconstruction of the radiation emergency medical system from the acute to the sub-acute phases after the Fukushima Nuclear Power Plant crisis. *Japan Medical Association Journal, 57*, 40–48.

Sano, S. Y., Tanigawa, T., Shigemura, J., Satoh, Y., Yoshino, A., Fujii, C., et al. (2012). Complexities of the stress experienced by employees of the Fukushima nuclear plants. *Seishin Shinkeigaku Zasshi, 114*, 1274–1283. (in Japanese).

Shigemura, J., Tanigawa, T., Nishi, D., Matsuoka, Y., Nomura, S., & Yoshino, A. (2014). Associations between disaster exposures, peritraumatic distress, and posttraumatic stress responses in Fukushima nuclear plant workers following the 2011 nuclear accident: The Fukushima NEWS Project study. *PLoS ONE, 9*, e87516.

Shigemura, J., Tanigawa, T., Saito, I., & Nomura, S. (2012). Psychological distress in workers at the Fukushima nuclear power plants. *Journal of the American Medical Association, 15*(308), 667–669.

Tanigawa, K., Hosoi, Y., Terasawa, S., Kondo, H., Asari, Y., Shishido, F., et al. (2011). Lessons learned from the Fukushima Daiichi nuclear power plant accident; the initial 5 days medical activities after the accident. *Journal of Japanese Association for Acute Medicine, 22*, 782–791. (in Japanese).

Tsubokura, M., Nihei, M., Sato, K., Masaki, S., Sakuma, Y., Kato, S., et al. (2013). Measurement of internal radiation exposure among decontamination workers in villages near the crippled Fukushima Daiichi Nuclear Power Plant. *Health Physics, 105*, 379–381.

Wada, K., Yoshikawa, T., Hayashi, T., & Aizawa, Y. (2012a). Emergency response technical work at Fukushima Daiichi nuclear power plant: Occupational health challenges posed by the nuclear disaster. *Occupational and Environmental Medicine, 69*, 599–602.

Wada, K., Yoshikawa, T., & Murata, M. (2012b). Decontamination work in the area surrounding Fukushima Daiichi Nuclear Power Plant: Another occupational health challenge of the nuclear disaster. *Archives of Environmental & Occupational Health, 67*, 128–132.

Yasui, S. (2013). Engineering case report: Lessons learned: Radiological protection for emergency workers at the TEPCO Fukushima Daiichi APP (part 1). *Journal of Occupational Environmental Hygiene, 10*, D151–D158.

Yasui, S. (2014). Lessons learned: Medical health care management for emergency workers at the TEPCO Fukushima Daiichi APP accident. *Journal of Occupational Environmental Hygiene, 11*, D49–D58.

Yasui, S. (2015). 250 mSv: Temporary increase in the emergency exposure dose limit in response to the TEPCO Fukushima Daiichi NPP accident and its decision making process. *Journal of Occupational Environmental Hygiene, 12*, D35–D42.

Chapter 18
The Effect of a Nation-Specific Stressor on Well-Being: Guanxi in Chinese Workplace

Qiao Hu, Wilmar B. Schaufeli and Toon W. Taris

Abstract This study differentiates between task resources and social resources and extends the Job Demands-Resources (JD-R) model with guanxi exchange. This is a typical Chinese form of social exchange between the employee and his or her supervisor that is based on the give-and-take of favors. Hypotheses were tested in two Chinese samples of police officers (N = 466) and nurses (N = 261). Multigroup structural equation analyses supported the distinction between social resources and task resources. Task resources predicted well-being in nurses, whereas social resources predicted well-being in police officers. Further, guanxi exchange with supervisors was associated with social as well as with task resources. Moreover, in nurses guanxi exchange was related with engagement, whereas in police officers it was related with burnout. In conclusion: (1) task and social resources are two distinct types of job resources that play a slightly different role in a law enforcement as compared to a health care setting; (2) guanxi exchange can be integrated into the JD-R model, thereby increasing its relevance for the Chinese work context.

Keywords Task resources · Social resources · Guanxi exchange · Job Demands-Resources model

Q. Hu (✉)
Global Institute for Zhejiang Merchant's Development, Zhejiang University of Technology, Hangzhou City 310023, Zhejiang Province, China
e-mail: qiaohu2005@aliyun.com

W.B. Schaufeli · T.W. Taris
Department of Work and Organizational Psychology, Utrecht University, Utrecht, The Netherlands

W.B. Schaufeli
Department of Work, Organizational and Personnel Psychology, University of Leuven, Leuven, Belgium

A. Shimazu et al. (eds.), *Psychosocial Factors at Work in the Asia Pacific*,
DOI 10.1007/978-3-319-44400-0_18

Introduction

Different culture leads to different values and beliefs, different communication, different norms of behaviors. China is a Confucian culture and significantly different from Western cultures. Guanxi has been considered as a product of Confucian values and is inherent in the work ethics of the Chinese people. Effective guanxi represents a long-term coalitional relationship among guanxi partners to deal with resource scarcity and environmental uncertainty. Employees use guanxi networks to overcome the uncertainty and distrust that plague the process of resources distribution, and to reduce the transaction costs of information search, relationship monitoring, and task enforcement.

The Job Demands-Resources (JD-R) model (Demerouti et al. 2001) posits that each and every job has particular job demands and particular job resources and that these demands and resources are the antecedents of employee well-being, motivation, and performance. Specifically, the JD-R model proposes that employee well-being is related to a wide range of workplace characteristics that can be conceptualized as either job demands or job resources. Job resources have been defined as those task and social job characteristics that support the employee in successfully coping with job demands, attaining work goals, and achieving personal growth and development (Schaufeli and Bakker 2004). Excess job demands and lacking job resources exert an energy-draining effect on employees through a stress process, while high levels of job resources are related to positive work outcomes through a motivational process. Although the JD-R model treats job demands and job resources as unitary concepts, a distinction has been made recently between challenge demands and hindrance demands (LePine et al. 2005). However, so far job resources have not yet been differentiated.

Task Resources and Social Resources in the JD-R Model

Studies using the JD-R model typically examine the indirect links between job characteristics and work outcomes via well-being. A high-resources job offers employees challenge and opportunities to cope successfully with job demands. Consequently, employees experience relatively little stress and feel engaged. This type of job fosters personal growth and development, leading to positive work outcomes such as high organizational commitment. However, many scholars voiced concerns that learning and growth do not happen solely as a function of task resources, arguing that this occurs in a social context. They suggested that personal learning and growth occur through social interaction with coworkers, while talking about work and observing others doing their work (Wenger 1998). Hence, scholars have recognized that both task and social resources are positively related to employee well-being. For example, Ouweneel et al. (2009) found that levels of job control among health care managers were not high enough to counteract the negative effects of job demands on learning, whereas additional supervisor support affected managers' on-the-job informal learning positively.

Accumulating evidence suggests that task resources (e.g., job control, participation in decision-making) as well as social resources (supervisor and co-worker support) are indirectly related to positive work outcomes (e.g., organizational commitment) through work engagement. The JD-R model assumes that these aggregated job (i.e., task and social) resources can be represented as a single composite dimension. Studies using the JD-R model thus usually combine different and quite heterogeneous job resources into one job resources factor. However, it has been argued that task and social resources are theoretically and conceptually distinct (e.g., Weigl et al. 2010): whereas task resources refer to the individual-level work context, social resources refer to interpersonal interactions and interdependencies that are related to the group-level work context. Task resources are therefore embedded in social resources.

The current study included two core task resources (job control and participation in decision-making) and two core social resources (social support from colleagues and from the supervisor). Based on the above reasoning, we expect a model in which two types of job resources are distinguished i.e., task resources (job control and participation in decision) versus social resources (supervisor support and colleague support) to fit better to the data than a model with a single composite resources factor (Hypothesis 1).

Guanxi Exchange in the JD-R Model

So far the JD-R model has been applied mainly in samples from western countries (e.g., Australia, Austria, Belgium, Germany, Finland, Netherlands, and Spain), and when it was applied to non-Western samples in its original form (e.g., Hu et al. 2011). The second objective of our study is to extend the original JD-R with a typical and important Chinese phenomenon—*guanxi* exchange—in order to increase its applicability in the Chinese context.

Interpersonal relationships exist in various forms in every human society, however, *guanxi* has been considered as a typical product of Confucian values and it is inherent in the work ethics of the Chinese people. As "the moral principles regarding interactive behaviors of related parties" (Chen and Chen 2004, p. 308), *guanxi* embodies a wide range of personal ties and nuanced patterns of interpersonal dynamics. Basically, *guanxi* is constituted by reciprocity, meaning that the behavior of petitioners is governed by the social norm known as "*renqing*" or "favors" (Hwang 1987). Providing benefits to somebody in one's *guanxi* network at a particular time will create a "debt" (i.e., an implicit obligation) to the petitioner, and the petitioner should return the *renqing* (favor) or else (s)he will be viewed as untrustworthy. *Renqing* is the most important aspect of *guanxi* exchange that emphasizes not only a normative standard for regulating social exchange, but also a social mechanism that an individual can use to strive for desirable resources in hierarchically structured relationships (Hwang 1987).

In contrast to western social exchange relations, which usually involve the exchange of equivalent value and timely return (Powell 1990), Chinese *guanxi* exchange involves special favors (e.g., bonuses, promotion, fringe benefits, etc.) that go beyond an equal exchange and which can be paid back in the long run (Yum 1988). *Renqing* ensures trust among the members of the *guanxi* network, which tends to minimize the risk of uncertainty (Lovett et al. 1999). *Guanxi* exchange is embedded in intricate and informal personal relationships, but these informal, unofficial relations are not easily separable from formal, official work relations, for instance at work. Management in China is thought to depend largely on interpersonal relationships (Hui and Lin 1996), and *guanxi* is considered as the basis for effective collaboration (Chen and Chen 2004). Because supervisors have limited time and energy, they can only develop close work relationships with a few employees whom they provide with material and immaterial resources to help them perform better. *Guanxi* exchange is a substitute for competitive disadvantages and employees use *renqing* to deal with resource scarcity and uncertainty. As a consequence, employees who have good *guanxi* with their supervisors tend to receive more bonuses and are more likely to be promoted (Law et al. 2000). Empirical research also attests that close *guanxi* bonds between coworkers facilitate job related support and recognition for each other (Cheung et al. 2009), and to social relations outside work (Law et al. 2000). *Guanxi* emphasizes emotional attachment and obligations, thus, the more supervisors and employees develop a high-quality work relationship and interact with each other, the more likely it is that employees exhibit organizational citizenship behavior (Wong et al. 2003), organizational commitment (Cheung et al. 2009) and work engagement. However, *guanxi* reciprocity requires that the individual continuously invests and puts effort into relationships with others, which might exhaust their energy (Warren et al. 2004). Moreover, in the process of *guanxi* exchange, supervisors make more generous resource allocations to those with whom they had frequent interactions and closer personal bonds, and interpersonal relationships may take precedence over the procedural justice rules (Tsui and Farh 1997; Zhang 2001), which is considered as a main antecedent of burnout (Liljegren and Ekberg 2009).

Based on the previous reasoning we formulate the following hypotheses: *guanxi* reciprocity is positively related to task resources (Hypothesis 2) and social resources (Hypothesis 3); *guanxi* reciprocity will be positively related with work engagement (Hypothesis 4) and negatively with burnout (Hypothesis 5), and guanxi reciprocity is positively related to organizational commitment (Hypothesis 6).

Methods

Sample and Procedure

All nurses from a general hospital and all officers from the police force in Yongkang city, China, received paper-and-pencil questionnaires. An accompanying letter introduced the goal of the study and emphasized the confidentiality and anonymity of the participants' answers. The nurse sample included 261 females (response rate 74.5 %; M_{age} = 28.38 years, SD = 7.47). The police officers sample included 401 males and 65 females (response rate 93.2 %; M_{age} = 36.76, SD = 9.82).

Measures

All job characteristics were assessed by the Chinese version of the Questionnaire on the Experience and Evaluation of Work (QEEW; Van Veldhoven et al. 2002) developed by Hu et al. (2011, 2013). These items were scored on 7-point rating scales (0 = "never", 6 = "always").

Three challenge *job demands* were included in the present study: workload (5 items, e.g., "Do you have too much work to do?"), physical load (7 items, e.g., "Does your work require physical strength?"), and mental demands (5 items, e.g., "Does your work demand a lot of concentration?").

Job resources included two task resources and two social resources. *Task resources* were job control (3 items, e.g., "Can you decide on your own how your work is executed?") and participation in decision-making (6 items, e.g., "Do you have a lot of say over what is going on in your work area?"). *Social resources* were supervisor support (3 items, e.g., "Can you count on your direct supervisor when you encounter difficulties in your work?") and colleague support (3 items, e.g., "If necessary, can you ask your colleagues for help?").

Burnout was assessed with the exhaustion and cynicism subscales of Hu and Schaufeli's (2011) Chinese version of the Maslach Burnout Inventory—General Survey (MBI-GS; Schaufeli et al. 1996). Exhaustion was assessed with five items (e.g., "I feel used up at the end of the workday") and cynicism with four items (e.g., "I have become less enthusiastic about my work") (0 = "never", 6 = "daily"). High scores on the exhaustion and cynicism subscales signify burnout.

Work Engagement was assessed with the Chinese version (Hu et al. 2011) of the Utrecht Work Engagement Scale (UWES-9; Schaufeli et al. 2006). The UWES-9 taps three underlying dimensions with three items each: vigor (e.g., "At my work, I feel bursting with energy"), dedication (e.g., "My job inspires me"), and absorption (e.g., "I get carried away when I am working"). A similar scoring was used as for burnout (see above).

Organizational Commitment (5 items, e.g., "I feel like 'a member of the family' in my workplace", 1 = "never", 5 = "always") was assessed by a scale from the QEEW (Hu et al. 2011, 2013).

A scale assessing *guanxi exchange* between employee and supervisor was developed based on the exchange of favors ("*renqing*"). Ten statements were derived from in-depth interviews held with Chinese employees. Four items referred to *renqing* investments, and the other 6 items referred to *renqing*-rewards (cf. Table 18.1). Participants used a 5-point scale (1 = "strongly disagree", 5 = "strongly agree") to

Table 18.1 The two *guanxi* exchange scales: renqing investment and renqing rewards

Renqing investment
1. I have to do a favor to my supervisor from time to maintain a good *guanxi*
2. I have to spend a lot of time and effort outside of my work to maintain a good *guanxi* with my supervisor
3. I have to express very often my understanding and empathy to my supervisor to maintain a good *guanxi*
4. I have to offer my supervisor gifts in the expectation that he/she will do me favor when I need it
Renqing rewards
1. I have developed a good *guanxi* with my supervisor whom I can call on for support when I need to get things done
2. I have developed a good *guanxi* with my supervisor which increases my social status in my work team
3. My supervisor will help me with my troubles at work because I have a good *guanxi* with him/her
4. My supervisor provides me with adequate and timely information because I have a good *guanxi* with him/her
5. My supervisor gives me my favorite tasks because I have a good *guanxi* with him/her
6. My supervisor supports my career because I have a good *guanxi* with him/her

rate their agreement with the statements. A confirmatory factor analysis of a correlated two-factor solution with *renqing*-investments and *renqing*–rewards as latent factors showed acceptable fit among nurses ($\chi^2(df = 34) = 35.22$, GFI = 0.97, TLI = 1.00, CFI = 1.00, RMSEA = 0.01) and police officers ($\chi^2(df = 34) = 150.31$, GFI = 0.94, TLI = 0.92, CFI = 0.94, RMSEA = 0.09).

The hypotheses were tested using Structural Equation Modeling techniques as implemented in the IBM SPSS AMOS 21 (IBM-SPSS Inc., Chicago, IL, USA).

Results

Table 18.2 provides the means, standard deviations, reliabilities (Cronbach's alphas), and correlation coefficients for the study variables.

Two separate confirmatory factor analyses using latent indicators showed good fit of the measurement model for both nurses ($\chi^2(df = 70) = 153.74$, GFI = 0.93, GFI = 0.93, CFI = 0.95, TLI = 0.93, RMSEA = 0.07) and police officers ($\chi^2(df = 70) = 293.95$, GFI = 0.92, CFI = 0.94, TLI = 0.91, RMSEA = 0.08). All correlations were in the expected direction, except for the correlation between *guanxi* and burnout that was significantly positive among police officers. The standardized parameter estimates are shown in Fig. 18.1.

Table 18.2 Means (*M*), standard deviations (SD), internal consistencies (Cronbach's α on the diagonal, in italics), and correlations between the study variables for police officers ($N = 463$, lower half) and nurses ($N = 261$, upper half)

	Police		Nurses								
	M	SD	*M*	SD	*t* (722)	1	2	3	4	5	6
1. Workload	3.87	1.08	3.82	0.96	0.64	*0.86–0.78*	0.47**	0.31**	0.15*	0.25**	0.08
2. Mental Demands	4.34	1.17	5.07	0.98	−8.91**	0.69**	*0.76–0.87*	0.39**	0.07	0.10	−0.04
3. Physical demands	2.82	1.07	4.22	1.10	−16.61**	0.41**	0.41**	*0.74–0.88*	0.07	0.10	−0.12
4. Supervisor support	3.37	1.28	3.16	1.14	2.28*	0.25**	0.31**	0.17**	*0.87–0.80*	0.60**	0.42**
5. Colleague support	3.56	1.17	3.22	1.11	3.88**	0.31**	0.29**	0.26**	0.68**	*0.62–0.84*	0.36**
6. Job control	2.51	1.30	2.36	1.28	1.51	−0.13**	−0.03	−0.07	0.19**	0.10*	*0.81–0.79*
7. Participation in decision	2.39	1.17	2.49	1.24	−1.06	−0.07	−0.04	−0.08	0.182*	0.12**	0.59**
8. *Renqing* Reward	3.12	1.27	2.96	1.33	1.58	0.21**	0.18**	0.16**	0.29**	0.28**	−0.09*
9. *Renqing* investment	2.61	1.25	2.59	1.31	0.20	0.29**	0.19**	0.25**	0.17**	0.20**	−0.12**
10. Vigor	3.08	1.32	2.37	2.13	4.88**	0.13**	0.18**	0.03	0.35**	0.34**	0.08
11. Dedication	2.90	1.33	2.10	1.26	8.04**	0.20**	0.24**	0.07	0.36**	0.35*	0.15**
12. Absorption	2.82	1.41	2.02	1.27	7.81**	0.10*	0.15**	0.03	0.34**	0.29**	0.06
13. Exhaustion	3.02	1.35	3.48	1.25	−4.62**	0.48**	0.32**	0.40**	0.13**	0.21**	−0.20**
14. Cynicism	2.55	1.48	3.05	1.39	−4.54**	0.35**	0.16**	0.30**	0.08	0.12**	−0.27**
15. Commitment	3.61	1.14	2.96	1.17	7.72**	0.11*	0.15**	0.01	0.33**	0.32**	−0.03

	Police		Nurses										
	M	SD	*M*	SD	7	8	9	10	11	12	13	14	15
1. Workload	3.87	1.08	3.82	0.96	0.08	0.17**	0.16**	0.05	−0.07	−0.05	0.40**	0.36**	−0.09
2. Mental Demands	4.34	1.17	5.07	0.98	−0.08	0.03	0.01	0.06	−0.03	−0.05	0.23**	0.16*	−0.04
3. Physical demands	2.82	1.07	4.22	1.10	−0.17**	0.14*	0.12*	−0.14*	−0.22**	−0.25**	0.36**	0.36**	−0.23**
4. Supervisor support	3.37	1.28	3.16	1.14	0.34**	0.16*	0.04	0.14*	0.05	0.06	0.05	−0.01	0.02

(continued)

Table 18.2 (continued)

	Police		Nurses										
	M	SD	*M*	SD	7	8	9	10	11	12	13	14	15
5. Colleague support	3.56	1.17	3.22	1.11	0.39**	0.23**	0.21**	0.23**	0.12	0.12*	0.06	0.04	0.11
6. Job control	2.51	1.30	2.36	1.28	0.53**	0.06	0.07	0.11	0.20**	0.21**	−0.15*	−0.17**	0.17**
7. Participation in decision	2.39	1.17	2.49	1.24	*0.84–0.92*	0.19**	0.15*	0.27**	0.29**	0.29**	−0.17**	−0.14*	0.31**
8. *Renqing* Reward	3.12	1.27	2.96	1.33	−0.04	*0.73–0.78*	0.53**	0.27**	0.20**	0.22**	−0.02	0.02	0.12*
9. *Renqing* investment	2.61	1.25	2.59	1.31	−0.06	0.62**	*0.66–0.77*	0.17**	0.09	0.14*	0.02	0.06	0.21**
10. Vigor	3.08	1.32	2.37	2.13	0.21**	0.23**	0.17**	*0.74–0.53*	0.58**	0.61**	−0.19**	−0.19**	0.27**
11. Dedication	2.90	1.33	2.10	1.26	0.22**	0.26**	0.25**	0.84**	*0.78–0.86*	0.87**	−0.37**	−0.31**	0.47**
12. Absorption	2.82	1.41	2.02	1.27	0.17**	0.20**	0.23**	0.79**	0.84**	*0.87–0.86*	−0.39**	−0.34**	0.45**
13. Exhaustion	3.02	1.35	3.48	1.25	−0.23**	0.25**	0.33**	−0.11*	0.00	−0.11*	*0.67–0.90*	0.86**	−0.30**
14. Cynicism	2.55	1.48	3.05	1.39	−0.29**	0.25**	0.37**	−0.20**	−0.08	−0.12**	0.84**	*0.70–0.92*	−0.32**
15. Commitment	3.61	1.14	2.96	1.17	0.17**	0.32**	0.26**	0.56**	0.53**	0.53**	−0.12**	−0.16**	*0.69–0.67*

Note The differences between the mean scores of police officers and nurses on the study variables was tested using *t* tests with 722 *df*

* $p < 0.05$; ** $p < 0.01$

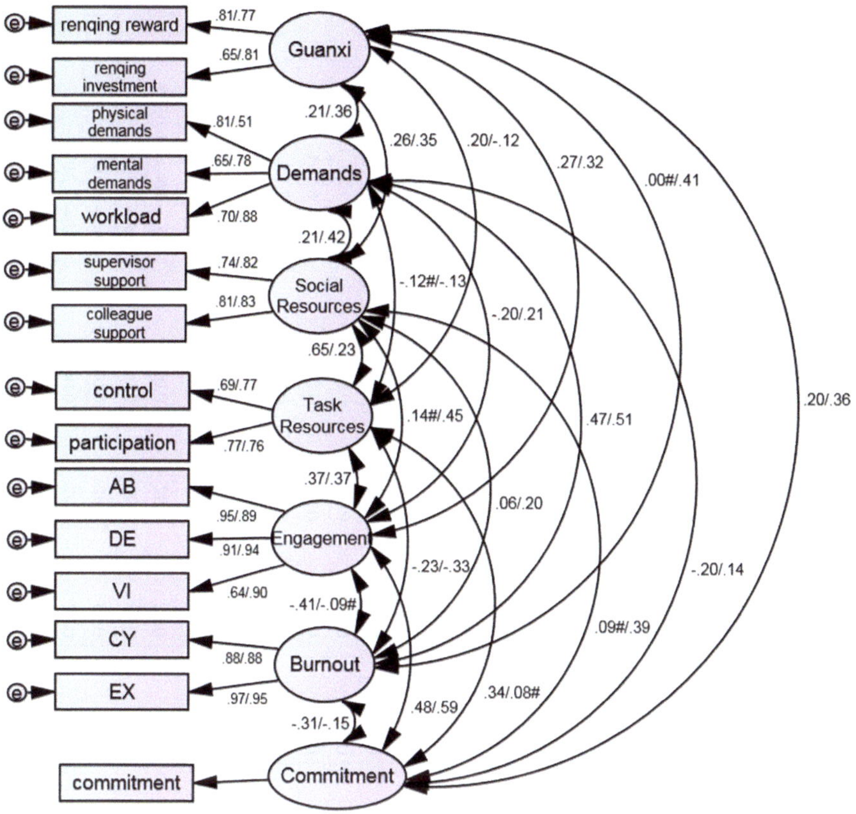

Fig. 18.1 Standardized estimates of the measurement model for 261 nurses (*left*) and 463 police officers (*right*), separately; *VI* vigor, *AB* absorption, *DE* dedication, *EX* exhaustion, *CY* cynicism; $^{\#}p \geq 0.05$

The presence or absence of common method variance was checked by conducting a multigroup Harman one-factor test. This test models the effect of the method factor at the measurement level. It does not require that the specific factor responsible for the method effect is measured, nor that the effects of the method factor on the measures are equal (cf. Podsakoff et al. 2012). A cross-sample one-factor model was estimated that was assumed to account for the associations among all latent factors. The poor fit of this model ($\chi^2(df = 171) = 1141.28$, GFI = 0.81, CFI = 0.82, TLI = 0.78, RMSEA = 0.09) implied that the associations among the measures were unlikely to be due to common method variance.

Next, model 2 (M_2) that included two types of resources (i.e., task resources and social resources) was tested and compared with the original JD-R model with one undifferentiated latent resources factor (M_1). Multigroup analysis indicated that the fit of M_2 was superior to that of M_1 across both samples; $\Delta\chi^2(\Delta df = 12) = 480.56$, $p < 0.001$ (cf. Table 18.3) (Hypothesis 1 confirmed).

Table 18.3 Multigroup analysis of the proposed JD-R model for nurses (N = 261) and police officers (N = 463)

Model	χ^2	*df*	CFI	GFI	TLI	RMSEA	$\Delta\chi^2$
Null model	5595.34	210	–	0.45		0.18	
M_1 (composite resources)	970.49	154	0.85	0.85	0.79	0.09	
M_2 (separated resources)	489.93	142	0.94	0.92	0.90	0.06	$M1 - M2$ = 480.56***
M_3 (correlated burnout and engagement)	447.68	140	0.94	0.93	0.91	0.06	$M2 - M3$ = 42.25***
M_4	450.08	144	0.94	0.93	0.92	0.05	$M4 - M3$ = 2.40, ns
M_5 (regression weights constrained)	514.96	158	0.94	0.92	0.91	0.06	$M5 - M4$ = 64.89***
$M_{5\ \text{Burnout} \to \text{commitment constrained}}$	453.31	145	0.94	0.93	0.92	0.05	ΔM = 3.23, ns
$M_{5\ \text{Engagement} \to \text{commitment constrained}}$	451.86	145	0.94	0.93	0.92	0.05	ΔM = 1.79, ns
$M_{5\ \text{Social resources} \to \text{commitment constrained}}$	457.77	145	0.94	0.92	0.92	0.06	ΔM = 7.69**
$M_{5\ \text{Task resources} \to \text{commitment constrained}}$	459.90	145	0.94	0.92	0.92	0.06	ΔM = 9.82**
$M_{5\ \textit{Guanxi} \to \text{commitment constrained}}$	452.31	145	0.94	0.93	0.92	0.05	ΔM = 2.23, ns
$M_{5\ \textit{Guanxi} \to \text{social resources constrained}}$	451.10	145	0.94	0.93	0.92	0.05	ΔM = 1.03, ns
$M_{5\ \textit{Guanxi} \to \text{task resources constrained}}$	459.56	145	0.94	0.93	0.92	0.05	ΔM = 9.49**
$M_{5\ \text{Demands} \to \text{burnout constrained}}$	454.84	145	0.94	0.93	0.92	0.05	ΔM = 4.76*
$M_{5\ \text{Task resources} \to \text{burnout constrained}}$	451.20	145	0.94	0.93	0.92	0.05	ΔM = 1.12, ns
$M_{5\ \text{Social resources} \to \text{engagement constrained}}$	456.33	145	0.94	0.92	0.92	0.05	ΔM = 6.26*
$M_{5\ \text{Task resources} \to \text{engagement constrained}}$	452.83	145	0.94	0.93	0.92	0.05	ΔM = 2.75, ns
$M_{5\ \text{Demands} \to \text{engagement constrained}}$	454.65	145	0.94	0.93	0.92	0.06	ΔM = 4.57*
$M_{5\ \textit{Guanxi} \to \text{burnout constrained}}$	460.32	145	0.94	0.92	0.92	0.05	ΔM = 10.24**
$M_{5\ \textit{Guanxi} \to \text{engagement constrained}}$	451.17	145	0.94	0.93	0.92	0.05	ΔM = 1.09 ns
M_6 (covariances constrained)	466.82	149	0.94	0.92	0.92	0.05	$M6 - M4$ = 16.63**
$M_{6\ \text{Burnout} \leftrightarrow \text{engagement constrained}}$	450.78	145	0.94	0.93	0.92	0.05	ΔM = 0.71, ns
$M_{6\ \text{Task resources} \leftrightarrow \text{social resources constrained}}$	451.47	145	0.94	0.93	0.92	0.05	ΔM = 1.40, ns
$M_{6\ \text{Demands} \leftrightarrow \text{social resources constrained}}$	457.30	145	0.94	0.92	0.92	0.06	ΔM = 7.21**
$M_{6\ \text{Demands} \leftrightarrow \text{task resources constrained}}$	450.19	145	0.94	0.93	0.92	0.05	ΔM = 0.12, ns
$M_{6\ \textit{Guanxi} \leftrightarrow \text{demands constrained}}$	456.87	145	0.94	0.92	0.92	0.06	ΔM = 6.79**

Note χ^2 chi-square, *df* degrees of freedom, *RMSEA* root mean square error of approximation, *TLI* Tucker–Lewis index, *CFI* comparative fit index

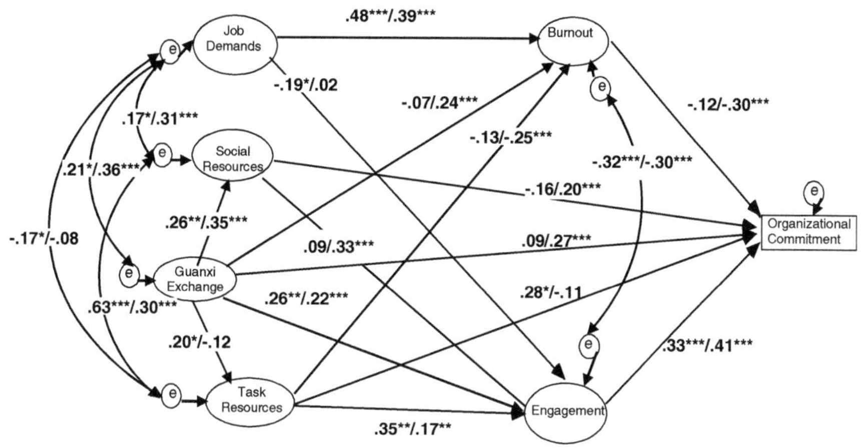

Fig. 18.2 The *multigroup* model with *guanxi* in the JD-R model for 261 nurses (*left*) and 463 police officers (*right*); $^{*}p < 0.05$; $^{**}p < 0.01$; $^{***}p < 0.001$

Since empirical studies found engagement and burnout might have part of their variance in common (Halbesleben 2010). Model (M_3) therefore allowed the residuals of burnout and engagement to correlate, showing a fit that was superior to that of M_2 ($\Delta\chi^2(\Delta df = 2) = 42.25$, $p < 0.001$).

After deleting two nonsignificant paths (demands → commitment, and social resources → burnout), Model 4 was accepted as the final model (cf. Fig. 18.2). The path linking *guanxi* to social resources was positive and significant among both nurses ($\beta = 0.26$, $p < 0.01$) and police officers ($\beta = 0.35$, $p < 0.001$) (Hypothesis 3 confirmed). Further, the path linking *guanxi* to task resources was positive and significant among nurses only ($\beta = 0.20$, $p < 0.05$) (*Hypothesis 2* partly confirmed). The path coefficient linking *guanxi* to work engagement was positive and significant among both nurses ($\beta = 0.26$, $p < 0.01$) and police officers ($\beta = 0.22$, $p < 0.001$) (Hypothesis 4 confirmed). The path linking *guanxi* to burnout was only positive and significant among police officers ($\beta = 0.24$, $p < 0.001$) (Hypothesis 5 not supported). Finally, the path linking *guanxi* to organizational commitment was positive and significant among police officers only ($\beta = 0.27$, $p < 0.001$) (Hypothesis 6 partly confirmed).

As two different samples were involved, the equivalence of M_4 across samples was tested with respect to the regression weights and the covariances. Compared to the unconstrained model (M_4), the fit of the models with equal regression weights (M_5) and with equal covariances (M_6) deteriorated significantly ($\Delta\chi^2(\Delta df = 14) = 64.89$, $p < 0.001$ and $\Delta\chi^2(\Delta df = 5) = 16.63$, $p < 0.01$, respectively). Thus, not all regression weights and covariances were the same for both samples.

Inspection of the separate covariances and regression weights revealed that two covariances and seven path coefficients were invariant across both samples (cf. Table 18.3). The correlations between job demands and social resources, and between job demands and *guanxi* exchange were both higher for police officers

(rs were 0.31 and 0.36, respectively, $p < 0.001$) than for nurses (rs were 0.17 and 0.21, $p < 0.05$). The path from job demands to burnout was positive and significant, but stronger for nurses ($\beta = 0.48$, $p < 0.001$) than for police officers ($\beta = 0.39$, $p < 0.001$). The path from job demands to engagement was only negative for nurses ($\beta = -0.19$, $p < 0.05$). Apparently, high job demands had stronger adverse effects for nurses than for police offices. The paths from social resources to work engagement and from social resources to commitment were positive and significant only for police officers ($\beta = 0.33$ and 0.20, $p < 0.001$, respectively), whereas the path from task resources to commitment was positive and significant only for nurses ($\beta = 0.28$, $p < 0.05$). Thus, task-related and social resources played a different role in both samples. This is exemplified by the fact that the path from *guanxi* to task resources was positive and only significant for nurses ($\beta = 0.20$, $p < 0.05$).

Sobel tests revealed that the indirect effects of *guanxi* on engagement and commitment (via social resources) were significant for police officers (Sobel = 3.88, $p < 0.001$ and Sobel = 3.15, $p < 0.01$, respectively). However, for nurses the indirect effects of *guanxi* on engagement and commitment (via task resources) were nonsignificant (Sobel = 1.76 and 1.70, ns). Hence, the indirect effect of *guanxi* on work outcomes occurred mainly through social resources.

Discussion

The current study contributes to the conceptual and cross-cultural development of the JD-R model by differentiating between task and social resources, and by including the typically Chinese interpersonal phenomenon of *guanxi*.

Main Findings

Multigroup analyses supported the distinction between social resources and task resources in both samples. The model with two separate types of job resources (i.e., social vs. task resources) fitted the data significantly better than a model with one, undifferentiated resource factor. Moreover, these two types of resources played different roles in the JD-R model. Whereas social resources were positively related to engagement and organizational commitment (for police officers), task resources were positively related to engagement (for both nurses and police officers), organizational commitment (for nurses), and negatively to burnout (for police officers).

Differences Between Nurses and Police Officers Although these findings show that social and task resources are distinct concepts, we found different patterns of results across both samples. Social resources were especially relevant as antecedents of engagement and commitment among police officers, whereas task resources took this place for nurses. These differences might be due to the different situations in which nurses and police officers find themselves in today's China. For nurses, China's health care reform program—"New Health Care Reform Plan" has taken place in China since 2009 to improve medical services to ensure both quality and efficiency in the health care sector. The traditional health professionals-centered service model is currently gradually being replaced with a patient-centered model, meaning that increased patient needs and the application of medical technology healthcare require redesign of the structure and the processes of care provision. As a result, nurses' job demands have increased, both in terms of patient care as well as in relation to new medical technology. This is exemplified by the fact that job demands had stronger adverse effects for nurses than for police offices. However, Maslach and Leiter (1997) proposed that a good fit between employees and their work environment would result in positive work outcomes. Task resources such as job control and participating in decision-making are critically important for nurses to deal adequately with these increased demands, to achieve work-related power, and to empower patients, which should lead to higher organizational effectiveness. Therefore, those with easy access to task resources in demanding environment are more motivated and committed in their jobs.

Compared with nurses, social resources were more important for police officers' levels of engagement and commitment. The higher their job demands, the more social resources they had. Previous research has shown that social coping resources, especially social support, are needed to deal with demanding situations and events (McCreary and Thompson 2006). For example, police officers often rely on supervisors for information to deal with violent crime, and talking things over among coworkers are the most frequent form of coping utilized while on duty. Police officers who feel marginalized or excluded from their peer group not only suffer from a lack of acceptance but are also denied information, sponsorship and promotion opportunities (Ellison and Genz 1983). Thus, for these reasons social resources could be particularly important for police to stay engaged.

Guanxi and the JD-R Model Our findings revealed that *guanxi* could be integrated into the JD-R model, although its patterns of associations with other concepts differed across samples. Specifically, (1) *guanxi* was positively related to social resources among nurses and police officers, and to task resources among nurses; and (2) *guanxi* was positively related with engagement among nurses and police officers, while positively related with burnout among police officers. (3) *guanxi* was positively related to commitment, but only for police officers.

Guanxi is embedded in informal personal social interactions that take place in formal work situations. The social resources included in our study were based on work-related interactions but their availability was to a large degree influenced by the quality of *guanxi*, as exemplified by the positive relation between *guanxi* and social resources in nurses and police officers. Furthermore, the basis for a high-quality *guanxi* exchange between supervisor and employees lies in mutual trust, loyalty and obligation. In this sense *Guanxi* can be viewed as a means for nurses and police officers in maintaining a well-balanced social exchange relationship with their supervisor to stay engaged. Interestingly, task resources were relatively important for nurses, suggesting that among nurses *guanxi* exchange with supervisors is more focused on task resources than among police officers. On the one hand, *guanxi* encourages perceptions of a relational psychological contract; that is, employees agree to contribute loyalty, trust, and continued membership while the organization provides competent management, participation, and a sense of belonging (Maguire 2002). On the other hand, the police subculture subjects its members to a strict operating code laden with discretion, secrecy, and solidarity in an attempt to insulate the officer from an uncaring and generally unsupported management structure, as well as a hostile public (Van Maanen 1978). This could explain why *guanxi* was associated with organizational commitment among police officers.

Guanxi exchange was positively associated with work engagement in both samples, but also was positively associated with burnout in police officers. It might reflect the complicated psychological dynamics involved in *guanxi.* On the one hand *guanxi* involves an emotional attachment that facilitates the development of high-trust workplaces, and people who report high levels of *guanxi* tend to believe they are being treated fairly (Chen et al. 2011), which can be assumed to lead to higher well-being (i.e., engagement). On the other hand, establishing high levels of *guanxi* requires high levels of effort, and these investments in the relationships with others are not always reciprocated equally—not even in the long run. Previous research has shown that investing much effort in a potentially unrewarding relationship can exhaust one's energy, elicit distress and negative emotions, and could lead to burnout. Thus, depending on the specific context, high levels of *guanxi* may have positive and/or negative effects on well-being.

Implications

Our findings have several implications for occupational stress research and practice. As regards theory, it seems that the dimensionality of the job resources concept should be reconsidered. Whereas previous research using the JD-R model usually focused on a compound job resources concept that included a wide variety of different resources, the current study suggests that a theoretical and empirical distinction between task resources and social resources is warranted. Further, in the practice of stress management, we propose to consider not only *formal* work-related interactions but also *informal* interpersonal relationships (such as *guanxi* reciprocity) when focusing on the effect of social resources on well-being. Particularly when these informal relations span organizational hierarchical boundaries, they may offer significant and rewarding benefits to individuals. From a societal perspective, it is important to acknowledge that *guanxi* exchange may promote employee well-being and work outcomes because good *guanxi* promotes trust and facilitates formal institutional support. It follows that employees and managers should be motivated to develop informal personal relationships in organizations as well, especially in work situations where it is difficult to increase task resources. However, note that *guanxi* exchange may potentially also affect employee well-being negatively, especially when interpersonal relationships take precedence over the procedural justice rules in the process of resources distribution.

Conclusion

The current study shows that social resources and task resources play a different role in the JD-R model. Moreover, the Chinese notion of *guanxi* (exchange of favors) was successfully integrated into the JD-R model. This not only increases the applicability of the JD-R model in China, but also exemplifies how the JD-R model can be extended by integrating notions from non-Western cultures.

References

Chen, X. P., & Chen, C. C. (2004). On the intricacies of the Chinese guanxi: A process model of guanxi development. *Asia Pacific Journal of Management, 21*, 305–324.

Chen, Y., Friedman, R., Yu, E., & Sun, F. (2011). Examining the positive and negative effects of *guanxi* practices: A multi-level analysis of *guanxi* practices and procedural justice perceptions. *Asia Pacific Journal of Management, 28*, 715–735.

Cheung, M. F. Y., Wu, W., Chan, A. K. K., & Wong, M. M. L. (2009). Supervior-subordinate Guanxi and employee work outcomes: The mediating role of job satisfaction. *Journal of Business Ethics, 88*, 77–89.

Demerouti, E., Bakker, A. B., Nachreiner, F., & Schaufeli, W. B. (2001). The Job Demands-Resources model of burnout. *Journal of Applied Psychology, 86*, 499–512.

Ellison, K. W., & Genz, J. (1983). *Stress and the police officer*. Springfield, IL: Thomas.

Halbesleben, J. R. B. (2010). A meta-analysis of work engagement: relationships with burnout, demands, resources, and consequences. In A. B. Bakker, & M. P. Leiter (Eds.), Work Engagement: A Handbook of Essential Theory and Research (pp. 102–117). New York, NY: Psychology Press.

Hu, Q., & Schaufeli, W. B. (2011). The convergent validity of four burnout measures in a Chinese sample A confirmatory factor-analytic approach. *Applied Psychology: An International Review, 60*, 87–111.

Hu, Q., Schaufeli, W. B., & Taris, T. W. (2011). The Job Demands-Resources Model: An analysis of additive and joint effects of demands and resources. *Journal of Vocational Behavior, 79*, 181–190.

Hu, Q., Schaufeli, W. B., & Taris, T. W. (2013). Does equity mediate the effects of job demands and job resources on work outcomes? An extension of the job demands-esources model. *Career Development International, 18*, 357–376.

Hui, C, & Lin, Z. (1996). *Regulating collective actions: A case of two cultural systems.* Paper presented at the Research Workshop on Global Organizations at Hong Kong University of Science & Technology.

Hwang, K. K. (1987). Face and favor: The Chinese power game. *American Journal of Sociology, 13*, 944–974.

Law, K. S., Wong, C. S., Wang, D., & Wang, L. (2000). Effect of supervisor–subordinate *guanxi* on supervisory decisions in China: An empirical investigation. *International Journal of Human Resource Management, 11*, 751–765.

LePine, J. A., Podsakoff, N. P., & LePine, M. A. (2005). A meta-analytic test of the challenge stressor–hindrance stressor framework: An explanation for inconsistent relationships among stressors and performance. *The Academy of Management Journal, 48*, 764–775.

Liljegren, M., & Ekberg, K. (2009). The associations between perceived distributive, procedural, and interactional organizational justice, self-rated health and burnout. *Work, 33*, 43–51.

Lovett, S., Simmons, L. C., & Kali, R. (1999). *Guanxi* versus the market: Ethics and efficiency. *Journal of International Business Studies, 30*, 231–247.

Maguire, H. (2002). Psychological contracts: Are they still relevant? *Career Development International, 7*, 167–180.

Maslach, C., & Leiter, M. P. (1997). *The truth about burnout*. San Francisco: Jossey-Bass.

McCreary, D. R., & Thompson, M. M. (2006). Development of two reliable and valid measures of stressors in policing: The operational and organizational police stress questionnaires. *International Journal of Stress Management, 13*, 494–518.

Ouweneel, A. P. E., Taris, T. W., van Zolingen, S. J., & Schreurs, P. J. G. (2009). How task characteristics and social support relate to managerial learning. *Journal of Psychology, 143*, 28–44.

Podsakoff, P. M., MacKenzie, S. B., & Podsakoff, N. P. (2012). Sources of method bias in social science research and recommendation on how to control it. *Annual Reviews of Psychology, 63*, 539–569.

Powell, W. W. (1990). Neither market nor hierarchy: Network forms of organization. *Research in Organizational Behavior, 12*, 295–336.

Schaufeli, W. B., & Bakker, A. B. (2004). Job demands, job resources, and their relation with burnout and engagement: A multi-sample study. *Journal of Organizational Behavior, 25*, 293–315.

Schaufeli, W. B., Bakker, A. B., & Salanova, M. (2006). The measurement of work engagement with a short questionnaire: A cross-national study. *Educational and Psychological Measurement, 66*, 701–716.

Schaufeli, W. B., Leiter, M. P., Maslach, C., & Jackson, S. E. (1996). *MBI—General survey*. Palo Alto, CA: Consulting Psychologists Press.

Tsui, A. S., & Farh, J. L. (1997). Where guanxi matters: Relational demography and guanxi in the Chinese context. *Work and Occupations, 24*, 56–79.

Van Maanen, J. (1978). People processing: Major strategies of organizational socialization and their consequences. In J. Paap (Ed.), *New directions in human resource management*. Englewood Cliffs, NJ: Prentice-Hall.

Van Veldhoven, M., De Jonge, J., Broersen, S., Kompier, M., & Meijman, T. (2002). Specific relations between psychosocial job conditions and job-related stress: a three-level analytic approach. *Work & Stress, 16*, 207–228.

Warren, D. E., Dunfee, T. W., & Li, N. (2004). Social exchange in China: The double-edged sword of *guanxi*. *Journal of Business Ethics, 55*, 355–372.

Weigl, M., Hornung, S., Parker, S. K., Petru, R., Glaser, J., & Angerer, P. (2010). Work engagement accumulation of task, social, personal resources: A three-wave structural equation model. *Journal of Vocational Behavior, 77*(1), 140–153.

Wenger, E. (1998). *Communities of practice: Learning, meaning and identity*. Cambridge: Cambridge University Press.

Wong, Y. T., Ngo, H. Y., & Wong, C. S. (2003). Antecedents and outcomes of employees' trust in Chinese joint ventures. *Asia Pacific Journal of Management, 20*, 481–499.

Yum, J. (1988). The impact of Confucianism on interpersonal relationships and communicative patterns in East Asia. *Communication Monographs, 55*, 374–388.

Zhang, K. Z. (2001). The history of china. Beijing: Advanced Education Press.

Chapter 19
Beneath the Surface: An Exploration of Remoteness and Work Stress in the Mines

Wesley P. McTernan, Maureen F. Dollard, Michelle R. Tuckey and Robert J. Vandenberg

Abstract The aim of this ethnographic study was to explore the experience of stress and remoteness amongst miners. Nineteen mining employees participated in semi-structured interviews; 11 remote miners were interviewed at their place of work in a South Australian mining company operating a fly-in/fly-out (FIFO) roster structure. Comparative perspectives were obtained from an additional eight miners working in Australia and the Philippines also operating within a FIFO roster, and Canada and Sweden where miners lived in neighbouring mining communities. We used a grounded theory approach and the job demands resources framework to identify the job demands, job resources and outcomes unique to mining work. Our analysis revealed that work stress was a common experience amongst mining workers, with the potential to manifest into impaired psychological well-being and sleep. Work pressure and environmental exposure were identified as the most prominent job demands. Remote workers additionally experienced work–family and work–life conflict. In relation to resources, remote miners reported a unique experience of social support. Remote miners frequently work away from the family which strains familial relationships. Facilitated by increased proximity, co-workers assume an intensified supportive role than would typically be provided by friends and family at home. Safety culture was identified as an upstream organisational factor that may precede or mitigate work stress and poor health outcomes.

Keywords Work stress · Well-being · Remote work · Mining · Social support

---

W.P. McTernan (✉) · M.F. Dollard · M.R. Tuckey
Asia Pacific Centre for Work Health and Safety, A WHO Collaborative Centre, University of South Australia, Adelaide, Australia
e-mail: Wes.McTernan@unisa.edu.au

R.J. Vandenberg
Terry College of Business, University of Georgia, Athens, USA

A. Shimazu et al. (eds.), *Psychosocial Factors at Work in the Asia Pacific*,
DOI 10.1007/978-3-319-44400-0_19

Introduction

Australia's vast landscape is abundant in valuable mineral deposits, presenting great potential for economic and industrial development. Problematically, however, the locations of these resources are largely dispersed inland at a great distance from Australia's coastal urban populations, creating an obstacle for organisations to recruit and deploy a workforce to operate within these remote regions. However, developments in transport and telecommunications services coupled with significant growth in Australia's mining industry in recent decades, has generated fly-in/fly-out (FIFO) and to a lesser extent drive-in/drive-out (DIDO; but also referred to as FIFO due to similarity) employment practices. These practices have become the industry standard in operating out of remote locations.

As a large number of new employees inexperienced with the machinery and industry practices required for operations having entered the mining workforce during the industry boom in recent decades, workplace safety is a substantial concern for employers. Further, lucrative employment prospects have stimulated a large number of workers to shift career paths, adding to the inexperience of the employee base. The safety risks are reflected in mining carrying the second highest fatality rate in Australian industries (SafeWork Australia 2011). A review of the literature investigating health hazards in the mining industry by Donaghue (2004) found quite an extensive range of research published; however little research was found investigating psychosocial risks to health.

Considering prevailing safety concerns within the industry, identifying psychosocial factors that contribute to psychological strain will allow organisations to target these safety factors to prevent on site accidents and injuries. Identifying and addressing concerning psychosocial factors, stands to help reduce future industry accidents and mitigate well-being-related productivity deficits. Understanding contributing factors that may mitigate these deleterious outcomes is therefore beneficial to employers and employees, as well as offering insight into primary industries that adopt FIFO rosters such as oil and gas.

To address this gap, an ethnographic explorative study was conducted in an Australian mining company, involving eleven semi-structured interviews. This was repeated in a follow-up online sample of eight participants across countries to cross-validate findings. As there is scarce available research on psychosocial health in the mining industry, a qualitative study provides not only descriptive insight into uncharted territory, but also a starting point for future quantitative investigation.

Theoretical Framework: The Job Demands Resources Model

The job demands resources model (JDR; Bakker and Demerouti 2007) is proposed as the theoretical scaffolding in the design and analysis for the present study. The JDR model has gained popularity in psychological stress research literature, due to its conceptual flexibility to occupational and organisational differences, as well as being theoretically harmonious with other contemporary work stress theories, i.e. the job demand control model (Karasek and Theorell 1990) and the effort rewards imbalance model (Siegrist et al. 1986). The JDR model posits two distinct yet interconnected pathways of psychosocial factors and outcomes: the health erosion pathway, where excessive workplace demands lead to psychological strain by way of heightened stress arousal that depletes energy reserves; and the motivational pathway, where workplace resources enable a worker to perform job tasks that lead to positive workplace outcomes, such as increased engagement. Further, research suggests that these two pathways are interconnected. A range of workplace resources have been found to buffer workplace demands thereby minimising psychological strain (Bakker et al. 2005).

Authors Bakker and Demerouti (2007) propose that workplaces are unique, and therefore that the types of workplace demands and resources experienced by workers is unique to the organisation and work role. With this in mind, Bakker and Demerouti identified the important role of qualitative investigation prior to conducting quantitative research, to explore and identify the core features of an unknown work environment. Given the unexplored psychosocial characteristics relating to mining work, the JDR model is an ideal framework for guiding conceptualisation in the present qualitative study.

The Extended Psychosocial Safety Climate: Job Demand Resource Model

Recent research by Dollard and colleagues (Dollard and Bakker 2010; Dollard and McTernan 2011) extends the JDR model to account for organisational system antecedents of workplace demands and resources. Psychosocial safety climate (PSC)—the policies, practices and procedures within an organisation relating to its attitude towards psychosocial health safety—is a distal predictor of both the health erosion and motivational pathways. Safety climate refers to the present state or 'temperature' of an organisational safety culture. By targeting upstream safety climate factors, organisations may minimise some of the negative downstream consequences. Therefore, an extended PSC–JDR model is used as a guiding theoretical framework for the present study (Fig. 19.1).

Using this model as a guide the authors aim to identify the key demands pertinent to remote and non-remote mining workers, the key resources that help workers manage job demands, and the form the job strain manifests.

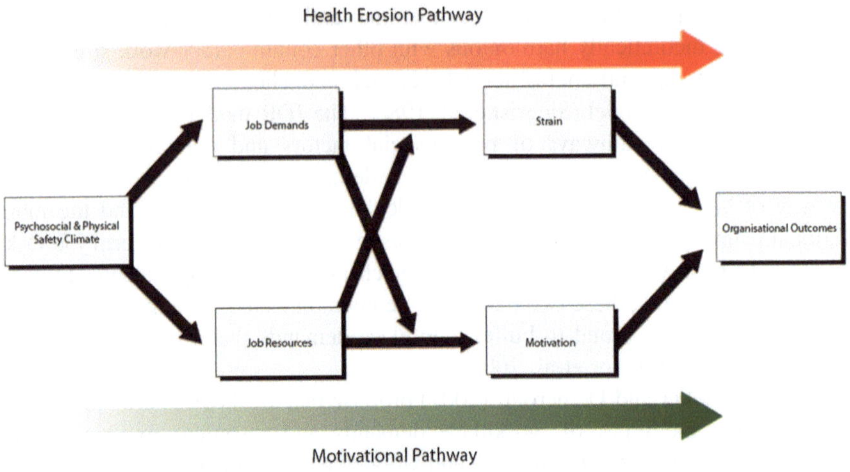

Fig. 19.1 The extended psychosocial safety climate—job demand resources model

Method

Sample I: Ethnographic

In early 2012 mining organisations with work sites located in South Australia were approached for involvement in this study. By mid to late 2012 a company had agreed to facilitate the interview process with its employees. Interviews were conducted on the mining site late 2012, with the exploration team at their central office early 2013. A purposeful sample was chosen to acquire a representation of typical company demographics (such as age, gender and occupation; see Table 19.1). To safeguard anonymity, further industry demographic identifiers (e.g. geographical region and minerals produced) are not disclosed. The total number of Sample I consisted of 11 employees.

Sample II: Comparative

A follow-up sample was used to cross-validate the findings of Sample I. An information letter targeting the network's mining community was posted online in a social media network website reddit.com. The interview techniques of the initial sample were repeated, except face-to-face communication was replaced with personal communications via the networks forum and email liaison. This resulted in an additional eight mining employees participating in Sample II from Australia ($n = 4$), Canada ($n = 2$), Sweden ($n = 1$) and the Philippines ($n = 1$). Two additional employees were removed from the United States and Brazil, due to insufficient data from interviews. A visual data map of the data origin is presented in Fig. 19.2.

Table 19.1 Job condition characteristics and illustrative quotes of distal (safety climate) and immediate (co-worker support) job resources

Job condition	Characteristics	Illustrative quotes
Safety climate	A concern for safety across organisational hierarchy Management makes the safety of workers a priority Employees are concerned for the safety of each other Attitudes towards safety are shared amongst workers Safety attitudes are predominantly towards physical safety, but psychosocial safety is an emerging area of attention	"That's management… A focus of trying to get everybody to think of safety as a package, not as a statistic." (P10.18.3) "The biggest thing is coming home safe. It's the most important thing." (P8.2.1) "That strong safety culture is something I like about this place." (P8.4.2) "For the mining practices, we are lagging in terms of safety… overall it's really not that great, at least compared to modern mines." (P20.1.5)
Co-worker support (FIFO)	Co-workers provided each other support on a range of work-related and personal issues Supportive relationships increased with their proximity to co-workers Co-workers adopted familial-like support roles on site, acting as surrogates for the social support they would typically receive from friends and family at home	"These people become your family essentially". (P11.1.6) "Because they're away from their families, people create a family". (P4.9.2)

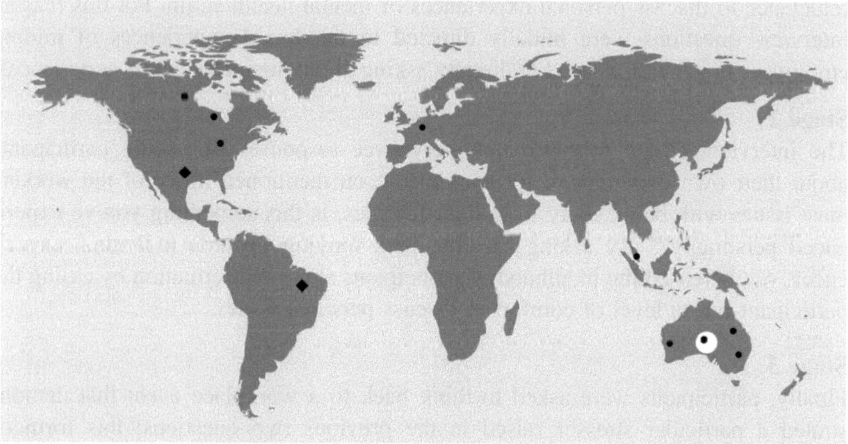

Fig. 19.2 Data map of ethnographic and transnational mining interview samples. *White circle* represents the location of ethnographic interviews. *Black circles* represent transnational comparative sample. *Black diamonds* represent interviews removed due to insufficient data

Materials

Questions from two previous grounded theory studies that also examined work stress (Idris et al. 2010; Kinman and Jones 2005) were used as a basis for interview question structure. Questions were modified and expanded to specifically draw out the types of demands, resources and outcomes as per the JDR framework. Participants were additionally asked to add any information they felt was relevant but not covered in the initial questions, as well as an opportunity for the interviewee to ask the interviewer questions about the research. Interviews in Sample I were recorded using a voice recorder with the participants' permission. Before commencing research ethics approval was obtained from the University Human Research Ethics Committee.

Procedure

A gradual mode of inquiry was introduced in the present study: successive stages of incremental questioning were adopted, to facilitate interviewee comfort and disclosure.

Stage 1
The first stage inquired about the general experiences of workers within the mining industry. Considering the stigma towards mental health in rural Australian communities (Rost et al. 1993), and the rural culture of mining sites, we anticipated reluctance to discuss personal experiences of mental health strain. For this reason, interview questions were initially directed to the broad experiences of mining employees in general, instead of directly asking about the interviewees experiences.

Stage 2
The interviewer then followed up interviewee responses by asking participants about their own experiences, for example: "you mentioned many of the workers have issues with being away from their families, is this something you've experienced personally?" By asking broadly, then moving towards individual experiences, we increased the likelihood of participants sharing information by easing the participant into a level of comfort to discuss personal issues.

Stage 3
Finally, participants were asked to think back to a workplace event that demonstrated a particular stressor raised in the previous two questions; this form of mentally reliving an event to trigger contextual memories is based on context-dependent memory theory (Smith 1994). Context-dependent memory theory proposes that contextual information is stored with the memories of a given phenomenon, and by thinking back on the environmental context, and mentally walking through the event, richer memory information will be triggered from the

arising contextual cues. A common example of this mechanism is retracing your steps when trying to remember where you placed your car keys.

We propose that this novel approach of gradually increasing the depth of inquiry will result in a better the quality of participant responses, and maximises interviewee comfort.

Before conducting the interviews, several trial interviews were conducted with peers of mixed age and gender. This allowed for a process question refinement to minimise unnecessary jargon, as well as rephrasing questions to improve the overall transition between questions and clarity.

Analysis

We aimed to develop a local theory of work stress in remote mining work, by identifying phenomena unique to remote mining workers and placing this within the broader JDR conceptual framework. Grounded theory (Glaser et al. 1968) was adopted as the framework for coding data and analysis. Grounded theory has been described as a form of reverse-hypothesis generation, where data is coded into emerging themes that then guide the development of theory.

Recorded interviews from Sample I were transcribed into the word processing software, Microsoft Word 2013. Interviews from Sample II were additionally transferred to Microsoft Word so that both sets of interviews could be formatted and checked for spelling before being transferred into NVivo version 10 for analysis. Key themes were then explored in terms of the over-arching extended JDR theoretical framework, creating a base for local theory development. After initial coding, a cluster analysis was conducted to identify overt node overlaps via word similarity.

Thematic analysis was conducted with consideration to Braun and Clarke (2006) discussion on appropriate theme identification and coding, where thematic classification is a process of examining intra and inter-interview theme frequency, as well as its relevance to the research questions. In consideration of these guidelines, identified themes were discussed by more than 50 % or more of interviews, and in most instances over 70 %. Consistency of responses emerging in the interview process with the comparative sample indicated a point of saturation had been reached.

Findings and Discussion

Using the extended job demand resource model as a guiding theoretical framework, several themes emerged (Fig. 19.3). A common experience of job demand was work pressure, physical environmental exposure, and work-family conflict. In terms of job resources, remote miners frequently reported social support from co-workers, which helped them cope with stress. Outside of job demands and resources, safety culture was identified as an organisational factor that may precede or reduce work

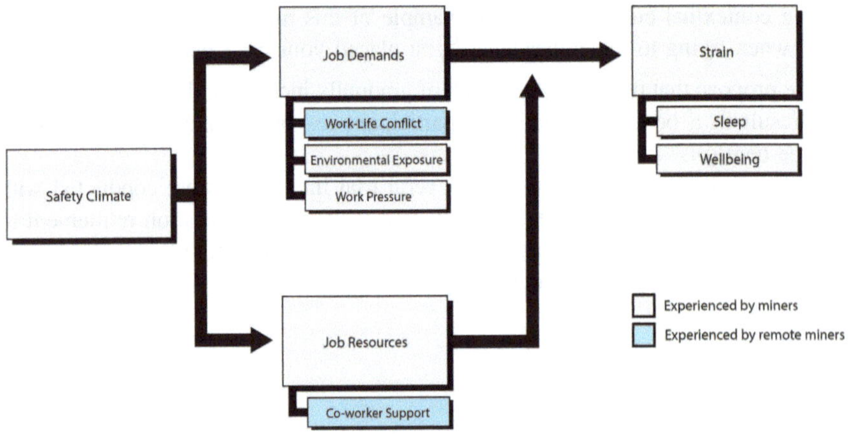

Fig. 19.3 Local model of work stress amongst mining workers

stress and poor health reactions. Interviewees identified management and employee attitudes towards safety as a cause of good safety practices and prevention of safety incidents. The most prominent strain-related outcomes related to well-being and sleep. Next we elaborated these themes, and mapped these with relevant literature.

Safety Climate

Safety climate, that is the present state or *temperature* of an organisation's safety culture, emerged as a prominent theme among the remote and non-remote mining workers. The remote Australian miners from Sample I and one from Sample II indicated that safety was a topic everyone cared about, that they felt responsible for the safety of their co-workers, and that their co-workers were responsible for their safety. Interviewees also described safety culture as something that was evident amongst employees on the ground, as well as a priority driven by management.

Both Zohar (2000) and Dollard and McTernan (2011), theorists in physical and psychosocial safety climate, respectively, propose that safety climate is a multilevel construct evident in unit level safety practices as well as top–down management driven policy implementation. Interviewee responses supported the multilevel interpretation, expressing a perspective that management was highly concerned with the safety of employees (Table 19.1: P10.18.3) as well as fellow co-workers (Table 19.1: P8.2.1) and that this cultural attitude spanned the entire worksite (Table 19.1: P8.4.2).

Comparatively, a non-FIFO miner in Canada and a FIFO miner in the Philippines from Sample II, both mentioned concerns regarding safety practices. The Canadian miner mentioned experiences of working on a sleep debt, and a concern that unsafe working conditions may lead to worker fatality. Similarly, a

FIFO Filipino miner raised similar concerns, suggesting the site was behind in safety practices compared to 'modern' mining sites (Table 19.1: P20.1.5). It's possible the strength of safety climate may then be partially explained by sociopolitical factors, rather than the influence of FIFO contracts. This supports the finding of national socio-political influences (e.g. union density) on safety climate, as elaborated by Dollard and Neser (2013).

Amongst the remote Australian miners, safety climate attitudes predominantly pertained to physical safety, however indicators of psychosocial safety climate emerged within interviews but to a lesser extent. Within one of the Australian mining organisations, employees were provided with telephone counselling services through an anonymous employee assistance program. One interviewee noted that although there was a high concern for physical safety, mental health was an area of growing area of interest within industry. Findings therefore suggest that psychosocial safety may be an underdeveloped but emerging area within the industry.

Aside from overt physical safety practices such as the effective use of personal protection equipment (PPE) and fatigue management, workers engaged in a variety of co-worker monitoring based physical safety practices. Interviewees mentioned the use of both formal and informal "buddy systems". A new employee might get paired with an experienced employee to help them transition into the job role. Additionally, it was common for employees to develop an informal relationship with another worker to check up on them in terms of their health and well-being. In this regard, safety culture (physical and psychosocial) was shared and active amongst employees.

Job Resources

Co-worker Support

Co-workers support was the most frequently reported, and multifaceted psychosocial job resource remote Australian interviewees discussed (it was not discussed by the remote Filipino worker). They reported that the physical proximity to their co-workers with whom they lived and worked for extended periods (typically between 8 and 14 days), led to an increased level of social proximity and more salient relationships compared to other previous work arrangements. Interviewees noted that they shared the same living, social and work environments as their colleagues, including sleeping areas, eating areas, and social areas (such as the recreational room and gym facilities). In this regard workers had a 24 h exposure to co-workers, leading to the formation of unique relationships.

The social support relationship between colleagues involved typical support roles, such as providing aid in completing work tasks, however several atypical behaviours were reported. Workers mentioned relying on each other to talk about personal problems such as issues with their family and home life. Additionally, workers reported 'watching out for each other' in terms of emotional and psychological well-being, and being highly aware of each other's mannerisms so that they would notice when they were struggling with home or work problems. The frequency that this level of disclosure was reported, and the degree of attention to their peers' psychological well-being, is indicative of a more personal rapport in mining site relationships compared to traditional work relationships.

Further, the majority of these workers reported that their co-workers were like *family* (Table 19.1: P11.1.6; P4.9.2; P2.5.6; P8.5.6).

This type of behaviour did not emerge in the interviews with workers that were not on FIFO contracts with exception of one interviewee. One non-Australian employee worked FIFO in the Philippines, however co-worker support did not emerge as salient during the interview process. It is likely that this type of behaviour is therefore directly due to the FIFO roster structure (which are typically longer in the Philippines), or perhaps specifically to FIFO in Australian work environments.

Work Demands

Work–Life Conflict

Australian workers expressed a variety of ways in which their work conflicted with their personal life, attributable to long working hours and the FIFO roster. Conflicts with their family role appeared to be the most severe form of personal life conflict, as being away from home created stress by not being available for a family member when they were needed to contribute to family duties or if there was an emergency. Workers with or without families both reported a difficulty in finding time to maintain personal relationships, and this inhibited workers from forming new relationships outside of work. Workers also reported that being away from their social circles most of the time meant friends assumed they were unavailable even when they were home, making their social life suffer. Although most workers could comment on these difficulties that a remote work schedule created, there was a strong sense of ownership towards their circumstances. Workers acknowledged remote mining as a lifestyle choice, albeit one not suitable for everyone—expressing the strain it places on families and personal relationships (Table 19.2: P5.5.2).

Outside of affecting personal relationships, workers also reported that FIFO rosters influenced their ability to maintain personal routines, in particular the ability to keep a consistent pattern within the week of allocating time to a personal activity or hobby. Workers mentioned that they could not commit to sport because they are not able to consistently make it to games or training sessions (Table 19.2: P9.3.1).

Workers also reported that work conflicted with their exercise routines, as they had far less time to exercise when on their swing (period of roster rotation on site) than when at home, making it difficult to allocate a consistent time during the week for exercise. Workers also reported that going back to the same sleep/wake cycle as partners and family members when off swing was difficult. In all of these cases,

Table 19.2 Job condition characteristics and illustrative quotes of job demands (work–life conflict, environmental exposure and work pressure)

Job condition	Characteristics	Illustrative quotes
Work–life conflict (FIFO)	Time and energy required for work makes it difficult to meet family commitments Workers experience strain on their relationships due to their work commitments Workers feel they do not have enough energy to talk to family members Workers find it difficult to maintain friendships Workers cannot commit to a routine, such as being part of a sporting team	"You've only got to look around the industry and most of the guys are in their fifties and on their second or third marriage." (P5.5.2) "Being out of the settings where you would normally exercise, it's hard to join a sports club, it's hard to live your lifestyle tailored to you." (P9.3.1)
Environmental exposure	Employees work outdoors, with a higher frequency of exposure to the environment Employees work in regions with more severe temperatures both hot and cold Workers are exposed to dust in sandy regions Workers are exposed to noise from the machinery and equipment	"…sometimes you may not realise it, it will creep up on you… It can be quite physically uncomfortable here. It's either extremely cold or extremely hot." (P4.4.10)
Work pressure	Workers are required to work long hours Workers are concerned that mistakes could cost their employer gross amounts due to the value of the material produced Workers are concerned that mistakes could cause serious injuries or fatalities	"This [job] puts a lot of pressure on you … every decision I make might cost millions… That's stressful." (P6.1.6) "Our work can be quite physical … mentally it's draining, because you're watching all the time. You know you don't want to run someone over…you've got to be quite vigilant." (P4.3.4)

it was the inability to maintain a consistent weekly routine, due to sporadic changes in use and availability of time that caused conflict with their personal life and created stress. Comparatively, mining employees from who did not operate on a FIFO roster did not report the same conflict with their personal life. Although this does not suggest that mining workers who are not on the isolated rosters do not experience some form of work–life interference, it is likely that it is a greater issue for remote miners.

Environmental Exposure

Remote FIFO Australian interviewees reported exposure to extreme temperatures when working outdoors where employees may spend 12 or 13 h. One worker reported that it was not uncommon for the temperature to reach upwards of 45 °C (113 °F) in summer. Conversely, at night the temperature can drop rapidly, presenting a robust range of temperature for the body to be exposed to, and to adapt to. One worker expressed the change between extreme heat and cold to be physically uncomfortable (Table 19.2: P4.4.10).

Wind and air particles (sand, dust) were additional forms of environmental conditions that affected employees amongst Australian FIFO employees. Heavy winds were discussed as something that exacerbated the heat. One employee noted that workers were more prone to get agitated or grumpy on a windy day. Similarly, employees were required to wear safety glasses, as a heavy wind could pick up sand and dust which could get in an employee's eyes.

Temperature related environmental exposures were also mentioned by a non-FIFO worker. One Canadian interviewee noted working in −30 °C was common, and that the cold can affect a worker mentally. Considering that many of the major mining nations (e.g. Russia, Australia, and Canada) have regions of extreme heat and cold, environmental exposure is likely a common job demand across the industry.

Several strategies were reported for reducing heat-related stress. One strategy was to work at a medium pace, so that a constant pace could be maintained and heat exhaustion avoided. Additionally, monitoring the water consumption of one another was also reported. One worker noted that it was difficult to monitor your own hydration, so workers would keep an eye on one another and watch for physical (e.g., lack of perspiration) and behavioural cues (e.g. a slower verbal response). This type of behaviour was suggestive of a strong over-arching safety culture within the organisation, as this was expressed by several employees from the same worksite.

Work Pressure

Remote Australian workers of Sample I and II reported working long days when on site, where a typical working day was described as 12–13 h. Interviewees working these hours reported this as a difficult aspect of their job role, whereas those who worked more typical hours on a non-rotational roster reported no difficulty with the work hours compared to their experience working long hours when engaged in a FIFO roster. Long hours were considered a difficult work demand for two reasons. First, they provided an extended exposure to work demands, and therefore elicited a long exposure to stress arousal. Second, working longer hours resulted in less time remaining in the day for recovery.

Both Australian miners, and miners interviewed from other regions in Sample II reported various types of work pressure. Employers were aware that should production be hindered, or that a mistake be made on their behalf, that the resulting effect on work production had major financial implications (Table 19.2: P6.1.6).

Other types of pressure included the responsibility of working with dangerous machinery. This included a concern of driving a truck into other machinery incurring large costs to the employer, or the risk of hitting a co-worker that could result in injury or death (Table 19.2: P4.3.4).

Health Outcomes

Sleep

Sleep disturbances were reported as not only a potential outcome of stress from work, but also something that can exacerbate it amongst both samples. Interviewees commented on how the thin walls of the living quarters allowed noise to transfer between adjacent rooms quite easily, so that workers had to be careful with the amount of noise that they made so not to disturb other employees (Table 19.3: P10.5.1). Further, having employees working different hours during the day meant a person's sleep patterns may be disturbed by their neighbours.

Table 19.3 Job condition characteristics and illustrative quotes of health outcomes (sleep and well-being)

Job condition	Characteristics	Illustrative quotes
Sleep	FIFO workers experience difficulty getting to sleep, and staying asleep due to noise permeating the thin walls of transportable accommodation Workers were more likely to make mistakes at work when they had inadequate sleep	"It can be hard to sleep. .you've got these dongers [with] four rooms per building, but the insulation in them is not all that flash, …they're noisy, they wobble if someone walks up one end. Everyone up the other end can feel them walking into their room." (P10.5.1) I have experienced irritability with co-workers while trying to perform physical tasks on a sleep debt many times " (P18.3.4)
Well-being	Experience of decreased mood or increase in anxiety Workers may withdraw socially due to a decrease in mood Experiences of increased temper, or becoming agitated more easily Difficulty concentrating on work tasks due to feeling down or depressed	"There are subtle signs you see… one of the signs is that they can go into their shell a little bit. They can get a little depressed a bit because they're not getting their point across, no one kind of understands them." (P11.3.4) "Your mood becomes affected so it's harder to work with everybody. [You] narrow down on little things that aren't such a big deal." (P9.8.7) I've just once seen and heard of a guy going nuts down there. He would stand in completely dark places and bark at the walls." (P14.3.2)

Several comments were made about how poor sleep can affect a workers job performance, by both remote Australian miners and non-Australian miners. One Canadian miner reported noticing workers on a sleep debt making frequent job errors, exacerbated by the cold (Table 19.3: P18.3.4). In this regard, although rotational shifts such as FIFO rosters may aggravate the sleep disturbances, sleep may be a particularly important concern for the industry as a whole.

Well-being

Several ways in which work demands affected worker well-being were discussed by both samples. Low mood, feelings of anxiety or feeling depressed were reported as a possible outcomes of stress that arises from work, in particular if an employee was having problems coping with working on a FIFO roster. Mood appeared to also be directly tied to co-worker relationships, as support or conflict from another co-worker would help or deteriorate mood (Table 19.3: P11.3.4; P9.8.7). In this regard well-being status may be preceded by work-family conflict issues that arise from FIFO rosters, but the negative impact could be mitigated by co-worker support.

In a severe example, a Swedish worker from Sample II working underground commented on the psychological effects of light deprivation and isolation, observing a co-worker 'bark' at the walls, from spending too much time underground (Table 19.3: P14.3.2).

These responses are not surprising, as a decline in well-being is a typical strain outcome of stress according to the JDR model of work stress. However, it may be the case that remoteness and isolation associated with mining work appears to exacerbate the concerns relating to mental well-being. Difficult working conditions, such as light deprivation, may pose further risks.

Conclusion

This study explored the unique working conditions of the mining industry and the implications of remoteness on workers, and aimed to build a local theory of stress framed on the psychosocial safety climate extended job demands resources model. The findings of our survey add qualitative support to the job demands resources model, in that interviewees reported a causal relationship between the discussed job demands and outcomes, as well as reporting a buffering effect from co-worker support. Further, the unique experience of certain demands and resources supports Bakker and Demerouti's (2007) proposition that industries will differ in the types of demands and resources experienced. Our study extends theory however by identifying a unique proximity effect to social support, discussed below.

The qualitative investigation reported here lays down the initial ground work for future quantitative research by identifying the key industry-specific constructs relating to the stress pathway for mining workers, in particular the areas more prevalent for remote miners. Further, qualitative data can help understand additional facets of issues within the industry that are already identified.

One such example within the present study was work–family/work–life conflict associated with remote work, which places strain not just on familial and peer relationships, but also on the worker's ability to maintain sporting and leisure hobbies. This disruption of personal routines, which goes beyond maintaining social relationships and into maintaining intrinsic self-actualisation processes from sport and leisure activities, is a previously undiscussed facet of work–life conflict that may warrant future investigation. Additionally, these types of activities aid in stress alleviation (Zuzanek et al. 1998). Inhibiting regular engagement in these activities may remove some of the pre-existing stress buffering mechanisms workers utilise.

Our findings on safety culture within the Australian mining sample also provide interesting insights into industry culture. Despite an awareness of physical risks associated with the job due to machinery and environmental exposure, employees felt there was a strong culture towards safety amongst employees and employers. It is important to note that safety climate was perceived to be enacted amongst employees as well as management. This adds qualitative support to safety climate theory, which is theorised to function across multiple levels of organisational hierarchy (Dollard and McTernan 2011).

Indicators of a psychosocial safety climate were evident but emerging, as one participant described it as a growing area of interest in the industry. This can be partially explained by mental health and well-being being relatively new concepts to the workplace, as well as the resistance towards addressing mental health in rural Australia where Australian mines are located. It may also be the case that stigma towards mental health may have prevented interviewees from discussing mental health to a further extent. In this regard, a lack of discussion makes it difficult to obtain an impression on the sample's psychosocial safety climate. However, as communication is a key element of psychosocial safety climate, a lack of discussion suggests that psychosocial safety climate may be underdeveloped.

One of the most unique themes to emerge was the close relationships FIFO miners had with co-workers, who were like 'family'. An explanation for the enhanced co-worker support roles could be accounted for by systems of group cohesion and the proximity principle. The proximity principle refers to the increased likelihood of people forming social bonds and establishing group cohesion when they are in frequent physical contact. Evidence for this phenomenon has been found in campus boarding facilities (Marmaros and Sacerdote 2006; Newcomb 1961; Priest and Sawyer 1967, Rubin and Shenker 1978), and has been associated with increased disclosure (Rubin and Shenker 1978), which may explain the enhanced support. As workers in isolated environments, such as remote miners, experience a similar living environment, this theoretical perspective could help explain this phenomenon. Future quantitative research should therefore assess whether greater co-worker support is reported amongst mining workers, and if this acts as a buffering resource for work stress.

The emerging theme of sleep disturbances amongst FIFO miners was anticipated by the authors, as rotational rosters, may result in inconsistent sleep cycles between their work sleep–wake cycle and that at home, as it needs to be harmonious with partners and family. Further transportable accommodation and noise on may also disturb sleep. As disturbed sleep can impact cognitive faculties such as attention and alertness (Miller et al. 2014), this could be an area mining organisations may wish to focus on.

Reports of changes in mood were anticipated; and are typical of a high stress environment such as mining work. Poor mood was mentioned more commonly, but not exclusively by the Australian FIFO miners. This may in part be due to the pressure a FIFO roster places on at-home relationships. Work-family conflict has been shown to be related to greater depression prevalence (Frone et al.1997; Hammer et al. 2005), and given that the interviewees reported FIFO roster placed pressure on home relationships, this may explain the reported mood disturbances. Future research should investigate this relationship, to identify if there is a quantitative correlation.

Theoretical Implications

The present study adds to the job demand resources (JDR) model, which is yet to be investigated in qualitative research. Interviewees reported casual pathways between demands and health outcomes, supporting the model's health erosion pathway. Further, co-worker support was identified as a situational resource, supporting the buffering pathway of the JDR model. In addition, we identified a local theory of work stress for remote and non-remote mining work, supporting the industry contextualisation of the occurrence of different demands and resources proposed by Bakker and Demerouti (2007).

Perhaps the most important theoretical implication of the present study was identifying a proximity effect of social support. Social support at work is a key construct in contemporary work stress theory; both in Karasek and Theorell's (1990) job demand control model, as well as an important resource of Bakker's job demand resources model. Considering the rise of transient work arrangements, both FIFO rosters adopted by mining companies as well as off shore drilling, as well as an emerging migrant workforce in China, remoteness and its effect on social support at work and home may become a growing issue. Work stress theory may need to accommodate these changing work structures as transport and telecommunication technologies that support these practices continue to develop.

Practical Implications

This proximity effect also carries concerns for organisational practices regarding co-worker relationships in remote workplaces, as well as policies and practices that may affect at home relationships. These findings such organisations stand to benefit from fostering positive co-worker relationships, which in turn buffers stress at work. Additionally, investing in infrastructure that helps minimised work-family conflict such as communication services, may reduce stress and stress-related outcomes.

Similarly, organisations may wish to focus their attention on other identified demands and outcomes that emerged in the interviews. Although it may be difficult to limit working hours that contribute to the employees experience of work pressure, efforts could be made to improve employee's quality of sleep. The reduction of sleep disturbances could be facilitated by ensuring the sleeping quarters of day and night shift workers are separated, so that their daily and nightly movements to not interfere with one another's sleep. Sound insulation would also restrict the amount of noise permeating through bedroom walls, helping improve the quality of sleep on site.

Limitations

One of the possible limitations of the present study is that individuals from the comparative sample could not be interviewed in person. Although this is not realistically possible, it may affect the types of, and depth of information people choose to disclose. Another limitation is that the potential for selection bias. Several organisations were approached for Sample I, and it may be that the selected company that chose to participate may represent a more positive work culture. Similarly, although Sample II was selected from a large online community of mining employees, it is possible that this may not reflect the ideas and opinions of those less engaged with social media. In both cases, a bias might occur where we are only receiving information from those that wish to share it rather than a representative sample. Nevertheless the sampling strategy in Sample I was purposively chosen to represent all of the major demographic categories of the sample.

Closing Remarks

It is important to note that each occupation and industry provides an environment of unique experiences of various job stressors and resources. What makes remote mining work so unique, is the way in which this remoteness changes an individual's relationships with both their family, and their co-workers. Although some of the difficulties that arise from this unique work structure are unavertable, understanding the way in which these factors interact help in both understanding the way in which stress arousal manifests, but also shines a light on what areas may be the best to focus efforts to reduce work-related stress.

References

Bakker, A. B., & Demerouti, E. (2007). The job demands-resources model: State of the art. *Journal of Managerial Psychology, 22*(3), 309–328.

Bakker, A. B., Demerouti, E., & Euwema, M. C. (2005). Job resources buffer the impact of job demands on burnout. *Journal of Occupational Health Psychology, 10*(2), 170.

Braun, V., & Clarke, V. (2006). Using thematic analysis in psychology. *Qualitative Research in Psychology, 3*(2), 77–101.

Dollard, M. F., & Bakker, A. B. (2010). Psychosocial safety climate as a precursor to conducive work environments, psychological health problems, and employee engagement. *Journal of Occupational and Organizational Psychology, 83*(3), 579–599.

Dollard, M. F., & McTernan, W. (2011). Psychosocial safety climate: A multilevel theory of work stress in the health and community service sector. *Epidemiology and Psychiatric Sciences, 20* (04), 287–293.

Dollard, M. F., & Neser, D. Y. (2013). Worker health is good for the economy: Union density and psychosocial safety climate as determinants of country differences in worker health and productivity in 31 European countries. *Social Science & Medicine, 92*, 114–123.

Donaghue, A. M. (2004). Occupational health hazards in mining: An overview. *Occupational Medicine, 54*(5), 283–289

Frone, M. R., Russell, M., & Cooper, M. L. (1997). Relation of work–family conflict to health outcomes: A four-year longitudinal study of employed parents. *Journal of Occupational and Organizational Psychology, 70*(4), 325–335.

Glaser, B. G., Strauss, A. L., & Strutzel, E. (1968). The discovery of grounded theory; strategies for qualitative research. *Nursing Research, 17*(4), 364.

Hammer, L. B., Cullen, J. C., Neal, M. B., Sinclair, R. R., & Shafiro, M. V. (2005). The longitudinal effects of work-family conflict and positive spillover on depressive symptoms among dual-earner couples. *Journal of Occupational Health Psychology, 10*(2), 138.

Idris, M. A., Dollard, M. F., & Winefield, A. H. (2010). Lay theory explanations of occupational stress: The Malaysian context. *Cross Cultural Management: An International Journal, 17*(2), 135–153.

Karasek, R., & Theorell, T. (1990). *Stress, productivity, and the reconstruction of working life.* New York: Basic Books Inc, Publishers.

Kinman, G., & Jones, F. (2005). Lay representations of workplace stress: What do people really mean when they say they are stressed? *Work and Stress, 19*(2), 101–120.

Marmaros, D., & Sacerdote, B. (2006). How do friendships form? *The Quarterly Journal of Economics, 121*(1) 79–119.

Miller, M. A., Wright, H., Hough, J., & Cappuccio, F. P. (2014). Sleep and cognition. In Idzikowski, C. (Ed.), *Sleep and its disorders affect society*. InTech. ISBN 9789535117254.

Newcomb, T. (1961). *The acquaintance process*. New York, NY: Holt, Rinehart & Winston.

Priest, R. F., & Sawyer, J. (1967). Proximity and peership: Bases of balance in interpersonal attraction. *American Journal of Sociology*, 633–649.

Rost, K., Smith, G. R., & Taylor, J. L. (1993). Rural-urban differences in stigma and the use of care for depressive disorders. *The Journal of Rural Health, 9*(1), 57–62.

Rubin, Z., & Shenker, S. (1978). Friendship, proximity, and self-disclosure. *Journal of Personality, 46*(1), 1–22.

SafeWork Australia. (2011). *Notified fatalities statistical report*. Canberra: SafeWork Australia.

Siegrist, J., Siegrist, K., & Weber, I. (1986). Sociological concepts in the etiology of chronic disease: The case of ischemic heart disease. *Social Science and Medicine, 22*, 247–253.

Smith, S. M. (1994). Theoretical principles of context-dependent memory. *Theoretical Aspects of Memory, 2*, 168–195.

Zohar, D. (2000). A group-level model of safety climate: Testing the effect of group climate on microaccidents in manufacturing jobs. *Journal of Applied Psychology, 85*(4), 587.

Zuzanek, J., Robinson, J. P., & Iwasaki, Y. (1998). The relationships between stress, health, and physically active leisure as a function of life-cycle. *Leisure Sciences, 20*(4), 253–275.

Part V
Conclusion

Chapter 20
Key Contributions and Future Research Directions

Akihito Shimazu, Jodi Oakman, Maureen F. Dollard and Rusli Bin Nordin

Abstract This chapter will refer to key contributions and future research directions on the basis of each chapter as a conclusion.

The Asia Pacific is the world's most populous region and many workers experience very poor work conditions and insecure employment. Yet in terms of global effort little attention is given to psychosocial factors at work in the region. The 19 chapters of the current book focused on practical approaches toward healthy workplaces and workers in the Asia Pacific. Multidisciplinary efforts to address worker occupational health were made by presenting examples of practical approaches from global or national perspectives, and examples involving specific conditions such as telework, small-medium sized enterprises, work in disaster areas, and workplace clients' violence.

The book begins with an introduction to issues relating to psychosocial factors at work in the Asia Pacific, building on the body of work presented in the first book: Psychosocial factors at work in the Asia Pacific (Dollard et al. 2014). In turn four major themes are addressed in the book.

A. Shimazu (✉)
Department of Mental Health, The University of Tokyo
Graduate School of Medicine, 7-3-1 Hongo,
Bunkyo-ku, Tokyo 113-0033, Japan
e-mail: ashimazu@m.u-tokyo.ac.jp

J. Oakman
Center for Ergonomics and Human Factors,
School of Psychology and Public Health,
La Trobe University, Melbourne, Australia

M.F. Dollard
Asia Pacific Center for Work Health and Safety,
School of Psychology, Social Work, and Social Policy,
University of South Australia, Adelaide, Australia

R.B. Nordin
Jeffrey Cheah School of Medicine and Health Sciences,
Monash University Malaysia, Johor Bahru, Malaysia

A. Shimazu et al. (eds.), *Psychosocial Factors at Work in the Asia Pacific*,
DOI 10.1007/978-3-319-44400-0_20

The first theme related to policy and practice frameworks in the Asia Pacific and beyond. In the Chap. 2, Leka and Jain undertook a comprehensive review of international initiatives for the management of psychosocial risks and the promotion of mental health in the workplace providing an important context for the book—later chapters examined psychosocial risk management more specifically in the Asia Pacific region. Policies discussed included legislation and also nonbinding voluntary policy initiatives, social partner agreements and some standards, providing an interesting overview for consideration within the region.

In Chap. 3, Bailey and colleagues examined macro-level policy and its influence on workplace practice in four countries across the Asia Pacific. A focus group was held to discuss key questions relating to the interpretation and practical application at the workplace level, of macro-level policy relating to psychosocial factors. Challenges were outlined, in particular some developing countries were identified as being in the early stages of identifying workplace psychosocial risk factors and it was noted that this is an emerging area which will be important to monitor in coming years.

Chapter 4 by Tsutsumi and Shimazu described guidelines for the prevention of mental health disorders at work. These guidelines are designed for use in workplaces who wish to implement programs to address workplace factors contributing to the development of adverse mental health. The authors acknowledged that these are a first step, and as the evidence base is limited, the guidelines will require refinement as they are trialed in workplaces.

In the final chapter (Chap. 5) on this theme, Park carefully outlined strategies to prevent work-related stress and cardiovascular disease in South Korea. She found that strategies designed to prevent work-related cardiovascular and cerebrovascular diseases in South Korea included: (1) the early detection of high risk groups with complex cardiovascular risk factors; (2) workplace health promotion through lifestyle modifications; (3) control of underlying disorders; and (4) assessing and promoting fitness for work. Strategies designed to manage job stress in South Korea include providing workplaces with Korea Occupational Safety and Health Agency (KOSHA) guides applicable to high risk industries and occupations. In addition, the Korean Ministry of Employment and Labor is preparing regulations to prevent job stress in workers involved in emotional labor such as call center workers and salespersons in department stores. Although South Korean made good progress in dealing with work-related cardiovascular and cerebrovascular diseases from 1999, it has lagged behind other developed countries in the development of guidelines for occupational safety and health that relate to work stress.

The next major theme related to psychosocial factors at work relevant to the global and regional context, with five chapters focused on this issue. Chapter 6, Yulita, Idris, and Dollard present a systematic narrative review of a facet-specific climate for psychosocial safety [psychosocial safety climate (PSC)] that has been featured in the literature. They reviewed 13 peer-reviewed empirical journal articles on PSC in terms of its history, role, impact, and research trend. Thirteen peer-reviewed journal articles qualified for the review. For comparative purposes they considered research on other climate facets, safety climate (n = 59), and psychological safety climate (n = 16), published from 1980 to 2016. Although safety climate remains the dominant research interest, PSC surpassed psychological safety climate in terms of publications from 2010. The researchers identified a specificity of outcomes related to PSC (e.g., physical health, psychological health, work motivation, work conditions). The main theorisation and operationalisation of PSC were as a group-level antecedent and moderator of work stress processes rather than as a mediator. Evidence strongly supported this dual function of PSC. Around half the studies were longitudinal, and all were published in either Australia or Malaysia. The authors provide insights into future research requirements to advance the field of PSC research such as the simultaneous use of multiple climates, multilevel modeling, research time lags, advanced research designs, and data analysis tools.

Parker and Zhang continue work on psychosocial factors in Chap. 7 by providing a state-of-the-art overview of job design aspects that work in the contemporary world. They highlight five key areas that need more attention from researchers and practitioners: putting work design into context to consider the effects of rapid current changes; identifying the value of work design from a longer term and more strategic perspective; paying more attention to employee-initiated forms of work design; giving greater attention to why poor work design continues; and estimating the effects of culture on work design and cross-cultural research on work design. The chapter concludes by suggesting the collaboration of researchers and practitioners to take up challenges of work design to achieve decent work for everyone.

In Chap. 8, a study of workplace violence in Taiwan, Cheng and Pien found in general, that women were more likely than men to experience workplace violence. In the healthcare sector, women had particularly higher prevalence rates of workplace violence than men, which may be attributed to a greater gender inequality in healthcare settings. Results from multilevel analyses with adjustment of workers' actual experiences of workplace violence showed that neighborhood-level workplace violence was positively associated with mental health risks in women but not in men. This finding suggests that working in a broader environment where aggressive or abusive behaviors are more prevalent may entail a greater mental health risk to women. Research improvements should be made in many aspects ranging from, the measures for workplace violence, study designs to investigate the casual mechanisms of workplace violence and health consequences, to the strategies for effective prevention. Furthermore, as workplace violence is embedded in a social context, researchers and occupational health practitioners should pay attention to contextual factors that might influence societal tolerance of abusive work practices.

Chapter 9 by Oakman, Maakip and Keegel found in their study of musculoskeletal disorders that despite similarities in the prevalence of musculoskeletal discomfort in both the Australian and Malaysian populations, differences were identified in the relative contribution of factors. Results from a qualitative study of female Malaysian office workers who were asked about their coping strategies for managing persistent musculoskeletal pain revealed that disclosure of conditions was limited. Without disclosure and organizational support, workplace accommodations were developed at an individual or peer-related level and changes to working conditions were rare. The findings from this study provide insights into future policy development of management of MSDs. Malaysia is at a formative stage in terms of risk management for MSDs and as such a different focus is needed to adequately address relevant workplace factors.

Chapter 10 on psychosocial safety climate (PSC) by Afsharian, Zadow, and Dollard extends the boundaries of PSC theory by pioneering an investigation into the role of PSC and its relationship with psychosocial risk factors and psychological health within the sociocultural contextual background of Iran. The findings provide evidence that PSC is a climate construct that exists as a group phenomenon cross-culturally. They found that PSC in Iran has group like properties with around 11 % (cf 15 % in Australia) of the variance in PSC due to group-level factors, with high levels of homogeneity of perceptions of PSC within groups (0.92 vs. 0.94 Australia).

Iranian hospital employees reported lower levels of PSC, skill discretion and decision authority, and higher levels of emotional demands, compared to the Australian sample. Evidence in support of the climate concept also came from the way it behaved in a nomological network of analyses. The major theoretical paths delineated in PSC theory were confirmed in the Iranian data. Multilevel analysis identified that as a between-group effect in Iran and Australia team PSC was significantly negatively related to psychological demands and emotional exhaustion, and positively related to job resources, decision authority, and work engagement. As a between-group effect Australian work teams with high PSC also reported higher levels of the job resource, skill discretion. Having confirmed the utility of PSC theory in Iran (at least among hospital workers), along with Australia and Malaysia, the authors argue that the assessment of PSC may enable the development of organizational systems to prevent workplace psychosocial risk factors across the Asia Pacific.

The third major theme describing practical approaches to reduce psychosocial risk factors and improve worker well-being at the employee and organizational level comprises five chapters. Searching the globe for information on psychosocial risk management tools to guide interventions for psychosocial risk management and prevention was the goal of Chap. 11 by Potter and colleagues. They conducted an exhaustive search to locate tools, using a mixed search strategy of online databases, snowballing, internet-based search engine (Google Scholar), websites of stakeholder organizations in occupational health and macro-level initiatives/standards. Eleven tools were identified from the European Union, Canada, and Australia and each tool is summarized individually. However, the results suggest that there is a general lack of scientific evidence regarding evaluation of the implementation of the psychosocial risk management processes outlined in the tools. Consequently, it is important that future research provides scientific evidence on the effectiveness of these practical approaches to address this major gap within the literature. As a result of developing greater evidence, more organizations will be encouraged to include the psychosocial risk management processes in their own organizational policies and practices, especially those in the Asia Pacific Region. Areas in the Asia Pacific Region may benefit from adapting these tools to fit the cultural context, or develop methods based on the psychosocial risk management paradigm (Dollard et al. 2007), and then, intervene to eliminate or reduce them through the necessary preventative or protective measures (Leka and Cox 2010).

In Chap. 12 by Inoue and colleagues, the New Brief Job Stress Questionnaire (BJSQ) was revised to assess a broader set of psychosocial factors at work compared to the current BJSQ in accordance with a proposed Japanese framework of prevention of job stress, the "Kenko-ikiiki Workplace model," a new Japanese framework for prevention of job stress and promotion of positive mental health based on the Job Demands-Resources (JD-R) model (Schaufeli and Bakker 2004). A nationally representative survey was administered to employees in Japan (n = 1633) in 2010/2011 to examine the reliability and construct validity. As a result, most scales showed acceptable levels of internal consistency (Cronbach's alpha) and test-retest reliability over one year. Principal component analyses showed that the first factor explained 50 % or greater proportion of the variance in most scales. A scale factor analysis and a correlation analysis showed that these scales fit the proposed theoretical framework. These findings provided evidence that the New BJSQ scales are reliable and valid. The New BJSQ is a useful instrument to evaluate psychosocial work environment and positive mental health outcomes in the workplace.

In Chap. 13 by Nordin and Ahin, a critical review of the literature on occupational stress and coping strategies among Malaysian employees identified significant occupational stressors that include unrealistic objectives, incompetent boss, time pressure and deadlines, work pressure, homework interface, performance pressure, excessive workload, long working hours, insufficient number of staff, competition in career development and progression, and role ambiguity in addition to lack of support from coworkers and supervisors, depression, anxiety, and use of avoidance coping strategies. Various coping strategies were adopted by employees in different industries in Malaysia to address their work-related stress: "divert thinking and disregarding" (by doing something fun), networking and learning more effective ways of communication, positive reframing, and emotional support. Cognitive, social, and emotional coping strategies, especially the former, were also found to positively influence occupational stress among managers in electronic firms (Sathasivam and Kumaraswamy 2014). However, the benefits of coping strategies and resilience on lowering the level of workplace stress among working mothers and working females have not gained much support from Malaysian organizations. Further research should examine the effectiveness of the psychosocial safety climate (PSC) framework (Idris et al. 2014; Dollard and Bailey 2014; Kortum and Leka 2014), if adopted, in preventing and reducing occupational stress and to involve managers. Organizations need to incorporate effective coping strategies into their intervention programs and to provide regular training and monitoring of their employees' well-being. As there is very little research in addressing occupational stress at the organizational level, particularly in Malaysia, it is suggested that organizations at the managerial level look into involving managers to understand the need for prevention and mitigation of occupational stress and intervention strategies to assess and address identified risks (Ahmad and Xavier 2010).

In Chap. 14 by Imamura and colleagues on the evaluation of whether computerized cognitive behavioral therapy delivered via the Internet is effective in improving depression in the general working population, three studies were examined: Study 1: The effects of the iCBT program on improving subthreshold depressive symptoms among healthy workers; Study 2: The effects of the iCBT program on preventing the onset of major depressive episode (MDE) among workers; and Study 3: The effects of the iCBT program on increasing work engagement among healthy workers. Results indicated that the (1) iCBT program showed a significant intervention effect on BDI-II ($t = 21.99$, $p < 0.05$) with small effect sizes (Cohen's d: 20.16, 95 % confidence interval: 20.32–0.00, at six-month follow-up); (2) intervention group had a significantly lower incidence of MDE at the 12-month follow-up than the control group (Log-rank $\chi^2 = 7.04$, $p < 0.01$) and the hazard ratio for the intervention group was 0.22 (95 % confidence interval 0. 06–0.75), when estimated by the Cox proportional hazard model; and (3) iCBT program showed a significant intervention effect on work engagement ($p = 0.04$) with small effect sizes (Cohen's $d = 0.16$) at 6 month follow-up. On the other hand, mediation analysis showed that a change in depression marginally significantly mediated the effect on work engagement, which explained 26–31 % of the total effect. Improved depression by the iCBT program might contribute to improvement of work engagement to some extent. This study first demonstrated that a computerized cognitive behavioral therapy delivered via the Internet is effective in improving depression in the general working population. It seems critical to improve program involvement of participants in order to enhance the effect size of an iCBT program. These findings indicate a possible large public health impact of applying an iCBT program in improving mental health among workers.

In Chap. 15 by Martin and colleagues, participants in a quasi experimental study assumed the role of a call center manager with an employee suffering from depression and were randomly assigned to a group where cues were provided to them that reflected an organizational context that was either supportive or unsupportive toward mental health. Hierarchical regression analyses revealed that participants in the "unsupportive" condition reported higher levels of cognitive stigma toward an employee with depression ($\beta = 0.126$; SE = 0.133; $p < 0.05$) and that the supportive or unsupportive nature of the cues participants received also moderated the relationship between an identified predisposing individual characteristic, help seeking reticence, and cognitive stigma ($\beta = 0.416$; SE = 0.122; $p < 0.01$). Affective stigma was associated with participants rating the performance of a depressed employee more negatively ($\beta = -0.189$; SE = 0.025; $p < 0.01$). These results provide impetus for organizations to develop work environments that signal support for employee mental health, strategies to reduce depression stigma among managers and appropriate mechanisms for dealing with employee depression in performance appraisal and performance management processes (Martin and Fisher 2014).

The fourth major theme related to describing practical approaches to improve psychosocial factors and worker well-being in specific conditions and comprised four chapters. The challenge of managing psychosocial factors in small-scale enterprises is of global importance. In Chap. 16, Moriguchi and his colleagues discussed pertinent issues for small-scale enterprises in Japan and the Asia Pacific region. In many countries occupational health service activities for small-scale and microscale enterprises are often insufficient (Bradshaw et al. 2001; Park et al. 2002; Houtman et al. 2007) as they have limited access to human, economic, and technical resources (Champoux and Brun 2003). Thus, the employer in these enterprises is the key player for any changes that need to be made. The researchers clarified the attitudes of employers and the situation regarding mental health activities in small-scale enterprises and microscale enterprises. They also developed educational tools for improving mental health conditions in microscale enterprises and small-scale enterprises.

In Chap. 17, Mori and his colleagues discussed health issues of workers engaged in operations related to the accident at the Fukushima Daiichi Nuclear Power Plant (NPP). They reviewed the health issues that occurred among the workers and described the actions taken to solve them. They also summarized the lessons learned from the experience for disasters in the future. After a large disaster, there are various trade-offs between health risks and other factors. After the Fukushima incident, personal protection against radiation exposure and contamination increased the risk of heat illness and accidents. The Tokyo Electric Power Company (TEPCO) was concerned that implementing a fitness for work evaluation program might result in manpower shortage and other issues. However, it was difficult to manage such issues when different departments or organizations share responsibility in a disaster situation. When the necessity for trade-offs becomes clear following a disaster, the departments or organizations concerned need to communicate positively with one another toward making the appropriate decisions.

In Chap. 18, Hu and her colleagues addressed the effect of a nation-specific stressor on well-being by focusing on Guanxi (i.e., human network, connection) in the Chinese workplace. Guanxi is considered a product of Confucian values and is inherent in the work ethics of the Chinese people. The researchers showed that social resources and task resources play a different role in the Job Demands-Resource model (Schaufeli and Bakker 2004). Moreover, the Chinese notion of Guanxi (exchange of favors) was successfully integrated into the JD-R model. This not only increases the applicability of the JD-R model in China, but also exemplifies how the JD-R model can be extended by integrating notions from non-western cultures.

Finally, in Chap. 19, McTernan and his colleagues discussed remoteness and work stress in the mines. They identified the key demands pertinent to remote and non-remote mining workers, the key resources that help workers manage job demands, and the form that job strain manifests. They claimed that each occupation and industry provides an environment of unique and job stressors and resources. What makes remote mining work so unique is the way in which remoteness changes an individual's relationships with both their family and their coworkers. Although some of the difficulties that arise from the unique work structure are unavertable, understanding the way in which these factors interact help in both understanding the way in which stress arousal manifests, and shining a light on what areas may be the best to focus efforts to reduce work-related stress.

Concluding Remarks

So far research and theorizing in the field of psychosocial factors at work has been dominated by North American and European scholars. Hence, it is important that scholars from other parts of the world contribute to that field as well. Although Asia Pacific is quite diverse, many economies in the region are emerging and growing fast, which creates particular challenges and opportunities, also with regard to psychosocial factors. On the other hand, basic psychological processes might be quite invariant across countries and regions. This book has succeeded in addressing a striking gap in the global stock of knowledge about psychosocial factors at work by presenting scholarly research from the Asia Pacific.

However, there are still several issues for future research and practice. First, more research is needed from the broader region such as South Asian countries in order to generalize findings in the book. Second, more cross-cultural collaboration in terms of research and practice are needed, given the increasing number of multinational enterprises and joint venture corporations in the region such as in Thailand, Vietnam, India, and Myanmar. Third, although most chapters in this book focused on psychological problems such as psychological distress and depression, more diverse outcomes can be focused on such as physical health and more positive aspects of well-being such as work engagement and job performance. Fourth, national surveillance of psychosocial factors at work using a common tool across Asia Pacific countries is needed to benchmark and draw national and international attention to prevalent psychosocial issues and poor working conditions, to highlight where action is required and where resources can be funneled.

We thank all our chapter authors for their contributions and congratulate them for the production of a valuable and unique reference book for researchers, professionals in occupational health and safety, human resource management, occupational health psychology, organizational psychology, students, and policymakers. We also thank Ms. Mayumi Watanabe for her hard work as a coordinator of the book and editing this international and interdisciplinary book.

We hope this book has been of value to you and that you find our contributions and observations useful in your own efforts to improve the psychological health of workers around the globe. We believe that this book is of interest to various audiences: it is difficult to tell for what audience it is NOT suitable! We also believe that it is most interesting to researchers, students, policymakers, and (occupational health and human resource management) professionals, both in the Asian Pacific region as well as elsewhere (Europe and North America).

References

Ahmad, S. Z., & Xavier, S. R. (2010). Stress and coping style of entrepreneurs: A Malaysian survey. *International Journal of Entrepreneurship, 14*, 25–36.

Bradshaw, L. M., Curran, A. D., Eskin, F., & Fishwick, D. (2001). Provision and perception of occupational health in small and medium-sized enterprises in Sheffield, UK. *Occupational Medicine, 51*, 39–44.

Champoux, D., & Brun, J. (2003). Occupational health and safety management in small size enterprises; an overview of the situation and avenues for intervention and research. *Safety Science, 41*, 301–318.

Dollard, M. F., & Bailey, T. S. (Eds.). (2014). *Australian workplace barometer: Psychosocial safety climate and working conditions in Australia*. Samford Valley, QLD: Australian Academic Press.

Dollard, M. F., Skinner, N., Tuckey, M. R., & Bailey, T. (2007). National surveillance of psychosocial risk factors in the workplace: An international overview. *Work and Stress, 21*, 1–29.

Dollard, M. F., Shimazu, S., Nordin, R. B., & Brough, P. (2014). The context of psychosocial factors at work in the Asia Pacific. In M. F. Dollard, A. Shimazu, R. B. Nordin, P. Brough, & M. R. Tuckey (Eds.), *Psychosocial factors at work in the Asia Pacific* (pp. 3–27). Dordrecht: Springer.

Houtman, I., Jettinghoff, K., & Cedillo, L. (2007). *Raising awareness of stress at work in develop-ing countries: A modern hazard in a traditional working environment: Advice to employers and worker representatives*. World Health Organization. http://www.who.int/occupational_health/publications/raisingawarenessofstress.pdf

Idris, M. A., Dollard, M. F., & Yulita, (2014). Psychosocial safety climate. Emotional demands, burnout, and depression: A longitudinal multilevel study in the Malaysian private sector. *Journal of Occupational Health Psychology, 19*, 291–302.

Kortum, E., & Leka, S. (2014). Tackling psychosocial risks and work-related stress in developing countries: The need for a multilevel intervention framework. *International Journal of Stress Management, 21*, 7–26.

Leka, S., & Cox, T. (2010). Psychosocial risk management at the workplace level. In S. Leka & J. Houdmont (Eds.), *Occupational health psychology*. Chichester: Wiley.

Martin, A., & Fisher, C. (2014). Understanding and improving managers' responses to employee depression. *Industrial and Organizational Psychology: Perspectives on Science and Practice*,. doi:10.1111/iops.12147.

Park, H., Ha, E., Kim, J., Jung, H., & Paek, D. (2002). Occupational health services for small-scale enterprises in Korea. *Industrial Health, 40*, 1–6.

Sathasivam, K., & Kumaraswamy, N. (2014). Coping strategies of job stress among managers of electronics industries in Malaysia. *Journal of Asian Scientific Research, 4*, 534–540.

Schaufeli, W. B., & Bakker, A. B. (2004). Job demands, job resources, and their relationship with burnout and engagement: A multi-sample study. *Journal of Organizational Behavior, 25*, 293–315.